HUMAN RESOURCE MANAGEMENT IN PRACTICE
with 300 Models, Techniques and Tools

SRINIVAS R. KANDULA

Director (Human Resource)
Sasken Communication
Technologies Limited
Bangalore

PHI Learning Private Limited

New Delhi-110001
2009

Rs. 350.00

HUMAN RESOURCE MANAGEMENT IN PRACTICE
with 300 Models, Techniques and Tools
by Srinivas R. Kandula

© 2003 by PHI Learning Private Limited, New Delhi. All rights reserved. No part of this book may be reproduced in any form, by mimeograph or any other means, without permission in writing from the publisher.

ISBN-978-81-203-2427-5

The export rights of this book are vested solely with the publisher.

Seventh Printing   ...   ...   **September, 2009**

Published by Asoke K. Ghosh, PHI Learning Private Limited, M-97, Connaught Circus, New Delhi-110001 and Printed by Rajkamal Electric Press, Plot No. 2, Phase IV, HSIDC, Kundli-131028, Sonepat, Haryana.

Contents

Chapter 3 Human Resource Planning and Sourcing Management *59*

Chapter 4 Career and Competency Management *73*

Chapter 5 Management Development and Training Management 88

Chapter 6 Performance Management 102

Chapter 12 Self-Management 227

Chapter 13 Selected Classics in OB and OD 235

Chapter 14 Organizational Learning and Knowledge Management 252

Chapter 15   Organizational Management   *275*

Chapter 16   Culture Management   *299*

Chapter 17   Change Management   *308*

Preface

Today, many books are available in the market which deal with Human Resource Management (HRM) providing different perspectives. These books are either too academically oriented, leaving little scope for pragmatic issues or too brief, neglecting basic concepts and theories. This book is an attempt to fill that gap. It is a unique blend of theory and practice and presents many facts of HRM, not found in other books on the subject. It is my conviction that any person aspiring to become a good human resource professional has to possess both knowledge of human resource management concepts and an awareness of the implications of such concepts in practice. Possessing merely either of this, i.e. conceptual knowledge without understanding practical implications or indulging in human resource management practice without possessing theoretical perspective can never be adequate. Keeping in view this reality, the book presents, in a vivid manner, both fundamental and advanced concepts of human resource management as also their implications in practice.

This comprehensive text which deals with HRM concepts and practices is the result of a two-year intentsive study on these concepts and practices. It traces the evolution of human resource management. The book with its rich content base comprises 18 chapters which describe 300 models, techniques and tools of human resource management in practice. In order to understand and practice human resource management in a systematic manner in the organizational context, it is necessary that we have knowledge about various models of HRM developed and practised worldwide. With this objective, Chapters 1 and 2 discuss 45 models, techniques and tools with their managerial implications for sound HRM practice. Human resource planning and sourcing are essential for people management. Recognizing this fact, 13 different techniques and tools applicable for varied contexts are dealt with in Chapter 3. Twelve contemporary models are described in Chapters 4 and 5 to emphasize the significant role of training, management development, competency and career management in sustaining the motivational level of human resource.

Academicians, consultants and practitioners of. HRM are constantly in search of new models, techniques and tools to enchance performance of human resource. This has contributed to the emergence of innumerable practices. Taking these into account, Chapter 6 presents 34 most effective techniques and tools of performance management, while Chapter 7, with the support of 19 best models in practice, deals with *Leadership*, the most important and talked about topic in HRM.

New generation human resource practices like team building, employee communication, involvement and empowerment are discussed in Chapters 8 and 9. Intelligence and motivational management are two strong pillars of human resource management and leaving them untouched can make any book dealing with the subject of human resource management incomplete. Therefore, with an objective to bring HR professionals back to basics, Chapter 10 describes 18 models of intelligence and motivational management. People are at the centre of creativity and decision-making practices. This is rightly brought out in Chapter 11 comprising 15 techniques and tools. Chapter 12 is devoted to the issue of self-management and a total of seven techniques are discussed as a part of this. Though organizational behaviour and organization development, organizational learning and knowledge management have acquired the status of independent disciplines with growing research, they remain an integral part of HRM, at least in practice. Every student and practitioner of HRD has to invariably possess the knowledge of these issuses. In order to facilitate this, 32 most relevant and essential models, techniques and tools are presented in Chapters 13 and 14. Unless we appreciate the interaction between the larger canvas of organizational management and human resource management, designing and executing organizationally relevant HR practices will remain a dream. In this context, 17 different models, techniques and tools are provided in Chapter 15, enabling a deeper understanding of the issue.

Culture is at the heart of HRM practice from the process perspective. Many organizations ascribe their success to good culture management. Recognizing this, Chapter 16 deals with culture management, presenting 16 models, techniques and tools. Change mangement is regarded as one of the principal constituents of HRM in practice since success of change initiatives is largely influenced by people practices. Thirteen models describing the role of human resource in change management are discussed in Chapter 17. Globally, measuring 'soft skills' through 'hard measures' has become an accepted method of establishing the efficacy of human resource management in practice. The final chapter (18) presents 30 powerful human resource assessment and evaluation techniques and tools which can be used by students and practitioners of HRM.

The book should prove useful to postgraduate students of management offering courses in HRM/HRD. It should also prove beneficial as a handbook to HR professionals. I sincerely hope this is one book that both students and practitioners alike would like to cherish as a classic in the practice of human resource management.

I am indebted to Administrative Staff College of India and the Centre for Organization Development, Hyderabad for allowing me to use their library facilities. I am thankful to Ashok Awasthi, B.B. Bhattacharya, G. Jawahar, K.V.V. Satyanarayana, Ritu Tather, Sandeep Chatterjee and Vinod P. Baxla, without whose help this work would not have been possible. I also wish to sincerely thank my wife and son for their encouragement and patience while I was writing this book.

Finally, I would like to thank the Publishers, Prentice-Hall of India, especially their editorial and production team, for the care they have taken in bringing out this text.

Srinivas R. Kandula

Chapter 1

Models of Human Resource Management

Understanding models in human resource management (HRM) is essential for any human resource practitioner for three reasons. Firstly, it provides a macro perspective of HRM practice in overall organizational set up. Secondly, the unity and diversity of these models serve as vital inputs in drafting tailor made HRM model for organizations. Thirdly, these models offer answers to quite a few dilemmas that practitioners encounter in their mission to pursue an organizationally dovetailed and business aligned human resource function.

With these objectives in view, this chapter deals with 30 different models in HRM practice. Each of these models illustrates HRM strategy from a particular perspective, its focus, and the principal elements, the overall philosophy and ultimate objective. These 30 models together present the spectrum of HRM practice that include soft and hard variants of HRM, quality enabled HRM, models drawn from religious scriptures, strategy, structure, process aligned HRM, and models based on employee commitment approach, capability driven, human potential oriented, profit motivated, and sectorial based HRM, thus giving a comprehensive and holistic approach to the subject.

BALDRIGE MODEL OF HRM

Malcolm Baldrige National Quality Award is regarded as the world's highest quality award that is given annually to an organization in recognition of its quality standards. HRM practices take a central place in quality movement of organizations. A maximum of 1000 points is allocated to different dimensions of quality management for assessment under Baldrige award. Out of these, HRM practices get 150 points. Further, these practices like employee development, involvement and empowerment, has potential to influence the other dimensions of the award like customer focus, leadership, and quality planning. Keeping in view its importance, Dr Christopher Hart, president of TQM Group-USA and Prof Leonard Schlesinger of Harvard Business School advocated for application of Baldrige framework to HR in their paper titled "Total Quality Management and the Human Resource Professional: Applying the Baldrige Framework to Human Resources" published in HRM in 1991. This orientation may help companies to not only strengthen their quality efforts but also give a purposeful shape to HR function.

In quality modelling, HR function needs to develop a new vision for itself as a customer focused service provider, in other words, setting 100 per cent customer satisfaction as HRM's ultimate goal which means, defining who the customers are and determining their precise needs. Baldrige award emphasizes the critical role of five HR practices in this endeavour. These are (i) HR planning, (ii) HR education and training, (iii) HR performance and recognition, (iv) HR involvement, and (v) HR well-being and morale. Again, each of these practices are broken into a number of activities. For example, HR planning practice is sub-divided into ·redefining job descriptions to increase clarity of job, steps to enrich jobs, lines of authority, organizational structure, etc. Similarly, education and training encompasses activities like leadership training, training in quality, communication, mentoring, job specific employee training, remedial training for career growth and so on. The quality modelled HRM activities would progress in tandem with quality efforts as illustrated in Table 1.1.

TABLE 1.1

Variables	Baldrige	HRM
Outcome	Customer focus and satisfaction	Employee performance, satisfaction, growth and motivation
System	Strategic quality planning	HR planning
Driver	Leadership	Employee characteristics

Managerial Implication

Baldrige model of HRM helps organizations in focusing their attention on attaining global standards in quality of products and services. HR managers have to understand quality systems and internalize the philosophy and mechanisms of Malcolm Baldrige award in order to apply the right HR practices. Quality specialists have taken over HR function wherever human resource professionals were not successful in applying quality reinforced HRM model. The lack of basic HRM foundation in quality specialists led to failures in integrating Quality-HRM partnership. Therefore, special attention must be paid to identify an HRM professional with requisite skills who can translate Baldrige HRM model into practice.

HARVARD MODEL OF HRM

The type of HRM policies and practices an organization prefers should be dependent upon its organizational vision, mission, strategy, goals, and objectives. In quite a few cases, such HR practices shall also be devised and adopted in tune with external environment of organizations. In other words, HR policies and practices are subject to be influenced by internal and external environment of organizations. Harvard model of HRM propounded by Michael Beer, Richard Walton, Quinn Mills, P. Lawrence and Bert Spector highlighted this influence of environment on HRM in their book titled *Managing Human Assets* published in 1984. This model also known as Soft Model of HRM/Harvard Map of HRM/Multiple Stakeholders Model, argues that human resources policies are to be influenced by two significant considerations:

1. *Situational factors.* The internal and external environment factors of organizations that include (i) labour market conditions, (ii) societal values, (iii) business strategies, (iv) technologies, (v) management philosophies, and (vi) market conditions will constrain the formation of HRM policies.

2. *Stakeholders' interests.* The stakeholders influence the short-term HRM policies. They include (i) management employees, (ii) unions, and (iii) government agencies.

Further, the model classifies HRM policies and practices into four themes as follows:

1. *HR flows.* Recruitment, selection, placement, promotion, appraisal and assessment, promotion, termination and the like.
2. *Reward systems.* Pay systems, non-monetary recognition schemes and so on.
3. *Employee influence.* Clarification of responsibility, authority, hierarchy and delegation of powers.
4. *Work systems.* Definition of work and alignment of people.

The above HR practices are centered on four C's as described in the following:

1. *Commitment.* HRM policies must contribute for infusing employee commitment to organization. The commitment will yield two benefits. Firstly, it will enhance the employee performance and loyalty to his/her work. Secondly, it will enhance the individual self-respect and worth.
2. *Competence.* HRM policies and practices will exist in such a way that they attract, develop and retain employees with valuable skills and knowledge.
3. *Cost effectiveness.* HRM policies must be evaluated in terms of wages, benefits, turnover, absenteeism, strikes, benefits etc.
4. *Congruence.* There must be congruence between and among various HRM policies as well as practices in operation.

Managerial Implication

The model helps HR managers in charting HR strategy for their organizations. This model offers three significant insights for practice. Firstly, HRM policies should be defined keeping in view the environmental factors and stakeholders' concerns. In other words, there must be a good fit between organizational environment and HR policies. Secondly, such HRM policies and practices must have a goal to achieve employee commitment, competence development, coherence among themselves and embrace cost effective methods. Thirdly, HRM that stems from environmental factors and is drawn based on four C's will result in employee and organizational effectiveness. This is a soft model as it is based on stakeholders' concerns and their commitment to organizational goals.

MICHIGAN MODEL OF HRM

The Michigan model has a harder, less humanistic touch, holding that employees are resources in the same way as any other business resource. They must be obtained (i) as cheaply as possible, (ii) used sparingly and (iii) developed and exploited as much as possible. John Storey, the outstanding scholar in the field of HRM termed it as *utilitarian instrumentalism.* From this point of view, for example, the object of formal human resource planning can be just that—largely a factor of production, along with land and capital. In the words of Karan Legge,

> the hard model of HRM emphasizes the quantitative, calculative and business strategic aspects of managing the headcount resource in a rational way as for any other economic factor.

This model stresses upon the crucial importance of the close integration of HR policies, systems and activities with business strategy. The Michigan theorists highlighted the following as being the most important HR issues to achieve such a match:

- Selection of the most suitable people to meet business needs.
- Performance in the pursuit of business objectives.
- Appraisal, monitoring performance and providing feedback to the organization and its employees.
- Rewards for appropriate performance.
- Development of skills and knowledge required to meet business objectives.

The essential features of this model are that it:

- is focused on individual and organizational performance.
- is based on strategic control, organizational structure, systems for managing people.
- concentrates on managing human assets to achieve strategic goals.
- contributes to human resource performance.
- has components such as organization structure, mission and strategy, human resource selection, performance appraisal, rewards and development.
- requires that personnel policies, practices and systems are not only consistent with the business objectives of the firm but should also have coherence among various sub-systems of HRM.

Michigan model of HRM has originated from the writings of C. Fombrun, Noel Tichy and M.A. Devanna, who discussed it in a detailed fashion in their book titled *Strategic Human Resource Management,* published in 1984.

Managerial Implication

This model has been lauded for its practical approach. In other words, this model is different from other employee relations oriented HRM models, which stress on the commitment and relationship factors rather than on business results. This is also most popular among practitioners, and many organizations have adopted it in practice. This model as indeed influenced the direction of HRM literature during the last two decades. Therefore, understanding and possesing complete knowledge of this model is essential for HR managers. Michigan model can offer a solution in attainment of organizational objectives to the satisfaction of all stakeholders.

TEN C MODEL OF HRM

The field of HRM has been evolving ever since it came into existence in 1970s. HRM experts have proposed many models to interpret, explain and also advocate HR policies and practices in tune with specific ideology and philosophy. Among this new genre of models, Ten C model of HRM is regarded as all encompassing and a pragmatic model. Alan Price is the architect of this model who presented it in his book titled *Human Resource Management in a Business Context,* published in 1997. There are ten essential principles—the Ten Cs—in this model. These are:

1. *Comprehensiveness.* The HRM strategy of an organization must include all the aspects of people management, typically starting from recruitment to post separation programmes.

2. *Credibility.* The HR practices must build trust between staff and top management and encourage employees' belief in HRM strategies.

3. *Communication.* The objectives of organization and that of HRM must be understood and accepted by all employees. The operating culture in organization must encourage openness and be free from all barriers.

4. *Cost effectiveness.* The reward and promotion system must be fair.

5. *Creativity.* The competitive advantage of the company must stem from its unique HR strategies.

6. *Coherence.* HRM activities and initiatives must form a meaningful whole.

7. *Competence.* HRM strategy will be crafted in such a way that organization becomes competent to achieve its objectives with the support of individual competencies.

8. *Control.* HRM policies and practices must ensure that performance of HR is consistent with business objectives.

9. *Change.* The basic premise of HRM strategy must be that continuous improvement and development is essential for survival.

10. *Commitment.* The last C stresses upon that employees are to be motivated to achieve organizational goals.

Alan Price 10 C model is measurable at the organizational level and success of the model lies in the tension and balance between the ten Cs.

Managerial Implication

The 10 C model is a comprehensive HR model that takes care of all aspects of a sound HRM programme in an organization. HR managers can draw two important lessons from this model. Firstly, this model serves as a measurable instrument to assess the status of HR function in organizations. Secondly, the model guides them in crafting an organization specific HRM strategy. HR strategy, policies and practices designed and implemented in consonance with this model would contribute for achieving coherence in HRM practices as well as organizational objectives.

TEN COMMANDMENTS MODEL OF HRM

It is widely acknowledged that religion has powerful influence over the human behaviour. Human beings carry these learnings to organizations, may be, in a dormant fashion. An interesting perspective is that we don't integrate these learnings with a firm's human resource strategy. All religions have put forth basic guiding principles or tenets for mankind to follow. Christians, Jews and Muslims each have their respective commandments. These commandments have influence on the outlook and behaviour of individuals and groups.

Three academicians namely Abbas Ali, Manton Gibbs and Robert Camp of University of Pennsylvania have given a shape in the form of religious foundations to human resource strategy in their paper titled 'Human Resource Strategy: The Ten Commandments Perspective', published in *International Journal of Sociology and Social Policy,* in 2000. They say the HR aspects of ten commandments in the three religions, center on loyalty, networking and minimization of the conflict to ensure survival and continuity. The implications of these Ten Commandments to HR strategy are given in Tables 1.2, 1.3 and 1.4.

TABLE 1.2 The New Commandments Propounded by Jesus Christ and their HR Implications

Ten commandments	Implications
1. Ye have heard that it was said by them of old time. Thou shalt not kill; and whosoever shall kill shall be in danger of the judgement;	Management should create an environment conducive to harmonious relationships; conflicts are a threat in group survival; due process enhances confidence and trust.
But say unto you. That whosoever is angry with his brother without a cause shall be in danger of the judgement.	
2. Ye have heard that they said it of old time. Thou shalt not commit adultery; but I say unto you. That whosoever looketh on a woman to lust after her hath committed adultery with her already in his heart.	Management and employees should observe the spirit and framework of their contract; sincere and honest relations are valid for a spirit of teamwork.
3. It hath been said. Whosoever shall put away his wife, let him give her a writing of divorcement; but I say unto you, that whosoever shall put away his wife, saying for the cause of fornication, causeth her to commit adultery: and whosoever shall marry her that is divorced committeth adultery.	Management should treat employees with fairness; management should not be motivated by mere short term cost reduction in conducting its HR strategies.
4. Swear not at all; neither by heaven; for it is God's throne.	Employees should trust management and not resent its instructions.
5. Ye have heard that it hath been said, an eye for an eye. And tooth for a tooth: but I say unto you, that ye resist not evil; but whosoever shall smile thee on thy right cheek turn to him the other also.	Employees should tolerate management even when affairs are carried out in an authoritarian style; employees should avoid conflicts among themselves and with management.
6. Ye have heard that it hath been said thou shalt love thy neighbour, and hate thine enemy. But I say unto you, love your enemies, bless them that curse you do good to them that hate you and prey for them which despite fully use you, and persecute you.	Tolerance for some abuse of power is vital for group and organizational survival. Resentment in the work place may lead to severe consequences.
7. That ye may be the children of your Father which is in heaven: for he maketh his sun to rise on the evil and on the good and send the rain on the just and on the unjust.	Management should treat employees equally and reward them. Interactions between management and employees needs to be just and equitable for building trust.
8. For if ye love them which love you, what reward have ye? Do not even the publicans the same?	Management should reward employees who are loyal and productive; fairness in conduct and tolerance for diversity strengthen the organizational culture.
9. And if he salute you brethren only, what do ye more than others? Do not even the publicans so?	There should be no discrimination in the work place; employees should be motivated to do their best as a team and be an example for new recruits to follow.
10. Be ye therefore perfect, even as your father which is in heaven is perfect.	Management should be the model that inspires employees to achieve perfection in their work.

TABLE 1.3 Ten Commandments in Islam: HR Implications

Ten commandments	Implications
1. Do not consider anything equal to god.	Respect for competent leadership; priority in hiring should be given to qualified individuals.
2. Be kind to your parents.	Disagreement with superiors should be voiced politely; employees should follow the instructions of their superiors.
3. Do not murder your children out of fear of poverty.	Management should consider employee layoffs and downsizing as a last resort to maintain business survival.
4. Do not even approach indecency either in public or in private.	Employees should be honest in dealing with management and should not sabotage property; management should show the utmost consideration for social norms, values and the rights of employees.
5. Do not murder for no reason anyone whom god has considered respectable. Thus, your lord guides so that you may think.	Management should establish a due process for dealing with employee grievances and should show justice and equity; performance should be the main criteria for evaluation.
6. Do not handle the property of the orphans except with a good reason until they become mature and strong.	Management should not abuse the rights of employees. Employee pension fund should be handled with utmost care.
7. Maintain equality in your dealings by the means of measurement and balance.	Management should be fair and just in recruiting, in giving compensation and in treatment of employees. Management should maintain a balanced programme to motivate and retain employees; employees should do their best to meet their commitments to their organizations.
8. Be just in your words even if the party involves is one of your relatives.	Management should avoid favouritism and nepotism; there should be no discrimination in the work place; supervisor should avoid misleading their subordinate; maintaining the dignity of employees in a virtue; diversity is essential for organizational growth.
9. Keep your promise with god. Does your lord guide you so that you may take heed.	Employees should observe both the letter and spirit of their agreement with their organizations, and should not violate any terms of agreement that would harm the organization.
10. This is my path and it is straight. Follow it and not other paths which will lead you far away from the god.	Management should device plans that motivate employees to be productive and loyal to their organizations; frankness in dealing with their subordinates is a virtue.

TABLE 1.4 The Original Ten Commandments Given to Moses by God: HR Implications

Ten Commandments	Implications
1. Thou shalt have no other gods before me.	Centrality of authority and leadership in organizational life, leaders play a vital role in motivating employees and in enhancing the cohesiveness of the group.
2. Thou shalt not make unto thee any graven image, or any likeness of anything that is in heaven above, or that is in the water under the earth.	Employees should be proud of their work and be loyal to authority; rewards are for those who obey and observe instructions.
3. Thou shalt not take the name of Lord thy God in vain; for the lord will not hold him guiltless that taketh his name in vain.	Employees should be respectful of their leaders and be loyal to them.
4. Remember the Sabbath day, to keep it holy, six days shalt thou labour, and do all thy work. But the seventh day is the Sabbath of the Lord thy God; in it thou shalt not do any work, thou, nor thy son, nor thy daughter, nor thy man servant, nor thy maid servant, nor thy cattle, nor thy stranger, that is within thy gates.	Flexible work schedule enhances commitment, group retreats are vital for spiritual renewal and commitment; leisure activity should be encouraged as it provides refreshment of energy and motivation.
5. Honour thy father and thy mother.	Employees should respect management and be loyal to their organization; they should honour their organizational contracts.
6. Thou shalt not kill.	Employees should not resort to violence to enforce their demands.
7. Thou shalt not commit adultery.	Management and employees should honour their contracts; both should not disturb work group norms and established procedures.
8. Thou shalt not steal.	Management and employees should not abuse organizational resources; sincerity to work groups increases turnover and enhances productivity.
9. Thou shalt not bear false witness against thy neighbour.	Employees should not provide false information that might demoralize their organization. Management and employees should negotiate in good faith.
10. Thou shalt not covet thy neighbour's wife, nor his manservant, nor his maidservant, nor his ox, nor his ass, nor anything that is thy neighbour's.	Management should not layoff employees just for the sake of it; neither management nor employees should pursue any desire that would weaken organizational cohesiveness.

Managerial Implication

The ultimate philosophy of any HR strategy will be similar to that of Ten Commandments—morality, honesty, sincerity and commitment. It may be easier to drive these points with the help of religious principles. A model of HRM integrating all the three religious commandments could be drawn to attain workforce commitment. The practical objective of such a model should be to transmit the central message of HRM in a language and manner the employees' respect.

TRIARCHIC MODEL OF HRM

There are many models and perspectives that are in existence to explain the nature, purpose and underlying assumptions of HRM. These perspectives include (i) Performance based HRM driven by American practices, (ii) Relationship based HRM supported by new generation practitioners, (iii) Learning oriented HRM promoted by academicians, (iv) Strategic HRM driven by economic models, (v) Reactive and proactive HRM models originated from industrial relations school etc. All these perspective have contributed for understanding of HRM as a systematic body of knowledge. However, each one of these provide only a singular view of HRM. Three experts from University of Limerick namely Thomas Garavan, Patrick Gunnigle and Michael Morley proposed a comprehensive view of HRM by bringing all the perspectives of HRD together in a meaningful fashion in a paper titled 'Contemporary HRD Research: A Triarchy of Theoretical Perspectives and their Prescriptions for HRD' published in *Journal of European Industrial Training in 2000*. Broadly, there are three models in HRM as described in Table 1.5.

TABLE 1.5

Theme	Model-I Capability-driven HRD	Model-II Psychological contact perspective	Model-III Learning organization perspective
Key underlying principles	HR is a critical source of sustained competitive advantage.	HR performance based on reciprocal, unwritten contract consisting of expectations, beliefs, promises and obligations.	Use collective knowledge to improve performance.
Prerequisites for HRD	Tangible and intangible capabilities defined clearly in strategy and appropriate human resource selected and fitted into jobs.	Fairness and trust in management. Commitment to career development of employees.	Integration of developmental activities with policy, practice and culture.
Target of HRD	Rather than focusing on past or current performance, HRD should focus on targeted future performance.	To facilitate the delivery of the deal for both employer and employee.	Activities aimed to improving the capacity for learning skills of employees.
Nature of HRD	HRD works directly with a central element of strategy: human behaviour. HRD does not merely assist or support strategy; it is a means of executing it.	Proactive life long learning and career development activities. Investment in general and advanced competencies.	Proactively working to create a work environmental that supports collective learning—formal and informal learning.
Daily task of HRD	Facilitate the daily execution of strategy by human resource.	Facilitate the creation of positive employee perceptions of their psychological contracts.	Facilitate employees to generate and utilize knowledge, establish appropriate networks and engage in double loop learning.
Basis for evaluating HRD	Delivery of targeted behaviours in line with strategy.	Contribution to outcomes such as job satisfaction, organizational commitment and citizenship, motivation and job involvement.	Extent to which knowledge creation occurs and brings about organizational change.

Managerial Implication

Top management in conjunction with HRM manager must decide the type of HRM model to be followed in the organization. Unfortunately, often organizations are not clear about the model they are pursuing. Sometimes, their HRM practices and principles do not progress in integrated fashion and may be conflictive. Similarly, evaluation model does not go in tune with the type of HRM model being executed. For example, assessing effectiveness of capability driven HRM practices through Psychological contract or learning organization evaluation models confuses the organizations. Therefore, organizations must adopt HRM model consciously that suits it most, based upon its internal and external environment encompassing nature, dominant culture, type of human resource, technology, products and customers. The practices, implementation and evaluation methods that are supportive and compatible to such adopted HRM model must be chosen.

TOYOTA MODEL OF HRM

Toyota is known for many world-class products and quality initiatives that include famous Toyota production system that later became popular as JIT (just-in-time inventory). Toyota maintains high profile in its HRM policies and practices too. Ian Winfield of University of Derby, UK who conducted a detailed field study on Toyota's HRM in 1994, strongly believes that human resource practices of this company can serve as a model, particularly in manufacturing and production oriented organizations. Toyota's HRM framework broadly comprises of four goals as described below:

1. *The goal of organizational integration.* The integration of employees at individual and collective level with organization is seen as the primary goal of Toyota HRM strategy. This goal has been achieved through extensive use of teams that are subordinate to organizational goals. Welfare of employees also received wide attention as a part of this goal.

2. *The goal of commitment.* In order to achieve this goal, a two-pronged strategy was followed. Firstly, Toyota preferred semi-rural workforce for induction in their plants. They believe that people who are not contaminated by industrial culture and influences tend to retain with them a kind of feudal value of loyalty, which can be converted into organizational commitment. Secondly, measures such as suggestion schemes, quality circles and employee involvement methods are used to gain commitment.

3. *The goal of flexibility and adaptability.* Team authority in place of single individual holding all the powers had paved way for realizing flexibility in the organization. These teams are task-based and can be dismantled or restructured, depending upon the situation. The adaptability trait is institutionalized through the approach of multi-skilling and job rotations.

4. *The goal of quality.* Self, peer and team surveillance techniques are used to ensure quality of products. Further, a series of measures employed, such as time and motion study, benchmarking, continuous process improvement and employee involvement contributed in the achievement of this goal.

Toyota has recomposed the aforementioned four HRM goals into 17 specific practices. These 17 practices are classified into production practices and employment practices. The production practices are: JIT, Kanban, Line stop, Level scheduling, Continuous flow and Processing. The employment practices are: Continuous improvement, Single status facilities, Performance appraisal, Daily team briefings, Temporary contracts, Performance related pay, Company council, Cross disciplinary teams, Single unions, Cross training and Group decision-making.

Managerial Implication

This model has two prime practical implications. Firstly, it serves as an ideal model in terms of how an HRM strategy must be made. In other words, a sound HRM strategy should have super ordinate goals linked to organizational goals and these goals must be rendered to core HRM practices. Secondly, the mix of local ethos with international practices to obtain commitment and organizational integration of workforce serves as a great learning tool. For example, Toyota used local cultural/rural ethos to launch its production system of international origin and obtain loyalty.

BUSINESS PROCESS MODEL OF HRM

The business process aligned HRM, which gathered momentum during the last decade, has strengthened in the new millennium on account of its efficacy. Figen Cakar and Umit Bititci of *University of Strathclyde* proposed and tested a new model called Business Process Model using hard systems approach. They also tested this model in a number of manufacturing organizations. Based on the results therein, the model was further refined. They presented this fully developed model in their paper titled "Human Resource Management as a Strategic Input to Manufacturing" in *International Working Conference on Strategic Manufacturing* held in 2001 in Denmark. The salient features of this model are:

1. *Make HRM strategy.* Use business strategy and objectives and requirements of key business processes to formulate an integrated HRM strategy by setting objectives, establishing current capabilities, negotiating appropriate budgets for realistic implementation of the plan, and setting HRM policies.

2. *Set HRM objective.* This activity interprets business strategy and objectives and requirements of other key business processes to formulate HRM requirements and objectives.

3. *Establish current capability.* This activity establishes the current HRM capability within business and its key processes to meet the set objectives.

4. *Plan.* This activity develops a plan, including budgets, which define courses of action the business is going to adopt to build upon its current capabilities and develop its HRM in line with the stated HRM objectives and requirements.

5. *Negotiate budget.* Uses requirements of the plan to negotiate for financial resources, which will lead to successful implementation of HRM strategy.

6. *Set HRM policies actively.* Set up types of compensation, staffing methods, appraisal methods, form of training and development, and working conditions of relevant strategic needs.

7. *Implement HRM strategy.* Implement HRM strategy by controlling HRM planning, assessing, recruiting, selecting, monitoring, and utilizing the right people in order to train, educate and develop them.

8. *Control HRM.* To make sure that HR strategy is planned, correctly applied and monitored in accordance with the objectives and requirements of the organization.

9. *Recruit.* Concerned with bringing in human resource into positions in line with its HRM requirements from internal and external sources.

10. *Train, educate, develop.* Activity concerned with upgrading existing people's capabilities within the business in line with its human resource objectives.

11. *Managing HRM performance.* Activity concerned with the setting up of targets for individuals, monitoring progress against the targets, and identifying necessary training, education and development needs as well as deciding reward and discipline action.

12. *Manage redeployment.* Facilitates to identify a deficiency in a job position, which cannot be rectified through training, education or redeployment of the current job holder within the organization.

13. *Monitor impact on business results.* This subprocess monitors the impact of the HRM process on business performance through monitoring its contribution to the business strategy and objectives and other key business processes.

14. *Monitor impact on business strategy.* Monitors the impact of the HRM strategy on business strategy as well as business performance.

15. *Monitor impact on people satisfaction.* Concerned with establishing how well the business satisfies its employees.

16. *Monitor impact on managerial process.* Concerned with monitoring how well the HRM strategy and its implementation is satisfying the requirements of managerial processes.

17. *Monitor impact on operational process.* Concerned with monitoring how well the HRM strategy and its implementation is satisfying the requirements of operational processes.

18. *Monitor impact on support processes.* Concerned with monitoring how well HRM strategy and its implementation is satisfying the requirements of support processes. The support processes mainly consist of staff functions.

Managerial Implication

The model explains how HRM strategy is to be devised, implemented and monitored. The experience of organizations indicates that this model has the potential to deliver positive results to the organization. The understanding of various steps involved and its orientation helps HR managers in their efforts to implement a business aligned HRM model in their organizations.

COMPETITIVE ADVANTAGE MODEL OF HRM

In our times, it is well acknowledged that HR function has the capability to sharpen a firm's competitive advantage over the rival firms and HR professionals have a strategic role in this process. However, the approaches in presenting the role of HR function in gaining competitive advantage have differed. Some of these approaches could not succeed in putting a convincing model because of ambiguity and inadequacy in defining what elements of HR can be a source for providing sustainable competitive advantage to firms. In order to overcome these gaps, Professor Jay Barney of Ohio State University and Professor Patrick Wright of Cornell University developed a comprehensive model in 1997 to establish HR as a competitive advantage of the firm. This model was built on the framework of VRIO (value, rareness, imitability and organization). In other words, the premise of the model is that it is the value, rareness, non-imitability and scientific organization of HR that provide sustainable competitive advantage to the firm to be precise, the model presents three elements of HRM that provide the competitive advantage as indicated in the following:

1. *Sustainable competitive advantage stems from firm-specific more than general skills.* All the firms possess general skills and they provide equal value to them. Thus, to seek sustained competitive advantage through general skills would be futile. On the other hand, this does not imply that these skills are not important. In contrast, specific skills provide value only to a particular firm that possess them.

2. *Sustainable competitive advantage comes from teams more than from individuals.* Individuals though quite valuable, it is the teamwork and teams that provide competitive advantage, because most of the tasks in organizations are interdependent. Further, team working promotes trust and bonds among employees. This team environment will be firm-specific, rare, valuable and difficult for the competitors to imitate or pirate them unlike a single individual or group of individuals.

3. *Sustainable competitive advantage stems from HRM systems more than single HRM practices.* The essence of it is no individual HRM practice like training, selection, reward etc., or a few HR practices however best they may be, can become source of competitive advantage. It is rather a well-integrated HRM system that produces a synergetic effect among all the HRM practices that would offer the competitive advantage.

HR managers have an important role to perform in shaping the HR system for a competitive advantage. They need to understand four critical elements in this endeavour indicated the

- value of people in the firm and their role in competitive advantage
- economic consequences of the HR practices in a firm
- comparative attributes of HR and practices in a firm with its competitors
- role of the HR function in building organizational capability for the future.

Managerial Implication

The VRIO framework helps organizations and HR managers in many ways. Firstly, as the model advocates, it is the rareness, value, non-imitability and well organized HR function that can keep an organization on a firm foot. Therefore, organizations must strive to achieve this distinction of VRIO in HRM through (i) nurturing organization specific skills by building HR competencies, (ii) infusing team work and (iii) implementing an integrated human resource system. Secondly, HR managers must acquire knowledge in the four areas as specified above. Unless, HR managers equip themselves with these strategic skills, they cannot even become partners in organizational strategy, leave aside guiding the competitive advantage initiative.

E-BUSINESS MODEL OF HRM

E-Commerce, E-Business, B2B (Business to Business), B2C (Business to Customer), etc. have become common focus of all organizations in the 21st century. Further, all organizations from brick and mortar companies to fully web-based companies, are equally struggling to build a compatible HRM model that reinforces their business strategy and operational plans. Organizations, when they adopt E-business model, typically encounter certain business challenges like uncertainty in the business environment, speed in decision making, frequently changing technology, maintaining integration of suppliers, distributors, customers, internal processes etc. and the need to maintain a project-based organization structure and working. Therefore, they need to build a HRM model that is drastically different from a traditional model in terms of focus and role. Based on an in-depth study of cross section of organizations in the year 2000, Professors Patrick Wright and Lee Dyer of Cornell University have developed a model for E-business organizations, which involves transformation of the focus and role of HRM as in Table 1.6.

TABLE 1.6

From	*To*
Focus	
• Programmes	• Deliverables
• Policies	• Solutions
• Paper	• Cyberspace
• Years	• Weeks
• Complexity	• Simplicity
• Analyze, then solve	• Solve, then analyze
• Analysis paralysis	• Action learning
Role	
• Strategic partner	• Change agent
• Change agent	• Strategic partner
• Employee advocate	• Employee advocate
• Administrative expert	• Administrative expert

Organizations shall also have to adhere to the following six principles in order to build an E-Business HRM model:

1. *Attain autonomy with accountability.* Every employee does whatever is necessary and appropriate to achieve organizational goals. Therefore, HRM policies, programmes and practices are designed and implemented in ways that promote individual autonomy along with personal accountability for outcomes, at all levels of the organization.

2. *Forge common purpose.* Every employee understands, embraces and lives the organization's vision and core values. HRM policies, programmes and practices should be designed and implemented to reinforce the organizational vision and core values.

3. *Achieve contextual clarity.* Every employee understands (i) the organization's business environment, (ii) strategic direction and domain, (iii) business models and results and (iv) knows how his/her contribution promotes business success. Achieving contextual clarity involves a change in the mindset. Some areas of emphasis include: participation, training and development, communication and compensation strategy.

4. *Promote personal growth.* Every employee takes personal responsibility for his/her professional development assisted by the organization, which provide the essential opportunities and resources. Organizations can encourage the employee's development through mentoring and forming communities of interest and communities of practice for critical skill areas.

5. *Develop mutual support.* Every employee feels that he/she is part of a caring community of which members are committed to one another's well being. There is a formidable challenge to ensure a mutually supportive environment where individuality triumphs. Organizations, therefore, must use team working, team performances and reward systems.

6. *Provide commensurate results.* Every employee perceives that the total resources (monetary and nonmonetary) provided by the organization are equal in value to the total contribution made to the organization. Organizations must make a balancing act to ensure the equitable compensation, incentives, career upgradations and other non-financial rewards on objective parameters in reference to performance.

Managerial Implication

The role of HR function and its managers will be different as elucidated above. The above model helps HRM managers in E-Business organizations to shape suitable HRM policies and practices. They must initiate three-pronged action strategy. Firstly, audit your HR function in reference to this model and chart the comparative differences and deficiencies. Secondly, prepare an action plan based on audited results vis-à-vis the critical elements of above model. Thirdly, commence the implementation in an evolutionary manner. In a nutshell, shift the focus of HRM from administrative and transactional-base, to that of knowledge and transformational-base.

HRM MODEL FOR DYNAMIC ORGANIZATIONS

It is widely believed that functioning of HRM department is the testimony of bureaucracy, and in a few cases, symbol of red tapism in organizations. There is also a perception that HRM departments are required and suitable only for stable and large-sized organizations. Fortunately, organizations of sun rise industry like hotel, hospitality, financial, retailing and software destroyed this myth by manifesting that the success of these organizations is contingent upon, to a considerable extent, how well HR function is organized. However, it is a fact that organizations operating in a dynamic environment need HRM policies and practices that are dynamic and different from HRM in stable organizations. Five experts namely Richard Shafer, Lee Dyer, Janine Kilty, Jaffrey Amos and G.A. Ericksen have highlighted five most important issues for formulating HR strategy in dynamic organizations based on an in-depth case study conducted in 2000 as a part of Cornell University working study series. These five critical issues are:

1. *Even in the most dynamic environment, not everything can be emergent.* In dynamic situations, extensive strategic planning will be futile. On the other hand, everything cannot be emergent. Therefore, organizations must create a vision and set of core values that provide skyhooks of stability for employees to hang onto as emergent business strategies are formed and the culture change progressed.

2. *Organizational agility doesn't just happen; it has to be deliberately pursued.* There may not be a master plan on paper but it must be in the minds of people. HR managers must lead transformations and changes in a deliberate and planned manner but that shall be engineered in a way that people own this process.

3. *Guiding models facilitate the formation of an agility-oriented human resource strategy.* The business model that is adopted in an organization must facilitate adoption of corresponding HR policies and practices. Further, there must be good rapport between the business and HRM models. The HRM model must draw guidelines from implicit and explicit objectives of the business model that is pursued in organization.

4. *A limited number of integrated or synergistic human resource initiatives define an agility-oriented human resource strategy.* Dynamic organizations need HR policies and practices that are flexible and efficient. These include: (i) enriching work and promoting personal growth, (ii) providing commensurate returns to employees who contribute to emergent strategies and (iii) providing autonomy to employees with accountability and (iv) involvement of employees at operational and strategic levels. There must also be sharp integration among all HRM practices horizontally and vertically.

5. *Key human resource initiatives guides the choice of human resource programmes and practices.* Often, there is a view that dynamic organizations need HRM practices that change in accordance with contextual demands. It may be true, but the practices must emanate from a broad framework and principles. For example, encouraging employee involvement is the standing principle but the application of it can change depending on the situation.

Managerial Implication

These five key lessons help HR managers to build a HR model that help organizations in a dynamic environment to stabilize themselves. This model provides a pragmatic perspective of how certainty can be brought otherwise in an uncertain environment by crafting an agile HRM strategy. The other insightful suggestion that emanates from this model is that few well-integrated HRM practices can yield valuable results to both employees and organizations. Therefore, the lesson is that it is not the quantity but the quality of HRM practices originating from sound principles that facilitate success.

MODEL FOR BUSINESS—HRM ALIGNMENT

A large number of HRM professionals, and strategic and corporate planners endorse that there must be a sharp linkage between business plans and HRM plans in an organization. They believe such an association not only strengthens the organizational functioning but also positions HRM in a strategic role. However, attaining such a linkage or alignment is easier said than done. The fundamental question that arises is how this alignment should be done, and what appropriate approach the organizations must follow. The fact, however, is that there is not even a single standard model which can be made universally applicable to all organizations and to all situations in the same organization. Therefore, the appropriateness would be contingent upon history, operating culture, technology, and internal and external environment of the organization. Thomas Garavan and Noreen Heraty of University of Limerick and Pat Costine, a management consultant based in Ireland have identified ten approaches that organizations can follow to establish the said linkage and presented them in a paper titled 'The Emergence of Strategic Human Resource Management' published in a *Journal of European Industrial Training* in 1995. These approaches are:

1. *Top down approach.* This approach involves three steps: (a) identification of business plans on long, medium and short terms, (b) formulation of HRM strategy corresponding to business plans at all the three term levels and (c) designing of HRM activities based on objectives of HRM strategy to make available the human talent when needed.

2. *Market driven approach.* HRM professionals here classify the employees into distinct skill and knowledge groups, assess the skills available with each group, predict what skills employees require to possess to meet the organizational market demands and decide how to close the gap between current human skills/competency and requirement in future.

3. *Career planning approach.* This approach advocates that human resource practitioner must work towards linking each employee career plans with that of business plans. In other words, the existence and growth of every employee flows from business plans of the organization.

4. *The futuring approach.* Here the alignment will be achieved at strategy formulation stage itself. In this process, sometimes HRM can itself become a major focus and ingredient of business plan.

5. *Performance diagnosis approach.* This approach proposes that linkage between the two can be achieved through HRM playing the facilitator role in formulation and execution of business plans. Here, HRM practitioners structure the meetings, interactions and exercises, enabling strategists to decide the business plans.

6. *Artificial experience approach.* HRM practitioners in this approach create simulation of future business plans and develop ways of HRM alignment. This is done through participation of line managers, corporate planners and top management using appropriate group meetings and exercises.

7. *Pulse taking approach.* Survey technique and training and development interventions will be employed in this approach to gauge implementation effectiveness of business plans. HRM department organize the analysis of data so obtained to gather solutions through appropriate measures that include small group meetings.

8. *The educational approach.* The linkage achieved in this approach mainly includes offering training and knowledge of strategic thinking, methods and management to prepare business plans and also equipping them with implementation skills.

9. *Interpersonal approach.* This approach is based on the premise that a substantial percentage of corporate strategy is informal and dynamic. Therefore, it is HRM

professionals who with their interpersonal approach can institutionalize this informal strategy in a planned and formal way.

10. *The rifle approach.* This approach is based on troubleshooting. In other words, HRM would be used to identify the problems and constraints in implementation of business plans and also to resolve them.

Managerial Implication

The above ten approaches present a comprehensive perspective of business-HRM alignment. It also illustrates different routes organizations can use to achieve the alignment. In practice, it may be difficult to decide what approach should be adopted to establish this linkage. Therefore, human resource managers must analyze all the related aspects such as operating culture, technology, the type of workforce, and the nature of business strategy, while embracing a particular approach. On the other hand, none of these approaches can be straight jacketed into the situation of organizations. In that case, a combination of approaches or an approach with necessary modifications may serve the purpose.

MODEL LINKING HRM WITH STRATEGY AND STRUCTURE

By now it is a fundamental knowledge that structure must follow the organizational strategy because structure is a means to operationalize the strategy. The logical consequential development in this approach is that there should be a sharp linkage between HRM policies and practices with organizational strategy and structure. This is because, both strategy and structure need strong support of HRM. Knowing the importance of linkage, J.R. Galbrith and D.A. Nathanson, way back in 1978, proposed a seminal model illustrating the role of HRM in strategy and structure in their book titled "Strategy Implementation: The Role of Structure and Process". The essential features of the model are summarized in Table 1.7.

TABLE 1.7   Human Resource Management Practices

Strategy	Structure	Selection	Appraisal	Rewards	Development
Single product	Functional	Functionally oriented; subjective criteria used	Subjective: measure via personal contact	Unsystematic; allocated in a paternalistic manner	Unsystematic; largely through job experiences; single function focus
Single product: Vertical integration	Functional	Functionally oriented: standardized criteria used	Impersonal: based on cost and productivity data	Related to performance and productivity	Functional specialists with some generalists: largely through job rotation
Growth through acquisition of unrelated businesses	Separate, self-contained businesses	Functionally oriented, but varies from business to business in terms of how systematic	Impersonal: based on return on investment and profitability	Formula-based and includes return on investment and profitability	Cross functional, but not cross business

TABLE 1.7 Human Resource Management Practices (*continued*)

Strategy	Structure	Selection	Appraisal	Rewards	Development
Related diversification of product lines through internal growth and acquisition	Multidivisional	Functionally and generalist oriented; systematic criteria used	Impersonal; based on return on investment, productivity and subjective assessment of contribution to overall company	Large bonuses; based on profitability and subjective assessment of contribution to overall company	Cross functional, cross divisional and cross corporate/divisional formal
Multiple products in multiple countries	Global organization (geographic center and worldwide)	Functionally and generalist oriented; systematic criteria used	Impersonal; based on multiple goals such as return on investment, profit tailored to product and country	Bonuses; based on multiple planned goals with moderate top management discretion	Cross-divisional and cross-subsidiary to corporate; formal and systematic

Managerial Implication

The above model clearly drives home three vital issues that have implications for managerial action. Firstly, it highlights that HRM activities must be pursued in tandem with organizational structure and strategy. Secondly, strategy and structure specific HRM activities ought to be adopted from time to time. It means HRM strategy should be subjected to change in tune with change in strategy. Thirdly, four functions, i.e. selection, appraisal, rewards and development of human resource are the critical activities that should be given utmost importance. Unfortunately, most of the human resource activities in organizations are implemented in a standalone format that serves purposes of low value.

PARALLELING HR PLANNING WITH BUSINESS PLANNING

In order to reap maximum benefits, HR planning should be carried out at the same time as strategic business planning in a parallel process. However, successful linking of HRM with Strategic Business Planning is dependent upon participation within and across the levels of organization. Though, it may appear as cumbersome process at the beginning, but can provide a meaningful direction and existence to human resource activities in organizations. This paralleling must be done step wise, prescribes James Niniger in his remarkable book titled *Managing Human Resources: A Strategic Perspective* published in 1982. The paralleling model is illustrated in Figure 1.1.

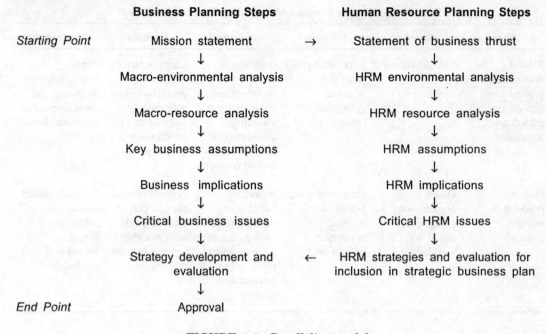

	Business Planning Steps		**Human Resource Planning Steps**
Starting Point	Mission statement	→	Statement of business thrust
	↓		↓
	Macro-environmental analysis		HRM environmental analysis
	↓		↓
	Macro-resource analysis		HRM resource analysis
	↓		↓
	Key business assumptions		HRM assumptions
	↓		↓
	Business implications		HRM implications
	↓		↓
	Critical business issues		Critical HRM issues
	↓		↓
	Strategy development and evaluation	←	HRM strategies and evaluation for inclusion in strategic business plan
	↓		
End Point	Approval		

FIGURE 1.1 Paralleling model.

The model clearly stipulates the progress of human resource strategy formulation movement. For example, the HRM environment and its resource allocation priority shall follow the macro environment and organizational resource allocation. In this process, at every stage, human resource strategy is built by seeking input from business strategy. This contributes for higher-level mutual bonding and compatibility between both of them.

Managerial Implication

The model comprises a practical framework for integrating HRM with strategy formulation itself. It has two prime practical implications for managerial action. Firstly, the step-wise model guides the HR managers in their efforts to integrate HR planning with business planning. Secondly, it presents a perspective of developing HR strategy in organizations. Undoubtedly, the model fuelled the practice of matching HR planning with business planning and facilitated to accord business status to HRM function.

MODEL FOR MATCHING HRM WITH LIFE CYCLE OF ORGANIZATION

One major problem with existing HRM systems is that they are fragmented, incomplete and sometimes built on faulty assumptions about human or organizational growth. Edger Schein, the legend in organizational behaviour and theory of our generation argues that successful organizations are those that are able to match organizational needs with individual needs, thus achieving organizational growth along with individual development, commitment, creativity etc.

He advocated a model aligning strategic HRM with life cycle stage of an organization in his book titled *Organizational Culture and Leadership* published in 1985. The model is summarized in Table 1.8.

TABLE 1.8

Life cycle stage	Key culture/Strategic features	Practical implications for HRM
Embryonic	• High levels of cohesion • Dominant role of founder • Outside help not valued • Lack of procedures and planning systems • Politics play an important role	• Owner may not perceive need for HRM • Limited management expertise and succession problems • Changes may be unplanned/ad hoc • HRM may have to market its services aggressively
Growth	• Large variety of cultural changes • Levels of cohesion decline • Emergence of middle management • Tensions/conflicts may arise in organizations • Need to get people to accept new ways of thinking • Diversification of business activities • Line/Staff differences	• Initiation of career development activities • Inducting new recruits • Management development activities • Development of high performing teams • Involvement in the management of change • Reinforcement and maintenance of cultural values and beliefs • Dealing with ambiguity and uncertainty
Maturity	• Institutionalization of values and beliefs • Evolutionary rather than revolutionary changes • Inertia may emerge in organization	• HRM function should be well established • Maintenance of HRM activities may be more appropriate • Lack of career opportunities may require novel HRM approaches
Decline	• Culture may act as a defence against a hostile environment • Major decisions may have to be taken • Readjustment necessary	• Management of change • Reassure employees that problems are being tackled • Organizing problem-centred project/task activities

Managerial Implication

The implications of this model for practitioners are self-explanatory. Nevertheless, two other benefits of this model to HR managers are: Firstly, the model enables to gain a perspective on how HR practices gain shape in correspondence with life cycle of organizations. Based on this, HR managers can critically examine the shape of HRM in their organizations vis-à-vis organizational stage. Secondly, it helps as a practical prescription to human resource and corporate planners in augmenting the needs of organizations at various stages.

MODEL FOR LINKING HRM PRACTICES WITH ORGANIZATIONAL STAGES

The most advocated approach in HRM practice during the last and current decades is linking HRM practices with growth stage of an organization. As an organization specialists put it, every organization will undergo different stages of growth in its life. Correspondingly, human resource needs of organizations also differ depending on this growth stage. According to Lloyd Baird and Ilan Mesholaum, organizations undergo five stages of development, with different HRM needs in each stage. One program or approach does not work everywhere; programs must fit at each stage. Based on this argument, they proposed a model to link HR practices with organizational stages in their path-breaking paper titled "Getting Pay Off from Investment in Human Resource Management" published in *Business Horizons* in 1992. They further point to a main advantage of viewing HRM in terms of developmental stages is, that it provides a way of understanding what an organization will need in the future. The essential features of this model are illustrated in Table 1.9.

TABLE 1.9

Organizational stage	*HRM practices*
Stage I: Start Up Entrepreneurship, founder management, inform-ality, limited products and markets	• Recruiting to find key people, basic compensation and administrative systems
Stage II: Growth Dynamic growth, technical specialization, expan-ded product lines and markets, added formality and structure, professional management introduced	• Advanced recruiting capability, training and socialization programs to adapt new employees to the organization
Stage III: Control Competition for resources, pressure to increase productivity, controlled investments.	• Cost control of HRM programs and controlled investment in business related skills. Computer used to analyze costs.
Stage IV: Integration Diversification, decentralization, product groups or divisions, project management. Focus on coordination and integration.	• Effective integration mechanisms between the various HRM components, planning and organization development capability.
Stage V: Flexibility Highly developed monitoring and scanning capability, flexibility to adjust to market and environmental needs, multiple products and markets.	• Adaptability, collaborative teamwork, team action, full integration across functional areas.

Managerial Implication

The simplicity of HRM lies in its integrative framework, i.e. managing activities ranging from attracting human resource talent to its separation from organization in mutually beneficial fashion. The complexity lies in its change of emphasis on HRM activities in tune with organizational stage. This is the insight this model provides to HR managers. Unfortunately, most of the HRM professionals either pursue HR practices in their own direction, conveniently leaving aside the dire need of its linkage with organization. When this linkage is absent, the irrelevance of HR existence in organization becomes apparent. Therefore, HR managers must drive organization stage specific HRM practices to establish its utility to organizations and employees.

MODEL FOR WORLD-CLASS HRM SYSTEMS

Studying best HRM practices of world-class companies provide some useful insights to all of us. A consultancy organization popular for its services in the area of benchmarking practices, namely Best Practices, LLC at Chapter Hill, NC studied HRM practices of world class companies and profiled best HRM practices of six multinationals such as Royal Dutch/Shell, Lucent Technologies, Motorola, Xerox, Federal Express and Saturn. These companies have maximized employees' potential through strong human resource programmes. Four out of these six companies: Lucent, Motorola, Xerox and Federal Express are recipients of Malcom Baldrige award for their quality standards and remaining two are well known for their HRM practices internationally. The key practices of these benchmark class organizations are:

1. Employee development

    (a) Recruiting and selecting excellent employees
    (b) Defining strategic direction for development programmes
    (c) Structuring the development of organization to facilitate effective delivery
    (d) Setting clear development goals
    (e) Aligning programmes to bridge developmental gaps
    (f) Deploying developmental programmes through innovative and effective methods
    (g) Measuring developmental programmes effectiveness
    (h) Reducing training cycle time

2. Leadership

    (a) Developing an integrated leadership model
    (b) Identifying and understanding key experiences associated with successful leaders
    (c) Evidence through actions are the key dimensions of leadership
    (d) Monitoring leadership and communication effectiveness
    (e) Employing flexible developmental programs to meet the needs of each type of leader

3. Reward and recognition

    (a) Developing innovative, broad based reward and recognition programmes to support employee satisfaction
    (b) Implementing innovative pay systems
    (c) Designing an organizational structure to support reward and recognition systems
    (d) Aligning empowerment programmes to drive employee satisfaction
    (e) Designing systems to maximize employee satisfaction
    (f) Designing performance review systems to allocate rewards and recognition

4. Teamwork

    (a) Fully integrating teams and teamwork into the company's operations, structure, and mission
    (b) Employing teams as primary means for delivering operating strategy
    (c) Creating common structure and support to ensure team's function efficiently
    (d) Developing team enabling tools and measurements

Managerial Implication

The study and understanding of these benchmarked HRM practices give HRM managers a practical perspective, insights and some innovative ideas to redefine their own HRM systems and processes. Many times, adopting the best HR practices with suitable modifications to suit in an organizational context may be much easier than following some abstract models. Certainly, these world-class HRM practices have the potential to inspire many organizations to reckon them as benchmarks in their journey to achieve high standards in HRM practices. The benchmark reports can be obtained from Best Practices, LLC, Quadrangle Drive, Suite 200, Chapel Hill, NC 27516.

MODEL FOR EFFECTIVE HRM PRACTICES

HRM encompasses a wide range of practices intended to attract, develop, reward, motivate, integrate and retain employees. However, practices that are effective in one organization/context may not evoke same or similar result in other organization/situation because of a number of factors. However, there are a few practices that have proved their universal appeal. In other words, studies and experiences of organizations point that there are a certain set of HRM practices that are sure to deliver effective results for all types of organizations. Professor Jeffrey Pfeffer, based on his comprehensive and intensive study of a number of organization, classified the following as the most effective HR practices in his book titled *Competitive Advantage through People: Unleashing the Power of the Workforce* published in 1994. These are as follows:

- Financial incentives for excellent performance
- Work organization practices that motivate employee effort and capture the benefits of know-how and skill
- Rigorous selection and selectivity in recruiting
- Higher than average wages
- Employee share-ownership plans
- Extensive information sharing
- Decentralization of decision making and empowerment
- Work organization based on self-managing teams
- High investment in training and skill development
- Having people do multiple jobs and job rotation
- Elimination of status symbols
- Compressed distribution of salaries across and within levels
- Promotion from within
- Long term perspective
- Measurement of HRM practices and policy implementation
- Coherent view of employment relations

These practices were identified as effective, based on their positive contribution to bottom line of organizations in terms of turnover, sales, market capitalization and profits. The author's series of research studies clearly establish this.

Managerial Implication

The above practices are categorized as effective HRM practices with lessons from live experiences. Therefore, it has immense practical value to all managers, particularly to HR managers. The critical analysis of these practices also reveals three essential aspects: Firstly, the practices figured are comprehensive in nature. They consist of practices from recruitment to separation and also measurement of these practices to assess their utility. Secondly, it strongly advocates the need to bring coherence among HR practices in organizations. Thirdly, it points out that effectiveness of practices is more dependent upon how we use these practices and what benefits we expect from them rather than the practices themselves.

MODEL FOR CAPABILITY DRIVEN HRM PRACTICE

The role of HRM in building internal capabilities of an organization has become a subject of interest to academicians, management consultants and practitioners. It is well acknowledged that HRM not only contributes in building these internal capabilities but also strengthens the organizational efforts in gaining strategic advantage over the competitors. This is because HRM can build organizational capability that is more than the sum of its employee's competencies. Many of the organizations, though convinced with this argument, are not quite clear as to what the capability-driven HRM is all about and how they can build such model in their organizations. Professor Mikko Luoma of University of Vaasa based on study of few organizations and practices had developed a capability driven HRM framework and presented a paper titled "Developing People for Business Success: Capability-Driven HRD in Practice" published in *Management Decision* in 2000. There are four critical elements in a capability-driven HRM model such as (i) clarity of HR development strategy, (ii) integration between corporate and HR function level issues, (iii) involvement of human resource and (iv) and evaluation of human resource approach to renew it timely. The determinants of capability-driven HRM, together with these four critical elements are illustrated in Table 1.10.

TABLE 1.10 Critical Features

Determinants	Clarity	Integration	Involvement	Evaluation
Strategy process	Documented, explicit approach to strategy formulation	Connection between corporate, business and function level issues	Participation of middle management and representatives of personnel	Evaluation of the functioning of current approach and sensitivity to new approaches
Sources of competitive advantage	Competitive factors identified and agreed on	Strengths supporting each other	Possibility of several key groups' contribution	Measurement of competitive position and identification of competitors' strengths
HRM strategy	Explicitly stated HRM strategy	HRM practices aligned with each other and the direction of business	Line managers as owners of HRM practices	Evaluation and reformulation of existing practices
HRM activities	Identified and retained as a comprehensive set of HRM activities	HRM activities linked to each other and to HRM strategy	Coverage of all personnel	Measurement of learning results and overall efficiency

TABLE 1.10   Critical Features (*continued*)

Determinants	Clarity	Integration	Involvement	Evaluation
Management development processes	Established and remain as an institutionalized management development processes	Management development processes embedded into the ongoing business	Active participation of senior management in the planning, execution and follow-up processes	Evaluation of management development . processes based on their ability to deliver business results
Expertise areas of HRM people	Business knowledge, collaboration skills, influencing skills, knowledge of organizations			

Managerial Implication

The above-mentioned model was created with the help of evidence from real companies. This can serve as a basic model for HR professionals to design their own model. There are two major implications for practitioners here. The first one is to build business capabilities in the organization through building hard and soft skills. Secondly, HR strategy must be subjected to audit and assessments on a continuous basis to measure its utility to the business improvement and to renew it based on the results.

MODEL FOR CUSTOMER FOCUSED HRM

The growing role of service sector such as hospitality, financial services, knowledge organizations, entertainment, tourism and transport in the economy, is an important development of the new millennium. Customers and their satisfaction have occupied a central role in survival and success of these service organizations. HRM has the potential to accomplish their organizational goal of customer satisfaction. The HR strategies apt for manufacturing organizations may not be compatible with service set up which requires different types of strategies. Therefore, they require HR strategies that support customer satisfaction and service excellence. Professor Benjamin Schneider of University of Maryland, based on a comprehensive study, identified five HRM practices that can result in customer delightfulness, and presented them in an analytical manner in the paper titled "HRM-A Service Perspective: Towards a Customer-focused HRM" published in *International Journal of Service and Industrial Management* in 1994. The practices are:

1. Supervision which provides feedback on performance, establishes reward contingencies and shares information
2. Organizational practices that facilitate personal career development and planning
3. Working for an organization that has a good status and image in the larger community
4. Organizational training and socialization practices that facilitate new entrants into the organization
5. Organizations, which, generally facilitate rather than inhibit job performance.

All except a few service organizations, have developed their HRM practices like recruitment, selection, compensation, training, communication, leadership, and socialization, focusing on production than delivery. Therefore, they need to shift themselves towards HR practices that can enhance an organization's capabilities to satisfy the external customers. There is clear evidence from successful service organizations that there is a direct and positive linkage between work climate and customer satisfaction. Hence organizations must take actions in two areas: (i) they must introduce the customer as a legitimate standard for evaluating the effectiveness of HRM practices and procedures and (ii) introduce employee perceptions and feelings into the logic of customer service quality.

Managerial Implication

Traditionally, HR strategies are mainly focused on internal processes and its employees than on external domain like customers. Therefore, it demands a 360-degree shift in their focus. The objective of creating a positive work environment may be same for all types of organizations but their *modus operandi* differ. Service organization requires HR policies and practices that are centered on customer satisfaction and quality excellence whereas enhancing production must be the corner stone of manufacturing sector. The practical implication of this model for HR managers is that they must evaluate their HR practices with customer as focus and adopt the practices that motivate employees to perform as vehicles of service excellence.

MODEL FOR HRM SCOREBOARD

Based on the survey of 3000 firms located in four countries conducted during the period 1992 to 1998, three experts namely Brian Becker, Mark Huselid and Dave Ulrich, introduced a measurement system that establishes how HRM impacts business performance. They authored a book titled *The HR Scoreboard: Linking People, Strategy and Performance* published in 2001. The book presents an incisive analysis of how each element of HRM system can be designed to enhance a firm's performance and maximize the overall quality of human capital.

This HR scoreboard model consists of following seven-step process that ties HR results to an organization's overall strategy:

1. Clearly define business strategy
2. Build a business case for HRM as a strategic asset
3. Create a strategy map
4. Identify HRM deliverables within the strategy map
5. Align the HRM architecture with HRM deliverables
6. Design the strategic HRM measurement system
7. Implement management by measurement

A sample HR Scorecard template is given in Figure 1.2.

Managerial Implication

Implementing an HRM Scoreboard will enable HRM professionals to become strategic partners in organizations. For that to happen HRM professional must acquire business related skills. Though most of the chief executives realize human resource as strategic asset of firm, they are not very conversant with how to realize this in practice. HRM Scoreboard can be an answer to

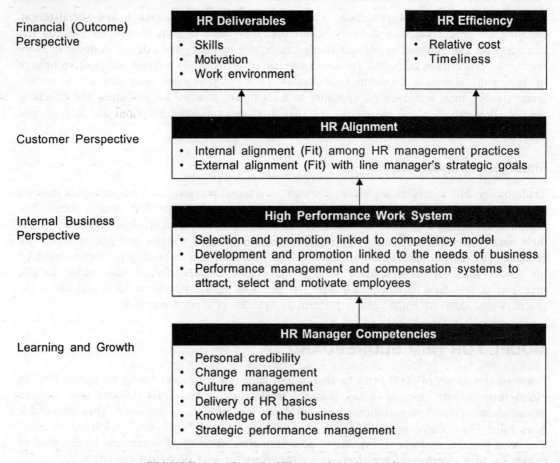

Financial (Outcome)
Perspective

HR Deliverables
• Skills
• Motivation
• Work environment

HR Efficiency
• Relative cost
• Timeliness

Customer Perspective

HR Alignment
• Internal alignment (Fit) among HR management practices
• External alignment (Fit) with line manager's strategic goals

Internal Business
Perspective

High Performance Work System
• Selection and promotion linked to competency model
• Development and promotion linked to the needs of business
• Performance management and compensation systems to attract, select and motivate employees

Learning and Growth

HR Manager Competencies
• Personal credibility
• Change management
• Culture management
• Delivery of HR basics
• Knowledge of the business
• Strategic performance management

FIGURE 1.2 Sample HR scoreboard template.

this question. HRM scoreboard, apart from building a culture of measurement-based management, also guides organizations through a quality-oriented human capital architecture. This assumes the status of greater business proposition, particularly in the light of startling revelation that 35 per cent improvement in human capital architecture can result in gaining 20 per cent shareholder value.

MODEL FOR REENGINEERING HRM

HRM departments should be restructured on a continuous basis in tandem with changing HRM focus in organizations. Most of HR departments have their origin to traditional administration, personnel, industrial relations and human relations orientation. This orientation ought to be altered to that of a value added function. HR departments must have professionals with right skills and competencies in order to transform the human resource department as partner in strategic management of organization. Professor Jac Fitz-Enz in his insightful paper titled "On the Edge of Oblivion", published in *HR Magazine* in 1996 presented a model of typical human resource department comprising of five types of HRM professionals:

1. *Superstars.* These are the people capable of seeing big picture of the organization. They understand the linkage of HRM activities with financial, marketing and technical functions of the organization. Their competencies include integrating HR strategy with business strategy. Generally, one or two per cent of HRM staff constitute this type.

2. *Treasurers.* These are practical, down to earth professionals who know how to get things done. They understand the basic rules of the game and good at implementation. But they feel inadequate to design HRM system on their own and do not bother about long-term perspective. Every HR department generally contains ten per cent of treasurers in the HRM department.

3. *Dependable.* They are dependable for executing any job. They need to be guided, clarified and motivated to do an activity. In other words, they can be faithful and loyal subordinates. Forty per cent of HR staff in HR department contain dependents.

4. *Wannabes.* About twenty per cent of human resource staff are wannabes. These people aspire to become dependents and struggle to achieve something but easily slips because of lack of effort.

5. *Zombies.* These are above average IQ professionals with adequate knowledge and HRM skills. But they do not know what their job is and what they are expected to do in an organization. About twenty five per cent of staff in HR departments spends the time without doing anything, in spite of their abilities.

In reengineered HR department, there is no place for Zombies. Wannabes and dependables must be trained on business skills that include inter disciplinary areas like finance, sales and technical issues and analytical skills. The amount of superstars and treasurers must be enhanced to sixty per cent.

Managerial Implication

With the increased emphasis on business role of human resource function, HRM departments need to undergo a massive restructuring in almost all the organizations. This model highlights two issues for action. Firstly, we must analyze the composition of our HRM departments in terms of these five roles and their percentage. Secondly, efforts must be made to redefine the composition to the extent that enables HR department to play a strategic and business role in the organization. The change of composition is the first step in the reengineering of HRM department.

TEN-STEP HRM MODEL FOR STRATEGIC ALLIANCES

Strategic alliances, collaborations, joint ventures and other form of partnerships have become more of a rule than an exception in modern industrial world. HRM has a distinct role to play in such situations. The accumulated evidence shows that a considerable number of strategic alliances weren't as successful as thought to be. This was mainly due to obstacles in the management of people, culture and processes. In the rush of launching strategic alliance, organizations pay low attention to HRM issues, and that in turn cause formidable obstacles in the way of strategic alliance maturity. Therefore, HRM ought to be involved right from the initial stages, and alliance specific practices must be drafted. Professor Vladimir Pucik of

Michigan University based on extensive study identified ten HRM steps that strengthen strategic alliances and presented them in his paper titled "Strategic Alliances, Organizational Learning, and Competitive Advantage: The HRM Agenda" published in *Human Resource Management* in 1988. These strategic alliance specific HRM practices are:

1. *Get involved early.* The HR function should be involved in the formation of the strategic alliance from the early planning stages.

2. *Build learning into the partnership agreement.* Provisions should be made in the joint agreement to ensure transfer of skills, knowledge and competencies. The process of joint and mutually inclusive learning must be made explicit.

3. *Communicate strategic intent.* HR managers, with the help of line managers, must communicate well with employees about strategic alliances and reasons for such an arrangement.

4. *Maintain HR input into the partnership.* Once the partnership agreement is created, HR managers must monitor the progress related HR practices in their respective organizations as stipulated in the agreement.

5. *Staff to learn.* This is an important step in joint venture formation. Efforts must be made to identify the required skills and gaps in competence areas in the light of new formation. Training programmes must be implemented to create these competencies.

6. *Set up learning driven career plans.* A comprehensive learning strategy is a must in alliances. This strategy can focus on cross-cultural learning in the beginning and functional learning tied to individual employee's career plans, as the alliance progresses.

7. *Use training to stimulate the learning process.* Learning environment and process must be infused through a continuous training of people. This must be a joint effort of both the organizations. The joint effort commences from imparting the skills of managing strategic alliances to managers, to transferring the technology related skills to new organization.

8. *Responsibility for learning should be specified.* Learning is not the responsibility of HR manager alone or a handful of managers but it is the responsibility of all the managers, for their own and also their subordinate employees' learning. This must be clearly specified.

9. *Reward learning activities.* Behaviour that promotes organizational learning must be rewarded. Long and short-term incentives can be used to motivate employees to acquire new skills and knowledge.

10. *Monitor the HRM practices of your partner.* Beginning with an HR audit prior to establishment of the partnership, attention should be given to the partner's HRM activities. Much insight can be gained from the continuous monitoring of the partner's human resource practices.

Managerial Implication

Organizations tend to pay exclusive attention to technological, financial and legal issues of joint ventures/strategic alliances at the cost of human resource related aspects. As a result, they may create a legally and technologically viable organization, but not a successful and market driven organization, because that comes from the contribution of human resource. The above ten steps were drawn from hard-core practice. Therefore, if these steps are followed they can give positive results for the companies. In practice, this works as an action planner for HR managers and top management in driving the HR function in strategic alliance in a systematic manner.

SEVEN-STEP HRM MODEL FOR TAKEOVERS

In a changing business environment, takeover of companies has become a vital strategy to expand one's influence over the industry as well as to consolidate the company's position in the shortest time. The role of HRM in takeover of companies, is so significant that it can make or mar the success chances of a takeover process. The history of takeovers points out that quite a few of them have failed to accrue the anticipated benefits due to mismanagement on human resource front. It doesn't mean that companies haven't put in efforts. It only implies that their efforts lacked purposeful direction and a practical human resource strategy. If it is so, what should be the right approach? Two experts namely Mike Burns and Adrienne Rosen of The Human Factor based on their in-depth study of Royal Bank of Canada takeover of Royal Trust Co. presented a human resource model in their paper titled "HR Aspects of a Takeover" published in *Career Development International* in 1997. The model comprises of seven steps as described below:

- Step-I: *Radical changes should be made swiftly.* Any radical change like closing down of overlapping business units should be done swiftly, ideally within six months from the takeover. Otherwise, there is a great risk that the uncertainty will result in low morale and the loss of valuable people.

- Step-II: *Focus on employee communication.* Communication with employees must be given high priority during and after the takeover process. HRM people should be used as conduits in this process.

- Step-III: *Harmonization of pay.* Harmonization of the existing pay and benefits should be considered at an early stage. This key area can consume much time and money, but has to be tackled. It also offers the opportunity to remove the anomalies and bring semblance in the compensation structure.

- Step-IV: *Mechanisms to deal with resistance.* Resistance to change varies from group to group. For example, people in senior management cadre may accept quickly comparing to their staff. Therefore, mechanisms should be developed to handle this resistance in a positive and systematic manner.

- Step-V: *Employee participation.* The process of changing the business and developing a clear vision of its future must be participative, with contributions from all levels and categories of employees. Suitable number of task forces consisting employees must be drawn and should be made responsible for managing the transition. Techniques like large-scale interactive process and future search conference can be used.

- Step-VI: *Managing survivor syndrome.* It is unsafe to assume that those who survive redundancy will be so grateful that their level of motivation will be high. Some will experience feelings of guilt that will affect productivity, unless dealt with understandingly. Companies involved in takeovers must introduce mechanisms to unbottle emotions and feelings, and acknowledge the concerns of survivors.

- **Step-VII:** *Global* vs *Local.* Every corporation will be different in terms of its operations and cultural and other HR related aspects. Therefore, whenever a takeover is affected, the whole process must be seen at global and multiunit level and at the same time local issues shall be taken into account to manage human related issues.

Managerial Implication

This model is drawn from a live case of Royal Bank involving 46000 people employed domestically and 3000 internationally. There is no need to emphasize its practical value to managers particularly to HR managers. The model, apart from setting actionable HRM guidelines to be followed in takeover scenarios, also presents two valuable insights. Firstly, the model highlights the importance of completing radical changes swiftly to avoid performance slow downs. It implies the need to have special attention on ongoing human resource actions. Secondly, it deliberates multiple HR actions like communication, participation and managing survivors effectively that helps in implementing takeover smoothly. The model is a flexible one in the sense that it provides space for HR managers to adopt their HR tactics that are compatible with the organizational reality.

PEOPLE-CAPABILITY MATURITY MODEL (P-CMM)

The P-CMM is a maturity framework, patterned after the structure of the Capability Maturity Model (CMM) of software engineering, focuses on continuously improving the ability of software organizations to attract, develop, motivate, organize and retain the talent needed to steadily improve their software development capability. Software Engineering Institute (SEI) of Carnegie Mellon University developed this model in 1992 and has been improving it since then under the stewardship of Bill Curtis.

Although the P-CMM has been developed keeping in mind the needs of the software engineering and information systems community, the key practices for developing the workforce can be applied to any knowledge based organization. The P-CMM can be utilized in two ways: (i) it can be applied by an organization as a standard of assessing status of workforce practices in a software organization, and (ii) it can guide in planning and implementing people capabilities improvement activities.

As a capability maturity model, the P-CMM guides organizations in establishing and improving their workforce practices through five evolutionary levels and each level comprises certain key HRM practices as shown in Table 1.11.

The P-CMM does not provide guidance on how to implement programme alone. It is a road map for organizational growth and needs to be coupled with a model of implementing an improvement programme. The maturity levels in the P-CMM describe the characteristic practices of an organization at that maturity level. Each level forms a foundation on which an organization can build workforce practices effectively and efficiently on succeeding maturity levels. The P-CMM was designed to develop the supporting foundation needed to ensure that higher level practices could achieve their full impact on raising workforce capability. The model should be applied with an understanding of an organization's potential capabilities within the constraints that affect it.

TABLE 1.11

Level	Maturity stage	Focus	Key HR practices
Level-1	Initial	Workforce practices applied without analysis of impact	
Level-2	Managed	Managers take responsibility for managing and developing their people	• Compensation • Training and Development • Performance management • Work environment • Communication and Coordination • Staffing
Level-3	Defined	Develop workforce competencies and workgroups, and align with strategy	• Participatory culture • Workgroup development • Competency based practices • Career development • Workforce planning • Competency planning
Level-4	Predictable	Empower and integrate workforce competencies and manage performance quantatively	• Quantitative performance management • Organizational capability management • Competency based assets • Mentoring • Empowered workgroups • Competency integration
Level-5	Optimizing	Continuously improve and align personal, workgroup, and organizational capability	• Continuous workforce innovation • Organizational performance alignment • Continuous capability improvement

Managerial Implication

Software and other knowledge-based companies should seriously consider implementing P-CMM model given its rational and pragmatic framework. It guides organizations with what should be done to build workforce competencies leaving how it has to be done to individual organizations. What factor can work as standard and how factor provides the much-required flexibility to organizations to draw its own implementation strategy. HR managers must start with assessing the current workforce maturity level using P-CMM assessment method. HRM practices in P-CMM model are built in evolutionary manner with clear foundation and vertical linkages. This helps organizations to pursue HR practices in a systematic manner. HR managers must bid farewell to ad hoc practices, and realize that it is time to embrace P-CMM for HR excellence.

HRM AS SHAREHOLDER VALUE

Research and number of empirical studies conducted on the role of HRM in firms by Prof. Brian Becker of State University of New York and Prof. Mark Huselid of Rutgers University and others reveal that, an internally coherent, externally aligned and effectively implemented HRM can be a source of shareholder value. This is because the changing market conditions have rendered many of the traditional sources of competitive advantage such as patents, economies of scale, access to capital etc. as less important, in comparison to core competencies and capabilities of employees that help to develop new products, provide world class customer service and implement organizational strategy. High Performance Work Systems such as rigorous recruitment and selection procedures, performance contingent incentive and compensation systems, management training and development activities linked to the key business priorities can drive profits, growth and ultimately market value. For example, it was observed that changes (a one standard deviation improvement) in the quality of a firm's HRM systems are associated with changes in the market value of $ 15000–$ 60000 per employee. For a firm with 10000 employees, this represents more than a billion dollars in market value. HRM managers have to perform a different role as described below to transform HRM function as a source of shareholder value, according to Becker and Huselid:

1. *HRM must focus on business level outcomes rather than HRM level inputs.* The number one priority for the value creating HR function is to develop the perspective and competency to solve business problems. HRM makes a difference when it can point to human capital problems that limit the ability of the firm to achieve important business priorities and can provide HRM solutions to those problems.

2. *HRM must become a strategic core competency rather than a market follower.* A high performance work system that creates real shareholder value is not a commodity that can be benchmarked from other organizations. Benchmarking might keep you in the game, but it will not provide the intellectual capital to create a sustained competitive advantage.

3. *Strategic competencies are more important than functional competencies.* The most important value creating HR competency and the one of the most underdeveloped in many firms, is the ability to understand the human capital dimension of each of the firm's key business priorities and be able to communicate, how solving these human capital problems will directly affect operating performance.

4. *The most important missing element in the HR functional expertise is a systems perspective.* Functional competencies must blend traditional HR functional expertise with a system perspective to avoid deadly combinations and identify powerful connections.

The irrefutable evidence in support of HRM as a shareholder value and components of high performance work system are presented in the paper titled "HR as a Source of Shareholder Value: Research and Recommendations" and paper titled "Strategic HRM In Five Leading Firms", both published in *HRM Journal* in 1997 and 1999, respectively.

Managerial Implication

HRM managers across the organizations are under tremendous pressure to prove the worth of HR function in terms of bottom line. For all of them it is good news that they can do so by playing business oriented HRM role. They just need to transform the HRM function from a traditional maintenance cost based function to market enhancing function, by implementing the afore-mentioned four dimensions.

HUMAN POTENTIAL MODEL

There has been a potential argument that calling people management as HRM merely illustrates an incremental development in our attitude towards human beings. Some also argue that defining human beings as resource is demeaning. Their arguments are based on the following logics:

1. HRM is like putting old wine into new bottle, i.e. merely changing name from personnel administration to HRM, yet retaining most of the traditional personnel administration functions.
2. HRM considers human beings as resource to be managed, implying they are incapable of self-management. In this sense, HRM deprives employees of using their superior mental acumen.
3. The definition of human beings merely as a resource is obsolete, demeaning and out of line with our sociological evolution.
4. HRM is defined as, the process of utilizing human resource to achieve organizational objectives. This definition does not exclude utilization through coercion. Therefore, utilization could lead to demoralization and lack of motivation, and ultimately be counter productive to organizational growth and development.
5. The expression HRM relegates people into the category of corporate resources. HRM conveys the idea that people are employed in order to be used to make profits.

To overcome these shortcomings, Professor Satish Kalra of Management Development Institute, India presented an alternative perspective called human potential model in his paper titled "Human Potential Management: Time to move beyond the concept of HRM?" published in Journal of *European Industrial Training* in 1997. The salient features of human potential model are:

1. *Human Potential Model (HPM) focuses on self-management*. It has an underlying belief that if human beings are provided with opportunities to use their potential, they can manage themselves.
2. *HPM does not use human beings as a resource*, but recognizes their potential. and enables them to utilize their potential.
3. *HPM is an integrative* and continuous process of enhancing human capabilities and capacities. HPM follows a continuous growth oriented approach
4. *HPM focuses more on turning employees' potential* to their own advantage, thereby leading automatically to the organization's advantage. HPM underplays the organization's advantage by implying that if employees' potential is taken care of, it is likely to enhance employees' sense of responsibility towards organizations, and create a feeling of organizational ownership.

5. *HPM focuses on the continuous updating* of organizational policies, structures and systems in such a way, that it helps employees to achieve their full potential and contribute their best to the organization.

Managerial Implication

The model, though appears in surface as conceptual or ideological but has immense practical value to HR managers. Firstly, the significant idea is that most of the organizations have altered the name of their staff departments from personnel to human resource development/management, but their policies and practices have remained unaltered. Secondly, there was change only 'in style' and not 'in spirit' has happened since the very term 'human resource' might have contributed for utilizing or deploying or treating human beings like any other resource in organizations. Thirdly, the model, presents a practical advice that focuses on maximizing and motivating people to realize their potential, and this automatically leads to fulfilment of organizational objectives. In other words, the model encourages treating the ultimate objective of organizations as human potential enhancement.

PEOPLE SIDE OF BUSINESS PROCESS OUTSOURCING

Business Process Outsourcing (BPO) has become a new weapon in the hands of organizations that are determined to beat the competition. The rate of outsourcing is growing so rapidly that it can fail the expectations of everybody. This is because, there is a popular belief that BPO offers myriad of advantages to the organizations, which includes: (i) enabling existing staff to concentrate on core activities of organizational specializations, (ii) focusing on achieving key strategic objectives, (iii) lowering or stabilizing overhead costs, thereby gaining cost advantage over the competitors, (iv) providing flexibility in response to changing market conditions, (v) reducing investment in high technology and (vi) decreasing the product/processes design cycle time. However, on the other hand, it is found that unplanned and ruthless BPO can cause irreparable damage to the human resource system in organizations which in turn can lead to great losses surpassing the short term benefits. Nada Kakabadse and Andrew Kakabadse, who dealt with the subject of outsourcing in great length, found that outsourcing would pose formidable challenges from HRM angle, and detailed them in their paper titled 'Outsourcing: A Paradigm Shift' published in *The Journal of Management Development* in 2000. These challenges are briefly described in the following:

1. *Changing social contract.* As the organizations increasingly adopt outsourcing practice, the employee commitment to organization weakens. This can only be reconstructed by forming a new social contract as indicated in Table 1.12.

2. *Disintegration of organizational culture.* BPO can lead to the disintegration of an existing organization's culture. Research evidence point out that outsourcing has the potential to break down a complex set of interconnections within the organization, and as such is strong enough to tear apart whole value system.

3. *Survivor's syndrome.* BPO commonly leads to staff downsizing. This will have an affect over the morale of survivors. This syndrome is considered to be a major factor that contributes to many organizations failure in achieving their corporate objectives.

TABLE 1.12

Old social contract	*New social contract*
• Employment	• Employability
• Permanent workforce	• Externalized workforce
• Job security	• Career resilience
• Career structure within organization. Managed by employer	• Career portfolio within market, employee's responsibility for assessing and designing their own careers
• Organization reliant employees	• Self-reliant employees
• Union based bargaining	• Individually based bargaining
• Loyalty to employer	• Loyalty to self and profession-specialization
• Commitment	• Flexibility and performance
• Limited availability of information to employees	• Disclosure of information to employees
• Employer assesses training needs and provides training and development	• Employer provides tools, open environment and the opportunities for assessing and developing skills
	• Individuals empowered to hone, redirect and expand their skills to stay competitive on the job market

4. *Mourning.* In order to overcome the negative consequences of outsourcing, organizations need to make significant investment in their employees. Displaced victims and survivors need to feel that management is concerned about their needs.

Managerial Implication

The above discussion clearly drives an issue of concern to all those involved in BPO, and particularly to HR managers, that outsourcing may contribute for business gains in short-term but has the potential to cause great damage in the long run. Similarly, outsourcing enables organizations to gain greater flexibility in its operations and business focus but would lead to organizational discommitment and weak organizational culture. However, it is also a fact that BPO is more a necessity than simply an organizational strategy. Therefore, organizations must carefully introduce BPO and align HR processes accordingly and facilitate to form new social contract in a smooth fashion.

PEOPLE SIDE OF KAIZEN

Kaizen is a long-term and long lasting Japanese strategy to bring continuous improvements in all aspects of organizational functioning that include HRM. In fact, people side of Kaizen play an important role than any other activity in the entire Kaizen management. In order to implement Kaizen successfully, all employees from top management to shop floor workers have to perform their roles systematically. Clive Mortan, the benchmarking specialist, has clearly defined these roles in the book titled *Becoming World Class* published in 1994. These are:

1. *Top management.* The top management responsibilities include: (i) be determined to introduce Kaizen as a corporate strategy, (ii) provide support and direction for Kaizen

by allocating resources, (iii) establish policy for Kaizen and cross-functional goals, (iv) realize Kaizen goals through policy deployment and audits and (v) build systems, procedures and structures conducive to Kaizen.

3. *Middle management and staff.* Their tasks include: (i) Deploy and implement Kaizen goals as directed by top management through policy deployment and cross-functional management, (ii) Use Kaizen in functional capabilities, (iii) Establish, maintain and upgrade standards, (iv) Make employees Kaizen-conscious through intensive training programmes and (v) Help employees develop skills and tools for problem solving.

4. *Supervisors.* Supervisors perform important functions such as (i) Use Kaizen in functional roles, (ii) Formulate plans for Kaizen and provide guidance to workers, (iii) Improve communication with workers and sustain high morale, (iv) Support small-group activities (such as Quality Circles) and the individual suggestion system, (v) Introduce discipline in the workshop, and (vi) Provide Kaizen suggestions.

5. *Workers.* These employees have to actively: (i) Engage in Kaizen through the suggestion system and small-group activities, (ii) Practice discipline in the workshop, (iii) Engage in continuous self-development to become better problem-solvers and (iv) Enhance skills and job performance expertise with cross-education.

Managerial Implication

The implementation of Kaizen calls for active partnership of HRM, particularly in its implementation. The human resource functions that particularly receive special attention in implementation of this strategy are: Team building, employee participation, empowerment, team reward system, quality training and employee communication. The other HR subsystems like human resource information system, employment security and employees' family welfare also accorded importance. Many of the Kaizen experts believe that it is the HR system that ensures transformation of an organization into Kaizen philosophy. Therefore, HR managers must clearly understand the principles and practices of Kaizen. In this endeavour, appreciating the role of various players such as the top management, middle managers, supervisors and workers is the first lesson.

THIRTEEN BEST PRACTICES IN TQM BASED PEOPLE MANAGEMENT

Much of the success of the quality initiatives in organizations is influenced by its approach to HRM. Organizations that achieved peak of quality standards admit that people come first in implementation of quality efforts and then only techniques like statistical quality control, benchmarks, logs etc. However, the interesting question is, what are those HRM practices that strengthen the quality efforts? Two experts namely A. Hamzah and M. Zairi of University of Bradford identified three categories consisting 13 human resource practices that play enabling role in successful adoption of TQM based on their study of organizations that won international quality awards. They presented the study results and their analysis in the paper titled 'People Management: Where is the Evidence of Best Practice?' published in *Training for Quality* in 1996. These thirteen practices are:

1. Top management commitment

2. Resource/assistance support in terms of allocation of financial budget for training of personnel and creation of infrastructure for introduction of TQM
3. Use of recognition/appreciation tools to motivate good performance
4. Existence of a clearly stated HRM policy in writing
5. Creation of management structures for implementation of stated HRM policy
6. Extensive use of training and development covering all the employees
7. Involvement of employees in TQM implementation at all levels
8. Communication with employees on a continuous basis
9. Empowerment of employees individually and through the method of self-directing teams
10. Use of a culture based teamwork rather than structure based small groups
11. Use of employee attitude surveys for communicating as well as gauging the progress of change process
12. Analysis of survey results through the technique of benchmarking
13. Self-assessment for monitoring people's satisfaction and effectiveness of human resource system in relation to both operational and strategic levels of the enterprise

The practices from 1 to 3 are classified as leadership issues, 4 to 10 as people management issues, and 11 to 13 labelled as people satisfaction. Organizations that were found implementing these practices strongly believe that these practices contributed in the realization of quality management objectives.

Managerial Implication

This is one more landmark study proving that good HRM practices lead to fulfilment of quality objectives. These findings have two implications for managerial action. Firstly, HR managers with the collaboration of line managers can push these 13 practices in their organizations, but of course, in a phased manner. These practices can be adopted, regardless of whether your organization is TQM driven or not, since they have the potential to build a conducive work environment for productivity. Secondly, the classification of these practices into three major areas imply that we must initiate actions in all the areas simultaneously, but in ascending hierarchy, in each phase, based on the intensity of the practices in your organization.

Chapter 2
Function and Profession of Human Resource Management

There are two prime approaches that every HR practitioner intending to excel in HRM profession must follow: First, keeping abreast with latest developments in the function and profession, both locally and globally. Second, acquiring the skills and competencies that are required to manage HR function effectively and efficiently.

With these twin objectives in view, this chapter presents sixteen classics that capture: (i) the changing profile of HRM practice, (ii) the latest trends in HRM, (iii) variants and levels in HRM strategy, (iv) the potential barriers every HR managers face in realizing HRM strategy in practice, (v) the syndromes and traps in HRM practice, (vi) the skills required to perform HRM role successfully, (vii) why and how some HRM managers fail in their responsibilities and contribute in the downfall, (viii) different roles HR managers perform to add value, (ix) how successful HRM professionals redefined the function and created a new path in the profession and (x) the competency required to become strategic HR leader in the present business environment.

PERSONNEL vs HRM

HRM has a long history of growing from a simple welfare and maintenance function to that of a board level activity of the companies. In recent years, the focus on people management from human capital/intellectual capital perspective is also shaping firmly. However, the hard fact is that this growth can be generally witnessed in management literature and rarely in practice. Peripheral observation of people management in organization can mislead the observers since, hardly there could be any organization that is yet to rename its old fashioned title of industrial relations/personnel/welfare/administration department into HRM department. But, in practice, these organizations continue to handle the people management activities the way they had been handling earlier. The reasons for this could be many and varied. Among them, the potential reason is lack of clear understanding about the differences between personnel/IR and HRM. Professor John Storey brilliantly portrayed these differences in 27 areas of people management in 1992 in his book titled *Developments in the Management of Human Resources*. These differences are illustrated in Table 2.1.

TABLE 2.1 27 Points of Difference

Dimensions	Personnel and IR	HRM
Beliefs and assumptions		
1. Contract	Careful delineation of written contracts	Aim to go beyond contract
2. Rules	Importance of devising clear rules/mutually	'Can-do' outlook; Impatience with 'rule'
3. Guide to management action	Procedures	'Business-need'
4. Behaviour referent	Norms/custom and practice	Values/mission
5. Managerial task vis-à-vis labour	Monitoring	Nurturing
6. Nature of relations	Pluralist	Unitarist
7. Conflict	Institutionalized	De-emphasized
Strategic aspects		
8. Key relations	Labour management	Customer
9. Initiatives	Piecemeal	Integrated
10. Corporate plan	Marginal	Central
11. Speed of decision	Slow	Fast
Line management		
12. Management role	Transactional	Transformational leadership
13. Key managers	Personnel/IR specialists	General/business/line managers
14. Communication	Indirect	Direct
15. Standardization	High (e.g. 'parity' an issue)	Low (e.g. 'parity' not seen as relevant)
16. Prized management skills	Negotiation	Facilitation
Key levers		
17. Selection	Separate, marginal task	Integrated, key task
18. Pay	Job evaluation (fixed grades)	Performance-related
19. Conditions	Separately negotiated	Harmonization
20. Labour-management	Collective bargaining contracts	Towards individual contracts
21. Thrust of relations with stewards	Regularized through facilities and training	Marginalized (with exception of some bargaining for change models)
22. Job categories and grades	Many	Few
23. Communication	Restricted flow	Increased flow
24. Job design	Division of labour	Teamwork
25. Conflict handling	Reach temporary truces	Manage climate and culture
26. Training and development	Controlled access to courses	Learning companies
27. Foci of attention for interventions	Personnel procedures	Wide ranging cultural, structural and personnel strategies

Managerial Implication

There is a huge difference in terms of approach, beliefs, and assumptions between these two schools of people management. It is no denying the fact that many organizations embraced HRM title without understanding the critical differences. Now, the key question is whether organizations are prepared to shift their beliefs and assumptions in handling people issues in the lines of HRM, or intended to continue the system of personnel. It is not an easy task to decide, obviously, as that of changing the title. Shifting from personnel to HRM, requires an organization wide revolution. Undoubtedly, it reaps rich benefits, when organizations shift to HRM in spirit. In this process, the 27 points of difference is of great practical value to HR managers and to their organizations.

FOUR TYPES IN HRM STRATEGY

The success of HRM lies in its flexibility in reorienting itself in tune with changing internal and external focus of organizations. HR strategy that is most suitable to a particular market condition like change in product strategy may not be suitable to a condition like organizational turnaround. In this context, D. Stace and D. Dunphy proposed four HRM strategies that can fit in with four different organizational conditions in their paper titled "Beyond Traditional Paternalistic and Developmental Approaches to Organizational Changes" published in *International Journal of HRM* in 1991. These are summarized in Table 2.2.

TABLE 2.2

HRM strategy type	Conditions for use
Task Focused HRM Strategy HRM strategy strongly focused on the business unit • Strong bottom line orientation • Emphasis on workforce planning, job redesign and work practice reviews • Focus on tangible reward structures • Internal or external recruitment • Functional skills training and formalized multi-skilling • Formalized industrial relations procedures • Strong business unit culture	Use when markets/products/services are undergoing major change and niche strategies is prevalent. HRM strategies must deliver the capacity for rapid structural, systems, skill and cultural changes. Strong emphasis on business unit autonomy, maximum devolution, rightsizing (continuous redeployment), outsourcing of labour.
Development HRM strategy is jointly carried out by the corporate HR unit and the business units • Emphasis on developing the individual, and the team • Internal recruitment, where possible • Extensive development programmes • Use of intrinsic rewards • Corporate organizational development given high priority • Strong emphasis on corporate culture	Use when markets are growing and product/market innovation is desired. HRM strategies must create cross-organizational synergy, and a market-leader culture. Strong emphasis on individual development, corporate culture management, developing strong internal labour market (promotions/appointments) and team skills.

TABLE 2.2   *(continued)*

HRM strategy type	*Conditions for use*
Turnaround HRM Strategy HRM strategy is driven for a short period by the executive leadership, characterized by challenging, restructuring or abolish-ing HR systems, structures and methodologies. • Major structural changes affecting the total organization and career structures • Downsizing, retrenchments • Lateral recruitment of key executives from outside • Executive team building, creating a new mindset • Breaking with the old culture	Use when the business environment changes dramatically, i.e. when the organization is not compatible with its environment, and when the business strategy of the organization radically changes. HRM strategies must break and abolish redundant HRM practices, structures, and redefine a new culture. Strong emphasis on forced downsizing, lateral recruitment, new HRM systems and radical work and job restructuring
Paternalistic HRM Strategy HRM practice is centrally administered • Centralist personnel orientation • Emphasis on procedures, precedent and uniformity • Organization and methods studies • Inflexible internal appointments policy • Emphasis on operational and supervisory training • Industrial awards and agreements set the HR framework	Use only in very limited mass production situations where the organization has an absolute monopoly on stable markets/ products, HRM strategies are used as devices for control and uniformity of procedures/ operations. Strong emphasis on formal, detailed job descriptions, formal employer–employee industrial relationships and industrial awards.

Managerial Implication

The model offers great insights to HR managers in adopting the most appropriate HR strategy suiting to their organizational context. Generally, organizations start with a particular type of HR strategy and continue with it regardless of change in organizational focus. This continuation weakens both: organizational progress as well as utility of HR efforts. The above four types provide a comprehensive perspective of HR strategies together with conditions to use that help managers as actionable steps. HR managers can make comparative analysis of their HRM strategy vis-à-vis organizational focus using the above framework.

THREE LOGICS OF HRM STRATEGIES

The type of HRM practices that an organization prefers would be contingent upon its HRM goals. In turn, the goals of an organization's HR strategy depends upon the logic it chooses. This is the argument brilliantly put forwarded by L. Dyer and G.W. Holder in their book titled *HRM: Evolving Rules and Responsibilities* published in 1988. According to them, the logic organizations follow in managing their HR falls into three types: (i) investment, (ii) inducement and (iii) involvement. These logics differ in their goals which in turn influences the type of HR practices that an organization chooses as illustrated in Table 2.3.

TABLE 2.3 Logic

Goals	Investment	Inducement	Involvement
Contribution	High initiative and creativity; high performance expectations; some flexibility	Some initiative and creativity; very high performance standards; modest flexibility	Very high initiative and creativity; very high performance expectations, high flexibility, self-managed
Composition	Comfortable head count (core and buffer); high skill mix; moderate staff	Lean head count (core and buffer); low skill mix; minimal staff	Comfortable head count; protected core; high skill mix; minimal staff
Competence	High	Adequate	Very high
Commitment	High; identification with company	High; instrumental	Very high; strong identification with work, team, and company
Practices			
Staffing	Careful selection; extensive career development; some flexibility; minimal layoffs	Careful selection; few career options; use of temps; minimal layoffs	Very careful selection; some career development; extreme flexibility; minimal (or no) layoffs
Development	Extensive; continuous learning	Minimal	Extensive; continuous learning
Rewards	Tall structure; competitive, fixed, job based, merit; many benefits	Flat structure; high; variable, piece rate; profit sharing; minimal benefits	Flat structure, high, partially capable, skill and competency based; gain sharing, flexible benefits
Work system	Broad jobs; employee initiative; some groups	Narrow jobs; employee paced; individualized	Enriched jobs; self-managed work teams
Supervision	Extensive, supportive	Minimal, directive	Minimal, facilitative
Employee relations	More communication; high voice; high due process; high employee assistance	Less communication; some voice; egalitarian	Open and extensive communication; high voice; some due process; egalitarian, some employee assistance
Labour relations	Nonissue	Union avoidance or conflict	Union avoidance and/or cooperation
Government relations	Over compliance	Compliance	Compliance

Managerial Implication

This may sound somewhat abstract but puts the practice of whole HRM into a pragmatic perspective. The application of this model enables HR managers to draft HR practices that have strong integration with overall organizational logic. The effectiveness of HRM practices to organization increases when they flow from the four basic goals as shown in the model.

Unfortunately, in practice, there are hardly any efforts to understand the organizational logic and its type and corresponding goals in order to adopt compatible HR practices. This failure may be the potential contributory factor for ineffectiveness of many HR practices.

THREE LEVELS OF HRM ACTIVITIES

HR managers need to acquire expertise in their field of work from two dimensions. Firstly, they must have thorough knowledge of HR systems horizontally, i.e. ability to handle HR functions from recruitment to separation. Secondly, they should acquire skills to perform the vertical role of HR manager, i.e. ability to perform at strategic, managerial and operational level. Each of these horizontal HR activities like recruitment, reward, development etc. will have a vertical divide in terms of its nature of activity. For example, recruitment has to be handled at three levels: (i) strategic level (defining objectives, parameters, policy, job descriptions), (ii) managerial level (developing recruitment plans for a particular period, quality and quantity of manpower required, analyzing market conditions) and (iii) operational level (implementing recruitment plans). Therefore, HR managers need to understand the vertical role in all critical HR functions. For this purpose, the three levels model of HRM developed by three original Strategic HRM experts namely Mary Devanna, Charles Fombrun and Noel Tichy in 1984 is of great relevance. These three levels in reference to four critical HR functions are indicated in Table 2.4.

TABLE 2.4

Management level	Recruitment	Performance appraisal	Compensation	Development
Strategic	• Developing characteristics of people needed to run business in long term • Designing internal and external systems to reflect future businesses	• In long term, what should be valued? • Developing means to appraise future dimensions • Early identification of potential	• In world as it might be in long term, how will force be rewarded? • Linking rewards to the long term business strategy	• Planning developmental experiences for people running business of the future • Designing systems with flexibility to adjust to change
Managerial	• Validation of selection criteria • Development of recruitment plan • New markets	• Designing systems to link current and future potential • Assessment centers for development	• Five-year compensation plans for individuals • Cafeteria style fringe benefits	• Organizing management development programmes • Organizing development activities • Fostering self development
Operational	• Staffing plans • Recruitment plans	• Annual appraisal systems • Day-to-day control systems	• Wage and salary administration • Benefit plans	• Delivering job skill training • On the job training

Managerial Implication

The model rightly highlights many issues that have implications for HRM practice. Firstly, it provides the much-required clarity of a HR manager's job in terms of horizontal functions and verticality in them. Secondly, the three levels model can serve as a functional plan for managers. Based on this example, HR managers can meaningfully define the role of each function they handle at three levels and work on them accordingly. In order to become a full-fledged HR professional, one need to acquire skills of HRM horizontally as well as vertically.

THREE BARRIERS TO EFFECTIVE HRM

Despite rhetoric that HR is strategic assets of the firm, human capital is something that can neither be substituted nor cloned, there are hardly handful of companies that implement effective HRM policies. In spite of clear evidence in support of organizational benefits on account of effective HRM practices, why organizations fail to adopt these practices is a question to many across the globe. The answers to these questions are provided by Bob Kane and John Crawford of University of Technology, Australia and David Grant of University of London. Based on their multination survey covering wide range of organizations, they found that major barriers to effective implementation of HRM practices are same across the industries and throughout the world. The results of this survey were published in their paper titled 'Barriers to Effective HRM' appeared in *International Journal of Manpower* in 1999. The barriers to effective HRM can be classified into three categories as follows:

1. The first barrier is lack of top management commitment to HRM. A lack of top management support for HRM may be attributed to two factors. Firstly, it may be that the HRM function in general and HR managers in particular lacks representation and power to influence events in the organization. This is because top management is more concerned with their own power and maintaining control than about the real needs of the organization. Secondly, it may be that top management takes a short-term perspective on HRM because they believe that the evidence of HRM having a long term and positive impact on individual or organization level performance is sketchy.

2. The second barrier is shortage of knowledge and skills among HRM managers to implement a credible HRM programme within their organization. In the above-mentioned multination survey, majority of HRM managers viewed their job as routine administration and agreed that they lacked the knowledge, skills and influence and credibility to develop and implement an HRM programme.

3. The third barrier to effective HRM is lack of proven knowledge about the long-term impact of HRM programmes. As a result, members of an organization may be sceptical of the benefits of major HRM initiatives. Both top and middle management may hold this scepticism. They are unable to discern tangible and positive performance outcomes related to HRM, so that their commitment to it wanes.

Managerial Implication

The implications are quite clear with regard to what HR managers need to do. The lack of commitment of top management (first barrier) is also attributed to HR managers because they could not demonstrate the value addition of HRM to the organization. Therefore, HR managers need to act on two areas with utmost sincerity. Firstly, they must acquire the knowledge and skills of HRM and related areas. Secondly, they must develop HRM programmes that have clear value linkages with organizational operations for short and long terms and implement them in a systematic manner. The competence of HR manager coupled with design of value added HRM programmes not only enhances its credibility but also the effectiveness of HRM.

OUTs AND INs OF HRM-TRENDS

HRM function is continuously evolving due to changing contours of internal and external environments of organizations. Therefore, the job of managers responsible for HR function is also continuously changing; Precedents that are generally useful to make predictions and manage current and future HR problems have become liabilities. Oren Harari listed some of important trends in HRM that affects the way we administer this function, in his article titled "Back to the Future of Work", which appeared in *Management Review* in 1993. These are as follows:

Out: chain of command, reporting relationships, department, and function, work as imposed from above tasks

In: self-management, responsiveness, proactivity, initiative, collaboration, egalitarianism, self-reliance, standards of excellence, personal responsibility, work as collection of self-initiated projects and teams

Out: stability, order, predictability, structure, better safe than sorry

In: flux, disorder, ambiguity, risk, better sorry than safe

Out: job titles and labels such as employee, manager, staff and professional

In: everyone as businessperson, an owner of a complete business process, and president of his/her job

Out: good citizenship—show up, be a good soldier, stay 9 to 5 in cubicle, don't make waves, wait for someone else to decide your fate, work in some organization for 30 years, retire with gold watch

In: Make a difference—add value, challenge the process, work four hours, or eighteen hours a day, accept the job site as wherever the action is, learn from mistakes, develop career mobility and fluidity, work your tail off and be intensely loyal to company X for one year or ten years, and then move on to company Y, a better, more marketable person.

Managerial Implication

The job of HR manager has become more challenging than ever, more multi-disciplinary than any other discipline, and more demanding than in the past. Hence, HR managers have to continuously update and upgrade themselves. Macro and micro perspectives of organizations and analytical skills to process culture specific information are imperative to perform the role of HR managers. Further, they need to keep track of changing scenario described as Outs and Ins. Knowledge of trends is essential to act proactively.

IBM—TOWERS PERRIN ON HRM ROLE

HR and their effective management are seen as a major source of competitive advantage since 1990s. However, using HR talent as a competitive advantage presupposes a paradigm shift in the approach and orientation of HR strategy. What is that shift required in HRM is a critical question to many. The answer came from global giants, i.e. IBM, in association with Towers Perrin, a consultancy firm that conducted a study with the twin objectives of: (i) to identify HRM's role in gaining competitive advantage, and (ii) to understand the HR related priorities of top leaders in running their organizations efficiently. The study was conducted in 1992 covering 3000 managers from 12 countries representing functions such as HRM, line management and consultancy. Important findings of the study were:

1. The biggest challenge for HR managers is to shift their attention from current operations to developing strategies for the future
2. HRM should focus on quality, customer service, employee involvement, productivity, teamwork, and creating a flexible workforce
3. HRM is no longer a stand-alone staff function. It has become an area that must work closely with all employees to develop partnerships and programmes that permit the firm to succeed in a highly competitive environment
4. HRM needs to develop and help to implement strategies and programmes that are responsive to the competitive nature of the market place
5. HRM practices and policies should be jointly developed and implemented by HR managers and line managers
6. Globalization of business, changing demographics of the workforce, downsizing where external forces are most likely to affect a firm's competitive advantage in the current century.

Managerial Implication

Two key issues that emerge from this study which have direct relevance to HR managers across the industry are: (i) Need for enhancing HR Line partnership in design and implementation of HR strategies to optimize aptitude-attitudinal profile of all employees and (ii) Need for replacing the existing HR policy framework in organizations in tandem with changing business realities (business aligned) as well as changing mix of HR and their behavioural-expectation paradigm (culture-oriented). In other words, HR managers must design and implement HR strategy in partnership with line management and such strategy shall be dovetailed with superordinate goal of the organization.

MULTIPLE ROLE MODEL OF HRM

Dave Ulrich, Professor of Business Administration at University of Michigan argues that the roles of HR professionals must be redefined to meet the competitive challenges organizations face today and are likely to face in the future in his remarkable and insightful book titled *Human Resource Champions: The Next Agenda for Adding Value and Delivering Results* published in 1997. Based on numerous examples from dozens of companies that have transformed their HRM functions, he provided a framework that identifies four distinct roles that HR professional must perform simultaneously in order to contribute fully to their organizations, i.e. adding value and delivering results. This framework called as multiple role models is illustrated here:

1. *Strategic partners.* This role involves systematically assessing and aligning HR practices with business strategy. They need to have skills to design, integrate and operate HR system to build new organizational capabilities. Building new organizational capabilities call for performance management programmes aligned with the desired outcomes. Here the deliverable outcome is *executing strategy.*

2. *Administrative experts.* This role is characterized by improving the processes, applying the principles of reengineering to HR processes, creating value in work performance, measuring HR results in terms of efficiency (cost) and effectiveness (quality). The deliverables in this role is *building an efficient infrastructure.*

3. *Employee champions.* Listening and responding to employees and finding the right balance between demands on employees and resources available to them are the characteristics of this role. The key deliverable is *increasing employee commitment and capability.*

4. *Change agents.* The deliverable in this role is *creating a renewed organization.* To this end, HR professionals need to understand the theory and application of tools for change. They lead transformation by doing it first within the HR function; they serve as catalysts and facilitators of change.

Apart from above, the model advocates mutually beneficial partnership between line and HR staff and prescribes guidelines on how to establish this partnership to deliver value and make their organizations more competitive.

Managerial Implication

As the author asserts, the HR function stands at crossroads. Unless HR professionals become accountable for defining the value they create for their organizations and the performance standards by which they should be measured, they will be ultimately outsourced. Therefore, it is imperative for HR professionals to add value in whatever they do. In order to make this happen, they must play multiple roles as described above and they need to acquire relevant skills to perform these roles. The acquisition of these skills and multiple performances transform human resource professionals as champions. To be precise, the essence of the model is, *move from what I do mind set to what I deliver mission.*

SKILL SET FOR HRM PROFESSIONAL IN ORGANIZATIONAL CHANGE

The role of HRM Professional has undergone a revolutionary change in the recent past fuelled by volatile changes in organizations. HR role is being placed on the forefront whether it is downsizing or experiencing economies of scale or technological change or business process reengineering or organizational restructuring. In other words, managing micro and macro level organizational change has become the primary role of HRM professionals in organizations. In order to manage these changes successfully, HRM professionals need to have the right mix of knowledge and skills. However, what kind of skills would be appropriate is a fundamental issue for many that include HRM professionals in practice, academics and consultancy. Professors Barbara Whitaker and Marshall Swift of Widener University, USA, based on intensive case study of three organizations: Compaq, IBM and Dowd developed a model that correlate HR skills with particular aspects of organizational change. This model was presented in their paper titled 'Choose an HR Star for Competitive Edge' published in *Management Decision* in 2000. HR Skills that are suggested for managing various reactions of employees and different organizational changes are summarized in Table 2.5.

TABLE 2.5

Aspects of organizational change	Reaction of employees to work place change	Knowledge and skills needed by HR professional
Values	Anger, resentment, reassurance	Knowledge of culture as to purpose, elements and bedrock nature
Information technology	Fear, anxiety, curiosity, information seeking, excited	Ergonomics. Open thinking where change of processes may be needed, understanding socio-technical systems, impact of information on culture
Work process	Resistance, group think, make sense, accountable	Team effectiveness, personality theory, empathy
Economic inclusion	Insecurity	Empathy, knowledge of inter-cultural difficulties, decision-making skills, persuading skills
Organization inclusion	Employees upset, out of the loop	Negotiation skills, influencing skills, empathy
Leadership style	No loyalty, hoping to leave, reassurance	Leadership development skills, self awareness
Employee/employer contact	Powerlessness	Self-awareness, decision making and behaviour interpretation skills
Company driver	Confusion	Understanding of financial systems that are foundations of the business. Continuously developing and updating information network

Managerial Implication

This model helps the practising HR managers to understand the type of skills that are required to manage the employee reactions as well as organization change programmes. This also serves the second purpose of understanding the type of employee reactions that a particular organization change programme can generate. In other words, human resource professionals who lack the relevant skills and knowledge, not only fail to manage the organizational change, but also the employee reactions. HRM professional can refer this model as a checklist or inventory of skills for managing change.

FIFTEEN KEY ROLES OF HRM PRACTITIONERS

It is interesting to note that the kind of assignments HR managers perform differ from organization to organization and situation to situation. Sometimes, we find it extremely difficult to profile the job of HR manager in definite terms. This is precisely the reason why HR manager is required to handle variety of functions, and in the process, performing different roles. This is more a necessity than an option for those HR managers who want to be complete HRM professionals. If it is so, what kind of roles HRM professionals may have to perform? American Society for Training and Development provides answer to this question based on surveying the job descriptions and job profiles of a large number of HRM managers. The survey identified fifteen key roles indicated in the following that HRM practitioners need to play.

1. *Evaluator.* The role of assessing the impact and utility of a programme and, service to the employees and organization.

2. *Group facilitator.* The role of managing group discussions and group process, so that individuals learn and group members feel the positive experience.

3. *Individual development counsellor.* The role of helping an individual to assess personal competencies, values, goals and identify and plan development and career actions.

4. *Instructional writer.* The role of preparing written learning and instructional material.

5. *Instructor.* The role of presenting information and directing structured learning experiences so that individuals learn.

6. *Manager of training and development.* The role of planning, organizing, staffing, controlling, training and development operations, or training and development projects, and of linking training and development operations with other organization units.

7. *Marketer.* The role of selling, training and development viewpoints, learning packages, programmes and services to target audiences outside one's own work unit.

8. *Media specialist.* The role of producing software and using audio, visual, computer, and other hardware based technologies for training and development.

9. *Needs analyst.* The role of defining gaps between ideal and actual performance and specify the cause of gaps.

10. *Programme administrator.* The role of ensuring that the facilities, equipment, materials, participants, and other components of a learning event are present and the programme logistics run smoothly.

11. *Programme designer.* The role of preparing objectives, defining content, and selecting and sequencing activities for a specific programme.

12. *Strategist.* The role of developing long range plans for what the training and development structure, organization, direction, policies, programmes, services and practices will be in order to accomplish the training and development mission.

13. *Task analyst.* The role of identifying activities, tasks, sub-tasks, human resource, and support requirements necessary to accomplish specific results in a job or organization.

14. *Theoretician.* The role of developing and testing theories of learning, training and development.

15. *Transfer agent.* The role of helping individuals to apply learning after their learning experience.

Managerial Implication

The above description of key HRM practitioners' role offers valuable learning to HR managers of all types of organizations. This illustration of roles especially helps HR managers in their own career mapping, apart from driving home the practical truth of the number of roles they need to play. Based on these roles HR managers can also plan their career as a HRM generalist or specialist in a given sub area/s. Further, this description has realistic value to all HRM professionals in understanding their role since it has come after surveying the HRM practitioners.

CORE COMPETENCIES MODEL FOR HRM PROFESSIONALS

The competencies required to perform the role of HRM professional is rapidly changing. Further, HR professionals perform different roles such as generalist, consultant, organization leader, strategist, and specialist in a particular area of HRM. However, what competencies are essential and desirable in order to perform these roles effectively is a big question to many across the discipline. Three HR experts namely Donna Blancero at Arizona State University, John Boroski of Eastman Kodak Company and Lee Dyer of Cornell University identified eleven core competencies and six leverage competencies that are commonly required for all types of roles within HRM function based on their research conducted in 1995. These are briefly explained in the following:

Core competencies

1. *Ethics.* Possesses fidelity to fundamental values (respect for the individual, responsibility of purpose and to constituencies, honesty, reliability, fairness, integrity, respect for property).

2. *Communication.* Uses language, style and effective expression (including non-verbal) in speaking and writing so that others can understand and take appropriate action.

3. *Listening.* Able to interpret and use information extracted from oral communication.

4. *Relationship building.* Able to establish rapport, relationships and networks across a broad range of people and groups.

5. *Teamwork.* Understanding how to collaborate and foster collaboration among others.

6. *Standards of quality.* Has high performance expectations for self and others.

7. *Judgement.* Able to make rational and realistic decisions based on logical assumptions which reflect factual information.

8. *Results orientation.* Knows how to work to get results.

9. *Initiative.* Able to go beyond the obvious requirements for a situation.

10. *Self confidence.* Possesses a high degree of confidence in own abilities.

11. *Enthusiasm and commitment.* Able to believe in employer, find enjoyment and involvement in work, and to be committed to quality performance.

Leverage competencies

1. *Influence.* Ability and skill to cause an effect in indirect ways. Ability to impact individuals and organizations without exercise of direct power or command.

2. *Utilization of resources.* Able to find, acquire and leverage appropriate resources, inside and outside the organization.

3. *Customer awareness.* Understand both internal and external customers and their needs.

4. *Creativity.* Ability to invent, explore, imagine new approaches, frameworks or solutions; ability to stimulate ideas in self and others.

5. *Questioning.* Ability to gather and interpret objective information through skilful questioning of individuals and groups.

6. *Organizational astuteness.* Understanding individual sensitivities, power dynamics, relationships, and how the organization operates.

Managerial Implication

This competency model helps organizations in many ways. This can be used for recruitment and development of HR managers and job analysis purposes. This also helps as a benchmarked competency set for HR professionals for charting their own development. HR professionals must make an assessment of themselves with reference to these competencies and work to acquire the missing ones. These competencies are commonly applicable across all the roles and managerial positions within HR function. Therefore, HR departments in organizations can draft training programmes to impart and develop their HR executives on these competencies.

PASSIVE HRM MANAGERS

The role of an HR manager is in fluid state, not just now, but has been so for some decades. Many CEOs claim HR as the most valuable and strategic asset of the firm. In practice, a good number of them do not even value HR equal to other resources in terms of allocation of time, budget sanctions and commitment of other resources. Two factors are responsible for this and HR managers themselves are accountable for them. Firstly, HR managers do not understand the fundamentals of their discipline and secondly, are passive towards needs and demands of their profession at organizational level. Abraham Zaleznik, Matsushita Professor of Leadership authored a critically acclaimed paper titled "What's Wrong with HRM" highlighting how HR managers misunder-stand their role and eventually fail in what they ought to achieve. They are as follows:

1. Most HR managers don't understand human beings because they won't confront aggression in themselves or in other people. Aggression is a potent factor in productive work. But most HR managers can't or won't deal with aggression as a universal human attribute. Instead, like corporate Caspar Milquetoasts, they try to keep peace at all costs. And when they deal with aggression, they do so indirectly in ways that can drive other corporate citizens mad.

2. The inabilities of HR managers reflect in their eagerness to engage consultants on a dizzying array of projects. Seeking services of consultants means deflecting responsibility and accountability. That way, if the project comes under fire—as at

some point almost every project will—the consultants are the targets, not the HR manager who brought them in.

3. HR managers think their job is to satisfy the needs of the client, the line managers. Their job should be to satisfy themselves by making independent judgments, making recommendations and accepting responsibility for their advice. In other words, making a real contribution to the organizational effectiveness.

4. In the real world, not every request can be granted. Not every subordinate will deserve promotion or even continued employment. If the news is bad, the HR manager delivers it and if the news is good, it is the boss. The boss avoids unpleasant acts and a reputation for blocking what people want to do. The HR managers become identified with all the ways organizations have of denying people what they want.

5. Worst of all, the way most HR managers react when a contentious question arises: they turn the problem into a moral issue and then get on the side of the angels.

Managerial Implication

The implication is quite clear. In a position of passiveness, neither HR managers will be able to justify themselves nor can ensure organizational effectiveness. HR managers must work on their competence to understand people and organizations and their needs. They must directly involve in the business of organization at operational and strategic level and contribute in a way that proves the worth of HR function. They also need to be plain spoken and project it as a business function than as a custodian of peace and morals. Appeasement is not a quality that should be practised always. One needs to be equitable always in order to emerge as active HR manager.

FIRST BREAK ALL THE RULES

Based on interviews of more than 80,000 managers in more than 400 companies besides 20 years of their own experience in studying the core characteristics of great managers and work places, two Gall up management consultants namely Marcus Buckingham and Curt Coffman published a remarkable book titled, *First, Break All The Rules: What The World's Greatest Managers Do Differently* in 1999. The study conducted by the authors is the largest of its kind ever undertaken which has great relevance to human resource practitioners. Some of the key observations of this work are:

1. Employee stock options and other benefit programmes, though can attract the people to join in a company, it is the quality of the immediate manager and the productive environment of the workplace that determine the retention of employees in the company.

2. Great managers break conventional wisdom in hiring norms. They do not hire a person based on his/her experience, intelligence and knowledge. They do so by identifying a person's talent. Talent here is defined as natural recurring patterns, feeling, or behaviour that can be productively applied.

3. Great managers do not believe that people can change much. They dismiss self-help and self-improvement programmes as ineffective. You can't just teach each employee the nine habits of an effective life and expect them to excel.

4. Great managers believe that performance is in the *synapses*, the connections between a

person's brain cells. This develops in early childhood. As a result of this some people are great strategic thinkers, some have talent for mathematics, others in social skills and so on and so forth. Trying to put someone in a function his/her brain cells do not match will result in job mismatch and on-the-job-failure.

5. Great managers follow some key practices: (i) Keep the focus on outcomes, (ii) Value world class performance, (iii) Study your best, (iv) Don't waste time trying to put in what was left, (v) Try to draw out what was left in.

Authors have presented the following 12 questions that can be used to measure whether your workplace is productive or not. Yours is a productive workplace if employees answer these questions affirmatively.

1. Do I know what is expected of me?
2. Do I have the materials and equipment I need to do my work right?
3. At work, do I have the opportunity to do what I do the best everyday?
4. In the last seven days. Have I received recognition or praise for doing good work?
5. Does my supervisor, or someone at work, seem to care about me as a person?
6. Is there someone at work who encourages my development?
7. At work, do my opinions seem to count?
8. Does the mission/purpose of my company, make me feel my job is important?
9. Are my co-workers committed to doing quality work?
10. Do I have a best friend at work?
11. In the last six months, has some one at work talked to me about my progress?
12. Last year, did I had opportunities at work to learn and grow?

Further, the authors have criticized the conventional career path of promoting people out of roles in which they excel and moving them into roles in which they struggle. In essence, great managers break one conventional golden rule a day to create benchmarks.

Managerial Implication

This book is a great tool for HR managers. It helps to draw pragmatic plans in the areas of (i) employee retentions, (ii) hiring of employees, (iii) matching the employees' competence profile with compatible job in the organization and (iv) career management. More importantly, it provides valuable information, on how a productive work place should be created, and its importance. The other insights it can offer are (i) why managers should be great managers, and their prominent role in organizational functioning and (ii) the limitations of behavioural interventions. This book may convince HR managers why they need to create managers who are capable of breaking conventional rules uninterruptedly for business excellence.

IRISH ELK SYNDROME

Through many generations, the Irish elk had become the victim of an evolutionary quirk that led to its demise. Each year its antlers grew longer, eventually becoming so heavy that it was unable to lift its head and forage for food. It became weak and eventually starved to death. The antlers that had helped elk survive in the first place became exaggerated over time, leading to its extinction. Dr. David Weiss, senior fellow at the Queen's University, has drawn this analogy to describe what will happen to HR function if it continues to do what it had been doing! He challenges the traditional view with a new vision of HR as an internal business accountable for the return on investment of essential corporate assets, people, and organizational processes in his best selling book titled *High Impact HR: Transforming Human Resources for Competitive Advantage* published in 1999.

The central theme of the book is that the traditional HR activities such as recruiting, employee relations, compensation and training are necessary but not sufficient to help organizations thrive in a new business environment. Therefore, organizations must abandon HR practices that don't yield any value to the strategic value of the company and to its customers. The new challenge for HR is to take accountability for the return on investment of essential corporate assets, people and organizational processes. To tackle this challenge, HR function in organizations should undergo transformation by changing its priorities, accountabilities and organizational design. This transformation emphasizes the following focuses:

1. *Strategic value.* The extent to which people and organizational processes provide competitive advantage.
2. *A competitive mindset.* Rather than the idea of being a monopoly service provider without competition.
3. *Process outcomes.* Creating a balance between excellence in process and the delivery of specific measurable outcomes.

This transformation is to be managed in three phases: (i) Handle the challenge of transformation, mainly the systematic abandonment of valueless HR practices and processes, (ii) Install high impact and value added HR practices and (iii) Bring sharper alignment between HR practices and strategic business goals.

Managerial Implication

The book provides a comprehensive action planner consisting three parts and organized into seven chapters to transform HR function in one's organization. In other words, it is a practical how-to-do guide in transforming the HR function from a mere service and maintenance function to a strategic player. The speciality of the models presented is, its focus on external customer to establish the contribution of HR practices and their value to organizations. It is critical phase for every HR professional that they should shift the focus of the HRM function by abandoning value free practices to value added, otherwise the Irish Elk Syndrome may attack them.

STRATEGIC HR LEADER

The role of HR professional has been evolving much faster during the current decade than it was ever. The changing environment and increased realization of human value at work have made HR function in general and its managers in particular, very critical to organizational success. In order to understand and map the role of HR professionals in coming years, Dr William Rothwell, professor at Pennsylvania State University in association with Society for HR Development conducted a broad based study in 1996. The study identified six major trends that will affect and drive HR function during the next ten years. These are:

1. *Globalization.* Every factor of production, other than workplace skills can be duplicated anywhere in the world. How the people are selected, trained and managed, determines to a large extent how successful an organization will be.

2. *Technology.* The study identified technology as miniaturization, communications, software, new ways to do things with the aid of computers and so on. The increasing technological change require more technical training and further flattening of organization and concomitant HR practices.

3. *Change.* This ever-happening change requires organizations to learn continuously, develop and deliver new products and services quickly. Therefore, the most critical process in the organization will be the transition of a corporate idea to its implementation within the organization.

4. *Knowledge capital.* Valuing what people know is a formidable challenge that contributes to capitalize on technology as well as to maintain the competitive advantage in a changing environment.

5. *Speed in market change.* It is being caused by network model of business that allows organization to build customer base across the globe. Organizations with flexibility and the infrastructure to make and implement decisions are the only ones likely to succeed.

6. *Cost control.* This continues to be a major trend and the prices of products will be determined more by customers and less by its producers.

HR professionals have a distinct role to play in this changing scenario. The study also identified a competency skill set for HR professional that is specifically required currently and 10 years from now for dealing with the above described trends. This is summarized in Table 2.6.

TABLE 2.6

Current skill set	10 years from now
People skills	Credibility
Understand the business	People skills
Credibility	Understand the business
Develop credibility	Consultative approach
Leadership	Developing credibility
Comfort with change and ambiguity	Comfort with change
Consultative approach	Visioning
Establish mutual faith and trust	

In a nutshell, Dr. William Rothwell says HR professionals need to emerge as strategic HR leaders. The study envisages more a strategic role than maintenance role for HR leader. These study results with a detailed description are given in the book titled *The Strategic Human Resource Leader* authored by William Rothwell, Robert Prescott and Maria Taylor in 1998.

Managerial Implication

Studies have highlighted the changing role of HR professional, particularly from a paper-pusher role to that of boardroom. This study is more relevant, since it specifically identified the competency skill of HR professional that are required in correspondence with major trends in the industry across the globe. HR professionals, in order to transform themselves as leaders, must focus on acquiring the above described skills. Especially, they must develop business skills and mere understanding of few rules, regulations, tools and techniques of HRM are not just enough.

Chapter 3

Human Resource Planning and Sourcing Management

Quality of HR in an organization, particularly in terms of talent availability, is largely contingent upon its HR planning and talent sourcing practices. When these practices get derailed or professional approach is missed, organization will be saddled with substandard manpower. When HR planning is absent or carried out in an unscientific manner, the dominant consequence will be imbalanced manpower, i.e. either surplus or deficit manpower, both in quality and quantity terms. The possibility of inducting wrong person to a right position or right person to a wrong position is fair when talent sourcing method lacks a rational base. Therefore, it is fundamental to all HR practitioners that contemporary and scientific approach is adopted in HR procurement. In order to make this happen, professionals must possess the knowledge of these practices.

This chapter is devoted to these practices. A range of thirteen classics are covered here that will enable (i) to understand the basics and common traps in HR planning and sourcing practices, (ii) professional methods and techniques in design and implementation of sound planning and sourcing practices and also (iii) the administration of HR information system etc.

HR PLANNING TECHNIQUES

The purpose of HR planning is to make available, right quality and quantity of manpower at right time in organization. With the increased pressure on companies to cut down manpower costs, it is also important to see that no surplus manpower exists. HR planning typically involves two steps: (i) HR demand forecasting and (ii) HR supply forecasting.

Demand forecasting has to be done based on a number of long- and short-term factors such as (i) changes in economy, (ii) technological trends, (iii) market trends, (iv) global trends, (v) strategic plans of organization, (vi) ongoing and immediate future projects/operations and (vii) production schedules. There are number of techniques in vogue across the organizations in Globe for forecasting HR demand. Some of them are quantitative and others are qualitative. Popularly used techniques are:

1. *Predictor variables.* This technique is akin to statistical tool of regression. Based upon past employment levels vis-à-vis sales/production, the future requirement can be forecasted. It is mere extrapolation of an assessment to similar situations.

2. *Zero-base technique.*   Here, the present level of employment is used to determine future requirement. Everything starts with zero. It implies that organization has zero manpower and starts analyzing manpower requirement for each operation carefully.

3. *Bottom-up technique.*   This is a widely used technique in our organizations. The process involved is, each manager gives his requirement of HR in operations he is responsible. Requirement projected by all managers will be aggregated to draw organizational level forecast.

4. *Simulation technique.*   It is a technique of experimentation. A real-time situation will be created and then forecast assessment will be made manipulating different quality and quantity of manpower.

Following factors are to be considered in HR supply forecasting:

- Employee turnover rate
- Absenteeism rate
- Current skill inventory
- Separations
- Productivity levels

Managerial Implication

A scientific HR planning helps organizations not only in ensuring timely availability of right manpower when needed, but also helps in reducing manpower costs and optimization of human talents. HR practitioners must acquire the skills of implementing forecasting techniques in particular. HR planning is a pivotal tool in proving the efficacy and value of HR function.

PARKINSON'S DISEASE

Parkinson disease is a common phenomenon that we observe with most organizations. The key principles of this model include the following:

1. Work tends to expand to fill the time available for its completion. In other words, the task to be completed increases in its perceived importance and complexity in a direct ratio with the time to be spent on its completion. For example, an architect who generally requires 7 days' time to complete a building plan tends to devote 20 days for the same task if time is available.

2. The number of people in any working group tends to increase regardless of the amount of work to be done. An official has to multiply subordinates and not rivals and officials have to work for each other. For example, a firm of 100 employees takes a decision to set up a time keeping office, and employs a junior assistant to look after the same. After 4 years, the junior assistant makes a representation to the management that lack of promotion prospects makes him demotivated. On consideration, management promotes him as senior assistant. Again, after a few months, on his requisition, a junior assistant gets added to the time office. This assistant also impresses upon the management that a precedent of promoting a junior assistant to senior on completion of 4 years exists. Accordingly, management promotes him as senior assistant and senior assistant as chief assistant and consequently adds up one

more junior assistant. At the end of 16 years, on manpower assessment, organization finds a total of 10 persons employed in time office and all of them busy with some or other works connected to time keeping policy work/implementation/interpretation/ modification. They also make employees working in other departments busy with time office problems (rules) and services (procedures).

3. An organization employing more than 1000 employees becomes a self-perpetuating empire, creating so much internal work that it no longer needs any contact with outside world. For example, some organizations end up creating so many ancillary services that, at one point of time, more employees find place in these services than principal operations of organization.

Cyril Nothcote Parkinson, Professor at University of Malaya was the one, who proposed this remarkable principle in his book titled *The Parkinson's Law* in 1958.

Managerial Implication

Managers in general and HR/industrial engineers in particular must be conscious of this principle. Most of our overmanning/staffing problems are outcomes of failure in arresting Parkinson disease. Organizations interested in rational manning should follow scientific method of carrying out workload and workforce analysis instead of deciding manpower additions based upon requisitions from managers. There should be a suggestive time schedules for completion of projects/operations/assignments wherever possible to avoid over time works by employees. Parkinson says if unnecessary departments/overstaffing is not eliminated, it will result in shortage of manpower where required and over staffing where it needs some pruning.

MYTHICAL MAN-MONTH

Mythical Man-Month, is an excellent book authored by Frederick P. Brooks, Jr., Kenan Professor of Computer Science at University of North Carolina in 1975. The book deals with different aspects of software engineering and programming that include importantly people related issues. Frederick asserts that *adding manpower to a late software project makes it later*. This finding, now known as Brook's Law in software and management circles, had shaken and continues to serve as a caution to software companies' worldwide. According to the author, the man-month as a unit for measuring size of job is a dangerous and deceptive myth, hence the name, The Mythical Man-Month.

What is so mythical about the man-month based planning? An example may help to understand this principle. Consider a moderately complex software application from the early microcomputer era, such as the Lotus 1-2-3 or WordStar. Assume that such a program might take one very smart, highly motivated, expert programmer approximately for a year to design, code, debug, and document. In other words, 12 months. Imagine that market pressures are such that we want to get the programme finished in a month, rather than a year. What is the solution? You might say, get 12 experienced coders, divide up the work and problem will be solved. But Brooks states that time cannot be warped so easily because 12 months does not equal to 12 programmers based on his experience as team leader managing the development of Operating System (OS/360) at IBM. Why it is so? Because more the team members are the communication and coordination problems. They tend to over spend time on meetings, drafting project plans, negotiating interfaces and progress may get adversely affected on account of group dynamics. Further, training requirements and performance speed of programmers also vary. In a nut shell, ancillary tasks will go up as size of team increases that include keeping one member of team as leader, one more for coordinating the team members' schedules and another for housekeeping and one more for updating progress charts and so on and so forth.

Managerial Implication

Brook's law is Parkinson's disease (work tends to expand to fill the time available) of software companies. Many of HR problems in the organizations are due to naïve assumptions of managers in understanding human behaviour at work. Presuming complex issues/relations in a linear way as that of man-month principle lands organizations in deep crisis. Therefore, HR managers must appreciate the vitality of a systematic HR planning and placement in software projects. Also, they should advise top management for undertaking work measurement studies and take up responsibility to draw, at least working job descriptions of key positions. These measures can help organizations to optimize HR and perform more effectively.

ERGONOMICS

Ergonomics is a field of study that is concerned with human-machine interaction. It is closely associated with industrial and experimental psychology. The aim of ergonomics is to design human-machine system involving the best combination of human and machine elements. Ergonomics is also called the science of human engineering, human factors or human machine systems. In designing a production system, the combinations of human-machine factors have to be harmonized for the best performance of both machine and human. The human and machine systems possess different characteristics as shown in Table 3.1. Ergonomics advocates using these

TABLE 3.1   Man vs Machines

Man excels in	Machines excels in
1. Detection of certain forms of very low energy levels	1. Monitoring (both men and machines)
2. Sensitivity to an extremely wide variety of stimuli	2. Performing routine, repetitive, or very precise operations
3. Perceiving patterns and making generalizations about them	3. Responding very quickly to control signals
4. Detecting signals in high noise levels	4. Exerting great force, smoothly and with precision
5. Ability to store large amounts of information for long periods and recalling relevant facts of appropriate moments	5. Storing and recalling large amounts of information in short time period
6. Ability to exercise judgment where events cannot be completely defined	6. Performing complex and rapid computation with high accuracy
7. Improvising and adopting flexible procedures	7. Doing many different things at one time
8. Ability to react to unexpected low-probability events	8. Deductive processes
9. Applying originality in solving problems: i.e. alternate solutions	9. Insensitivity to extraneous factors
10. Ability to profit from experience and alter course of action	10. Ability to repeat operations very rapidly, continuously, and precisely the same way over a long period
11. Ability to perform fine manipulation, especially where misalignment appears unexpectedly	11. Operating in environments, which are hostile to man or beyond human tolerance
12. Ability to continue to perform even when overloaded	
13. Ability to reason inductively	

Source: Woodson, Wesley E. and Donald W. Conover (1964), *Human Engineering Guide for Equipment Designers*, University of California Press, Berkeley.

characteristics in a complimentary manner while designing and implementing any production and mechanical operations.

Managerial Implication

Though Ergonomics is a specialized area, HR managers should have sufficient familiarization with this technique of man-machine interaction. Because, joy at work is contingent upon ergonomics and ensuring joyful working is the primary responsibility of HRD.

MOTION STUDY

The essence of motion study is analysis of fundamental motions of human activity to find out the best way of doing any job. In other words, it is a process of analyzing a job to find the easiest, most effective, and most economical way of doing it. Gilbreth classified the basic motions into what he called *therbligs* (which is gilbreths spelled back), such as search, find, transport empty, preposition, grasp, and so forth.

Frank B. Gilbreth, an inquisitive Industrial engineer, had pioneered the technique of Motion Study in association with his wife Lillian Moller Gilbreth during 1902–12. Prior to use of Gilbreth's standard method, 120 bricks laid per worker were considered to be normal. Gilbreth's development of *standard method* using motion study resulted in an average production rate of 350 bricks per worker per hour. This increase was not achieved by making bricklayers work faster but through most effective way of doing it. For example, Gilbreth reduced the number of motions from 18 to 5 in laying the bricks. Traditionally, a bricklayer would bend over and pick up a brick from a pile of bricks on a relatively unadjustable scaffold, rotate the brick to find the best side, and then lay the brick by tapping with mortar of often poor consistency. Gilbreth suggested a different pattern. Consider that bricks brought to a site are density arranged, all touching one another, on a pallet. Gilbreth wanted bricklayers to be able to pick up a brick most efficiently. Therefore, he had minimum-cost labourers arranging the bricks on a pallet for ease of pick up by the master bricklayer. He then provided adjustable scaffolds, the proper location of bricks and mortar, and mortar of proper consistency. The result was a vast improvement in productivity with less fatigue.

Managerial Implication

There may be many operations in organizations, which need to be studied in order to establish a scientific mode of carrying them for optimization of HR efforts. Definition and renewal of existing work methods could give a fillip to improvement in productivity. Unfortunately, most of the activities and operations in organizations are carried out based on precedence and in a conventional way resulting in machine and human inefficiency. In a cost cutting era, organizations just can't afford such inefficient method and approach. Therefore, HR managers must influence their management in implementing motion studies in order to establish new benchmarks and method of doing work.

PRINCIPLES OF MOTION ECONOMY

The standard principles of good design are referred to as principles of motion economy. Workstations that are designed in consonance with these principles generally result in greater optimization. There are twenty-two motion economy principles according to Ralph Barnes who dealt with these issues in the book *Motion and Time Study: Design and Measurement of Work* published in 1968. They are:

1. The two hands should begin as well as complete their motions at the same time
2. The two hands should not be idle at the same time except during rest periods
3. Motions of the arms should be made in opposite and symmetrical directions, and should be made simultaneously
4. Hand and body motions should be confined to the lowest classification with which it is possible to perform the work satisfactorily
5. Momentum should be employed to assist the worker wherever possible, and it should be reduced to a minimum if it must be overcome by muscle effort
6. Smooth continuous curved motions of the hands are preferable to straight-line motions involving sudden and sharp changes in direction
7. Ballistic movements are faster, easier, and more accurate than restricted or controlled movements
8. Work should be arranged to permit easy and natural rhythm wherever possible
9. Eye fixations should be as few and as close together as possible
10. There should be a definite and fixed place for all tools and materials
11. Tools, materials, and controls should be located close to the point of use
12. Gravity feed bins and containers should be used to deliver the material close to the point of use
13. Drop deliveries should be used wherever possible
14. Materials and tools should be located to permit the best sequence of motions
15. Provisions should be made for adequate conditions for seeing. Good illumination is the first requirement for satisfactory visual perception
16. The height of the work place and the chair should preferably be so arranged that alternate sitting and standing at work are easily possible
17. A chair of the type and height to permit good posture should be provided for every worker
18. The hands should be relieved of all work that can be done more advantageously by a jig, a fixture, or a foot operated device
19. Two or more tools should be combined wherever possible
20. Tools and materials should be pre-positioned wherever possible
21. Where each finger performs some specific movement, such as in type writing, the lead should be distributed in accordance with the inherent capacities of the fingers
22. Levers, hand wheels, and other controls should be located in such positions that the operator can manipulate them with the least change in body position and with the greatest speed and ease.

Managerial Implication

The use of these principles would be productive in developing efficient workstation designs. Choose a sample unit in your organization and re-design the same in consonance with the above principles. Then compare the results of this workstation with others for assessing the benefits.

SCIENTIFIC MANAGEMENT

Frederick Winslow Taylor had pioneered the popularly known comprehensive technique called Scientific Management in 1911 as a result of his keen research in different areas of industrial activity. He is also regarded as father of Scientific Management. The main aim of scientific management was to maximize the production and efficiency of each worker and to design a system, which would maximize the carrying of employees and employers. Scientific management involves a complete mental revolution on the part of workmen engaged in any establishment or industry towards their work, fellow workmen, and toward their employers. And it involves equally complete mental revolution on the part of those on the management's side towards their workers and their daily problems. The principles of scientific management are:

- Science in the place of rule of thumb
- Harmony; not discord
- Co-operation; not individualism
- Establishment of standards for performance
- Greater specialization of activities
- Emphasis on fitting workers to particular tasks
- Elimination of waste efforts
- Maximum output in the place of restricted output
- Development of each man to his greatest efficiency and prosperity
- Collection of data to support decisions rather than reliance on casual judegment

Taylor's Scientific Management has strengthened the process of assembly line and mass production. The techniques such as piece rate wage system, time study, standardization of tools, costing methods etc., also originated from scientific management practices. Scientific Management was criticized mainly for its lack of human concern/approach. In 1911 and 1912 Taylor was questioned at length by a special committee of the U.S. House of Representatives concerned about the Taylor system, particularly time study of operations, piece rate system standardization etc. U.S. Government also had brought a law banning the use of stopwatch for time study of operations. Despite these bans and criticism by many, Scientific Management grew and prospered, and radically changed the structure, people and the way jobs were carried out in organizations.

Managerial Implication

This model gave birth to the task-oriented management. This has relevance even in today's organizations. Many of the quality models, benchmarking practices, and just-in-time techniques have similarity with scientific management principles. Importantly some of the principles like, (i) co-operation in the place of individualism, (ii) development of each man to his greatest efficiency and prosperity, and (iii) science in the place of rule of thumb have great relevance to the practice of HRM.

JOB EVALUATION TECHNIQUES

Job evaluation is a process of evaluating the worth of a job in an organization. Though job evaluation measures worth of a job in an administrative sense, it is often used for the purpose of compensation design by translating the administrative worth into monetary terms. Many companies use job evaluation to

- establish worth of a job in comparison to other jobs in organization
- develop hierarchy of jobs
- develop an organizational structure
- establish relationships between jobs
- facilitate compensation design
- eliminate inequity in compensation

There are four techniques in evaluation of jobs that firms follow. These are described in Table 3.2.

TABLE 3.2

Technique	Useful to	Steps involved	Advantages	Disadvantages
Job ranking	Small firms	(a) Develop brief job descriptions for each job (b) Appoint a cross-functional committee to select top and bottom most job benchmarks (c) Compare jobs to these benchmarks and rank them.	(a) Simple (b) Inexpensive	(a) Crude method (b) Subjectivity
Job classification/ grading	Medium and large sized firms	(a) Develop a yardstick/standard for each job based on job description (b) Create a scale of value for the standard/yardstick job (c) Compare jobs to standard and assign value (d) Based on value, draw classification of jobs	(a) Simple (b) Easy to understand and communicate (c) Inexpensive	(a) Classification requires multiple yardsticks and values to evaluate jobs like production, marketing, personnel (b) Only generalizations could be used in defining grades (c) Subjectivity
Point system	All types of firms	(a) Develop detailed job descriptions (b) Interview job occupants to understand the jobs (c) Create benchmark points for each skills (skills, physical, mental, cognitive) in terms of quality and quantity (d) Assign points to each job based on requirement levels of skills	(a) Comparatively objective (b) Easy to interpret	(a) Time consuming (b) Expensive

TABLE 3.2 *(continued)*

Technique	Useful to	Steps involved	Advantages	Disadvantages
Factor comparison	All types of firms	(a) Compare each job with five universal job factors such as: (i) Responsibilities, (ii) Skill (iii) Physical effort, (iv) Mental effort and (v) Working conditions (b) Assign value to determine worth of the job	(a) Step-by-step formal method, systematic (b) Easy to translate into monetary terms	(a) Complexity (b) Time consuming

Managerial Implication

Job evaluation has assumed greater significance in organizations currently due to its multifaceted usefulness in HRM. HR managers when launching job evaluation exercise must take note of (i) job that should be evaluated and not the person performing it, (ii) defining clearly purpose of evaluation (iii) adoption of one of the four job evaluation techniques based upon company size, internal needs and organizational culture and (iv) allocation of sufficient resources for the exercise.

JOB ANALYSIS TECHNIQUES

Job analysis is a process of identifying of duties, responsibilities and knowledge of a job. This is considered as a basic tool of HRM and provides comprehensive information that has impact on almost all HR sub-systems. For example, it is useful to following HR functions:

1. *Preparation of job specifications.* Job analysis data enables to write minimum required qualities to perform a job that is called as job specification.

2. *HR planning.* Job analysis is a major technique in assessing quantity and quality of HR for carrying out particular operations.

3. *Recruitment and selection.* Data provided by job analysis forms as basis to design employment tests and selection methods.

4. *Training and development.* Job analysis data can be used as a benchmark to determine training needs of employees and jobs.

5. *Compensation.* Job evaluation, a technique widely used to establish relative worth of a job is dependent upon the data provided through job analysis.

6. *Performance appraisal.* Here also job analysis data forms as a benchmark to assess performance level of employees on a particular job.

7. *Career planning.* Job analysis provides information of all related jobs based on which movements of employees can be planned in addition to determining hierarchy of a particular job.

A number of techniques including the following are employed in analyzing jobs in an organization:

1. *Questionnaire.* It is an extensively used method. Based on need, open end or

structured questionnaire is prepared to which present incumbent of a job answers. The questionnaire generally includes items such as technical, administrative duties, working conditions, academic specifications, equipment used etc., popular ones are position analysis questionnaire (PAQ) developed by researchers at Purdue University, management position description questionnaire (MPDQ) developed by Control Data Corporation.

2. *Observation.* A specialist observes an incumbent performing a job and records the observations. The log thus prepared yields great deal of information. This technique is used for every routine, and standardized jobs.

3. *Interview.* Interactions with incumbents and associated people are carried out to determine and explain the duties, responsibilities and knowledge standards required to perform a job. The advantage is that a direct interaction is feasible with people associated with the job directly and indirectly.

4. *Combination.* A combination of all the above mentioned techniques can be used.

Managerial Implication

Job analysis exercise should be conducted at regular intervals since change in profile of jobs is happening speedily than in the past. Absence of job analysis data can cost organizations dearly and HRM decisions will be based upon approximates and not on accuracy. HR managers in association with line managers and industrial engineers must develop position analysis questionnaires relevant to their organizations to begin within this direction.

HUMAN RESOURCE INFORMATION SYSTEM (HRIS) TECHNIQUE

HR information system is much more than computerizing the payroll or skill inventory in organization. It is an integrated approach aimed at accelerating the decision-making process concerning HR and improvement of two-way communication. Software packages such as HRMS ORACLE, People soft-HR, and SAP-HR are available which are relevant for creating HRIS. The system is used in following areas:

- Recruitments, particularly pre-employment application process
- Training need analysis
- HR planning, particularly in forecast techniques
- Payroll
- Skill inventory
- Career and succession planning
- Employee benefit administration and services
- Two-way communication in organization
- HR personal data
- Job evaluation
- Compensation management
- Employee surveys

Areas of utilization of this technique are on the rise during the current decade. Many organizations have reported huge savings and improved decision-making in terms of quality and speed. For example, Chevron estimated that it saved to the tune of $2000 per employee consequent upon integration of employee information through HRIS. Philips Petroleum reported saving of over $100 million by ensuring availability of information needed directly to managers.

HRIS is particularly useful to organizations whose geographical spread is vast or employing large manpower. HRIS, apart from using computers is meant to integrate the employee related information in a meaningful fashion. HRIS also can be used for generating various reports and analyzing HR information with different permutations and combinations to draw inferences not possible by manual operations. Organizations generally allow three types of accessibility of HR information, which include: (i) information meant to all employees, (ii) Information accessibility restricted to managers and (iii) information accessibility to only top managers. Employee interaction online is also possible to receive services, communicate with management and receive bulletins. One time investment on HRIS will dramatically increase effectiveness of HR management and saves the more money than invested on it.

Managerial Implication

A number of organizations end up making a wrong or not very rational decision because of limited information available with them regarding HR. It is difficult for some organizations to establish exact strength of manpower on roll in a given day. Further, the rise of variables in HR data makes it impossible for organizations to leave the data uncomputerized and unprocessed. However, computerization of HR data is just a beginning in the direction of HRIS creation. HRIS is a combination of factors that provide information timely, accurately, meaningfully, completely and in a concise manner.

SAP HR

SAP HR is an integrated software module developed by SAP AG that enables medium and large size organizations to maintain a common HR database in a scientific manner. This software helps organizations in efficiently managing a wide spectrum of HR functions that include the following:

1. *Organizational management.* This tool offers a variety of organizational models like matrix, project organizations, flat structure etc. We can construct and maintain entire organizational structure, including organizational units, positions, jobs, tasks and the reporting structure with ease and efficiency with its graphical planning tool. It allows model the organizational structure and modify it as required to reflect its dynamic development and can determine the current staffing situation, future requirements, vacant positions, qualification deficits.

2. *Personnel administration.* This tool enables to achieve a streamlined, comprehensive and fully integrated HR data structure. It allows to store all data with effective dates, carry out validity checks, and maintains a precise log of data entered. Data entry can be streamlined and accelerated with the help of fast data entry functions for mass data input, standardized default values to facilitate data maintenance, customizable menus that are user specific. Further, this system empowers employees to view, create and maintain their own data at any time, from their workstations, anywhere in the world.

3. *Recruitment.* This component provides recruiters with all the necessary data on vacant positions, the required skills, educational requirements and job descriptions to facilitate both internal and external job posting. Its processes are automated and streamlined.

4. *Personnel development.* This system consists of tools to manage (i) career and succession planning, (ii) individual developmental plans, (iii) appraisal systems monitoring, (iv) skills profile in the organization and (v) planning training events.

5. *Compensation management.* This provides three flexible application components to develop and establish individual remuneration policies, long term incentives and performance and success oriented compensation strategies These are: (i) SAP HR Compensation management, (ii) SAP HR Benefits administration and (iii) SAP HR Personnel cost planning.

6. *Time management.* An automatic planning table that is inbuilt here provides an overview of the HRs available at a given moment. It helps in planning shifts, absentee management, recording working times and compliance of labour laws.

7. *Payroll.* Country specific versions are available to handle the payroll function. This can take care of all components and multiple factors such as valuation of time data, partial payment calculation, reductions or company loans etc. Lock mechanisms can ensure that data relevant to the payroll run is changed when the program runs and at the same time they allow you to enter and edit data relevant for future runs.

8. *Additional components.* This package additionally provides services in the areas of travel management, event management, intranet employee self-service and business workflows.

Managerial Implication

This integrated software tool will be highly useful to organizations which are multi-unit and whose operations are spread geographically. Many of HR decisions are databased and foolproof maintenance of the same is imperative. Disintegration of HR related data like payroll from compensation policy/career planning from training and development data is often a common feature with organizations. Therefore, integration of data helps for rational decisions. It can also save companies from duplication of efforts, man-hours and consequential financial costs. Circulations of data, transparency and online employee communications are inbuilt benefits with the system.

TALENT IDENTIFICATION TOOLS

There are a number of traditional and modern tools organizations used to assess aptitude and attitude of people. These tools are briefly presented below:

1. *Simulation.* In these tests, individuals are exposed to hypothetically real-life situations. In-basket exercises and role-plays are examples of this method. This test reveals abilities of persons with high predictive validity since they perform on the job/task. For example, a person's web designing skills can be assessed through assigning a defined web-related task with time as deadlines. Similarly, a person's decision-making

capabilities can be assessed through seeking solutions to an organizational problem built on real life.

2. *Job knowledge tests.* These tests measure the level of knowledge a person possesses in a given area of work/field. Tests can be designed based upon job analysis reports. Competitive tests, departmental examinations and other paper based/trade tests are examples of this type of tests.

3. *Personality tests.* To understand the personality characteristics, this method is used. Myers-Briggs Type Indicator (MBTI), Personality Factor-16, Killman's conflict inventory, FIRO-B etc. are examples of this test.

4. *Skill inventory tests.* To understand the areas of interest of a person, this method is used. Campbell skill inventory tests are examples of this.

5. *Cognitive aptitude tests.* These tests are used to determine reasoning abilities, memory, and linguistic and numerical abilities. Examples include competitive and employment tests which different recruitment agencies conduct.

6. *Psychomotor abilities tests.* These tests are used to measure dexterity and coordination abilities. There are no standard tests that are universally applicable. Depending upon a job requirement, test is to be designed.

Managerial Implication

Attitude measurement tests such as personality and psychomotor tests are as important as aptitude tests like job knowledge, simulator and cognitive tests for correct assessment of a person and for identification of talents. Unfortunately, organizations are yet show keen determination in conduct of attitude tests. Negligence of this assessment already resulted in some kind of managerial imbalance in a few organizations. HR managers must work on developing organization and job specific talent identification tools for optimization of human talents.

TOOL TO CHECK ERRORS IN RECRUITMENT INTERVIEWS

Interview method is one of the commonly used selection techniques in recruitment of people worldwide. There are many benefits with the technique of interview in selection tests such as (i) opportunity to interact with the person directly and (ii) test the candidate's functional as well as interpersonal orientation. But it is also fraught with many disadvantages such as (i) inconsistency in accuracy, (ii) personal bias, (iii) interviewer's inability etc. Robert Gatewood and Hubert Field in their book titled *Human Resource Selection* published in 1994 have listed the errors that can occur in the employment interviews. These are:

1. *Stereotyping.* Applying generalizations and allowing personal bias to influence evaluations.

2. *Halo effect.* Evaluating the personality/candidature based on one or two characteristics.

3. *First impression error.* Drawing conclusion based on the interaction of first few minutes.

4. *Similar-to-me error.* Evaluating a candidate favourably or disfavourably because he or she is similar or like you.

5. *Contrast effect.* Allowing the quality of the applicants who preceded the present applicant to influence the ratings of the present applicant.

6. *Leniency error.* Evaluating liberally thereby converting low standards as superior.

7. *Central tendency error.* Evaluating all as average thereby denting the difference between good and bad candidates.

8. *Stringency error.* Evaluating candidates against high standards instead of solicited standards.

9. *Excessive talking.* Interviewer indulging in excessive talking hereby limiting the interviewee time and resulting in poor understanding of candidate.

10. *Irrelevant information.* Seeking answers or collecting information that has no relevance to the job the candidate is being interviewed for.

11. *Inconsistency.* Inconsistency of the questions in terms of quality and quantity posed to candidates yield information that could be incomparable.

12. *Non-verbal influence.* Evaluating under the influence of non-verbal behaviour.

13. *Inability of interviewer.* Inability/overconfidence of the interviewer in evaluation of candidates resulting in hasty decisions.

Managerial Implication

Interviewers need to be trained in the technique of interview method and in the use of structured and unstructured interview patterns. More importantly they should be appraised and exposed to the pitfalls of interview method in terms of above checklist. Interviewers who are conscious of these pitfalls could keep a self-check on themselves. Such a self-check will contribute for rational selection decisions. HR managers apart from themselves being fully aware of these pitfalls must also keep other managers involved in interview and selection procedures well informed about these.

Chapter 4

Career and Competency Management

Career and Competency management has assumed greater importance in present day organizations. It is one of those toughest functions that HR managers handle. This is tough because they are responsible for two conflicting functions at the same time, i.e. flattening organizational structures and downsizing of manpower on one side and ensuring career opportunities to the employees on the other side. In order to manage these functions effectively, HR managers need to redefine career management and provide a new meaning to it. The new meaning should be centered around competence enhancement in the place of hierarchical advancement. Therefore, there is need to juxtapose competence management with career planning to derive maximum benefits.

In consonance with this objective, the present chapter encompasses twelve classics covering (i) career planning fundamentals, process, techniques, best practices, (ii) employee coaching and succession planning practices and (iii) mapping of competency management, required managerial competencies in globalized environment and also presents the common management competencies that ought to be available in every organization.

SUSTAINABLE CAREER DEVELOPMENT MODEL

Career planning and development is one of the functions of HR management that came under intense pressure in the changing environment. Restructuring programmes, downsizing and delayerings, adoption of flat and matrix structures, flexible work practices, outsourcing and contingent employment practices have derailed the traditional career planning in many organizations. Added to this, some organizations launched a quick fix career solution called high-flyer programmes/accelerated promotions etc. to obtain superior performance, which also further strained the career system in organizations. The experience of many organizations reveal two important things: (i) the traditional career planning simply based on hierarchical structure lost its relevance and (ii) the high potential/high flyer career programmes generated problems for both organizations and employees. Professor Paul Iles of Liverpool Business School based on indepth study presented a resource based career development in the paper titled "Sustainable High Potential Career Development: A Resource Based View" published in *Career Development Journal* in 1997. This model is drawn from two schools of thought: (i) the first is based on environmentalism which believes that all economic and social development should be sustainable, that is, it must not reduce the options open to future generations, (ii) the second is based on strategic management literature or resource based view, which promotes treating career development as a competitive advantage to both individuals and organizations. The salient features of the model are:

1. The career development must bear a long-term focus, not just a focus on the immediate exploitation of resources. This requires attention to developing the whole organization and not just high flyers. A greater focus on learning communities, rather than on fast track elite development, can be a sustainable proposition for organizations.
2. The model suggests that career management practices based on the notion of sustainable career development, life long learning and development and mentoring may help in the development of a more appropriate response to the challenges of high potential career management.
3. The high potential/flyer programmes encourage individualism, elitism, a failure to develop knowledge and skill in depth, short-term career focus, lack of loyalty, focus on upward management of the boss with neglect of subordinate development through empowerment, coaching, monitoring and team building and an excessive focus on work and career as to neglect family and personal life.
4. Existing models of high potential career development may discourage innovation and experimentation, may inhibit improvement, teamwork and organizational learning, and may not develop sustainable careers.

Managerial Implication

This model rightly highlights the pitfalls with existing career development practices in organizations. The traditional career planning methods that are based on parent-child relationship provides no opportunity and freedom to the individual to shape his/her career. Therefore, this approach needs to be recast. The so called modern approach based on parent-parent principle, though provides defined opportunity and freedom to the individual, where as high-flyer programmes, lacks long-term focus. Therefore, organizations cannot sustain it on long term. Hence, the practical prescription is to develop a career planning that encompasses learning, skill and competence enhancement. In other words, a career development that hinges on competence rather than on organizational ladder.

TARGETED CAREER DEVELOPMENT MODEL

Career development is a critical activity in the management of HR. However, a majority of managers simply perceive career planning as vertical movement conveniently sidelining the development part of it. Objectively speaking, career upgradations without development opportunities and orientation have no meaning in terms of competence building. The career movements that are not accompanied by competence building lack vitality and employees tend to feel inadequate and meaningless. Therefore, career movement and competence acquisition should either proceed parallely or competence possession must precede career movement. This can be possible only through a clearly targeted career development plan. How such a targeted career development is to be developed? Manuel London of AT&T and Stephan Stumpf of New York

University presented a model of targeted career development in their book titled *Managing Careers* published in 1982. This is illustrated in Table 4.1 in precise manner:

TABLE 4.1

Guidelines	Activities
Have an accurate and thorough understanding of skills and abilities required for each targeted position	Prepare well documented job descriptions
Provide development activities that reflect individual strengths, weaknesses, preferences and goals	Use learning contracts that specify a logical sequence of training experience
Set target jobs and specific time frames for reaching those jobs	Discuss and establish as part of career planning
Provide challenging job assignments as early as possible	Identify jobs and projects with components critical to the individual and the organization. Redesign jobs and projects along critical dimensions
Assign the individual to effective role models who can provide enabling resources	Assign individuals to managers who are known to be good role models
Provide job performance feed back	Train managers to give meaningful feed back
Ensure accuracy and realism of expectations	Clearly communicate expectations. Encourage job visits
Expose the individual to a variety of functional areas within a department or in different departments	Vary assignments along dimensions such as line-staff, technical-nontechnical, working with others and alone etc. Take advantage of variation between jobs within departments for easy transfers
Encourage a high level of commitment and involvement on the part of top management and participants	Involve managers and subordinates in designing and carrying out the career development programme. Reward managers for developing subordinates
Allow periodic evaluation and redirection of career plans	Annual examination of career progress. Rewrite learning contract and reset targets

Managerial Implication

The above model helps practicing managers in multiple ways. Firstly, it drives an important point that career planning should be centered on development rather than hierarchical movements. Secondly, it provides ten essential guidelines in designing a targeted career development model that can be followed as the basis for developing such plans for your managers. Thirdly, it illustrates how the profile of employees is to be matched with job responsibilities as a precursor for career development of employees. Fourthly, this model helps managers in providing competence based career to all employees in the place of few opportunities when followed vertical oriented career planning.

CAREER MANAGEMENT PROCESS MAP

An international best practices consulting organization, Best Practices, LLC based at Chapel Hill, NC conducted a performance management benchmarking study using a wide range of resources that include primary research, online data searches, conference proceedings, professional journals and books, academic research, consulting assignments. The study identified a multi-industry group of seventy one companies implementing best practices in the area of performance management. Based on this study, the consultancy organization has drawn a career management process map as shown in Figure 4.1.

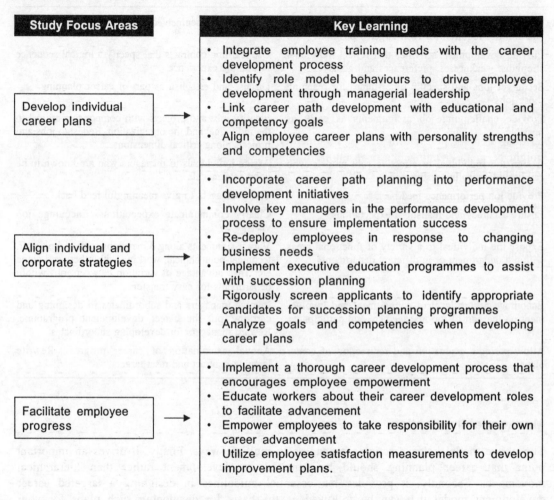

Study Focus Areas	Key Learning
Develop individual career plans	• Integrate employee training needs with the career development process • Identify role model behaviours to drive employee development through managerial leadership • Link career path development with educational and competency goals • Align employee career plans with personality strengths and competencies
Align individual and corporate strategies	• Incorporate career path planning into performance development initiatives • Involve key managers in the performance development process to ensure implementation success • Re-deploy employees in response to changing business needs • Implement executive education programmes to assist with succession planning • Rigorously screen applicants to identify appropriate candidates for succession planning programmes • Analyze goals and competencies when developing career plans
Facilitate employee progress	• Implement a thorough career development process that encourages employee empowerment • Educate workers about their career development roles to facilitate advancement • Empower employees to take responsibility for their own career advancement • Utilize employee satisfaction measurements to develop improvement plans.

FIGURE 4.1 Career management process map.

Managerial Implication

Career management means just promotions and upgradations for many organizations. In other words, it is simply a vertical movement of employees. This approach has resulted in shortage of competent managers in many organizations. Also there will be a wide gap between quantity and quality of managers when a competency based career plan is nonexistent. Absence of a clearly defined and planned career management programme also contributes for skill stagnation and consequential frustration among employees. The above described process model has originated from of the best practices implemented across world-class companies. This model will work as a base for all those organizations intended to draw a career management plan that is not only beneficial but also of strategic advantage to the company. HR managers must renew the existing career plans in line with the spirit of the best practices process model.

NINETEEN CAREER PLANNING TECHNIQUES

Career planning is dual responsibility of employees as well as employer. Unfortunately, most of the managers consider the vertical upgradation as the only career planning technique. They also behave in a manner as it individual employees have got nothing much to do with this and should be left to organizations. This attitude caused many problems to career management. In fact, career management requires comprehensive treatment because of its importance as the critical element in performance of organizations. There are many elements that organizations might be imple-menting like counselling, training, appraisal system, mentoring and so on. These elements can also be used as techniques in career planning of employees without incurring any additional over heads. Yehuda Baruch of London Business School identified nineteen of such techniques that organizations can use for effective career planning and management based on a study of 57 organizations. These techniques are presented in the paper titled "Organizational Career Planning and Management Techniques and Activities in Use in High-Tech Organi-zations", published in *Career Development Journal* in 1996. These are:

- Use of performance appraisal as a basis for career planning
- Career counselling by direct supervisor
- Career counselling by HRM department
- Books and or pamphlets on career issues
- Common career paths
- Assessment center
- Dual ladder (parallel hierarchy for professional staff)
- Postings regarding internal job openings (internal advertisement of vacant jobs)
- Appraisal committees
- Formal education as a part of career development
- Career workshops
- Written personal career planning programmes
- Retirement preparation programmes
- Mentoring
- Performance appraisal as a basis for salary review
- Management inventory (succession planning)
- Quality circles as a source for identification of management potential
- Training programmes for managers (to give them the skills needed for taking care of their employees' careers)
- Self-career management

Managerial Implication

Managers need to take career planning more seriously and adopt a professional approach. Use of more number of techniques can increase the effectiveness of career planning. This is because relying on just two or three techniques to plan career of employees can be misleading at times. The data obtained using one technique needs to be cross-verified with other techniques. Therefore, managers must select a combination of techniques to use it as a methodology in career planning. The above 19 techniques can be of immense help in this direction. Further, managers must provide space for individual employees to participate in their career planning. Career planning is a continuous process and it should not be treated as a one-time activity.

FOUR COMPETENCIES IN CAREER MANAGEMENT

Career management assumed new dimension in the current scenario of downsizing and flat organizational structures. It is clear by now that organizations will no longer be able to make and offer career planning based on tall hierarchies and prolonged employments. The solution is that career planning must be centered around building competencies instead of hierarchical positions. Further, individual employee has a significant role in self-career management as that of the organization. The successful self-career management supported by organization requires four competencies according to Ben Ball of University of Sussex who presented them in his paper titled "Career Management Competencies—The Individual Perspective" published in *Career Development International* in 1997. These are:

1. *Optimizing career prospects.*   This competence involves the ability to envision future opportunities, and having determined broadly defined goals, to create and make own chances. It represents a form of well-considered opportunism. To undertake optimizing process successfully, a particular set of skills and behaviour need to be brought into play. These skills include (i) the ability to take a goal directed approach to career planning, (ii) to anticipate future business and life changes and (iii) to promote one's own career interests. The other behaviour skills include: (i) making use of formally assigned or informal mentors, (ii) projecting a positive self-image by gaining attention for one's achievements and (iii) working alongside the staff who are seen as high performers.

2. *Career planning-plying to your strengths.*   In career planning of employees, four steps are involved viz., (i) review how far their work is using their skills and satisfying their needs and interests, (ii) identify their own development needs and what is required for effective performance, (iii) obtain data from the experience of mentors, partners and other work colleagues and (iv) anticipate future changes and prepare for job opportunities that might arise. The development of career planning competence should go some way to help individuals to take ownership and management of their own career development.

3. *Engaging in personal development.*   Employers are no longer able to guarantee life long continuity of employment or upward career progression. Therefore, more attention is to be paid to personal development rather than career development alone. The forms of personal development vary, but the range is increasing. For this purpose firstly, employees need to have a sufficient self-awareness to review and identify their development needs. Secondly, they need to be effective learners with a positive attitude towards the learning process. Learning seldom happens in a vacuum; it takes place in a social context and those in the workplace may need to gather around them

a supportive network in order to understand personal development activity of a challenging nature.

4. *Balancing work and non-work.* The concern to balance work and non-work is clearly a function of career stage. Being able to define one's own work priorities and maintain one's motivation in the absence of externally defined checks on performance become increasingly important. The issue of balancing work and non-work is problematic because of the competing demands of work and personal life. The competence to balance work and non-work is required by all those in the workplace because the relationship between the two is never static, but ever changing.

Managerial Implication

HR managers must equip their employees with the above four competencies for effective career management. Days are over when employers take sole responsibility for their employees' career management. Further, it is time the employees are facilitated to plan their career in the most systematic manner. In other words, career planning shall be dealt in a different way from that of the past. The focus is on making employees masters of their career. The route to this is in acquiring above described four competencies.

TWENTY PRACTICAL STEPS IN EMPLOYEES' COACHING

Coaching is an important function that shall be carried out by all managers. The importance of coaching has grown in the recent past due to fast changes in job and skill profile of employees. We need to distinguish the coaching from mentoring and counselling. The former deals with emotional state of employees, whereas the latter with employees' performance. John Burdett of Orxestra Consulting, based on years of experience prescribed twenty practical steps that a manager must follow in coaching for effective results:

1. Coaching is exclusively a process focused on enhanced performance. The first step in the coaching relationship is for the coach to share his/her vision of what future success looks like.

2. The emotional genesis of the coaching must be the employee's needs-not those of the coach.

3. Coaching agenda must reflect a robust appreciation of the context, including the organizational mission, strategic intent, beliefs and values.

4. The essential tools the coach has to work with are: trust, mutual respect, a sense of common purpose, integrity, openness and honesty.

5. Any durable coaching must contain three elements: (i) managing expectations, (ii) monitoring performance, and (iii) giving feedback.

6. Unless the coach and the employee can define specifically what behaviour should change, nothing changes.

7. If the coach's own behaviour is not congruent with the espoused values coaching becomes a manipulative process.

8. Not all employees can be or want to be coached.

9. Time, place and interpersonal rapport are variables that significantly impact the effectiveness of feedback.

10. Start with ending.

11. It is important that early on in the coaching relationship, ownership of the problem or opportunity passes to the employee.

12. The coach should bear in mind that all learning aspects start with a question.

13. The coach should not be reticent in giving what he/she believes to be possible remedies to performance difficulties.

14. Negative feedback is most valuable when delivered with honesty, sensitivity and is reflective of more than one input.

15. Even when the tone of feedback is critical, the communication should avoid damaging the employee's self-esteem.

16. The greatest limitation to coaching success lies on the fact as to what the employee believes is possible.

17. The coach must understand that before the employee can change, three conditions must be met with: (i) there must be a will to change, (ii) the employee must have the capability to act in the way agreed and (iii) the employee must be given the opportunity to practice the new behaviour.

18. Exploration and play are invariably far more meaningful, as learning interventions than instruction.

19. The most powerful form of coaching is, a team members coaching each other.

20. When the coaching has been carried through with purpose, subtley and character, and the behaviour does not change still, it would have to be concluded that the employee is in the wrong role.

Managerial Implication

The implication of this for managerial practice is self-explanatory. Firstly, managers must realize the significance of coaching their employees and coaching as a prime tool in the development of their employees. Secondly, for coaching to be effective, some basic rules as explained above should be adhered to. In a competitive world, where every organization tries to be different, certainly coaching can be one that has enough potential to accrue that distinction to organizations. In order to make this happen, all mangers must be trained to practice the above twenty steps to begin with.

CAREER ANCHORS

Edgar Schein found in a longitudinal study he conducted that attitudes that guide career interest of persons are formed in early stage of life. Results of the study are presented in his paper titled "How Career Anchors hold Executives to their Career Paths" published in *Personnel Journal* in 1975. These early-formed attitudes consist of values, needs and talents of a person and serve to anchor the person to hold to particular type of career. Hence, these are called as career anchors. According to Schein, career anchors are of five types as described in Table 4.2.

TABLE 4.2

Career anchor	Characteristics	Typical career paths
Technical/Functional competence	• Excited by work itself • Willing to forego promotions • Dislikes general management and corporate politics	• Research-oriented positions • Functional department jobs • Specialized consulting and project management
Managerial competence	• Likes to analyze and solve knotty business problems • Likes to influence and harness people to work together • Enjoys the exercise of power	• Vice-presidencies • Plant management and sales management • Large, prestigious firms
Security and Stability	• Motivated by job security and long-term careers with one firm • Dislikes travel and relocation • Tends to be conformist and complaint to the organization	• Government jobs • Small, family-owned businesses • Large government-regulated industries
Creativity/Entrepreneurship	• Enjoys launching own business • Restless; moves from project to project • Prefers small, up coming firms to well-established ones	• Entrepreneurial ventures • Stock options, arbitrage, mergers and acquisitions • General management consulting
Autonomy and Independence	• Desires freedom from organizational constraints • Wants to be on own and set own pace • Avoids large businesses and governmental agencies	• Academia • Writing and publishing • Small business proprietorships

Managerial Implication

Knowledge of career anchors is important to HR managers in placing right people to right jobs. This information also serves in deciding recruitment and career-related issues. Unfortunately, lack of proper assessment and systematic study on the career anchors of employees in organizations often lead to placing right people in wrong assignments and sub-optimal utilization of HR talents. Therefore, an assessment of career anchors situation in the organization is advisable in order to (i) ensure optimum utilization of HR, (ii) plan right mix of people for running the organization and (iii) also to initiate action to ensure availability of right mix.

DOW CHEMICAL MODEL FOR SUCCESSION PLANNING

Succession planning plays a key role in the companies' ability to pursue their long-term strategies and achieve lasting results. Many companies have realized the importance of succession planning during the current decade. However, succession planning is one of the toughest managerial assignments. It requires many things: top management commitment and personal involvement in grooming their successors, every manager grooming at least one successor for him/her and a grand strategy and an impeccable implementation plan are a few to name. Dow Chemical is one organization that realized a world-class succession-planning model that can offer lessons to many. According to the chief executive of Dow, Frank Popoff this model is built on six critical practices as described in the following:

1. *From an annual event to a continuous process.* Companies need to create an environment of continuous succession thinking rather than an annual succession planning. There should be more frequent senior management meetings, more time devoted to follow up at regular staff meetings, more emphasis on succession issues in business planning and greater incorporation of succession issues into performance evaluation and management.

2. *From a short-term replacement strategy to a long-term development and retention strategy.* A balance must be struck between need for immediate replacements and the need for a steady supply of ready talent. Employees will obviously appreciate the attention paid to their development and continuous improvement.

3. *From an emphasis on whom a company has to an emphasis on what a firm needs.* Companies must create an atmosphere in which external talent can be hired to fill critical skill gaps, independent of job openings.

4. *From position blockage to appropriate turnover in key positions.* Companies must promote and reward capable managers of people, rather than emphasizing technical over managerial skills. If all managers of the company are good at managing people, they can routinely assess the potential of incumbents in key positions, develop appropriate action plans, avoid positions becoming blocked and generate appropriate turnover.

5. *From insufficient bench strength to a pool of ready talent.* Dow has created a Genesis award to recognize people development. In a company with many highly competent technical and professional people, the award programme provides insight on who is actually practising good people management.

6. *From subjective evaluation to an emphasis on results.* Dow has established specific measurements to evaluate succession results. The measurements include: the percentage of key jobs which have at least two ready successors; the percentage of development action plans implemented; and the extent to which the process contributes positively to business results.

Managerial Implication

A number of companies though eager to put in place a systematic succession planning, often refrain because it involves massive efforts. The fact remains that good management will not happen just by itself but it will certainly demands sustained efforts. The experience of Dow chemical is the testimony to this. This model can be helpful to all those managers involved in succession planning and implementation. The six-step formula, if followed can equip the organization with leadership abundance. Therefore, HR managers based on this can develop their own succession strategy.

MODEL FOR COMPETENCY MAPPING

Competency modelling or competency mapping has assumed greater significance in order to optimize not only the HR but also to provide meaningful job understanding to its incumbents. Further, good number of organizations are also intending to use the data obtained through competency modelling for the purpose of decisions relating to rewards, promotions, recruitment, training and motivational aspects. HR professional must choose an appropriate model while building competency models in organizations according to Richard Mansfield who advocated it in his paper titled "Building Competency Models: Approaches for HR Professionals" published in *Human Resource Management* in 1996.

A competency mapping is a description of skills, traits, experiences and knowledge required for a person to be effective in a job. There are three models in mapping the competencies described as follows:

1. *The One-Size-Fits-All Competency Model.* This model uses the data obtained from existing job descriptions and job analysis. The data pertaining to a class of jobs, for example civil structural engineers/sales representatives will be consolidated and key features will be identified to convert them into competency traits. The general features like organizational mission, objectives and culture related competence would be added to build a competency model for a civil structural engineer/sales representative likewise.

2. *The Multiple Job Competency Model.* There are three steps in this. In the first step, competencies required for organizational function will be identified. Secondly, these competencies will be classified into technical, social, marketing, management, finance and general. In the third step, combination of competencies will be grouped to draw a particular role like finance manager, technical manager, quality manager likewise.

3. *The Single Job Competency Model.* This is a traditional, time tested and commonly used method. A position that is most important and being performed well will be identified from a class of positions (jobs). Data will be obtained observing its incumbent while performing the job, discussing with him/her and other related departments, past records, decisions taken by that person, formal job description etc. The data so obtained will be used to build competency model for that particular position.

Managerial Implication

Competency mapping is an ongoing process in contrast to what most of the managers believe it as a one-time exercise. HR managers have an important role here in terms of (i) identifying right method for competency modelling based on internal conditions of the organization and type of competency modelling, (ii) executing the mapping in a scientific manner particularly during data collection and competence building and (iii) mapping so finalized and put into practice is evaluated and renewed in regular intervals in tandem with changing competence profiles. They also must put efforts in creating documentation of competencies like competency dictionary or inventory that will be helpful as a basis for future exercises.

MODEL OF COMMON MANAGEMENT COMPETENCIES

The availability of right quality and quantity of management competence is the key factor in business success of organizations. This realization struck many organizations during the current decade and efforts made to tone up their managers. A common issue across all the organizations is, managers should be equipped with what kind of competencies. It is also a fact that managers must possess the competencies specific to their organizational need and environment. According to Andrew May of London Business School, there is a competence set that is applicable to all organizations and he illustrated them in his paper titled "Developing Management Competencies for Fast Changing Organizations" published in *Career Development International* in 1999. These are:

1. *Operations management*

    (a) Managing time effectively such as control of time scheduling and project control

    (b) Planning and decision-making consisting (i) controlling planning, (ii) option evaluation and (iii) evaluation of plan performance

    (c) Managing change consisting (i) identifying improvement opportunities, (ii) formulating change objectives and (iii) monitoring and evaluating change

    (d) Quality management consisting (i) quality measurement, (ii) conditions monitoring and diagnostics and (iii) systems control

2. *People management*

    (a) Team leadership indicating (i) leadership styles, (ii) structured teams, (iii) delegation, (iv) counselling and (v) meeting participation

    (b) Performance management consisting of (i) assessing competencies, (ii) job design and review, (iii) target setting and review and (iv) motivation of staff

    (c) Influencing others like (i) planning process management and (ii) negotiating

    (d) Legal issues of employment that includes (i) health and safety, (ii) recruitment and employment conditions and (iii) industrial relations

3. *Financial management*

    (a) Financial control that includes (i) cost monitoring, (ii) financial statement analysis, (iii) results presentation and (iv) financial systems awareness

    (b) Financial planning including (i) investment appraisal, (ii) systems development and (iii) managing outsourcing

4. *Information management*

    (a) Communications that includes (i) presenting information, (ii) selling ideas and behaviour interpretation

    (b) Marketing consisting of marketing strategies

5. *Behavioural competencies*

This includes (i) entrepreneurial, (ii) creative thinking, (iii) management synergy, (iv) logical thinking and (v) analytical ability

Managerial Implication

The above framework of management competencies is useful to practicing managers, particularly those involved in competence development. The framework and its itemwise description of competence can be used in building competence development plan for your organization. This is a comprehensive model since it has taken care of cross-functional needs and skills such as operations, finance, HRM, change management and information technology. In other words, it can serve as a basis for designing a competence plan for managers.

FIVE CORE MANAGERIAL COMPETENCIES FOR GLOBAL MARKETS

The managerial competencies essential and desirable for managing the organizations in changing globalized scenario are different from that of traditional managerial job descriptions. Managers recruited and groomed in consonance with the conventional job profiles will feel inadequate to manage the new economy organizations. Therefore, every organization that intends to occupy a place in the changed business scenario must restructure its managerial job inventories. Organization Development specialists, Wendell French, Cecil Bell Jr. and Robert Zawacki listed five areas as core managerial competencies that are most appropriate in managing organizations in the current generation in their book titled *Organizational Development and Transformation* published in 2000. These are described in the following:

1. *Gaining access to, and absorbing new knowledge.* The most obvious way to gain access to the new knowledge stream is to recruit people with the required new knowledge. However, it is not enough that the need for new knowledge is recognized and steps are taken to acquire them, but fundamental legitimacy and urgency must be assigned to that task. In order to be successful, the progress of the task of instituting and melding the new knowledge into the different traditional intellectual cultures must be continuously monitored.

2. *Integrating multiple streams of knowledge.* Acquiring new knowledge is a difficult process, and actively integrating it with traditional knowledge to create new business opportunities is even harder. Organizations learn by doing. Therefore, it is critical that top managers set up specific, bite-size projects. Projects are the carriers of new learning. They focus the organization's attention on solving the problems of integrating the new knowledge with the old. Project teams with cross-disciplinary membership are critical for successful learning and application.

3. *Sharing across cultures and distance.* Different cultures have different implicit priorities. No manager lives in a vacuum. While collaboration is initiated in the context of evolving knowledge, across multiple cultures, conflicts and misunderstanding is bound to arise. A deeper and explicit understanding of the socialization patterns of groups involved becomes a necessity. Moreover, managers must avoid stereotyping the other groups. Cross-cultural collaborative activity is emerging as a critical skill in the new economy.

4. *Learning to forget.* It is easy to exhort an individual or an organization to learn. But forgetting may be equally important. Many times forgetting is more difficult than learning new things. The dominant logic of the firm, or the recipes people use to learn, can become a major impediment to learning. Therefore, managers must be trained first to learn to forget. In most organizations, the forgetting curve is flat; in an age of

discontinuities, a flat forgetting curve is a serious problem to compete in the new economy, it is essential to forget the old patterns.

5. *Deploying competence across business unit boundaries.* The more the large organizations move toward business unit based strategies and measurement systems, the harder it is to focus on sharing across business unit boundaries. In order to have a system of deployment of competencies, all business units must have a common understanding of the patterns of market and technology evolution. Without such understanding, the conceptual framework for sharing does not exist. But a conceptual framework, without organizational systems, is unlikely to work.

Managerial Implication

This five-core competence managerial framework has many practical implications. This impresses the need for revising the managerial job profiles. The key difference between the conventional competence and globalized competence of managers is that the former is oriented towards internal needs of the organization whereas the latter is crafted around the external demands of the organization. However, revamping the managerial competence is the toughest and most challenging task. This can happen only through well planned and well organized strategy that include development of managerial competency profile in line with above five competencies and training the managers on them.

MICROSOFT'S COMPETENCY DEVELOPMENT MODEL

Microsoft steadily maintained an edge over its competitors because of its competence advantage. The company achieved this competence advantage through a well crafted and implemented competency development model. Microsoft has a specific programme for development of competencies called Skills Development Programme. It is also called as SKUD within Microsoft terminology. This programme consists of five components as described below. Thomas Davenport conducted a detailed case study on Microsoft competency and knowledge management initiatives and published it in 1997 along with other cases with the title *Knowledge Management Case Studies.*

1. *Development of a structure of competency types and levels.* In developing the competency structure, Microsoft used a four type hierarchy model which included: (i) Foundation skills-base level skills, (ii) Local advanced skills that apply to a particular job, (iii) Global skills that are present in all employees within a particular function and (iv) Universal skills present in all employees within the entire company.

2. *Defining the competencies required for particular jobs.* While matching jobs and competencies, Microsoft IT developed templates to measure competencies; the average template contained 40 to 60 competencies.

3. *Rating the performance of individual employees in a particular jobs based on competencies.* The goal of the employee rating process was to build a competency inventory that could be used all across Microsoft. For example, a manager who was building a new team for a specific project could query an online database for the employees who were qualified for the project.

4. *Implementing the competencies in an online system.*   Skills planning and development involved building an online system that contained the competency structure, the job rating system and rating database, and the competency levels for employees. The system had Web enabled front-end for easy access through Microsoft's intranet.

5. *Linkages to education resources.*   Microsoft's goal was to be able to recommend not only specific courses, but also even specific material or segments within a course that would be aimed at the targeted competency levels. Microsoft hoped to use the system to assess course demand on the basis of role descriptions and the competencies required.

Managerial Implication

The above Microsoft competency development model has been implemented involving large number of employees on a global level and the evaluation reports reveal that the programme is successful and contributed in keeping the company in high competency zone. This model will be helpful to HR managers who can draw a number of lessons from this experience. The detailed study of this model can be considered as an important step in developing competency model for your organization.

Chapter 5

Management Development and Training Management

With the rapid changes in business environment, the needs of management development and training are also changing fast. A few years back, it is left to individual managers themselves to develop their managerial competencies. There was hardly handful of organizations, which had put in place a well-articulated management development programme. However, with the increasing competition and growing realization of HR as a strategic advantage, many trends and experiments are happening, especially in management development and in training management in general. It is imperative for HR practitioners to keep themselves abreast with latest developments and practices in use in order to develop a business aligned and organizationally embedded management development strategy for their organizations.

Eleven classics are presented in this chapter to broadly illustrate: (i) the trends in management development, (ii) practical tips in developing management development strategy, (iii) best practices in management development to serve as inspiration, (iv) basics and fundamentals in developing managers, (v) behavioural and online training methods and (vi) practical tips in developing training programmes.

SIX MEGA TRENDS IN EXECUTIVE DEVELOPMENT

All organizations have become susceptible to international pressures with the increased pace of business globalization. Some of these pressures are mega in their scale and implication. In consonance with these mega trends, the approaches to executive development are also changing. Heather Cairns, Director of IMD, Lausanne, Switzerland based on the study of 200 companies conducted in 1997 and 1998, identified six mega global trends in executive development. These are as follows:

1. *Processes to align executive development to the business objectives.* In many organizations, executive development has become a part of the strategic agenda. In this way, a learning agenda is created which is flexible enough to change with the business priorities, rather than lagging behind. One powerful tool that an organization adopting to align learning with the business is the balanced scorecard approach. This tool recognizes that a purely financial driven strategic plan does not accurately reflect the vision and operational needs of the company which encompasses understanding

customers' perceptions, improving internal processes and knowing how to create future value through innovation and value.

2. *The parallel development of individuals and learning organizations.* The organizations seek to gain competitive advantage from learning more quickly than its competitors. Individuals seek to remain employable through the continuous development of their skills. As both parties have a need for development, there is increased interest in a deliberate approach to learning that accomplishes these in parallel, through planned processes that support both individual growth and organizational learning.

3. *The development of critical individual competencies.* Many companies are turning to competencies as a way of developing key behavioural skills that will assist managers to deal with the future. The managers are expected to acquire the skills to balance the complexity and paradoxes of management that relate to the more analytical aspects of understanding and running a global business and the soft aspects of managing people.

4. *A select but comprehensive menu of development options.* This involves use of both internal and external sources for executive development on careful scrutiny of their value addition. This implies developing a new mindset in which the organization is viewed as a system of rich learning opportunities, which are focused on the business priorities.

5. *The development of global partnerships, networks and alliances.* Global companies are seeking to create partnerships or alliances worldwide in support of a global learning strategy. These partnerships may be created with other companies in the form of a consortium in order to expose managers to different company cultures, different national cultures and a broad spectrum of perspectives.

6. *The need to create competitive advantage through executive development.* Global companies are using executive development in four key ways to create competitive advantage. These are: (i) partnership programmes focused on strategic implementation, (ii) shorter programmes cascaded to large numbers of managers in the organization, (iii) coordinating learning activities globally and (iv) a wide variety of opportunities for learning.

Managerial Implication

The awareness and understanding of these trends helps HR managers to assess where they are. It also enables them to pick up the relevant ideas to adopt a business aligned executive development programme within their organizations. The other important implications for practice are: (i) need to focus on developing critical competencies in an integrated fashion and (ii) encourage collaborations within and outside the organization for learning effectiveness.

EIGHT PRACTICAL LESSONS IN MANAGEMENT DEVELOPMENT

Managers themselves are primarily responsible for their development. Therefore, the first step in the journey of management development is that the views and assessments of managers must be obtained, analyzed and then strategies should be drawn. The programmes that are developed without taking into account the feedback of managers may end up as futile exercises. In contrast, the programmes designed based on the feedback of managers will greatly contribute in not only addressing the needs of managers but also the organization. Clinton Longenecker and Laurence Fink of The University of Toledo proved it in their study of 59 organizations in United States covering 433 managers conducted in 2001 that management development programmes developed based on feedback of managers tend to be highly successful. Based on this study, they presented the following eight practical lessons:

1. *In periods of rapid change, management development needs are large.* The competitive pressures from today's business environment are causing many organizations to make fundamental changes in their operations and the way they interact with customers and stakeholders. Responses to competition have emphasized total quality management, continuous improvement efforts, reengineering, downsizing, working with a diverse workforce, culture change and implementation of new technology. Extensive retraining of managers is necessary if these initiatives are to be effectively implemented.

2. *Always clarify the manager's role(s) in your changing organization.* Changes in strategy, structure, and work processes often leave managers unsure of their roles and related responsibilities. Role ambiguity can be a major obstacle to organizational performance improvement, innovation and change efforts. Only with a clear understanding of their role in particular change effort can managers reasonably be expected to either develop strategies for implementing a new business project or change effort.

3. *Managers learn by doing.* Giving managers a chance to learn by tackling real world problems (action learning or learning by doing) is a very effective method of management development. Some examples of learning by doing include: (i) fixing or stabilizing a failing operation, department or product, (ii) working on adhoc projects alone or with a group, (iii) developing a new product or implementing a new programme and (iv) job rotation or cross training.

4. *Do not underestimate the importance of ongoing performance measurement and feedback.* Organizations which do not integrate ongoing performance measurement and feedback into their management development programmes tend to experience lower than expected performance improvements and higher dissatisfaction and turnover of their managers. Therefore, top management should increase both the quality and quantity of performance feedback to improve management performance during periods of raid change.

5. *Managers are seeking mentors and career guidance in periods of change.* Being mentored by senior managers and formal career planning discussions are both treated as the most desirable and preferred approaches to improving managerial performance. For mentoring programmes to work effectively, you need committed mentors who are willing to give time to those they are developing, and are ready to be held accountable for their developmental activities and the progress.

6. *Do not develop an overdependence on seminars and workshops as primary development vehicles.* Formal training methods are among the lowest rated in terms of importance in improving management performance in rapidly changing organizations.

While formal training programmes have their own usefulness, they are not necessarily perceived to be a critical factor in helping managers to improve their performance in periods of rapid change. Thus, organizations should not develop an over reliance on those types of efforts to improve managerial performance despite the fact that they are relatively easy to implement.

7. *Assess the needs of your managers and develop an action plan to meet them when going into periods of large scale change.*   Careful assessment needs is /the essential foundation to designing any effective management development programme. No management development programme should be persued before the connections between the new attitudes, behaviours, knowledge and skills taught in the programme and their relationship to managerial success and achievement of organizational goals or effective implementation of change efforts in the organization are established.

8. *Create development plans around the needs of individual managers.*   One of the key to successful management development is to assess each manager on his/her own particular strengths and weaknesses and to match the proper learning experience with each manager's developmental needs. Managers at all levels must become more proactive in managing their own career development because, in the end, no one else in their organization will ultimately care about their success as much as they should.

Managerial Implication

The implication of above eight lessons for management development in your organizations is profound. These lessons have emerged from a systematic study conducted on a number of organizations. Therefore, HR managers must consider these issues carefully while designing and implementing management development programmes.

MODEL FOR EXECUTIVE DEVELOPMENT STRATEGY

The success of new economy organizations such as knowledge and service driven firms is largely contingent upon the performance of its executive personnel. Therefore, these organizations must develop and implement an executive development strategy that ensures attraction, development and retention of competent executive HR. However, crafting an exclusive executive development strategy calls for an integrated developmental approach. If succeeded, this can provide significant advantage to the organization. For this purpose, the model executive development strategy proposed by Robert Barner in his book titled *Executive Resource Management: Building An Exceptional Leadership Team* published in 2001 will be of immense value to HRM practitioners. This model consists of six key principles as described below:

1. *Executive development strategy must provide logical linkages between your company's business objectives and important executive selection and development decisions.*   An effective executive development strategy should be able to tell how anticipated changes in business conditions are likely to modify the required composition of your executive team. An effective executive development strategy guards against business failures by forcing senior teams to measure existing leadership competencies found in their executive talent pools against their leadership requirements for key initiatives.

2. *Executive development strategy must employ a data-driven competency assessment process that enables senior managers to make well informed decisions on executive placement and development.* The engine that powers an effective executive development strategy is a well constructed database. A comprehensive database provides employees in the organization with a common language and assessment methodology for evaluating the comparative performance of executive incumbents and candidates.

3. *Executive development strategy must reflect a tightly orchestrated HR systems that ties together company's selection, recruitment, and development components.* The test of this integration is that your executive development strategy should allow to easily match and compare data that reside within different components of HR system. In a valid system, executives are not expected to use one set of competencies when conducting performance appraisals, a second set of competencies when participating in selection interviewing, and still another one in their succession planning process. Instead, there should be same set of competency metrics for calibrating HR actions across the organization.

4. *Executive development strategy must incorporate inputs from key organizational stakeholders, including board members, senior managers, executives and high potential managers.* If your organizational stakeholders buy into the design process for executive development strategy, they will be more likely to accept and support decisions regarding executive placement and development.

5. *Executive development strategy must reflect a decision process that goes well beyond immediate concerns and short-term business pressures to address the long term needs of organization.* A more effective approach is to use the executive development strategy to do an assessment of both your company's short-term and long-term leadership requirements. This approach can help you determine, the degree to which organization's current leadership talent pool poses a serious constraint on its ability to pursue critical long-term goals.

6. *Executive development strategy must allow to focus executive resource efforts to obtain the most effective overall team.* The most distinguishing charac-teristic of a viable executive development strategy is that it can leverage talent and ability through a focused and sustainable game plan.

Managerial Implication

The six-step executive development model is useful in introducing an effective executive development strategy or in improving the strategy if it is already existing. The six-principle framework can also be adopted as basis for evaluating the impact of executive development strategy. In precise, the above model would be useful as a practical guideline in pursuing a systematic executive development strategy that can make right leadership competency available at right time to the organization.

UNILEVER MODEL FOR MANAGEMENT DEVELOPMENT

Management development can be a strategic tool to achieve the objectives of both organization and its employees, if a systematic approach is adopted. Management development calls for a dynamic approach that matches with the changing environment of organizations. Further, there must be an integrated approach that encompasses functions like training, performance targets setting and evaluation, job clarity and enrichment and succession planning. In recent years, Unilever is one organization that successfully used management development as a prime tool to steer the changes in organization. S.G. Reitsma, executive of Unilever at Netherlands presented this much acclaimed model in his paper titled "Management Development in Unilever" published in *Journal of Management Development* in 2001. The salient features of this model are described below:

1. Unilever moved from a job evaluation system consisting of 17 job classes at managerial level to a system containing 4 managerial work levels below business group president. The difference between two work levels is marked by the expected level of accountability, by differences in task horizon, the nature of problems addressed (operational vs strategic), the extent to which the individual can decide on resources like money and people, the amount of interaction with the environment and so on.

2. Moving from one work level to the next therefore is a significant career milestone for a manager, a real change, and not just more of the same. Decisions to move people from one work to the next therefore are absolutely critical. An approach was developed to ensure these decisions concerning high potential assessment could be made in as objective a way as possible.

3. The drive towards professionalism initially sparked an analysis of the various professional fields (marketing, logistics, HR). These analyses then became the foundation for developing career patterns in these fields, for training, and least for allowing the individual manager to drive his own learning and development.

4. Professionalism is not necessarily specific to functional areas only. There are also more of generic ways to operate as a managers. To help drive the individual's development of these aspects, Unilever developed a competency dictionary which now forms an important ingredient for performance discussions, training decisions and high potential assessments.

5. Unilever's statements that performance, professionalism and potential are important have implications for the remuneration system. The company therefore, developed a new system, which explicitly includes among other features considerable scope for salary addition for managers who show sustained high performance, and for those who are considered of high potential.

6. Unilever's stringent focus and results orientation meant that target-setting and target achievement had to become part of normal management practice in all countries and at all managerial levels.

7. The focus on individual development, and on factoring in individual wishes and limitations into the management development system, required a different approach to the appraisal system. Unilever shifted from a system with an emphasis on looking back on last year, to a system that used last year's performance merely as an input for the development discussion, i.e. for looking ahead. The ultimate consequence of this shift would be able to abolish the appraisal grades.

8. Unilever wants its managers to take an active role in their development. This requires Unilever to be completely open about such things as the systems and criteria used and views about the individual in terms of potential.

Managerial Implication

The success of management development is totally dependent upon the way it is designed and implemented. Most of the organizations tend to adopt a singular approach in management development efforts, which can produce negligible impact. For example, some organizations equate management development with training alone and some others only performance setting and evaluation. Therefore, organizations must accord a comprehensive and all encompassing approach to management development to shape it as a real strategic tool. In such an effort, the Unilever model of management development can serve as guide.

PWC MODEL FOR MANAGEMENT DEVELOPMENT

The forces of globalization forced organizations to operate everything at global level. As a result, more and more organizations have become international. This internationalization has brought its own problems such as (i) diversity in work culture across the units of the organizations, (ii) different HR systems and (iii) coordination of problems among managers working in different units of the same organizations. Many multinational organizations encounter these problems and Pricewaterhouse Coopers (PWC) is no exception. The only exception is that this management consultancy firm solved these problems through a five step model of management development. The salient features of the model are:

1. Management development is a powerful instrument to optimize international coordination, which can be achieved along three different channels:
   (a) Focusing on shared standards and values
   (b) Focusing on the specific development of common management development instruments and procedures
   (c) Ensuring mutual coordination and (international) commitment.
2. The most powerful management development instrument is the work itself, the experience gained in projects and with clients. This instrument can be managed by:
   (a) Closely linking strategic objectives to job content
   (b) Defining the experience that is required for making the next career move (e.g. project leadership or product development)
   (c) Ensuring that individuals have a clear understanding of the experience needed to allow their development.
3. The big pitfall encountered in developing common instruments is the bureaucracy it may involve. It is therefore very important to monitor the balance between costs and benefits.
4. Another drawback of the systems related to the pitfall referred to above, is the amount of time involved. Training, assessment and updating one's own competencies takes time, and often disturbs the work life balance, as many people will find that this reduces their leisure time, even though training and instruction are always included in the work schedule.
5. Another factor to be taken into account of is the cultural diversity. This can be explained by the fact that instruments have a "cultural" change in themselves. This may lead to aversion in some countries and cultures.

Managerial Implication

Management development plays an important role in a company's successful functioning. The importance grows many folds in international companies. The experiences also show that management development requires a different kind of treatment in these organizations. When poorly managed or when adequate attention is not paid, managerial confusions across the organizations arise because of diversity in understanding and practicing the organizational functions. Therefore, multinational organizations must commit sufficient resources to this aspect and must develop and adopt a sound approach. Pricewaterhouse Coopers model is a well researched and well built model that can stand as a benchmark. The insights offered by this model as above are of immense help to all those involved in management development function.

ROYAL DUTCH/SHELL MODEL FOR MANAGEMENT DEVELOPMENT

In tune with changing business scenario, Shell embarked on a transformation journey, mainly with the help of a management development strategy. Carla Mahieu has chronicled this journey in the paper titled "Management Development in Royal Dutch/Shell" published in *Journal of Management Development* published in 2001. The management development model is driven by the following factors:

1. General drive for more openness and transparency within the company
2. The need for immediate success to maintain and build market position, leading to more emphasis on performance, rather than just long term potential
3. Changing values of the workforce-staff wanting more control over their own careers and in many cases indicating more limited mobility
4. Constant new skills requirements in the awakening of new and changing business needs and new business directions
5. A more nimble, less centrally driven approach to talent identification and development and
6. New IT technology, most notably the use of intranet, as an important enhancing factor to do things differently.

Based on the above-described emerging reality, Shell planned a strategy to move the organization from a state of static to dynamic as indicated in Table 5.1.

TABLE 5.1

From	To
Potential full	Performance push
Fully growing our own timber	Attraction of talent at different levels into the organization
Central planning by HR staff	Local and individual initiatives
Control	Coaching
Being moved	Moving yourself
Closed system	Open system, with internal competition
Responsibility with line and HR	Responsibility with line and individual

The strategies used to achieve these new management development goals include:

1. *Open resourcing.* Open resourcing is essentially a process where all vacancies are posted and people are free to apply, within certain rules of the game. One such rule is that people who apply should be near the end of their current assignment, preventing people from rotating quickly. The hiring manager selects the preferred candidate and provides feedback to those who didn't make the cut.

2. *Performance management.* The whole performance management cycle stretches from target setting to appraisal to reward. In line with the overall transformation process, self appraisal tools, competency frameworks, 360 degrees feedback and variable pay were introduced, all stressing the responsibility of the individual and underlining the notion of performance management.

3. *Management learning.* The fixed curriculum and formalized training programmes were abandoned in favour of flexible and action learning oriented training. Leadership programmes were implemented not just for the most senior executives but also for all staff who consider themselves to be leaders in their fields. These leadership programmes are run within the context of the business, focusing on real business issues.

4. *Not everything changed.* Amidst all these changes some elements have been retained to include: (i) the flux culture providing the environment where open resourcing is accepted and valued, (ii) the commitment to still grow our own people, encouraging on the job learning, (iii) succession planning for the top 200 positions and (iv) managing the talent pipeline.

Managerial Implication

The above model captures all the events that include the basis, goals and steps taken for management development. This model has many practical implications. Primarily, the journey presents a picture of how management development needs to be analyzed, objectives to be drawn and to be implemented without disturbing the existing system. The model can be helpful to many organizations having similar environment to draft a few lessons from it.

PURPOSIVE BEHAVIOURISM MODEL

Learning is acquired through meaningful behaviour is the idea behind the theory of purposive behaviourism. Edward C. Tolman, an American Psychologist, is the originator of this seminal concept who gave a detailed illustration of it in his book titled *Purposive Behaviour in Animals and Man* published in 1932. The model consists of five types of learning: (i) Approach learning, (ii) Escape learning, (iii) Avoidance learning, (iv) Choice point learning and (v) Latent behaviour.

It emphasizes that all behaviour is getting towards or getting away from something, securing something or avoiding something. All these behaviours have a purpose, a goal. For example, Tolman trained rats to run a maze with alternate routes in order to obtain reinforcer (food). After learning, the rats always choose the shortest route. However, when this route was blocked off, the rats immediately switched to the next shortest route and successfully obtained the reward. Tolman observed that the animals developed a cognitive map of the layout of the maze. He also argued that this behaviour couldn't be explained in terms of learned stimulus-response habit.

Another interesting finding was concerned with reward. Tolman established that reward is not required for learning. He formed three groups of rats and placed them in a complex maze. There was no reward for Group A, reward for every trial to Group B and one reward on every eleventh day to Group C for reaching to a particular location. Both Groups B and C were found to be almost equally fast on twelfth day of trial to imply that reward affects what the animal does more than what the animal learns. Based on these studies, principles of purposive behaviourism were defined in the following manner:

- Learning is always purposive and goal directed
- Learning often involves the use of environmental factors to achieve goal
- Organizations will select the shortest or easiest path to achieve a goal

Managerial Implication

Theory of purposive behaviourism has multifacet implication to the practice of HRM functions. Significant of them are two: Firstly reward can motivate the learning behaviour but not learning itself. It means by way of reward we may be able to motivate the people to learn behaviour not master it. Whereas in this competitive era, organizations need people with matured competence not superficial. Hence, work itself should be a prime motivator. Secondly, behaviour is basically purposive. Therefore, it entirely depends on organizations as what kind of environment they provide. It means the performance of an organization is equal to the environment it creates for its employees.

SOCIAL LEARNING MODEL

It is a behaviour predicting formula developed by Julian B. Rotter, a Clinical Psychologist at University of Connecticut who described it for the first time in his book titled *Social Learning and Clinical Psychology* published in 1954. The essence of this model is that personality represents an interaction of an individual with his or her environment. One cannot speak of personality, internal to the individual that is independent of the environment. To understand behaviour, we must take both the individual, i.e. a person's life history of learning and experience and the environment, i.e. those stimuli that the person is aware of and responding to into account. Rotter says, change the way a person thinks or change the environment a person is responding to, and the behaviour will change. He believes that change in behaviour can be brought in regardless of how old a person is. But the higher the life experience the more the efforts required for change to happen. The model comprises of four main components for predicting the behaviour as indicated here:

1. *Behaviour potential.* It is the likelihood of a person getting engaged in a particular behaviour in a particular situation.
2. *Expectancy.* A subjective probability that a given behaviour will lead to a particular outcome. There can be high, average or low expectation on any outcome based on the confidence of a person that a particular behaviour will or will not lead to the outcome.

3. *Reinforcement value.* Reinforcement refers to the desirability of outcome. Reinforcement will be high if we are attracted to the outcome and it will be low if not attracted.

By combining these three factors, behaviour of a person towards a particular situation could be predicted.

Managerial Implication

Two important lessons of this model to all involved in managing people are: Firstly, changes in behaviour could be brought about however old or strong people may be or however strong their behaviour towards a particular issue may be. Sincere and systematic efforts are the prerequisites. Secondly, we have an option either to change the way people think or the environment surrounding people. Based on principles of this model, strategies to deal with behaviour at work can be drafted in a meaningful manner.

MODEL FOR DESIGNING A TRAINING PLAN

Training has a distinction of being most widely used HR function as well as most disputed in terms of its contribution/effectiveness. Unlike most managers tend to believe, the effectiveness of training function is contingent upon itself. In other words, the overall training plan of an organization must be systematic, comprehensive and the utility must be self-evident. Though managers agree to this view, the oft-raised question is how to design such self-demonstrated training plan? What elements should be taken into account? What are the Do's and Don'ts etc. Based on their insightful study of large number of organizational training plans, Aaron Hughey and Kenneth Mussnug of Western Kentucky University provided convincing explanations to all these questions as indicated below in their paper titled "Designing Effective Employee Training Programmes" published in *Training for Quality* in 1997. They include the following:

1. The goals of training must be tied with the company's strategic plan. These goals reinforce the larger mission of the company and are also vital to the continued viability of the training programmes. Equally important is the ability to track both individual and collective employee progress to show explicitly how the acquisition of new skills and competences have a positive impact on productivity and quality.

2. The training plan should identify and detail any specific problem or problems that are currently impeding the company's potential for maximum profitability. These problems should constitute the core of the training programme.

3. The training plan also should address how progress towards elimination of skill/competence deficient problems via training will be assessed. Evaluation should be at both microcosmic and macrocosmic levels, i.e. both individual sessions as well as the overall thrust should be continually assessed for their effectiveness and overall impact.

4. The plan for employee training should address departmental goals and outline the various objectives that will be employed in attempting to meet these objectives. Both a short-term of two to four months and long-term of three to five years timetables are necessary to ensure meaningful results. The plan should be formalized and agreed by company personnel at all levels.

5. Always bear in mind that the training plan is subject to constant updating and revision as new data are acquired. It is not an immutable agenda regardless of changes in interpersonal or structure, external market conditions. As new information becomes available, the plan must necessarily adapt.

6. Progress towards the attainment of training goals and objectives should be monitored on an ongoing basis. Accountability is a never-ending process. Detailed records must be maintained that provide evidence concerning the impact of training activities on the bottom line.

7. Training managers have to avoid becoming so wrapped up in the details of day-to-day training functions that they forget to stop occasionally and assess the overall progress of the training programmes. Time must be made for reflection and analysis.

8. The training plan should serve as a reference point for determining success or failure of the training programme. Several critical questions must be continuously asked. Have the employees learned actually to do something new? Does what they have learned represent a better way of doing things? Do their new skill sets have a positive impact from a cost/benefit perspective? Are successes being documented/rewarded? How can the training be more effective?

Managerial Implication

The above eight elements of training plan helps training managers in designing a systematic training plan for their organizations. If already training plans exists, managers could examine the quality of such training plan in the light of these eight parameters. As rightly pointed out, such a systematic plan serves dual purpose: firstly establishing the worth of the training plan and secondly, it makes job of training managers in seeking resources easy.

ONLINE TRAINING

With the emergence of Internet and intranet, online training has become a prime medium of training. This has many advantages to organizations operating in multilocations with the employees spread in a number of locations. This medium can be used to deliver training without dislocating the trainees. Further, employees can be provided same quality and quantity of training, regardless of their location. However, online training, is not devoid of some grey shades. The advantages and disadvantages of this type of training are given below:

Advantages

1. The capabilities of technology have advanced significantly in recent years and in conjunction with delivery technologies such as the world wide web, they offer vast opportunities for training. It is possible to view IT networks as a medium through which entire learning programmes can be conducted remotely.

2. Increased understanding of the Internet as a mechanism to facilitate training through discussions, access to course materials, online libraries and global forums are enabling organizations to become enterprise schools of management.

3. The Internet generally has a level playing field and an open library ambience where information is free. It also provides an opportunity to collaborate on a project with

another classroom over great distances. There are several telecollaborative projects available online that are sponsored by educational networks and organizations.

4. Telementoring is emerging as one of the most educationally valuable and technically implementable models for collaboration.

5. For any educational course to be effective, it must be adaptive to the needs of each student, as each student will have different goals, and will take different paths when attempting to reach those goals. The Web's use of hypermedia enables courseware to be developed with links that can enable the student to navigate through the course in whichever direction they feel most comfortable with.

6. Online training provides access to appropriate expertise and resources irrespective of distance. This access from within the workplace significantly assists in the realization of concepts such as life long training.

Disadvantages

1. Delivery of training via online will lead to dilution of the learning experience and the associated educational value.

2. Trainees may suffer a lack of interaction with their peers, which would be implicit in classroom situation. This may result in reduced opportunities for acquiring skills that involve interaction.

3. Creating right content in user-friendly manner is a tough job. All organizations may not be able to create such content. Particularly, designing and developing hypertext is a specialized activity.

4. In order to avail online training, trainees require being familiar with computer operation and they need to be provided with equipment that will not be always possible.

5. Online training may lead to isolation as this restricts the opportunities of discussion and learning from others.

Managerial Implication

Online training system offers much flexibility—time, venue, and delivery style, matching with individual pace of learning and interactive course delivery. However, as illustrated above, this deprives the employees of interaction and mutual discussions. Many skill development activities involve good exchange of experiences. Therefore, online training can be considered as one of the methods through which training is delivered and not as a substitute to traditional method of training. This is effective to impart a common kind of training where large number of employees are involved and work at different locations.

SENSITIVITY TRAINING

Sensitivity training also referred to as *t*-group training, and laboratory training, is intended to enhance the personal and interpersonal effectiveness. Kenneth Benne, Leland Bradford and Ronald Lippitt are the founders of this method of training who presented it for the first time in 1964. Sensitivity training provides an intensive exposure to aspects such as how to transact with others and understand one's deep feelings and personality preferences. Usually, this training is conducted in a group consisting ten to fourteen members who help each other in mirroring their personality facilitated by a professional member of behavioural society such as NTL/ISABS. Further, according to the founders of this approach, sensitivity training focuses on the following:

(a) Increased sensitivity to emotional reactions and expressions in oneself and in others

(b) Greater ability to perceive and learn from the consequences of one's actions through attention to feelings, of one's own and of others

(c) Clarification and development of personal values and goals in consonance with a democratic and scientific approach to problems of social and personal decision and action

(d) Development of concepts and theoretical insights as tools in linking personal values, goals and intentions to actions consistent with these inner factors and with situation requirements

(e) Development of behavioural skills to support better integration of intentions and actions

(f) Ability to transfer laboratory learning to back home situations

(g) Learning how to learn; to continue to be analyst of one's own behaviour and to become the kind of self the learner is seeking to become.

The most hotly debated aspect in sensitivity training is its effectiveness and usefulness to the participants. The answer to this is that how much a participant can be benefited is equal to his/her involvement and degree of participation in the *t*-group session. The facilitator and the group members cannot help an individual member change and improve his/her ways of behaving unless they have opportunity to see and react to what is to be changed. The important steps the group members of a *t*-group include: (i) faith in *t*-training methodology, (ii) trusting group members, (iii) active listening and (iv) openness. The sensitivity training is a deeply involving experience. These activities are designed to make sense of the group experiences. They include sessions such as role-playing, participative cases, simulation exercises, problem analysis and consultation. In nutshell, sensitivity training provide opportunities to practice new approaches, new ways of behaving and coping with interpersonal and group behavioural problems.

Managerial Implication

It is well known that most of the HR related problems in organizations arise due to interpersonal ineffectiveness of its people. Further, most of the irrational expectations and behaviour have origins to lack of self-understanding. Organizations tend to down with emotional problems, and managers lose balance in decision-making when they are indifferent to sensitivity. This is hundred per cent true in case of all the managers supposed to deal with people as a part of their job. Therefore, all the managers need to be exposed to sensitivity training in a systematic manner. This certainly helps to promote healthy relationships and quality of behaviour of its personnel.

Chapter 6

Performance Management

Performance management is the backbone of HRM practice in any organization. There is a widespread realization that performance management practices have the capability to determine the motivational level of employees and could be a powerful vehicle in conversion of employees' potential into performance. A variety of approaches and practices are being followed in different organizations as a part of performance management. However, experts conclude that there is no single strategy or model in performance management that can be qualify as universally applicable and workable. Therefore, practitioners need to understand and practice divergent issues that include compensation, reward and recognition techniques, setting of performance goals and their appraisal, quality of work life, facilitation of task execution, and being aware of pitfalls in assessing people, so on and so forth. All these individual practices should be carefully aligned to create a single performance management strategy.

In tandem with these individual practices and integrated approach in performance management, this chapter comprises of thirty-five classics focusing on: (i) models of performance management, (ii) high performance work practices, (iii) compensation issues that include stock options, (iv) individual and group goal settings, (v) appraisals and feedback, both conventional and 360 degree methods, (vi) mentoring and facilitations methods, (vii) basic tenets in understanding the human work behaviour, (viii) fallacies and facts in performance management, (ix) rewards and recognitions and (x) surgical side of performance management like downsizing etc.

INTEGRATED PERFORMANCE MANAGEMENT MODEL

Organizations expend considerable amount of efforts, time and money in order to motivate and utilize the human talents optimally in the name of performance management. Unfortunately, most of these attempts have not succeeded in producing the anticipated and desired results, as pointed out by few research studies. The major reasons for this include lack of coherence among HR initiatives and misdirected or random efforts. Integration of performance management activities with a specific objective and its alignment with strategic planning of organization can (i) minimize these negative outcomes and (ii) contribute effectively for organizational effectiveness. There are numerous performance management models in circulation, mostly at conceptual level. In this context, a pragmatic and integrated performance management model developed, implemented and evaluated by Les Pickett, President-elect of ARTDO and President of HR International, Australia can serve as the best example and basis. The model had received wide appreciation during its presentation at 25th Annual International Symposium on personnel Administration held in 2000. The overview of this model is illustrated in Figure 6.1.

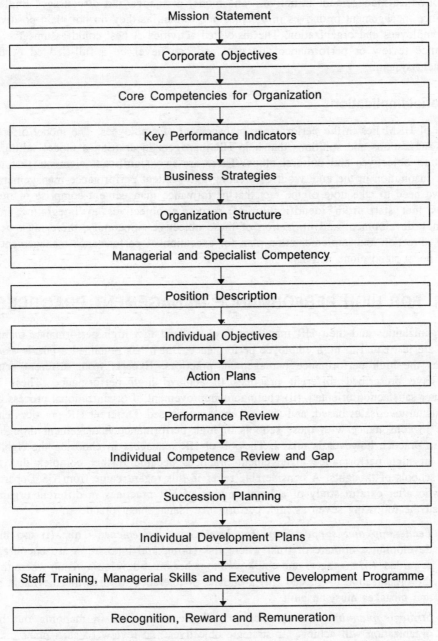

FIGURE 6.1 Integrated performance management—An overview.

The above illustration clearly suggests that there must be (i) identification of corporate objectives that should provide a framework for setting performance targets and a review of achievements against these agreed objectives, (ii) developmental plans for all the employees at individual levels, based on the competency mapping and (iii) a logical flow and integration in the performance management initiatives. The model dissuades and discourages implementing performance management initiatives in a standalone format, as they do not yield positive results to both employees and organization. The disjointed activities at best could assume the status of performance review or performance appraisal and can never be a full-fledged performance management system.

Managerial Implication

The core of HRM lies in the performance management of employees. The model offered many practical suggestions and solutions that help HR managers in drafting a model suiting to their organization objectives and cultural ethos. There are two significant elements that could be drawn as inspiration in the endeavour of creating an excellent performance management model. Firstly, we need to take note of the fact that performance management comprise of number of initiatives that start from identification of corporate objectives to integrating individual competency development and utilization of these objectives. Secondly, there must be a clear objective, direction and implementation plan for execution of performance management system, and it is not a stand alone activity.

MODEL FOR HIGH PERFORMANCE MANAGEMENT PRACTICES

Many organizations and their HR managers have realized that high performance management practices are just equal to high employee performance. But it has remained a puzzle as to, what constitutes the high performance management practices. Experts from different schools of thought have prescribed different practices to achieve high performance. These include: (i) customer satisfaction oriented, (ii) continuous improvement of organizational process oriented, (iii) profits/turnover/sales based, and (iv) stakeholders focused. Different HR practices came into existence in consonance with these schools of high performance management thought. Their efficacy in practice however is mixed. The job of HR managers in choosing the right mix of practices or high performance management practices became further complex due to these different schools of thoughts. A considerable relief in this regard came from US Department of Labour who after careful study of a large number of HR practices in different organizations categorized the following seven as high performance management practices:

1. *Leadership and support from top levels of management.* This: (i) top managers developing a climate of trust where risk-taking and innovation are encouraged and rewarded, (ii) managers and employees together must develop a vision where they want the organization to go and (iii) a climate of tolerance towards the inevitable setbacks and mistakes must be built.

2. *Strategic planning.* Involvement of all the employees in mapping out how the organization will achieve its strategic objectives and review of such plans constantly.

3. *Continuous development of employees.* All employees from top to bottom must be covered individually and collectively as far as training and development practice is concerned. Organization must withstand the pressure from budget cutters to reduce training levels as an easy way of reducing costs.

4. *Focus on the customer.* This include internal as well as external customers. The objective of HRM sub practices here is not just meeting the customer expectations but exceeding them. The techniques such as survey, feedback, and other process studies should be employed to gauge satisfaction of customers.

5. *Focus on quality.* There has to be HR practices that support an overall TQM type quality initiative in the organization. These HR practices should also be subjected to such quality standards and brought under the quality programme.

6. *Empowering frontline employees and an emphasis on teamwork.* The intelligence of frontline employees must be harnessed through programmes like empowerment and involvement. These also help converting potential into performance.

7. *Developing measures of progress.* There must be benchmarks in all HR practices. On the other hand, performance management practices also must promote benchmarking of various manufacturing and managerial aspects in organizations. These measures should have an ultimate goal like customer delightness.

Managerial Implication

The above seven practices summarize the essence of high performance management practices in organization. These practices together can produce high performance of employees in organizations. In a competitive environment, all organizations need to build high commitment work environment. In order to achieve this, just maintenance oriented HRM would be insufficient. There must be well-planned HR measures, called high performance management practices. In this process, the above model serves as a basis to HR managers to draw inspiration, if not its adoption. We must note that this model addresses all the vital aspects of modern work organization: Quality, Customer Satisfaction and Evaluation of benchmarks through high performance management practices.

SEVEN TENETS OF PERFORMANCE MANAGEMENT

Performance management has gained prominence in the current decade as a result of organizations' thrust to obtain the superior employee performance. This has also become the potential and reliable mechanism to attain the dual objective of fulfilling employee and organizational needs. However, experts came up with different models of performance management and different organizations adopted different approaches for performance management. These differences in approaches and models are well understandable but the matter of concern is that these approaches and models have generated certain misconceptions in the minds of practitioners. Therefore, the first step in the direction of design and implementation of performance management should clearly be understanding what it is? And what it is not? Two world renowned performance management experts namely Tracey Weiss and Franklin Hartle had propounded seven tenets of performance management that clarify many of basic and critical aspects of performance management in their book titled *Reengineering Performance Management: Breakthrough in Achieving Strategy through People* published in 1997. These seven tenets are:

1. *Performance management is a core business process.* Performance management is the

driving force in successful organizations. Performance management needs to be driven by top management and linked to the business planning process. It becomes the way in which strategic change is achieved, new cultures are built and business initiatives are turned from ideas into reality.

2. *There is no one-size-fits-all answer.* There cannot be one perfect model for all organizations. It is important for every organization to develop and refine its own approach to performance management. Each organization needs to assess how performance should be managed and then designed accordingly with contributions from line managers and staff.

3. *All aspects of performance matter.* Many approaches to performance management fail because they only capture the hard elements of performance that can be targeted and measured. The performance management process must reflect a balance between measurable results and demonstration of the right stuff that lead to individual and organizational success.

4. *Discretionary effort drives success.* The success of performance management lies in the abilities of managers in distinguishing good performance from that of satisfactory and rewarding correspondingly. In other words, raising the level of performance is all about getting discretionary effort from people.

5. *Effective links with rewards get important messages across.* Training, career development, and non financial personal and team rewards are at least as important as financial incentives and performance related pay. Getting the right balance is critical. Performance management plays a vital role in reinforcing the link between compensation and the strategy and culture of the organization.

6. *Ownership of the process is key.* The most effective and enduring performance management processes are developed with line managers and staff so that there is a proper fit between the process and the real time working practices. It is the day-to-day performance dialogue, the quality of discussion, the focus on development and providing recognition that are the real signs of a flourishing performance culture.

7. *Performance management is about relationships.* Effective performance management requires communication and feedback. This requires rapport, candour, honesty, and a genuine sense of caring. The caring creates a foundation for an open dialogue, where both parties feel that their opinions can be heard and understood in a non-defensive atmosphere.

Managerial Implication

The above-described seven tenets have two important insights for managers. Firstly, every organization should develop its own performance management model fitting to its organizational culture and objectives. Adoption of standard models or from other organizational practice may result in mismatch. Secondly, managers must be realistic while developing and executing a performance management strategy. The seven tenets offer these realistic parameters.

ALLIED SIGNAL'S PERFORMANCE MANAGEMENT MODEL

The success and sanctity of performance management of managerial personnel centers around its objectivity and fairness. The objectivity can be ensured only through measurable parameters. Further, these measures must be comprehensive and encompass all those attributes essential for organizational effectiveness. However, developing these parameters and deciding upon desirable behavioural attributes is a herculean task. Allied Signal is one organization that successfully made this a possible task by introducing world acclaimed performance management measures. These are illustrated in Table 6.1.

TABLE 6.1

Success attribute	Parameters
1. Business acumen	• Demonstrates knowledge, interest and aptitude for business • Knows competition • Familiar with strategies and tactics • Manages by fact
2. Customer focus	• Focuses on work processes for customer satisfaction • Meets internal and external expectations • Promotes and maintains strong customer relationships
3. Vision and purpose	• Sees possibilities; optimistic • Creates and communicates compelling vision • Inspires and motivates • Aligns the organization
4. Values and ethics	• Lives by company values • Adheres to code of conduct • Rewards right behaviours • Ensures that laws are obeyed
5. Bias for action	• Demonstrates a sense of urgency to achieve important goals • Sets priorities • Focuses on speed • High energy • Reduces cycle time and bureaucracy • Eliminates waste and unnecessary work
6. Commitment	• Widely trusted • Takes ownership • Candid and forthcoming • Delivers on commitments
7. Teamwork	• Initiates and supports meaningful projects • Demonstrates trust in team members • Serves on teams • Celebrates success
8. Innovation	• Promotes creativity and informed risk taking • Strives for technical and market leadership • Establishes processes for continuous improvement
9. Developing people	• Assembles strong teams • Empowers and trains people • Communicates effectively • Provides rewards, feedback and recognition • Demonstrates and stimulates passion and commitment
10. Performance	• Sets and achieves ambitious goals • Listens and responds • Drives for continuous improvement • Measures the right things • Gets results
11. Technical	• Has function or job specific competencies

Managerial Implication

The above-described eleven success attributes of Allied Signal's performance management serve as a practical dictionary to all those intending to develop objective and measurable performance factors. HR managers must note that these parameters in fact serve as means to achieve the organizational goals and also guide the managers in their performance. It generates great awareness, and clarifies what is expected out of managers' performance, apart from guiding them in their career. Of course, it undoubtedly sets the basis for performance assessment of managers. Every organization that wants to be successful and is determined to practice a scientific HRM must create a performance management model that is comparable to the present one.

HRM MODELS FOR PERFORMANCE EXCELLENCE

Apart from realizing the strategic value of HR and their management, organizations are also searching for HRM models that strengthen their bid for competitive advantage. However, there is no standard model that could be made applicable to all types of organizations and to all types of situations in the same organization. This non-existence of standard model is more due to the dynamic nature of organizations and cultural differences among the workforce rather than due to dearth of research or absence of sound practices. Philip Wright of Hong Kong University and Gary Geroy and Maura MacPhee of Colorado State University captured five types of HRM models that organizations adopt with a goal to achieve performance excellence, in their paper titled "A HRs Model for Excellence in Global Organization Performance" published in *Management Decision* in 2000. These are:

1. *The learning system model.* HR strategy stemmed from organizational learning school promotes the organizational flexibility through three factors: (a) well developed core competencies that instigate new products and services, (b) an organizational culture that fosters continuous improvement and (c) the ability to exit outmoded lines and enter new ones.

2. *The task model.* The core objective of HR strategy based on the task model to provide sufficient quantity and quality of HR to meet various organizational demands. This is achieved through acquisition, development and retention of human talent. This model emphasizes in two types of fits: internal and external. Internals implies that there must be compatibility between organizational tasks and HR strengths and external fit refers to match between external environment and HR strategy.

3. *The capabilities model.* This is based on concept of core competencies. HR strategy, policies and practices are centered on creating unique organizational capabilities that are difficult to be duplicated. HRM here facilitates employees to acquire the skills that provide organizations these unique capabilities.

4. *The core/flexible ring model.* HR strategy based on this model simultaneously pursues two approaches. One is a flexible model that focuses on contingent employees and the second is core model that is devoted to permanent employees. HR initiatives also accordingly differ between these two groups, typically having a long-term focus and short-term focus.

5. *The behaviour-engineering model.* HR strategy here promotes the key behaviour

attributes that enable the performance excellence. These attributes are promoted through practices such as employee communication, incentives, knowledge building, motivational management etc.

Managerial Implication

The above-described models illustrate different perspectives, different routes, and different methods to achieve the same goal, i.e. performance excellence. Organizations differ so much that it may be difficult for HR managers to adopt any of these models but certainly they can draw lessons from them. Sometimes, top management and HR managers may not be quite conscious to the extent as to what type of HRM model they are operating in the organization. It will not be advisable to have a HR system whose objective is unclear at macro and micro level. Therefore, HR managers must bring coherence in their strategy and give a shape to it to achieve performance excellence. In this process, they can choose a suitable model out of the five or combination of them.

BELL LABS MODEL FOR STAR PERFORMANCE

"Stars are made; not born" is the argument advanced by Robert E. Kelley, Professor at Carnegie Mellon University, based on his ten years of research on the subject of star performance. Prof. Kelley in association with his colleagues Janet Kaplan from the New School for Social Research and Dick Hayes of Carnegie Mellon University conducted a study on star performance at Bell Labs in order to understand (i) what is that separates star performers from mediocre and (ii) what are the special characteristics of star performers. The study led to gain the following valuable insights into the issue:

- The factors that distinguishes star performers from average employees are not cognitive, psychological, social or environmental. In other words, there are no differences in IQ (aptitude), reasoning, risk taking, leadership, and motivational aspects between the two. The factors that differentiated are patterns of behaviour on the job. It is not what is in the head but how it is used in day-to-day work.

Nine work strategies that characterize star performers are:

1. *Taking initiative*—accepting responsibility above and beyond your stated job, volunteering for additional activities, and promoting new ideas.

2. *Networking*—getting direct and immediate access to co-workers with technical expertise and sharing your own knowledge with those who need it.

3. *Self-management*—regulating your own work commitments, time, performance level, and career growth.

4. *Teamwork effectiveness*—assuming joint responsibility for work activities, coordinating efforts, and accomplishing shared goals with workers.

5. *Leadership*—formulating, stating, and building consensus on common goals and working to accomplish them.

6. *Followership*—helping the leader to accomplish the organization's goals and thinking for yourself rather than relying solely on managerial direction.

7. *Perspective*—seeking your job in its larger context and taking on other viewpoints like those of the customers, managers and work teams.

8. *Show-and-tell*—presenting your ideas persuasively in written or oral forms.

9. *Organizational savvy*—navigating the competing interests in an organization, be they individual or group, to promote cooperation, address conflicts and get things done.

Robert Kelley who continued his work on star performers, published a book titled *How To Be A Star At Work* in 1999 with more insights particularly focusing on training for creating star performers in organizations.

Managerial Implication

The study conclusively proved that actual performance is more important and not potential; that is just a fundamental. The implication for organizational practice is that average employees can be turned into star performers through a combination of training and reward-oriented strategies. The investment on these efforts will be worth keeping in view the finding that the star performers outperform moderate performers by a margin of 8:1. In other words, you can add 70 employees by turning 10 moderate employees as star performers without actually increasing your employee strength.

MODEL FOR COLLABORATIVE MBO

Management By Objectives (MBO), one of the oldest management tools that has been extensively used in organizations for more than five decades now. However, the traditional form of MBO could be utilized only in the context of a direct superior-subordinate relationship and where the task assignment is individual based. With the extensive use of teams and increased interdependence of tasks, a new approach ought to be followed in performance management. The OD legends, Wendell French and Robert Hallman proposed a team based MBO called Collaborative Management By Objectives (CMBO) way back in 70s which is catching up in practice during the current decade. They presented this model in their paper titled "Management By objectives: The Team approach" published in *California Management Review* in 1975. The MBO process consists of nine phases:

- Phase-I: *Diagnosis of organizational problems.* Collaborative mechanisms such as group surveys, small group meetings, large group interactions are used to identify the organizational and group level problems.

- Phase-II: *Information and dialogue.* Workshops with an objective to train employees at all levels on the technique of CMBO and problem solving skills will be conducted. This process first involves training a few people as resource persons who in turn will train others.

- Phase-III: *Diagnosis of organizational readiness.* The diagnostic techniques such as interviews and group meetings will be used to assess the willingness at organizational level for using CMBO approach. If readiness is low, workshops can be repeated especially covering the unwilling employees.

- Phase-IV: *Goal setting—Overall organizational level.* Based on the data received at phase-I, and other external sources like market data, objectives and goals that are identified at organizational level are to be set with defined timeframe. This process involves extensive interaction among all the employees.

- Phase-V: *Goal setting—Unit level.* Every organization has different functional units. Therefore, unit level objectives and goals are to be set which flows from organizational objectives and goals. Here also, group consensus method is followed.

- Phase-VI: *Goal setting—Individual level.* All individual employees set their objectives and goals keeping in view the unit and organizational level goals. These individual goals are reviewed by groups and finalized with group consensus.

- Phase-VII: *Performance review.* All employees prepare a kind of progress report of their activities on continuous basis. The designated groups of employees review these reports. Similarly, groups will prepare reports for group and organizational level performance, which are reviewed.

- Phase-VIII: *Rediagnosis.* A repeat diagnosis process will be initiated at organizational level to assess whether there is any change and improvement since the period CMBO method is used and in general the efficacy of this method in terms of organizational improvements.

- Phase-IX: *Recycle.* The process CMBO as described above will be repeated from phase-IV if the reports received at phase-IX are positive and it will be from phase-II if results are not encouraging enough.

Managerial Implication

This nine phase CMBO model offer many benefits to organizations, particularly the technology and knowledge driven. CMBO can also remove the dysfunctional effects of traditional MBO method due to its team and involvement based approach. There are three principle implications for organizations. Firstly, this helps in setting targets at multiple levels (organizational, unit and individual) through voluntary participation of all the employees. Secondly, it ensures that the goals of every employee is tied to that organization. Thirdly, it breeds a sense of oneness in organization. However, CMBO introduction must be preceded by proper preparation on the part of organization in terms of matching the other managerial systems and practices.

MOTIVE-BASED MODEL OF OCB

Organizational Citizenship Behaviour (OCB) is generally viewed as all positive and idealistic because it is defined in terms of socially desirable behaviour as performance beyond role requirements, willingness to cooperate, commitment to work and organization. The socially desirable definition of OCB led to view it as all positive. But OCB is not necessarily a positive behaviour all the time, at least for organizations. Professor Brian Niehoff of Kansas State University brought an interesting perspective to the whole issue saying the antecedents of OCB determines whether it is positive or negative to the organization. In his insightful paper titled *A Motive Based View of Organizational Citizenship Behaviours: Applying Old Lens to a New Class of Organizational Behaviours*, he presented a model of OCB that is, motive based. There are three motives that cause three different types of OCB in organizations as illustrated in Table 6.2:

TABLE 6.2 Organizational Citizenship Behaviour

Achievement motive	*Affiliation motive*	*Power motive*
Exhibit OCB as a means for (i) task accomplishment and (ii) success of the organization	Exhibit OCB as means for (i) establishing and maintaining relationships and (ii) receiving approvals	Exhibit OCB as means for (i) gaining power and status and (ii) present a favourable or positive impression
Behavioural traits include conscientiousness, field depen-dence, (a doer)	Behavioural traits include: service orientation, trusting, agreeable, extraversion, positive affectively (a people pleaser)	Behavioural traits include: Machiavellian, self monitor, political savvy (a shrewd politician)

Achievement motive leads to achievement motivated organizational citizenship behaviour. The achievement oriented citizen will persist in exhibiting OCB as long as there is sufficient challenge which includes clearly defined tasks, assignments and feedback on performance. Affiliation motive leads to affiliation-oriented OCB. The affiliation-oriented citizen is not much bothered about own performance but is concerned about others. Power motive leads to power oriented OCB. The power oriented citizen sees OCB as a means to acquire power and status with authority in the organization. Acts of OCB are driven by a commitment to self and one's own career agenda.

Managerial Implication

Organizations, particularly of new economy class have been focusing on OCB. Their efforts are mainly concerned with improving OCB among their employees. The motive-based model of OCB provides very practical view in two respects: firstly, the classification of OCB and traits enable HR managers to understand an employee's OCB type and create conducive environment so that they continuously exhibit OCB. Secondly, the model also gives the negative perspective of OCB. Therefore, efforts can be made to discourage the negative OCB like power-oriented OCB.

HEALTHY SCORECARD

Managers, consultants and academicians including those who put massive efforts to leverage everything in order to improve the profitability of organizations have not thought of something that is crucial for enhancing the well being of both employees and organizations. That is the link between employee's health and organizational performance. Danielle Pratt presented a remarkable approach labelled as Healthy Scorecard using Balanced Scorecard methodology that proves improving health of your employees can enhance the profits of organizations in astronomical figures. She authored a book titled *The Healthy Scorecard: Delivering Breakthrough Results that Employees and Investors will Love* demonstrating the colossal positive impact of health management of employees over the bottom line of organizations. The book secured number 4 position among the books released in 2001 in terms of sales. The central principles of this approach are:

1. High quality health care education and management in organizations, can reduce the severity and frequency of diseases dramatically and there is great evidence which shows that these measures are good for the bottom line. For example, effective asthma management reduces days hospitalized by 77 per cent, asthma related emergency visits by 48 per cent and urgent care visits by 32 per cent. This affects workplace productivity significantly.
2. The greatest beneficiaries are the organizations, which slash event rates for stress, illness and injury, and costs per event. This approach has a multiplier effect, and organizations, which chose this route, enjoy a stunning buffer from health cost inflation.
3. Health is viewed as a fixed, if not constantly increasing cost. How can we justify a health investment strategy based on failure costs, and at the same time pursue six-sigma process quality. By giving up control over investments in employee health, work places lose the ability to stop the bleeding in their opportunity costs. They lose a powerful lever for cost effective heath decisions.
4. Good health is good leadership, and good leadership means great business. Effective leadership programmes can dramatically reduce health care costs. Companies can reduce burnout, absenteeism and health problems by developing leadership programmes and supporting metrics. There is a direct positive relationship between leadership and employee welfare, which, in turn affects the HR process and measures of environmental health and safety. These would drive bottom line results.

Managerial Implication

The healthy scorecard offers one more opportunity to HR professionals to build the business case out of good HR practices in the form of health management of employees. The healthy strategy map, a prime tool of healthy score card will be of great help in this direction. HR professionals need to shift their focus from reimbursement of medical expenditure/insurance premiums to investment in proactive health management that reduces the reimbursement expenditure and increases productivity. This also presents an opportunity to emphasize that employees and organization are not two separate entities: employee's health is organization's health. In other words, this approach rightly highlights the old saying that 'health is wealth'.

PERFORMANCE EVALUATION TECHNIQUES

There are a number of evaluation techniques organizations employ to assess the performance of employees. These techniques include:

1. *Graphic rating scale.*   Most popular among the methods. Appraiser is asked to assess the appraise by assigning numerical value (e.g. outstanding = 5, average = 2 likewise).
2. *Forced choice.*   Appraiser is provided with a set of statements describing performance standards of a job from which he/she should choose a specified number of statements in reference to appraise.
3. *Management by objective.*   Mutually (appraiser-appraise) assessing the performance of appraisal against the mutually set targets.

4. *Essay.* Appraiser describes strengths and weakness of appraisal in a descriptive form.

5. *Critical incident technique.* Appraiser writes about key performance incidents/achievements of appraisee.

6. *Weighted checklist.* The appraiser will be provided with a list of performance traits against which assessment is to be carried out.

7. *Behaviourally anchored rating scales.* Appraiser assesses appraisee's performance against defined, specified and pre-set measurable performance items.

8. *Behavioural observation scales.* Appraise assess performance in reference to predetermined performance behaviour standards.

9. *Ranking.* Based on overall criteria, appraiser generates list of appraisees in order of ranking with respect to their performance.

10. *Paired comparison.* Each time appraise is presented with two names of appraisees from whom he/she should choose the high performer. Based on this exercise, overall ranking will be done.

11. *Forced distribution.* The percentage of appraisees to be assessed as outstanding, good, average, etc. will be predecided in this method against which appraiser should distribute.

12. *Performance test.* A combination of paper and simulator based tests will be conducted to assess the performance.

A model evaluation chart is given in Table 6.3.

TABLE 6.3

Evaluative base	Graphic rating scale	Forced choice	MBO	Essay	Critical incident	Weighted	BARS	BOS	Ranking	Paired comparison	Forced distribution	Performance test	Field review
Developmental cost	Moderate	High	Moderate	Low	Moderate	Moderate	High	High	Low	Low	Low	High	Moderate
Using cost	Low	Low	High	High supervisory costs	High	Low	Low	Low	Low	Low	Low	High	High
Ease of use by rater	Easy	Moderately difficult	Moderate	Difficult	Difficult	Easy	Easy	Easy	Easy	Easy	Easy	Moderately difficult	Easy
Ease of understanding by those evaluated	Easy	Difficult	Moderate	Easy	Easy	Easy	Moderate	Moderate	Easy	Easy	Easy	Easy	Easy
Useful in promotion decisions	Yes	Yes	Yes	Not easily	Yes	Moderate	Yes	Yes	Yes	Yes	Yes	Yes	Yes
Useful in compensation and reward decisions	Yes	Moderate	Yes	Not easily	Yes	Moderate	Yes	Yes	Not easily	Not easily	Yes	Yes	Yes
Useful in counselling and development of employees	Moderate	Moderate	Yes	Yes	Yes	Moderate	Yes	Yes	No	No	No	Moderate	Yes

Managerial Implication

All the above-discussed techniques are useful. However, the usefulness of these techniques is contingent upon purpose/context for which these are applied. Any of these techniques can fail when there is a mismatch between the technique used and the purpose and context in which it is used. Most of the organizations fall in a trap while implementing a particular technique for performance assessment of all categories of employees and for all kind of jobs. It is advisable to use a combination of techniques for good results and based upon job, assignment and context.

MODEL FOR A FAIR PERFORMANCE APPRAISAL

There may be very few performance appraisal exercises that are devoid of criticism of bias and subjectivity. However, most of the efforts to dispel the bias and subjectivity are restricted to changing appraisal formats and systems that include switching over to techniques like 360 degree appraisal and team assessments or using MBO criteria. These changes again have their own inbuilt limitation because change in the system alone is not just sufficient to bring transition. This change should be accompanied by change in the processes that include the manner in which the appraisal is carried out, involvement of appraisee and using constructive criticism inter alia others. Robert Folger and Russell Cropanzano in their book titled "Organizational Justice and HR Management" published in 1998, prescribed a criterion for launching a fair performance appraisal. The essence of this prescription is threefold as indicated below:

1. Adhere to the following basic rules:

   (a) If you promise to do a performance appraisal, then do it
   (b) Appraise subordinates on the appropriate criteria
   (c) Have knowledgable appraisers
   (d) Use a fair rating format
   (e) Maintain interpersonal fairness in the performance appraisal interview
   (f) Train subordinates to participate

2. Adhere to the following while conducting appraisal interview/discussion:

   (a) Be supportive
   (b) Be participative
   (c) If desired, you can discuss both developmental information and the subordinate's evaluation

3. Use only constructive criticism in appraisal process and avoid destructive criticism. The differences are:

   (a) Constructive criticism are represented by: (i) specific focus on the behaviour in question, (ii) not attacking the person as a cause of the poor performance, (iii) not making threats, (iv) considerate in tone and content, (v) delivery in a timely fashion and (vi) delivery in an appropriate setting
   (b) Destructive criticism are represented by: (i) general in content, (ii) blaming the person or attributes of the person as the cause of poor performance, (iii) making threats, (iv) inconsiderate in tone and tenor, (v) delivered after too much time has passed since the negative behaviour and (vi) delivered in an inappropriate setting.

Managerial Implication

Performance appraisal is largely an infamous activity with a great cause in majority of our organizations, whatever may be the contributory reason. Therefore, organizations must check the pitfalls in processes apart from identifying the shortfalls in the appraisal formats. In this effort, the above prescription helps all the managers in implementing performance appraisal in an objective and fair manner. The three dimensional prescription also helps HR managers as actionable guidelines in their endeavour. The above description provides a valuable insight that focuses on the processes to ensure fairness in the performance appraisal.

MODEL FOR APPRAISAL INTERVIEWS

As an essential part of performance management, managers have an important role in conducting the appraisal interviews at the end of the appraisal period. This would be critical in understanding the employee's performance behaviour and developmental needs. Cessna Aircraft Company encourages its supervisors to observe the following guidelines in conducting the interviews:

1. Give the employees a few days notice of the discussion and its purpose. Encourage the employees to give some preparatory thought to his or her job performance and development plans. In some cases, have employees read their written performance evaluation prior to the meeting.

2. Prepare notices and use the completed performance appraisal form as a discussion guide so that each important topic is covered. Be ready to answer questions employees may ask about why you appraised them as you did. Encourage your employees to ask questions.

3. Be ready to suggest specific developmental activities suitable to each employee's needs. When there are specific performance problems, remember to attack the problem, not the person.

4. Establish a friendly, helpful, and purposeful tone at the outset of the discussion. Recognize that it is not unusual for you and your employee to be nervous at the discussion, and use suitable techniques to put you both more at ease.

5. Assure your employees that every one on Cessna's management team is being evaluated so that opportunities for improvement and development will not be overlooked and each person's performance will be fully recognized.

6. Make sure that the session is truly a discussion. Encourage employees to talk about how they feel doing their job, how they might improve, and what developmental activities they might undertake. Often an employee's viewpoints on these matters will be quite close to your own.

7. When your appraisal differs from the employee's, discuss these differences. Sometimes employees have hidden reasons for performing in a certain manner or using certain methods. This is an opportunity to find out if such reasons exist.

8. These discussions should contain both constructive complements and constructive criticism. Be sure to discuss the employee's strength as well as weakness. Your employee should have clear picture of how you view his/her performance when the discussions are concluded.

9. Occasionally the appraisal interview will uncover strong emotions. This is one of the

values of regular appraisals; since they can bring out bothersome feelings, they can be dealt with honesty. The emotional dimension of managing is very important. Ignoring it can lead to poor performance. Deal with emotional issues when they arise because they block a person's ability to concentrate on other issues.

10. Make certain that your employees fully understand your appraisal of their performance. Sometimes it helps to have an employee orally summarize the appraisal, as he or she understands it. If there are any misunderstandings, they can be cleared up on the spot. Ask questions to make sure you have been fully understood.

11. Discuss the future as well as the past. Plan with the employee specific changes in performance or specific developmental activities that will allow fuller use of potential. Ask what you can do to help.

12. End the discussion on a positive and future improvement oriented note. You and your employee are a team, working towards the development of everyone involved.

Managerial Implication

Cessna model is helpful to all those involved in conducting appraisal interviews. The implications in this regard are quite obvious. An objective interview facilitates deep understanding between the boss and his subordinate in terms of performance assessment, developmental needs and future work plans. It also unearths the issues so far swept under the carpet. On the other hand, an arbitrary interview would result in heart burning and can be a cause for poor performance. Therefore, organizations committed for fair appraisal interviews may like to look at the Cessna model.

FOURTEEN ESSENTIALS FOR EFFECTIVENESS OF 360-DEGREE FEEDBACK

During the last two decades, the popularity and application of multi- rater and multi-feedback system in business organizations has grown many folds. 360-degree feedback system is the most widespread among the several instruments that came into existence for this purpose. However, the failures with this system are also widespread. This is mainly due to the inadequate preparation and less care exercised by managers. 360-degree feedback system can deliver the anticipated benefits only when certain fundamental rules are followed. The question will be what these are. Based on the extensive study of 360-degree feedback practices done under the auspices of Center for Creative Leadership Institute, M.A. Dalton and G.P. Hollenback stipulated fourteen essentials that can ensure successful implementation of 360-degree feedback system. These are:

1. *Prepare the participants.* Orientation to the 360 degree instrument as well as rater training should be planned in advance.

2. *Make top management visible players.* In many companies senior executives get feedback first, to model openness to the process.

3. *Tie feedback data to a larger programme.* Be clear about how this specific assessment activity fits in to the business need and the overall development plan.

4. *Clarify ownership of data.* Clearly state who owns the feedback data.

5. *Insist upon integrity.* It is crucial to maintain the integrity of the process through confidential handling of sensitive material.

6. *Commit 100 per cent accuracy.* Implement administrative checklists to ensure that all raters have the correct materials and know how and when to return them.

7. *Make administration as soon as possible and user friendly.* Find ways to make it simple for people to participate. Plan ahead, give lead time, and use postage-paid return envelops.

8. *Provide a safety net.* Make sure that there is always a human contact with everyone involved, both raters and participants. Always build time into feedback programs for individual consultation, should someone have a strong emotional reaction to the feedback.

9. *Check the timing.* Be sensitive to what else is going on in the organization. Midway through a downsizing is probably not the best time to conduct this activity.

10. *Provide confidentiality and anonymity.* A process that permits direct return to the scoring organization gives a greater perception of rater anonymity. Confidentiality of results should be clarified before planning the event.

11. *Have a sunset clause on data.* What is the shelf life of an individual's report data? This varies from person to person, but a reasonable rule of thumb is not to use data that were collected more than a month ago.

12. *Anticipate what will go wrong.* Plan for unexpected events such as facilitators becoming ill, snag in mailing systems and so on. Have backup facilitation ready.

13. *Start small.* An organization's first 360-degree intervention should start with a small pilot group, to work out the systems before rolling out a large initiative.

14. *Integrate with other interventions.* Be sensitive to other ongoing activities within the organization that might get in the way of successful implementation.

Managerial Implication

The adherence to the above principles can guarantee not only the successful implementation but also its effectiveness. These practices are drawn from observing the best practices of 360-degree feedback system in several organizations. Therefore, managers can check their implementation process in the light of these fourteen essential practices. Managers who intend to introduce 360-degree feedback system can adopt them as guidelines.

THIRTEEN MISTAKES IN 360-DEGREE FEEDBACK

Multi-rater and multi-assessment systems assumed vital importance in managing performance of employees. As a consequence, 360-degree feedback has received wide attention and many organizations have started implementing it. The experience of organizations with this system is mixed. The failures can cost organizations very dearly due to two reasons. Firstly, organizations might be unsettling the existing appraisal and feedback system to pave a way for 360-degree feedback introduction. They will be left with no working performance system if the experiment fails. Secondly, the failure could lead to confusion and chaos in assessment of employees' performance that some people can use the situation for their personal advantages. Both these developments will have adverse impact on motivation of employees. Therefore, organizations must carefully analyze all the issues before adopting 360-degree feedback system. In this context, two experts namely Scott Wimer and Kenneth Nowack caution managers about common pitfalls that occur in their paper titled "13 Common Mistakes Using 360 Degree Feedback" published in *Training & Development Journal* in 1998. These are:

1. *Having no clear purpose.* Organizations tend to adopt (i) for goodwill purpose (ii) since it is a latest technique, (iii) based on a consultant's advice or (iv) without a clear aim.

2. *Using it as a substitute.* Some managers think and use it, as substitute to manage poor performers and as a motivational tool.

3. *Not conducting pilot test.* Implementing straight away without understanding the difficulties that are likely to arise in the field.

4. *Not involving key stakeholders.* Unilateral decision to implement the system.

5. *Having insufficient communication.* No communication or incomplete communication with all the employees.

6. *Compromising confidentiality.* Not taking due care to thwart the exposure of appraisers wherever required.

7. *Not making clear the feedback's use.* Confusing people about its purpose, whether it is for reward, development or both, or none.

8. *Not giving people sufficient resources.* Not proving resources to deal with the information provided about strengths and weaknesses of an employee.

9. *Not clarifying who owns the feedback.* Questions about access to and ownership of data are fraught with difficulties.

10. *Having unfriendly administration and scoring.* The process of 360-degree is made of complicated procedures, paper intensive and ambiguities.

11. *Linking to existing systems without a pilot.* Casually integrating 360-degree is system with other existing HR systems without a detailed study.

12. *Making it an event rather than a process.* Treating 360-degree feedback system as flavour of the month to try, taste and discard.

13. *Not evaluating effectiveness.* No efforts to systematically evaluate the effectiveness of the system at regular intervals.

Managerial Implication

As stated above, an organization must be prepared for a radical change in terms of culture if it intends to adopt 360-degree feedback system. Secondly, HR managers must take full care to avoid these 13 classical mistakes that can happen while proceeding with this system. It may be wise for organizations to continue with the existing appraisal system instead of making half-hearted attempts to implement 360-degree feedback system. Look for the presence of these mistakes if you are already in the category of 360-degree implementers.

MENTORING PRACTICES

Mentoring is an age-old practice that could offer significant benefits to both employees and organization. Despite its value, the practice is restricted to a few companies. This is mainly due to the perception among some managers that implementation of mentoring programme is cumbersome and the benefits that accrue are not proportionate to the resources invested. Many studies and experiences of organizations have proved this perception as misplaced. For example, Monica Forret of Long Island University and Daniel Turban and Thomas Dougherty of University of Missouri, based on their study of mentoring practices in a number of Fortune 500 companies reported that mentoring contributes for the following benefits:

- Enhances employees' performance
- A better understanding of corporate culture and organizational structure
- Increases feelings of support and friendship
- Better awareness of what new employees experience
- The acquisition of new skills
- An improved network of contacts
- A better understanding of others' work styles
- Improvement in intra company communications
- Emergence of unified work culture

However, mentoring programmes implemented without adequate preparation, particularly placing managers as mentors without adequate training tend to provide no benefit. Further, both mentors and mentees may treat it as a burden. Therefore, managers must be trained before asking them to be mentors. Companies such as Hallmark Cards, Texaco Trading and Transportation, Imperial Oil Limited, Shell Oil Company and the like, are using the following training methods to train mentors:

- Role plays to train mentors in coaching and providing effective feedback, and to train protégés how to receive feedback
- Videos which illustrate effective mentoring relationships
- Handbooks which discuss issues such as understanding the mentor's role, confronting others' productively and checking expectations
- Lectures to describe what mentoring is, and some of the benefits and pitfalls.

In addition, these companies have a clearly defined mentoring policies clarifying (i) how mentors and mentees select each other, (ii) how profile sheets of potential mentors and mentees are to be compiled in a book, (iii) how mentor profile sheets are to be prepared collecting details such as why someone want to be mentor, what he/she hopes to gain from the experience, what is the mentor's position in the company, what type of experience he/she have had and what his/her hobbies and interests are.

Managerial Implication

The experiences of companies show that mentoring offers valuable benefits to organization when implemented with a clear policy and practice framework. The experiences also illustrate that simply telling employees that they are now a mentor or protégé can never be enough. Like in the case of many HR functions, here also there is no short cut for success. Therefore, companies, which decided to pursue a mentoring strategy, must do so with a clearly constructed plan. Mentoring can be a potential strategy to overcome many maladies that include weak organizational citizenship behaviour, weak organizational commitment, poor interpersonal relationships and poor integration of employees with organization apart from performance related issues.

SEVEN DETERMINANTS OF EMPLOYEE COMPENSATION

Compensation system is the backbone of HRM. It wields the real power to attract, retain and motivate employees to give outstanding performance. It is important to both employees and employer. For employees, compensation is an important issue since pay is perceived to be an indication of their personal and market value. It is important for employers since they have to strike balance between earnings of stockholders and stakeholders of the organization. Therefore, compensation management is a challenging job that shall be dealt in a systematic manner. HR/ compensation managers must make a comprehensive study of all relevant factors to design the compensation system. Steven Applebaum of Concordia University and Loring Mackenzie of Allied Signal based on their study of number of compensation systems operating in organizations identified seven principle factors that determine the compensation system in their paper titled "Compensation in the Year 2000: Pay for Performance?" published in *Manpower Management* in 1996. These are:

1. *Labour/product market conditions.* This includes (a) the demographics of the employee force and the significance of their skills, (b) the supply and demand situation in relation to critical skills and (c) the pay levels and practices of competitors.

2. *Economic and sociopolitical environment.* This includes the influence of the business cycle and the power of organized labour.

3. *Employees characteristics.* This includes education, seniority, qualifications, experience etc.

4. *Industry characteristics.* Industry standard wages vary considerably. Highly competitive industries, such as soft goods manufacturing, pay in response to changing conditions in their labour market. Less competitive industries, such as hard goods manufacturing, typically pay somewhat more than the minimum required by the labour market.

5. *Enterprise style.* The list includes culture (management style), organizational structure, objectives, policies and strategies, technology, size, profitability (ability to pay, competitive labour strategy, salary compression (inequitable pay differentials when pay rates for new hires are too close to those of experienced employees and when subordinate pay rates are too close to those of supervisors).

6. *Job characteristics.* This includes factors such as mental requirements (problem solving), physical requirements, skill requirements, responsibility/accountability, working conditions, level of public contact, and the effort required to carry out the work. Factors such as responsibility and decision-making would appear in evaluation systems for managerial jobs; physical demands and skill might appear in factory jobs;

and accuracy and amount of supervision received might appear as factors in clerical and technical evaluation systems.

7. *Employee behaviour characteristics.* This includes performance, absenteeism, and turnover.

Managerial Implication

Compensation is a critical issue for organizational effectiveness. Dissatisfaction or perceived inequity in compensation system can cause number of HR related problems. Unless compensation system is effective, the other interventions such as development, empowerment, communication, career planning etc., will not yield any positive results for the organization. In other words, compensation can be equated as basic foundation of HR system. In order to ensure, an equitable and rationalistic compensation policy, managers must take all the determinants into account and accord its due in pay design. In such efforts, the above description of compensation determinants help practising managers.

PERFORMANCE RELATED PAY—FOURTEEN ESSENTIALS

Performance related pay, though an old technique in the form of variable pay has assumed renewed importance in the new economy organizations. Performance related pay can yield many advantages that includes (i) rewarding people proportionate to their contribution and efforts, (ii) providing means to achieve equity in reward and (iii) working as a real motivator. However, it is a double-edged sword. This can create bigger problems in terms of demotivation, inequity and industrial unrest if the basis and administration of performance related pay is not free from pitfalls. Therefore, all the related aspects shall be critically examined before adoption of this kind of pay. Michael Armstrong prescribed fourteen essentials that can make performance related pay as an effective compensation strategy in his book titled *Management Techniques* published in 2001. These are briefly indicated here:

1. It is appropriate to the type of work carried out and the people employed on it and fits the culture of the organization
2. The reward is clearly and closely linked to the effort of the individual or team
3. The reward follows as closely as possible, the accomplishment which generated it
4. Employees are in a position to influence their performance by changing their behaviour
5. They are clear about the targets and standards of performance required
6. They can track their performance against these targets and standards
7. Fair and consistent means are available for measuring performance
8. The reward is clearly and closely linked and proportionate to the efforts of the individual or team
9. Employees expect that effective performance (or specified behaviour) will certainly lead to worthwhile rewards
10. The performance related pay scheme operates by means of a defined and easily understood formula
11. Provisions are in built in the scheme for amending the formula in specified circumstances
12. Constraints are built into the scheme which ensure that employees cannot receive inflated rewards which are not related to their own performance

13. The scheme is properly designed, installed and maintained
14. Employees covered by the scheme are involved in its development and operation

Managerial Implication

There is a realization that there must be a component of performance related pay in order to drive the employees for higher performance. However, experience of organization point out two critical issues: (i) performance related pay preferably should constitute fifty per cent of the total compensation, rest being basic compensation items and (ii) the scheme must be designed and installed scientifically. The above fourteen principles help managers in designing and installing a sound performance related pay. Further, managers must test the efficacy of such scheme before it is made as a company policy.

GAIN SHARING TECHNIQUES

Gain sharing plans are also known as production incentives, profit sharing plans and team incentives. The basic objective of any gain sharing programme is to provide incentives to employees on achievement of unit/organization level targets in terms of production schedules, project executions, customer satisfaction, improvements in quality standards, better safety records, optimization of company resources, cost saving measures of course bottom line improvements. Such gain-sharing plan generally involves all employees working in organization. Three commonly used gain sharing techniques are:

1. *Scanlon technique.* The first formal gain sharing plan was developed by Joseph Scanlon in 1930 to encourage employees to subscribe suggestions for cost cutting in operations which is now known as Scanlon incentive. This incentive is monthly payable based on gains an organization accrues on account of such employees' suggestions. A committee consisting of employee and management representatives evaluates benefits of suggestions in terms organizational gains.

2. *Rucker technique.* This is an economic incentive given to employees on improving productivity. The gain sharing incentive will be based on financial performance of organization. Here also a screening committee evaluates benefit of employees' suggestions in terms of bottom line. Employees' participation in the committee that assesses suggestions will be minimal and unlike Scanlon plan, it is just an economic plan.

3. *Improshare.* Basic philosophy of this technique is encouraging consultative process. The technique developed by Mitchell Fein is also intended to create work motivation. Factors such as basic productivity factor involving engineering time standards, absorption of indirect hours, actual hours worked are used to decide the incentive.

In 1991, Charles Gowen had identified following 20 characteristics associated with successful gain sharing plans:

1. Organizational unit of less than 500 employees
2. Stable productivity
3. Simple financial measures of productivity and costs
4. Growing or expandable market for the firm's products or services

5. Product costs affected by employee's behaviour
6. Organizational climate characterized by openness and high level of trust
7. Participative style of management
8. No union or a union favourable to cooperative efforts
9. Limited or no use of overtime
10. Seasonal stability of sales or production
11. High to moderate interdependence among employee's tasks
12. Low capital investment changes for the past few years and next few years
13. Few product changes in near past and near future
14. Corporate financial staff trusted by employees and able to communicate financial information about productivity and costs
15. Willingness on the part of management to disclose corporate financial results to employees
16. Trusted plant manager able to communicate production goals and results
17. Management able to work with critical suggestions for change
18. Supportive attitude by the parent corporation towards the organizational unit's change and development
19. Employees who are technically knowledgeable and motivated by participation and greater financial incentives
20. Maintenance and engineering staff component and willing to respond to new challenges

Managerial Implication

A gain sharing plan is more than a simple monetary incentive or bonus. It is a comprehensive technique that can bring sound HR management into action and promote a salutary work culture. The above-discussed gain sharing techniques are only representative and every organization needed to develop its own in tune with internal needs and conditions. When implemented or if already in implementation, check it with the above characteristics to assess the success with your gain sharing plan.

EMPLOYEE STOCK OWNERSHIP PLAN (ESOP)

Employee Stock Ownership Plan has become an essential ingredient in compensation design, and grown as a critical element of performance management system of new economy organizations. It is not difficult to understand why. In the face of falling strength of various motivational techniques, organizations had started looking at different options. This option search led to ESOPs. The idea of stock ownership, though initiated during 1930s, was actually observed in practice in 1960s and became a popular strategy with the advent of software industry.

ESOP is a right granted to an employee to purchase a specified number of shares of stock of the company at a predetermined price during a specific period. The benefits of ESOP include:

(a) Using stock based compensation plans, which allows the company to provide employee benefits with a lower cash outlay. As the company's stock value rises, employees participating in the plan can see their worth increasing. When the company gives shares of stock or options to employees, the employees benefit from price appreciation without the company having to lay out cash individually.

(b) Companies with ESOP have a growth rate of 8% to 11% faster than companies without them. A survey of 54 employee ownership firms reveal that, productivity in companies with ownership culture increased at the rate of 4 per cent annually, i.e. more than double of the non ESOP companies.

(c) The creation of employee ownership plan is viewed as the catalyst enabling socio-technical change process.

However, ESOP poses many challenges to companies such as the following:

(a) ESOPs can fall flat in delivering anticipated benefits. ESOP creates high employee expectation about ownership that may be difficult to coordinate with the evolving, long-term needs of the company. Meeting some of the ownership expectations in the face of layoffs and changing economic circumstances would be extremely difficult situation.

(b) Rules and Regulations such as Income Tax laws, company rules, stock formula and scheme etc., that make ESOP difficult to understand and dilute the emotional content of it.

(c) The fluctuation of the stock price can have an affect on the attitude and morale of the whole company.

Managerial Implication

Top management in conjunction with HR managers must take care of four aspects while adopting ESOPs: (i) creation and implementation of ESOP shall be aligned with broader people management in the organization. It must be consciously embedded in overall HR strategy or at least in combination with other commitment programmes like empowerment, involvement and performance management, (ii) employees shall be well informed about pros and cons of ESOP particularly in view of popular misnotion that all ESOPs will lead to monetary benefits to employees, (iii) make sure that everybody understands the rules of ESOPs as to. How does the plan work, how do employees cash out and (iv) manage psychological side of it because employees naturally demand more information and more details about company's functioning which means more participation in decision making.

MODEL FOR EMPLOYEE RECOGNITION SCHEME

Proper recognition of employee performance is vital to keep the employees motivated. However, in practice, recognition management is difficult, because it is a double-edged sword. No recognition can be as harmful as improper recognition. The motivational power of recognition lies in how we treat and handle it. Experiences of many organizations reveal that recognition schemes have become rituals and lost the power of motivating employees. Recognitions schemes when mismanaged, tend to give scope for dysfunctional politicking in the organizations. Ultimately, recognition schemes not only fail to serve the purpose but also become a hurdle in obtaining employee performances. Therefore, we need to manage employee recognition with utmost care and believe that recognition measures are instruments to ensure equity in HRM in organizations. G.H. Milas, an expert on employee recognition programmes presented a model in the paper titled "How to Develop a Meaningful Employee Recognition Programme" in *Quality*

Progress in 1995. The following guidelines are prescribed in this paper, which help in designing a recognition scheme:

1. Criteria and process must be made known publicly
2. Recognition is not compensation. It is highly personalized, flexible and based on immediate individual/team accomplishment
3. There are no winners and losers. Organizations should avoid ranking people or groups in any manner
4. Not all success is based on quantitative measurements. To accommodate intangible results, recognition can be made on above average expanded efforts
5. Recognition is not a form of manipulation. It should not be used to force behavioural changes or to reorganise the employees' task priority
6. Recognition is not based on luck or fate. It is based on documented accomplishment which deserves recognition
7. Employees must contribute to the recognition strategy to create ownership and commitment to the recognition programme
8. Recognition is personal experience
9. Recognition is fun. Ceremonies must be planned and the recipient must be made the guest of honour
10. Innovative forms of recognition, such as prepay taxes for recipients, gifts to charities of recipient's choice, involving recipient' family in the award and so forth should be experimented
11. Recognition is a continuous process even though the forms of recognition may change

Managerial Implication

In fact, some of the recognition measures could be more powerful in terms of its implications for motivation and encouraging high performance acts. HR managers, while launching the scheme, must train managers on administering and using the benefits of the scheme. They must be essentially trained on appropriateness, timeliness, consistency and fairness in handling the recognition tool. Any improper use can lead to inequity and demotivation among employees, apart from loss of managerial credibility.

MODEL FOR NON-FINANCIAL INCENTIVES

Research and surveys over the years have established the power of non-financial reward in motivating the work behaviour. People who are familiar with Herzberg's motivation theory know that non-financial reward in the form of recognition is crucial for obtaining the higher-level performance of employees. In contrast to the limited choice of financial rewards, the non-financial ones can offer a wide range of high impact incentives that include: (i) feedback to an employee about his/her good performance, (ii) congratulating in public, (iii) conferring social recognition, (iv) publishing about good performance/achievement of an employee in house journal/circular, (v) felicitating in special gatherings, (vi) recording in personal folders, (vii) sending employee with family on paid vacation, (viii) sending congratulatory communication to employee's family members directly and the like. However, the real impact of such non-financial incentives depends upon its execution. Nelson B. presented a model that characterizes an effective non-financial incentive in the paper titled "Motivating Employees with Informal Awards" published in *Management Accounting* in 1995. The salient features of this model are:

1. *Recognition should be immediate.* Recognition should be given as soon as possible after a desired behaviour has occurred. Increasing the time between the targeted behaviour and reward devalues the reward and diminishes the reinforcement value.

2. *Recognition should be delivered personally.* The power of social rewards derives from the way they are delivered. The fact that a manager is taking time to recognize or praise an employee drives the importance of the activity to the employee. In addition, time taken by a peer or subordinate to recognize a job done well can also be very effective.

3. *Recognition should be valuable.* Social rewards should be valued and made meaningful to the individuals who receive them. For example, some employees may value their autonomy and would prefer to be thanked in private. Other employees may be interested in having the recognition highly public to increase their promotion opportunities. Finally, some may prefer rewards that recognize the team or group contributions. Whatever the case might be, tailoring the rewards to the needs of the recipients is a good idea.

4. *Recognition should be a direct reinforce of desired behaviour.* Recognition should not be phony or given superficially. The key is to give rewards, which positively reinforce desired behaviours.

Managerial Implication

Despite knowing the powerful role of non-financial incentives in overall reward management, nothing much seems to be happening on the ground. This is a voluntary and credible method that can realize higher level of performance. In effect it can function as good as financial incentives and in some situations can perform outstandingly. Therefore, HR managers must generate organization and work specific non-financial incentive and implement its delivery in a way that reinforces the spirit of such reward.

PHENOMENON OF FORTY-FIRST CHAIR

This phenomenon deals with psychosocial processes that affect the allocation of rewards to scientists for their contributions: an allocation that in turn affects the flow of ideas and findings through the communication network of science. This, also known as *The Matthew Effect* in Science, published in the journal *Science,* was authored by Robert E. Merton, Giddings Professor of Sociology at Columbia University in 1968. This has an important teaching to all the organizations in terms of performance management. The central theme of this phenomenon is as follows:

The ultimate in the world of awards, the Nobel prize, is often assumed to mark off its recipients from all the other scientists of the time. Yet, this assumption is at odds with the well-known fact that a good number of scientists who have not received the prize and will not receive it have contributed as much to the advancement of science as some of the recipients or more.

This can be described as the 41st chair. This is derived from French Academy, which decided that a cohort of 40 could qualify for being awarded the prize in any year. This limitation of numbers made inevitable, of course, the exclusion through the centuries of many talented individuals who have done remarkable service. What holds for the French Academy holds in varying degree for every other institution designed to identify and reward talent. In all of them, there are occupants of the 41st chair, men outside the Academy having at least the same order of talent as those inside it. The phenomenon of the 41st chair is an artefact of having a fixed number of places available at the summit of recognition. Moreover, when a particular generation is rich in achievements of a high order, it follows from the rule of fixed numbers that some men whose accomplishments rank as high as those actually given the award will be excluded from the honorific ranks. Indeed, their accomplishments sometime far outrank those, which in a time of less creativity, proved enough to qualify for this high order of recognition. However, the tragedy is that people who are awarded the prize will attract more attention to their work, draw more and more awards, and receive more grants—all regardless of actual worth and at the cost of someone's more deserving work.

Managerial Implication

As stated by the author himself, 41st chair phenomenon is applicable to all organizations in varying degree. Most of the evaluation committees and managers try to escape the burden of real evaluation under the guise of reconfirming the performing person who is already confirmed, because to declare a person as outstanding who is already confirmed as outstanding will neither involve serious analysis nor the risk of controversy. This attitude of managers and evaluation committees in organizations create severe imbalances in performance management. Secondly, it is also a trap that if someone is declared as high performing, he/she is likely to draw plum assignments and more recognition/credits to their work than actually they deserve. Thirdly, many organizations practice fixed quota system in many areas of HRM that include promotions, rewards, recognitions and allocation of assignments. All such organizations need to mind the 41st chair phenomenon.

THEORY X AND Y

Based on his experience and observing the practices of managers, Douglas McGregor proposed a seminal framework about the nature of people. This is popularly known as *Theory X* and *Theory Y* representing the two set of assumptions about human behaviour at work. The two set of assumptions are fundamentally different and opposite to each other. Theory X is rigid, closed, and a kind of pessimistic model, whereas Y is optimistic, flexible and matured. These assumptions are:

Theory X assumptions

1. Average human beings have an inherent dislike for work and will avoid if they can
2. Because of this human characteristic of dislike for work, most people must be coerced, controlled, directed, and threatened with punishment to get them to put forth adequate effort toward the achievement of organizational objectives

3. Average human beings prefer to be directed, wish to avoid responsibility, have relatively little ambition, and want security above all.

Theory Y assumptions

1. The expenditure of physical effort and mental effort in work is as natural as play or rest
2. External control and threat of punishment are not the only means for producing effort toward organizational objectives. People will exercise self-direction and self-control in the service of objectives to which they are committed
3. The degree of commitment to objectives is in proportion to the size of the rewards associated with their achievement
4. Average human being learns, under proper conditions, not only to accept but also to seek responsibility
5. The capacity to exercise a relatively high degree of imagination, ingenuity, and creativity in the solution of organizational problems is widely, not narrowly, distributed in the population
6. Under the conditions of modern industrial life, the intellectual potentialities of an average human being are only partially utilized.

This theory became popular through McGregor's book titled *The Human Side of Enterprise* published in 1960. These X and Y are just a set of assumptions only and they are not managerial strategies.

Managerial Implication

X and Y may be only assumptions but have tremendous value for managerial practice. Probably, McGregor presented two extreme opposite assumptions that provide a picture of two worlds. Undoubtedly, these two worlds enable managers to gain a comprehensive perspective of human behaviour at work. There may not be an employee who possesses all the characteristics of X or Y alone and generally combination of both. The knowledge of this theory helps in understanding how an employee behaves in a particular situation: in X mode or Y? This understanding helps for effective management in various spheres of managerial activities: planning, organizing, directing and controlling of HR appropriately.

EIGHT PRACTICES OF QUALITY OF WORK LIFE (QWL)

Quality of working life though came into circulation in 1970s became popular only in 90s and organizations realized its potential to enhance the productivity in the new century. This works as a comprehensive model to those employers who want to ensure quality in working life of their employees. An ideal quality of work life programme will encompass practices in eight major areas as discussed below:

1. *Adequate and fair compensation.* This is fundamental to QWL. Human beings work for livelihood. Therefore success of rest of the initiatives depends upon fulfilment of this. However, important here is that compensation offered must be adequate implying it must be proportionate to labour, and there should be internal consistency among salaries of employees.

2. *Safe and healthy working conditions.* Unsafe and hazardous working conditions cause problems to both employers and employees. There may be little benefit to the employers in short-term but in medium- and long-terms, it adversely affects the productivity. Therefore, adequate investment must be made to ensure safe and healthy working conditions.

3. *Immediate opportunity to use and develop human capacities.* The jobs have become routine, meaningless and too specialized, depriving the employees of fulfilment satisfaction. Therefore, efforts should be made to increase the autonomy, perspective and exposure to multiple skills.

4. *Future opportunity for continued growth and security.* This is related to career aspects of employees. Meaningful career paths must be laid down and career mapping of employees is to be followed. The provision of advancement opportunities play a central role in QWL.

5. *Social integration in the work organization.* Relationships between and among the employees is an indicator of healthy work organization. Therefore, opportunities must be provided for formal and informal interactions. All kind of classes' religions, races, crafts, and designations must be treated equally on a social platform. In other words, it creates egalitarian environment.

6. *Constitutionalism in the work organization.* This is related to organizational norms that affect the freedom of an individual employee. Efforts must be made to see right norms are formed in the organization. It means norms that accommodate the privacy of an individual employee, freedom of speech, equity and freedom to dissent on some aspects.

7. *Work and the total life space.* Employees should not be allowed to continuously exert themselves. The continuous hard work causes psychological and physical strains. Therefore, there has to be a balance between personal and professional life. Organization must create proper work offs to enrich the life of employees.

8. *The social relevance of work life.* Employees must be given the perspective of how his/her work in the organization helps the society. This is essential to build relevance of the employee's existence to the society he/she lives in.

Managerial Implication

QWL is more relevant now than in the past because of two prime reasons. Firstly, it is well established that QWL leads to enhanced productivity. Secondly, QWL helps organization in many ways like building image of the company as best in recruitment, retention, and in general motivation of employees. This is one comprehensive strategy available with HR managers to achieve many things on employer as well as employees side.

EIGHT BEST DOWNSIZING PRACTICES

The new managerial thoughts and strategies of current decade almost turned 360 degree reverse from the thoughts and strategies of past five decades. Not long ago, large organizations, more manpower, permanency consistency and the like were considered as sources of organizational flexibility and agility. The same is now being rejected as causes of organizational competitive backwardness, business redundancies and managerial ineffectiveness. The prominent among new strategies that can ensure organizational flexibility and competitiveness is downsizing. However, experiences of organizations with downsizing are mixed. Some succeeded in achieving anticipated results while others encountered new problems. This is due to adoption of unsound downsizing practices, claim experts on the subject. It is no denying the fact that, more and more organizations have to offload more and more manpower in coming years due to the fast developments in technologies, markets and managerial systems. Therefore, we need to understand and follow the practices regarded as best in downsizing efforts. Professor Kim Cameron of Michigan University, based on a study of 30 organizations that were engaged in downsizing, identified eight best practices in downsizing, and enumerated them in his paper titled "Strategies for Successful Downsizing" published in *Human Resource Management* in 1994. These are:

1. *Approach.* This practice advocates (i) to approaching downsizing as a long-term strategy, (ii) to approaching HR as assets rather than as liabilities and (iii) approaching downsizing as an opportunity rather than as reaction to crisis.

2. *Preparation.* It consists of three activities: (i) involving employees in downsizing implementation rather than driving as top down, (ii) seeking involvement and suggestions from suppliers and customers and (iii) treating downsizing as everybody's activity rather than only of top management.

3. *Leadership.* During downsizing process, leaders must be quite visible and accessible, and they must personally communicate with all the employees. They must seek feedback continuously from all the people and find out ways to motivate people in downsizing situation.

4. *Communication.* Employees particularly need to be overcommunicated in downsizing process. Further, the communication must be fast and honest. It must be truly a system of multiple communications.

5. *Support.* It involves (i) providing safety net to those being downsized, (ii) training and retraining to ensure uninterrupted availability of skills and (iii) pay attention to people who stay in organization.

6. *Cost cutting.* In order to realize the benefits of downsizing, simultaneously three actions must be initiated: (i) analyze all the activities in the organization to eliminate inefficiencies, non-value added services, redundant processes and (ii) institute a variety of cost cutting measures.

7. *Measurement.* We need to develop the measures and parameters and also decide on methodology that facilitates in realistic assessment of various things connected with downsizing in pre, present and post scenarios. For example, there must be a system of measurement to understand what skills of employees are value added and redundant in order to draft appropriate actions.

8. *Implementation.* This is a critical practice in the entire downsizing programme. It should be implemented with all fairness. HR practices such as appraisal, reward, selection, development and communication must be reoriented to reflect the goals and objectives of downsizing. Employee involvement and participation must be paid full attention in the implementation phase.

Managerial Implication

This has many practical implications. For example, it emphasizes that downsizing in action must be presented and treated as big opportunity to recast the organization's focus rather than a reaction coming from a desperate company. This is a mistake many organizations commit in practice. Secondly, administer the whole programme from a positive perspective rather than in paranoid style. Thirdly, downsizing must be understood as an organizational programme comprising many strategies such as revamping managerial systems, shifting market focus, altering the company objectives and of course, reducing the manpower. In practice, organizations make the mistake of limiting themselves to manpower cuts and forget redefining the downsized organization. Therefore, these eight best downsizing practices have valuable practical value for managers.

MANAGING BY WALKING AROUND

Bill Hewlett and his colleagues at Hewlett-Packard who developed this technique in 1970's have been practising it since then in their organization as a multiple strategy of communication and shop floor accessibility. However, Tom Peters and Robert Waterman were the ones who popularized this technique by describing the largesse benefits of it in their book titled *In Search of Excellence* published in 1982. The process of this technique is simple—managers spend substantial amount of time every day in wandering around the workplace wishing the employees and generally ascertaining their comfort instead of closing themselves in their chambers all the time. However, this should not be practised as a ritual or just for the sake of it or as a mere goodwill measure. In other words, you need to be yourself walking throughout the organization looking for opportunities to make positive comments and to receive input and feedback. This allows managers to have direct contact with all employees, and also enables them to have first hand information on many things.

This approach is found to be very effective particularly in the organizations with many layers of hierarchy. A vice-president of Hewlett-Packard described Management By Walking Around as 'the business of staying in touch with the territory all the time'. Many benefits were reported with this approach. For example, Peters and Waterman discovered that companies that had top managers engaged in interacting with employees and customers were more successful than those with isolated management. This success was due to the leadership that wandered outside the executive suite. However, this is not as simple as it appears. Many managers do not know how to wander! Some get into the trap of inspecting progress of work and sometimes publicly criticize it. These actions defeat the spirit of the technique. The approach is successful with Hewlett-Packard because of its compatibility with their culture of mutual respect and teamwork.

Managerial Implication

Management By Walking Around as described above, offers multiple benefits in the shape of two way communication and timely decisions on many issues. It allows managers to communicate directly the management philosophy and organizational values. This also helps employees to access the top management on a regular basis. In effect, this reduces proxy management, widens the reality window of managers, and enhances the employees' involvement.

We must also remember the rider, i.e. the technique should have consonance with overall culture of the organization. The absence of such integration may produce counter results.

SMART-DUMB RULE

Simple but powerful, the concept called Smart-Dumb Rule is presented in the book titled, *In Search of Excellence* authored by Tom Peters and Robert Waterman. This concept drives a point that being simplistic in organizations should be a *no negative* connotation though it is treated as one. The simplistic people are those whose area of influence is wide in comparison to area of concern and they do not believe that some things could be impossible. Let us understand the smart-dumb features:

Many of today's managers—MBA trained and the like—may be little too smart for their own good. The smart ones are the ones who

(a) shift direction all the time, based upon the latest output from the expected value equation
(b) juggle hundred-variable models with facility
(c) design complicated incentive systems
(d) wire up matrix structures
(e) have 200 page strategic plans and 500 page market requirement documents that are but step one in product development exercises.

Dumber ones are those who don't understand why

(a) every product can't be of the highest quality
(b) every customer can't get personalized service
(c) a regular flow of new products is not possible, or why a worker can't contribute a suggestion every couple of weeks.

Managerial Implication

Managers are required to be conscious of the smart-dumb rule in recruitments, performance assessments and other evaluations of HR. People who are found to be smart during evaluation may not necessarily be performers and action-oriented and may be dumb. Merely being quick on a few aspects and having good vocabulary are not just sufficient to deliver performance. The dominant problem with many of our recruitment tests, interviews and performance testing exercises is that these are favourably disposed towards linguistic and articulation abilities. Undoubtedly, articulation, presentation and expression skills are important to managers but they should not become ends in themselves because they alone cannot guarantee the results. Equally important are down-to-earth and pragmatic approach, coupled with perseverance. Be cautious that those people with articulation skills can sometimes be otherwise in intelligence, still convince you and be presentable.

MICHAEL JORDAN EFFECT

The classic mistake of assuming if someone is technically good. This necessarily means he/she has the ability to lead people. This is called Michael Jordan Effect according to

Dr. Daniel Goleman who coined the term in his book titled *Working with Emotional Intelligence*. Michael Jordan was a famous basketball player in America whom the whole nation revered for his scintillating performances. Goleman takes Michael Jordan's name to drive home his point. Chicago Bulls lost their basketball coach. Therefore, they chose Michael Jordan as their coach. Though he's a brilliant player, he doesn't know how to coach others because the game comes to him so naturally. He would have been better of on the ground as a player than as a coach.

This phenomenon is commonly found in our organizations. We tend to make technically competent people/engineers as head of organizations, competent teachers as vice chancellors, scientists as directors of research institutes and so on without understanding their competence to motivate and lead the people. One needs to possess social skills and empathy to succeed in people management in organizations including even those which are highly technological. Goleman makes another potential observation through live examples that at the extreme high end of the scale, there is often lack of social skills. The smarter the people are in their functional areas, very often, the less competent they are emotionally, and in handling people. Mastery of these technical pursuits demands long hours spent working alone, often beginning in childhood or the early teen years—a period of life when, ordinarily, people learn vital social skills from interacting with friends. This does not mean, of course, that all high IQ technical people are socially incompetent. But it does not mean people with high skills in their fields make them high in people skills. We rarely find people with both the set of skills in high measure.

Managerial Implication

This concept provides two learnings for practice in organizations. Firstly, we must recognize that people skills are different from technical skills. Secondly, people skills are more important than technical skills to lead teams/groups/organizations. However, it does not mean that persons with people skills alone and without even minimum skills of relevant discipline must be chosen for leadership roles. In fact, they ought to have reasonable competence in the relevant field to understand and assess various issues involved in managing the project/work. It only drives a point that social skills are more important than technical skills to successfully motivate and manage the people.

PETER'S PRINCIPLE

Peter Principle is regarded as the most penetrating social and psychological discovery of the century. Laurence J. Peter, Professor at University of Southern California, was originator of this model and made it popular worldwide through his book titled, *The Peter Principle* published in 1969. The important Peter's laws include the following:

1. Managers tend to be promoted to their level of incompetence. The idea is that people are often promoted for their past performance and not for their competence to handle the promoted level which is usually more complex and demand more skills. Every position tends to be filled by an employee incompetent to execute the duties. The net result is that most of the higher levels of bureaucracy will be filled by incompetent people, who got there because they were quite good at doing a different task than the one they are expected to do.

2. Work is accomplished by those who have not yet reached to their level of incompetence: This is obvious because only competent people can deliver the goods.

3. Competence always contains the seed of incompetence. In other words, an employee who is competent in a particular skill/discipline not necessarily makes him as competent in other skills. In contrast, his/her total occupation with acquiring mastery in a given skill makes them ignorant of other things.

4. Employees in hierarchy do not really object to incompetence in their colleagues.

5. Internal consistency is more valued than efficiency.

6. Impostors tend to congregate in the mid to upper levels of large organizations because one impostor cannot spot another impostor.

Managerial Implication

Peter's laws have great relevance even in today's modern organizations. These laws should be taken as warnings. Number of consultants an organization engages, despite having full time managers in such functions, is an indicator of Peter Principle in action. Wrong recruitments, failure to place right people to right positions, poor training of managers, promotions without talent assessment and sometime indifference to capabilities are a few reasons for being trapped into Peter's laws. The taller the hierarchy of an organization, the higher the chances of having more incompetent managers. Middle level positions are more prone to this syndrome though other levels are no exception. HR managers have fundamental responsibility to see that right decisions are taken and scientific processes are adopted in organization that ensures job fitness across all the functions.

DILBERT PRINCIPLE

The most ineffective workers will be systematically moved to the place where they can do the least damage, i.e. Damage Management is the central principle of Dilbert. This phenomenon though similar to Peter's Principle is different in its core premise according to Scott Adams, who vividly described the model in his book titled *The Dilbert Principle* published in 1996. The difference is that, during Peter Principle days, bosses were good at least in some aspects. Now, apparently, the incompetent workers are promoted directly to management without they ever passing through the temporary competence stage. The author uses humour to illustrate the foibles and fallacies of the modern business world and rampant management fads which include such aspects as management incompetence, overbearing egos, a cubicle view of bosses, bottomless bureaucracies, petrifying performance reviews, long hour meetings, confusion of information super highways, ineffective teams, downsizing to grow sick, absurd corporate reengineering, quality free total quality, employee empowerment drama, fiction styled vision statements, unplanned business plans. In a nut shell, The Dilbert Principle portrays the absurdities of the 90's work place in a light hearted manner. According to Adams,

> people are idiots, including me, no matter how smart you are, you spend much of your day being an idiot is the chief assumption behind this principle. He further observes, no matter how absurd I try to make the comic strip of management, I can't stay ahead of what people are actually experiencing in their own work places.

Managerial Implication

All the managers, for more than one valid reason, should take the principle and its message seriously. The book is written, based upon not only the experiences of its author while working in a company called Pacific Blue, but also more importantly, the experiences of several thousands of people working in several hundred organizations who vented out their feelings and shared observations through e-mails to the author. Further, the book received overwhelming response expressing whether its author ever worked in their companies and with their bosses. This implies that a large number of people agree with salient observations of Dilbert Principle. Therefore, top managers in general and HR managers in particular must see that their organizations will not become victims of this principle. This is possible only through a systematic competence management in organizations, apart from building a performance based work culture.

PYGMALION EFFECT

It is a self-fulfilling prophecy. The name originated from a Greek mythological story and became popular in George Bernard Shaw's writings before its adoption in management. History of this concept makes explanation easy. Pygmalion, prince of Cyrus, who is also a sculptor by passion, creates an ivory statue of a girl. He names the statue of the beautiful girl as Galatea. He likes the statue so much that it culminates in deep love. He prays to Goddess Venus to breathe life into Galatea so that he can marry her and lead a happy life. Venus grants life to the statue and they live together. The essence of this story is that we tend to live up to the expectation of somebody as that of Goddess.

We convey our expectations through manifestation of various cues—verbally and non-verbally—which people pick up and behave accordingly. Findings of many studies prove that employees perform as expected of them by their managers/bosses. The case is same with children who behave in a way that proves the expectation of their parents and teachers. The simple truth is that all of us mostly behave the way expected of us. Therefore, success or failure of a person is a reflection of the image thus created by people. The process by which expectations turn into reality can be described as follows:

- We form certain expectations of people
- We communicate these expectations in various ways
- People tend to respond to these by adjusting their behaviour to match
- Expectations become true

Managerial Implication

There is a saying that performing managers produce performing employees and non-performing managers that of non-performing employees. Management is a process of making expectations, of course that are reasonable. An employee tends to behave well, who so far may have earned bad reputation, when a new manager expects nice of him. We come across many instances of employees delivering excellent performance when expected the same and treated confidently. Managers also need to remember that categorizing employees like good or satisfactory while assessing employees' performance is more an expectation of employees' future behaviour than assessment of past performance. Employees perform poor when managers expect poor results.

JOB ENRICHMENT MISUNDERSTOOD

The primary dissatisfaction of employees in organizations is attributable to lack of job enrichment or due to job erosion that include repetitive, boring work, less challenging job, minimal freedom, little employee control over the work, meaningless tasks, lack of employee participation etc. We come across many such remarks, inferences and conclusions in the management literature and reports. Therefore, redesign of job for enrichment is the key solution. This is what managements of many organizations would like to believe, but this is not necessarily what employees want. Because their primary dissatisfaction is neither with variety of work nor with challenges in the job connected to the practice of job enrichment. This is something to do with more basic—proper working conditions of work, pay and job security, reveals Mitchell Fein in his path breaking writing titled "Job Enrichment: A Re-evaluation" published in *Sloan Management Review* in 1974. Following findings support this point of view:

1. A study conducted by Michigan University covering 60,000 employees in more than fifty counties found that majority of employees ranked their needs in this order: physical conditions first, security second, earnings third and benefits fourth. The factor labelled *interesting work* was ranked far below the above indicated four needs.

2. Most of all, the job enrichment experiments, except that of Michigan study, were initiated by management, never by workers or unions. Further, most of these studies were conducted with handpicked employees, who were usually working in areas or plants isolated from the main operations and thus did not represent a cross section of the working population

3. The success reported by companies like General Foods, Procter & Gamble, Polaroid Corporation, Texas Instruments, AT&T etc. with job enrichment initiative also confined to miniscule of employees in their companies. It had never a company wide initiative. Therefore, difficult to draw valid inferences.

4. Studies from around the world, including the communist countries, demonstrate that the concepts of McGregor and Herzberg regarding workers' need to find fulfilment through work hold only for those workers who choose to find fulfilment through their work. Contrary to the more popular belief, the vast majority of workers seek fulfilment outside their work.

5. Further, there are many factors that constrain the philosophy of job enrichment in practice. In most instances it is impossible to add to jobs decisionmaking that job enrichment theorists call for, simply because of the growing automated technology of work. Relatively there will be few changes that need a high skill content which are in any case already enriched. Whereas most of the jobs by nature need only low skill content and enriching them will be counter productive. Job enrichment predicts that increased job satisfaction will increase motivation and raise productivity. However, workers know that if they increase production, reduce delays and waiting time, reduce crew sizes or cooperate in any way, less overtime will be available, some employees will be displaced, and the plant will require few employees.

Managerial Implication

HR managers particularly those involved in HR planning and job design must identify the jobs that are required to be enriched in the real sense instead of extending it to all sections of employees. Enrichment should not be adopted for the sake of generating good will. Managers also should be conscious of being trapped into job enrichment, relying upon its face value as a positive tool. Misplaced job enrichment can frustrate not only its initiators but also the employees.

RATCHET EFFECT

The essence of this concept is threefold.

Firstly, any temporary help that is extended to an individual or to an organization from outside in managing a crisis will lead to bigger crisis. For example, organizations tend to outsource and depend upon external sources for accomplishing its objectives. This may happen due to shortage of human skills or sometimes as a planned strategy to keep the organization slim and agile. This in turn will result in a strong weakness for the organization, eventually because of a number of reasons that include:

1. Neither employees nor employer will ever realize the need to build these skills internally since they do not feel the need of it until it becomes a major crisis;
2. The dependence of organization tend to increase many fold and any dependence create uncertainty that can grow as a crisis;
3. The uniqueness of an organization's products/services may vanish since the external agency services are also available to other organizations;
4. Outside intervention adversely affects the learning of employees. This includes learning related to their own work, technology and related aspects which may debilitate their capabilities in handling all the situations.

Secondly, failure of any party to follow its obligation in a mutual commitment will result in higher losses. For example, workers paid by the piecemeal should be happy to introduce new techniques that increase output. Organizations tend to reduce the piecerate when workers start earning too much money. Workers respond to this by restricting output and keeping new ideas to themselves. This ultimately lead to lower output compared to the level of the pre-commitment period.

Thirdly, a benefit introduced to attain a goal may work against attaining that goal. For example, it was thought that inefficiencies of central planning are related to absence of incentives like in many government bureaucracies. Paradoxically, it was found that there were incentives but they worked in wrong direction and were the source of many of the observed inefficiencies.

Hardin Garrett, a Biologist, conceived this concept to explain the effect of food aid in times of crisis on a nation's population that was borrowed in Industrial and Labour Economics.

Managerial Implication

It helps managers to understand their own internal situations in many ways. Firstly, ruthless outsourcing practices should be carefully studied in terms of its effect on competitiveness of an organization. Sometimes the services that are thought of as ancillary may become vital to the success of an organization. Secondly, its effect on skill gaps of employees in this field also should be audited to assess its extent. Thirdly, the efficacy of incentives and rewards must be studied at regular intervals to minimize the ratchet effect. Fourthly, never break a commitment—whether written or oral.

LAWS OF STUPIDITY

Walter Pitkin of Columbia University once stated, probably in 1934, that four people out of five are stupid enough to be called stupid.

However, Carlo M. Cipolla, Professor of Economic History at University of Berkeley, has developed a universally applicable model explaining human stupidity in 1988. He says that there is a remarkable character with a stupid, which no body has that a stupid person doesn't know that he/she is stupid. That makes things more difficult in organizations. Further, he brilliantly portrays five laws of stupidity as indicated here:

1. We always underestimate the number of stupid people. For example, people whom we had thought to be rational and intelligent suddenly turn out to be unquestionably stupid
2. The probability of a person being stupid is independent of any characteristic of that person. It can be found in all, irrespective of race, age, gender, education and occupation
3. A stupid person is someone who causes damage to another person, or a group of people, without any advantage accruing to himself/herself, or even with some resultant self-damage
4. Non-stupid people always underestimates the damaging power of stupid people. They constantly forget that at any moment, and in any circumstance, associating with stupid people invariably constitutes an expensive mistake
5. A stupid person is the most dangerous person in existence. For example, even intelligent people, however hostile they may be, are still predictable but stupid persons are not.

Managerial Implication

We must make efforts to minimize stupidity and number of stupids in organizations. As stated by an expert on stupidity, it has always been obvious that stupidity is the biggest destructive force in the history of humanity. The elements of stupidity exist in every human being. Therefore, we need to bring awareness in everybody to be conscious of this. When people act in stupid way, it could be difficult to ensure fairness in administration and semblance in managerial decisions. Further, the essence of this law is that we all are susceptible to make stupid decisions and act in stupid manner regardless of our proficiency and mastery in a given discipline, regardless of our formal position, irrespective of our seniority, and independent of general intelligence. Therefore, periodically managers need to introspect themselves that help at least to identify acts of stupidity and consequentially minimise them.

TELECOMMUTING

Telecommuting, also known as telework, is the new addition to HRM practices born out of information technology revolution. It is described as enabling your employees to work from home and occasionally visiting workplace. This is also referred as working in and for the organization form anywhere and at anytime. This type of work is best suited to backoffice operations, offsite business consultants, self-employed contractors who work for a number of companies, and also to regular employees in certain categories. Telework can be adopted with the use of Internet and intranet technologies to derive greater organizational and employee benefits. According to Canadian Telework Association, telework offers the following advantages:

- Saves office space and parking requirements estimated to be $ 2000 per employee per annum
- Increases productivity and job performance by 20 per cent on an average
- Reduces absenteeism and healthcare related costs, one or two days per employee per year on an average
- Reduces business disruptions due to emergencies (strikes, viral and other illness, natural calamities etc.)
- Can reduce long-term disability costs
- Savings reduce need to downsize
- Increases flexibility to staff during peak workloads
- Recognizes growing importance of family, increases single/dual career households
- Accommodates those with health problems or disabilities and improves morale and job satisfaction
- Improves recruitment and retention of key employees. Reduces hiring and training costs
- Taps labour markets from geographically remote areas
- An option to relocating employees.

However, telework has its share of challenges and should not be taken something that offers only advantages. It can pose challenges mainly to HRM aspects that include:

- Reduced social interaction can lead to social and professional isolation
- Fewer career and promotional opportunities
- Monitoring performance can be tricky
- Potential for long hours of work
- Work/family or life balance may be affected if teleworker becomes a work addict
- Organizational culture
- Some colleagues can be jealous, especially if they are refused the chance to telework

Managerial Implication

HR managers who want their organizations to adopt telework must work on three aspects. Firstly, identify the operations/works and jobs within the organizations, that can be performed through telework with the help of line managers. Secondly, study various legal, financial, and administrative related aspects of telework in the context of the organization. Thirdly, develop a telework HR policy and plan consisting the first and second aspects above and issues like hours of work, performance management and culture requirements. The most important is check whether telework has any substantial benefits to offer to your organization before venturing for it.

Chapter 7

Leadership Development

Undoubtedly, Leadership is the most talked and written about subject in various disciplines: History, Sociology, Psychology, Religion and importantly in the Management. However, the issue of leadership has remained an enigma for many. The questions that often surface are: whether leadership is a born talent or learned? Whether there is any universally applicable leadership style or effectiveness of style situational dependent? What is the standard leadership personality? What are the appropriate leadership traits? Who is an effective leader—a person who is loved by the people or one whom people are forced to admire, a person with sound technical knowledge in a given field or a person with people skills? Does leaders bound by moral values and ethics or simply one who leads the group to a particular direction which he/she perceives as right? Whether leadership is a matter of rank, privilege or responsibility? Whether leadership is everyone's business or only a handful in the organization? Who is important for organizations: leader or followers? Whether effective leader is one who is diligent in take accomplishment alone or a person with futuristic vision? What is the determinant of leader's success—follower's intelligence or leadership quality?

Often, HR professionals encounter these questions in practice. However, these questions are not left without answers. This chapter deals with such answers in a practitioner's language and also presents some successful models and leadership development practices. It also covers the contemporary leadership skill and competency profile that is required to be built in organizations.

GLOBAL LITERACIES MODEL FOR LEADERSHIP

Whether organizations are globalized or not, certainly their employees, suppliers and customers have become truly global in their expectations and behaviours. Therefore, organizations that have decided to be local also need leadership of global mode. In regard to organizations which operate in a global scenario, the global leadership is fundamental to their survival and strategic imperative to its success. But how to nurture global leadership is a tough question to many. Based on their comprehensive study involving face-to-face interviews with CEOs of more than 75 companies in 28 countries and a survey of 1000 senior executives around the world Robert Rosen and Patricia Digh provide answer to this in their book titled *Global Literacies: Lessons on Business Leadership and National Cultures* published in 2000. The answer is leaders need to be trained on four literacies as indicated below that allow them to (i) seeing, (ii) thinking, (iii) acting and (iv) mobilizing in culturally mindful ways.

Personal literacy

It refers to understanding and valuing oneself. The key behaviours include:

(a) *Aggressive insight*—committing to a continuous process of self-awareness and renewal

(b) *Confident humility*—being self-confident, yet humble enough to listen and learn from other people

(c) *Authentic flexibility*—understanding and accepting the attitudes, beliefs and behaviours of other people without compromising your own

(d) *Reflective decisiveness*—balancing thoughtful consideration of all options by acting boldly and forcefully

(e) *Realistic optimism*—envisioning a better future while acknowledging the constraints of current realities

Social literacy

It refers to engaging and challenging other people. The key behaviours are:

(a) *Pragmatic trust*—combining the attitudes of trusting believers and sceptical pragmatists

(b) *Urgent listening*—balancing the urgent demands of business with deep listening to the concerns of other people

(c) *Constructive impatience*—being impatient enough to inspire greater performance without damaging constructive attitudes and relationships

(d) *Connective teaching*—creating learning networks that enable to learn collaboratively across organizational and cultural boundaries

(e) *Collaborative individualism*—uniting the diverse skills and interests of individuals in a common purpose

Business literacy

It refers to focusing and mobilizing the business. The key roles are as follows:

(a) *Chaos navigator*—guiding people through change and managing unexpected

(b) *Business geographer*—understanding the business context of the regions and countries where your products and services are made, bought or sold

(c) *Technology steward*—learning the e-business and internet skills required in a technological world

(d) *Leadership liberator*—creating leaders every day and at every level of the business

(e) *Economic integrator*—aligning and connecting people, systems and processes in support of the vision and goals of the organization

Cultural literacy

It refers to understanding and leveraging cultural differences. The key roles:

(a) *Proud ancestor*—valuing your cultural heritage while acknowledging its shortcomings as well as its strengths

(b) *Inquisitive internationalist*—looking beyond one's own culture for business opportunities and resources

(c) *Respectful modernizer*—retaining the best of one's culture while using the knowledge and resources of others to modernize for the future

(d) *Culture bridger*—forming alliances and connections across cultures

(e) *Global capitalist*—bringing global resources to local problems and opportunities and local resources to global ones.

Managerial Implication

This model makes the job of HR managers easy on one hand and challenging on the other. It is easy because we have a readymade blueprint in the form of four global literacies to build global leadership. This is challenging because the model is different in its perspective, premises and behaviours from other conventional and contemporary models. This distinctiveness demands HR managers to grasp and build implementing strategy that can deliver these literacies. In the end, we must be happy for the brilliant model offered by its authors based on rigorous research.

COGNITIVE RESOURCE MODEL OF LEADERSHIP

This is also known as Cognitive Resource Theory (CRT), an update of Contingency Theory of Leadership. Fred Fielder who initially advanced this model of leadership in his book titled, *Leadership* published in 1971, stated that it is impossible to change the style of leadership, and therefore, situation is to be changed to attain the effectiveness of leadership. In other words, place a manager with a particular style of leadership in a situation where that style suits or is appropriate. The central theme of this model is that leadership effectiveness is dependent upon two factors: (i) situational control (in other words, the degree of leader control over a situation) and (ii) leadership style suiting to the situation. These two factors are briefly discussed here:

Situational control

The following three factors will determine who has control over the situation—Is it the supervisor who has control over the subordinates (group) or subordinates that have control over the supervisor?

1. *Leader-Member relations.* This indicates acceptance of an individual as leader by the group in terms of respect, confidence and trust the group has towards the leader.

2. *Position power.* This indicates the competency of leader to wield and exercise power in terms of rewarding or punishing the group members. The more the powerlessness of the leader, the greater will be the leadership ineffectiveness.

3. *Task structure.* This indicates how clear the group members are about their tasks and goals. Better the clarity, higher the leadership effectives and higher the ambiguity, lesser the effectiveness.

Leadership will be effective where leader-members relationship is good, leader's power is strong and task structure is high.

Leadership orientation

Broadly, there are two orientations in leadership—one is relationship oriented and the other is task oriented. Both are effective conceptually, but their actual effectiveness is wholly contingent upon the situation. For example, task orientation is suitable for a routine work where task definition and methods of performing is highly structured. It is the relationship orientation that works in unstructured and dynamic environment.

Fielder, in association with Joe E. Garcia remodelled the contingency model as cognitive model to explain the process by which a leader obtains effective group performance in their book titled, *New approaches to Effective Leadership: Cognitive Resources and Organisational Performance* published in 1987. The key aspects of this new model are:

1. The effectiveness of leadership is contingent upon abilities of leaders to develop plans, strategies and their overall knowledge of the task
2. Performance of group members will be high if their relations with leader is stress-free
3. There is a direct correlation between leadership effectiveness and leader's intellectual abilities.

Managerial Implication

There are three major implications for organizational practice in the area of leadership development. Firstly, leadership development efforts must focus on building the technical/functional skills, which the cognitive model aptly highlighted. Secondly, leader's adaptability must be enhanced because it is the situation that plays an important role in leadership success rather than the style itself. Thirdly, relationship (social skills) skills must be imparted because it is the relationship that frees group members from stress.

CHARISMATIC LEADERSHIP MODEL

We rarely come across leaders who are revered by followers and who can obtain absolute commitment, trust and confidence of the followers. Such people are called as charismatic leaders. There will be many mythical and heroic stories revolving around them and their deeds. Charismatic leaders can stimulate the followers to perform and achieve beyond expectations. The charismatic leadership, though as old as human civilization, it was Robert House who first made a systematic study of this phenomenon in business organizations in 1976. However, two professors at Mc Gill University namely J.A. Conger and R.N. Kanungo had developed the comprehensive charismatic leadership model and presented it in their paper titled "Toward a Behavioural Theory of Charismatic Leadership in Organizational Settings" published in *Academy of Management Review* in 1987. The key characteristics of charismatic leaders are:

1. *Self-confidence.* Charismatic leaders possess complete confidence in their abilities, decisions, judgements and behaviour.
2. *Vision.* They have far-sightedness and so can set goals that bring significant transformation from the current reality.
3. *Articulation of the vision.* They can take their vision to the followers with ease and with great clarity. Charismatic leaders use vision communication to motivate the followers.

4. *Conviction.* This is characterized by leader's commitment, willingness to make sacrifices, incur costs and put themselves in highly uncomfortable and dangerous positions. Charismatic leaders demonstrate this behaviour to achieve their vision.

5. *Unconventional behaviour.* Charismatic leaders behave in an unconventional manner; break the conventional norms in contrast to commonly accepted mode.

6. *Change agent.* They bring transformational changes into the system in contrast to the normal style of maintaining *status quo* or incremental changes.

7. *Sensitivity to surroundings.* Charismatic leaders are a well-informed lot and often assess the environment in a systematic manner. Based on this, they plan the action plan for changes.

The research studies established clear correlation between charismatic leadership and high performance and satisfaction among followers. However, charismatic leadership is not necessarily a moralistic style because they can be unethical also to achieve what they believe as right or essentially to serve their personal ends and incidentally organization's.

Managerial Implication

The important issue for managers is whether employees can be trained on charismatic leadership and how far it will be beneficial in practice. The relevant literature and studies reveal that employees can be trained to learn some of the charismatic leadership qualities and characteristics. But transforming somebody into charismatic leaders is just impossible unless they are basically charismatic oriented. However, the learned charismatic leadership qualities will be immensely helpful to all managers to motivate the employees. Therefore, HR managers and leadership trainers must consider imparting the ingredients of this model to all managers.

SITUATIONAL MODEL OF LEADERSHIP

This falls in the category of contingency leadership models, which argues that the effectiveness of a leadership style is wholly dependent upon the situational compatibility than the style itself. This model further adds that the effectiveness of leadership is contingent upon the acceptance of followers. Therefore, it is the quality and actions of the followers that determines the effectiveness of leaders. This is what authors of this model call as maturity of followers. There are two types of maturity of this kind. The first is job maturity characterized by the education level, job related skills and competence of followers. The second is psychological maturity that refers to willingness to perform and achievement motivation. In other words, leaders will be effective wherever followers job and psychological maturity is at a desirable level.

This model has been adopted by many corporate organizations as a standard module in their training programmes. Paul Hersey and Kenneth Blanchard who developed this model presented it in their book titled *Management of Organizational Behaviour* published in 1982. This model proposes four leadership styles based upon two leadership dimensions. These are: (i) task orientation and (ii) people orientation. The four leadership styles are:

1. *Telling.* This is called as high task—low relationship management style. This type of managers only give instructions and directions of what employees should do, and define their duties and responsibilities. This style is effective when maturity level of followers are very low.

2. *Selling.* This is popularly known as high task–high relationship style. Managers in this style guide as well as direct the subordinates. This style is effective when the maturity level of followers is low.

3. *Participating.* This is known as low task–high relationship style. Here, managers are more bothered about the comforts and welfare of followers than their performance level on the job. This style is effective when followers' maturity is on higher side.

4. *Delegating.* This is low task–low relationship style. Managers provide very little direction and support to the employees. This style is effective when followers' maturity is at a very higher level.

Managerial Implication

This model has two important lessons to offer for practice in organizations. Firstly, this model was the first that brought a new and very important variable in understanding the effectiveness of leadership styles, i.e. maturity of followers. It is the maturity of followers that decides which leadership style matches them rather reverse of the order. Secondly, there is nothing that can be categorized as a standalone ideal leadership style because, any style that matches the situation of followers is the ideal style. This is more a practitioners model than of researcher's. Therefore, HR managers can adopt it for leadership training in their organizations.

FOUR SYSTEMS MODEL OF LEADERSHIP

Based on years of leadership research at Michigan University, Rensis Likert developed a model known as Likert's four systems of management leadership and detailed it in his book titled *The Human Organization* published in 1967. The model presents four different systems demonstrating four different styles of leadership. He casted these four styles on a continuum representing autocratic style on one extreme end and democratic style on the other end. These four leadership systems are:

System 1

It is labelled as *Exploitative-Autocratic* leadership style. The style is characterized by lack of trust and confidence in the abilities of employees. Subordinates are not granted freedom to access the boss on any job related issue particularly in problem solving situations. Employees are not consulted before or during taking of decisions.

System 2

It is labelled as *Benevolent-Autocratic* leadership style. Managers of this category demonstrate a paternalistic approach. They have confidence in their subordinates but more in terms of their loyalty than in their abilities. Therefore, they consult them seldom in problem solving and while arriving at any decisions. Employees will have limited freedom to directly approach the manager.

System 3

This is labelled as *Participative* style. Employees under this style of managerialism are free to approach and discuss with management. Managers also seek views of subordinates and they exhibit a controlled confidence in the employees.

System 4

This is labelled as Democratic style. In this style, manager will have complete confidence and trust in the abilities of employees. Managers always seek their views and take decisions in consonance with such views. Employees feel free to discuss anything with the bosses.

Likert and his colleagues continued research on the above styles especially focusing on to understand which is the most preferred leadership style. Their large-scale survey revealed that managers in large sized organizations preferred System 3 and 4 styles, whereas managers in small organizations favoured System 1 and 2 styles.

Managerial Implication

This model was built based on several years of rigorous research on the issue of managerial leadership at Michigan University. This has great value to practitioners in terms of getting a perspective of leadership. The choice of leadership system out of the above indicated four are left to individual organizations to decide and adopt the appropriate one. It is always better to understand different leadership styles and exercise choice rather than pursuing what we believe simply as right and effective style. Therefore, HR managers must create the awareness and knowledge of leadership among managers through training and development measures.

FIVE GREAT MYTHS OF LEADERSHIP IN PRACTICE

Undoubtedly, leadership is much talked and written about subject in the management literature. In behavioural training too, leadership has the top priority. There are many models and theories that have come into existence highlighting the different facets of leadership. But leadership remained an enigma for many. This is due to creation of leadership that is not in reality. There are many managers who still believe that leadership is a born talent, leadership is only for top management and one should have an inbuilt charismatic personality to be a leader. This belief has negative ramification to leadership development efforts in organizations. Two of the most insightful leadership theorists, namely Warren Bennis and Burt Nanus in their book titled *Leaders: The Strategies for Taking Charge* published in 1985 identified five great leadership myths:

- Myth-I: *Leadership is a rare skill.* There is a widespread belief that leadership is rare because leadership skills are rare with people in organization. But the fact remain is that many people possess leadership competency within them. We realize this when opportunities are extended to them to demonstrate their leadership prowess. The formal organizational structures discourage people to exhibit leadership behaviour.

- Myth-II: *Leaders are born, not made.* Biographies of great leaders and stories surrounding them create a picture that leadership is a born talent. But the fact is that many leadership skills and competencies can be learned. However, there is no simple formula or model through which leadership can be developed. This involves a rigorous process and many times a lifetime effort is required.

- Myth-III: *Leaders are charismatic.* There is a tendency to think that one need to be stylish, smart, and charming in appearance to become a leader. This is only half true. In reality, successful leadership practices and behaviours contribute for a leadership rather than charisma selfleading a person to effective leadership behaviour.

- Myth-IV: *Leadership exists only at the top of an organization.* Organizations have played into this myth by focusing leadership efforts only on top management. The fact is that leadership is required at every level of operation in the organization. One has to be a good leader even in a single person operation to excel in that. Therefore, there must be multiplication of leadership roles.

- Myth-V: *The leader controls, directs and manipulates.* Leadership is a role of empowering the followers as opposed to popular misnomer leadership as power seeking role. Leadership is epitome of equity, fairplay and sacrifice and not the act of manipulation. Effective leaders ensure rewards to others at the cost of self-comfort. Further, facilitation is what leaders engage in and not controlling and directing.

Managerial Implication

The practical utility of five great myths will be enormous to all managers, particularly for HR managers. Organizations pay heavily, when we believe in something that is not real. For example, our leadership efforts may lack conviction if we believe that leadership is merely a born talent. Therefore, leadership development programme in any organization must commence with dispelling these myths. The other valuable insight that managers must put into action is that leadership must be the business of everybody in the organization and not be confined to top echelons or a handful of managers.

FIVE PRACTICAL APPROACHES OF CEOs

One of the top most critical factors that influence the success of HRM activity in organizations is commitment and support of its chief executive. Even the brightest and the most tactful HR managers also feel inadequate in pushing through the HR agenda without the active involvement of CEOs. However, the tactful HR managers know that their job start from drawing the support of CEOs. In order to achieve this, they need to understand the approach their CEOs adopt in leading the organization. Three experts on business leadership namely Charles Farkas, Philippe Backer and Allen Sheppard based on their study of 160 top class CEOs worldwide in 1995 had identified five different approaches CEOs adopt in achieving the organizational success. These are briefly described here:

1. *The strategic approach.* CEOs who fall in this category are basically strategists. They manage for success by acting as the company's top strategist, systematically envisioning the future, and specifically mapping out how to get there. Strategic CEOs focus bulk of their energies on determining how their company can be the market leader of tomorrow, and then structure the organization around this. They believe in delegation and involvement of employees in all aspects of organizational functioning. They make personal efforts to communicate the long-term strategy of the company that includes compatible HR policies and practices.

2. *The human assets approach.* There are CEOs who strongly believe that organizational success comes from people policies, programmes and principles. CEOs of this school keep information such as competencies of people, their development needs and motivational strategies on finger tips. In other words, CEOs of this type practice an organizational learning approach to achieve objectives.

3. *The expertise approach.* CEOs here achieve success by becoming the champion of a specific, proprietary expertise, and using it to focus the organization. They identify critical competencies of the organization that enable them to attain competitive advantage and spending energies in further developing and spreading it throughout the organization. They also promote a work culture that disseminates this critical knowledge of core competencies.

4. *The box approach.* This approach is represented by a behaviour in which CEOs manage the organization by building a set of rules, systems, procedures and values that essentially control behaviour and outcomes within well-defined boundaries. CEOs of this approach concentrate their energies on control issues that include culture of the organization as the best means to sustainable competitive advantage.

5. *The change approach.* CEOs who act as agents of radical change and who transform bureaucracies into organizations that embrace the new and different, fall in this approach. They continuously look for opportunity to bring change in the organization. Their organizations need not be in crisis but their leaders still see the need for continuous and significant change. They believe in the saying, *if you're not a change agent, you're at best a steward of something which is going to erode.*

Managerial Implication

Each of these approaches CEOs practise have different implications for HRM system. For example, CEOs of box approach may insist for a formal and rule bound HR system whereas CEOs of change may invite flexible and informal HR system and strategist CEOs may call for HR role in strategy formulation. Therefore, smart HR managers must first understand the CEOs style and augment his/her style accordingly for tangible results out of HR system. Otherwise, both their styles and approaches may come into conflict that can dilute HR programmes.

TEN TRAITS OF BEST OF WORLD BUSINESS LEADERS

It is an interesting question for many that include academicians, consultants and practitioners of management that whether the successful business leaders possess distinct personality traits or simply they are like other managers, may be with more drive for achievement and more luckier than others. If they possess distinct traits, how distinct are they and whether there is any commonality in the personality traits of business leaders across the world? Based on the study of 50 top world-class business leaders, Thomas Neft and James Citrin clarified many of these issues. They found that best of world business leaders possess some distinct traits and there is commonality in these traits across the business leaders. They also identified ten traits that all these leaders seemed to hold in common and presented them in their book titled *Lessons from the Top* published in 2001. These ten traits are:

1. *Passion.* No trait is more noticeable in the top business leaders than the passion they share for their people and their companies. Quite simply, they love what they do.

2. *Intelligence and clarity of thinking.* Most successful business leaders are highly intelligent. Some of their intelligence is clearly the kind of raw intellectual horsepower that is innate. However, equally as important as their native smarts is their ability to make the complex seem simple.

3. *Great communication skills.* One of the common traits among the 50 business leaders identified in this study is ability to communicate well. The best business leaders can effectively explain business fundamentals, strategy, alternatives and a course of action in ways that tap the employees' sense of meaning.

4. *High energy level.* On an average, the world-class business leaders work more than 65 hours a week. The line between work and private life is more blurry. The physical strain of developing strategy, forging consensus, making decisions, building a management team, dealing with regulators, communicating with institutional investors, lobbying the government, travelling—all that require enormous amounts of stamina seem to be not enormous to these leaders.

5. *Egos in check.* When you are the ultimate boss, it is tempting to take credit for the success of your organization. In contrast, the best of business leaders were human of small egos. Many were quite humble about what they have accomplished, crediting hard work, good timing, a healthy dose of luck and efforts of family members and colleagues for their success.

6. *Inner peace.* The most successful leaders appear to be the least stressed. They are frenetic, more self aware, and more in harmony than most of the managers.

7. *Capitalizing on formative early life experiences.* The study found that these leaders believe in the idea, *we cannot control who our parents are, what order we are born in, or what economic stratum we grow up in but we can control what we make of our early life experiences.*

8. *Strong family lives.* Comparatively, the divorce rate among managers is much higher. However, it is almost zero in case of top class business leaders. More important than the mere statistics, however, many of these leaders cite the balancing effect of a strong family life and the quality of objective advice they get from an intelligent spouse as key ingredients in their success.

9. *Positive attitude.* Another trait that is shared by these business leaders is their positive attitude. As a general rule, these people tend to look at challenges as opportunities and seek to make the best out of difficult situations. Their outlook and commitment to capitalizing, rather than punishing mistakes, help give employees a sense of the possible.

10. *Focus on doing the right things right.* The great business leaders achieve their results by focusing on the right things day in and day out that include: (i) living with integrity and leading by example, (ii) developing a winning strategy or big idea, (iii) building a great management team, (iv) inspiring employees to achieve greatness and (v) creating a flexible, responsible organization.

Managerial Implication

The above study that identified ten traits of world-class business leaders have many practical implications to managers that include firstly, the leadership development programmes could be developed seeking these ten traits as vital inputs. Secondly, these descriptions can be used to inspire the managers to adopt these personality and behavioural characteristics and thirdly, these remarkable findings of business leadership clarifies many of doubts and clears many apprehensions.

LEADERSHIP TRANSITION—SEVEN FUNDAMENTAL PROPOSITIONS

There would be hardly any leader who might have not experienced resistance from the system and people who haven't experienced moments of anxiety and fear of failure when they newly take over as manager or leader of a group/organization. The leadership transition is a challenging task for any manager. When a new leader assumes the responsibility of managing, particularly when he or she wants to bring change or transformation in the organization, he/she has to encounter many odds. However, with a systematic plan in mind, the new leaders can engineer transformation in the organization and emerge as successful. Dan Ciampa and Michael Watkins, based on their study of a number of leadership transitions distilled seven key propositions for managing leadership transition successfully in their book titled *Right from the Start* published in 1999. These are:

1. A new leader has two to three years to make measurable progress in changing the culture and improving financial performance

2. On arrival, the new leader should have already understood the organization's current strategy and associated goals and challenges, and should have formed hypotheses about its operating priorities. During the first six months, these hypotheses must be tested and either validated or changed

3. New leaders must balance an intense, single-minded focus on a few vital priorities about when and how they are implemented

4. Within the first six months, the new leader must make key decisions about the organizational architecture of people, structure, and systems. Most crucially, the new leader must decide whether the composition of the inherited team is appropriate, and whether the organizational structure must change

5. By the end of the first six months, the new leader must also have built some personal credibility and momentum. Early wins are crucial, as that lays a foundation for sustained improvements in performance

6. The new leader must earn the right to transform the organization. The initial mandate from the board and chief executive officer is never sufficient, nor will it remain static. It must be diligently and regularly reassessed. The new leader must also work actively to build coalitions supportive of change

7. There is no single way to manage a leadership transition. New leaders' approaches will inevitably be shaped by the situations they face, their prior experience and their leadership styles.

Managerial Implication

One common issue in leadership and overlooked by companies is the importance of leadership transition. Most of them believe that placing a new manager and leaving it to that person to manage by himself is more than enough. This belief may be rational but care must be taken in preparing them for managing this transition. As the above content indicates there may not be any universally applicable model that can enable managers to manage this transition. But preparing them with relevant tips can broaden their perspective and insight. Therefore, HR managers must ensure that their managers are familiarized with the above proposition of leadership transition.

CLASSIC SKILLS OF CHANGE LEADERS

Undoubtedly, Leadership and Change are two issues written and talked about extensively. Whatever the length and depth of these writings and talkings, the issues remain complex and inconclusive. This is precisely due to the reason that change is changing fast. Leadership that can transform people in organizations in tandem with this speed of change is scarce. It is not that managers are not putting sustainable efforts, but it is only not in right direction using right skills. They make efforts to change merely the systems, policies, and infrastructure and leave people to themselves to defend against the changes. This is found to be largely due to lack of skills in leading the people's transition. Therefore, in the first place, they must acquire these skills. Thought leader Professor Rosabeth Moss Kanter based on her decades of experience of working with leaders prescribed a set of seven enduring skills that are equally useful to CEOs, senior executives and middle managers who want to manage the transition in people. These are:

1. *Turning in to the environment.* Create a network of listening posts to know what is happening inside and outside the organization. Look not just at how the pieces of your business model fit together but for what doesn't fit.

2. *Challenging the prevailing organizational wisdom.* In Kanter's language, leaders need to develop Kaleidoscope thinking—a way of constructing patterns from the fragments of data available, and manipulating them to form different patterns.

3. *Communicating a compelling aspiration.* Leaders talk about communicating a vision as an instrument of change, but the ideal is the notion of communicating an aspiration. Because it is not just a picture of what could be; it is an appeal to our better selves, a call to become something more.

4. *Building coalitions.* Build the coalitions that support the change movement because the involvement of people who have the resources, the knowledge and political clout are crucial for implementing the change process.

5. *Transferring ownership to a working team.* Encourage the teams to forge their own identity, build a sense of membership and extend the protection they need in order to implement changes.

6. *Learning to persevere.* Many times, leaders launch something and leave it to the people undefined. It is the hard work and persistence that are essential to achieve the goal because every change is like a long march.

7. *Making everyone a hero.* In a change programme, a leader needs skills, talents and energies on a continuous basis for a long time. Therefore, they must remember to recognize, reward and celebrate accomplishments of individuals and groups.

Managerial Implication

Top management, other senior managers and consultants involved in change management must pay attention to these seven skills that play key role in implementing a change programme successfully. These are pure practitioner skills and developed in consonance with hard-core ground realities. Many change efforts failed on account of failure to enthuse and lead the transition in people. HR managers must take initiative in generating awareness as well as training managers on the above skills.

MANAGERIAL GRID

This is a leadership model that captures all the possible leadership styles that managers practice in organizations. The model also prescribes the favourable situations for practice of these styles in organizational settings. Robert Blake and Jane Mouton developed Managerial Grid and presented it in their book tiled *The Managerial Grid* published in 1964. This is a comprehensive framework that illustrates all the styles and range of leadership. There are five leadership styles in the grid model based on two leadership dimensions. These are: (i) concern for people and (ii) concern for task. The five leadership styles are:

- *1, 1 style.* This is also called as deserter style/impoverished management style. The leader will have concern neither for people nor for the task. It is the exertion of minimum effort to get required work done that is appropriate to sustain organization membership.

- *9, 1 style.* This is also called as autocrat style. Here, the leader is concerned with production only and minimum concern for human elements. In Blake and Mouton's terms, it is the efficiency in operations results from arranging conditions of work in such a way that human elements interfere to a minimum degree.

- *1, 9 style.* This is also called as country club management/missionary style. This type of leader's chief concern is human beings. They do not mind to place the comfort of employees before the organizational goals. It is termed as; thoughtful attention to needs of people for satisfying relationships, leads to a comfortable, friendly organization atmosphere and work tempo.

- *5, 5 style.* This is also called as compromiser/man organizational management style. Leaders of this style try to balance both the organizational and employees objectives. They believe that adequate organizational performance is possible through balancing the necessity to get work done while maintaining morale of people at a satisfactory level.

- *9, 9 style.* This is also called as executive style/team management. Here, leaders seek task achievement through a highly committed workforce. They use teams for interdependent tasks and nurture a culture of trust and mutual respect. This is represented by such terms as, work accomplishments is from committed people, interdependence through a common stake and purpose leads to relationships of trust and respect.

The leadership style labelled as 9, 9 is considered to be the most effective out of above five styles.

Managerial Implication

The authors of the model have also converted the above described leadership styles into a training module consisting six phases to impart leadership training called Grid training. There is emperical evidence which shows, that the manager who received Grid training adopted 9, 9 leadership style whereas others believed that either 5, 5 or 9, 1 leadership style is effective. Therefore, HR managers must take initiative at least to generate awareness about different leadership styles and relative effectiveness of each style. Managerial Grid training significantly helps in this effort.

REAL CHANGE LEADERS

Traditionally, it has been believed for decades that a manager who (i) is strategy driven, (ii) is committed to enhance the earnings per share, and (iii) who avoids mistake making is an ideal manager that organizations directly need and look forward to. Ironically, studies and organizational experiences clearly pointed out that this profile of ideal manager win just not suit for organizational change management which need all together a different style of leading. Based on an in-depth study of this issue, Jon Katzenbach, the revolutionary management expert came up with a style that is apt for change management called Real Change Leader in his book titled *Real Change Leaders* published in 1996. The characteristics of these real change leaders in comparison to the ideal manager profile on a set of five key issues are indicated in Table 7.1.

TABLE 7.1

Key issues	Traditional good manager view	Emerging real change leader view
Basic mindset	Analyze, leverage, optimise, delegate, organize, and control it—I know best.	Do it, fix it, try it, Change it—and do it all over again; no one person knows best.
"End-game" Assumptions	1. Earnings per share 2. Market share 3. Resource advantage 4. Personal promotions	1. Value to customers, employees, and owners 2. Customer loyalty 3. Core skill advantage 4. Personal growth
	Always make the numbers	Satisfy customers and workers
Leadership Philosophy	1. Strategy driven 2. Decide, delegate, monitor, and review 3. Spend time on important matters 4. Leverages his/her time	1. Aspiration driven 2. Do real work 3. Spend time on what matters to people 4. Expand leadership capacity
	A few good men will get it done for me	I must get the best out of all my people
Sources of productivity and innovation	1. Investment turnover 2. Superior technology 3. Process control 4. Leverage the people	1. Productivity 2. People superiority 3. Process innovation 4. Develop the people
	People = exploitable resource	People = critical resource
Accountability Measures	1. Comprehensive measures across all areas 2. Clear individual accountability	1. A few key measures in the most critical areas 2. Individual and mutual accountability
	I hold you accountable	We hold ourselves accountable

TABLE 7.1 (*continued*)

Key issues	Traditional good manager view	Emerging real change leader view
Risk/reward trade-off	1. Avoid failure and mistake at all cost 2. Rely on proven approaches 3. Limit career risks 4. Analyze until sure I cannot afford to fail—or to leave	1. Expect, learn from, and build on "failures" 2. Try whatever appears promising 3. Take career risks 4. If in doubt, try and see I can work here—or elsewhere

Managerial Implication

The model of real change leader has two significant learnings for practicing managers, particularly for managers engaged in leadership and management development. Firstly, we must note that the traditional style of leadership howsoever ideal it may appear will not match the requirement of managing uncertainties and handling challenges of change. This is because managing a relatively stable and predictable situation is totally different from that of managing volatile situations like change. Secondly, organizations must identify a selective group of managers who can be exposed to the tactics and behavioural characteristics of change management in the lines of real change leadership profile.

NURTURANT TASK LEADER

There are many leadership styles: participative, authoritarian, democratic, consultative, situational etc. There are also some divergent views about effectiveness of each of these styles. However, all the theorists and experts of leadership agree on one aspect that leadership style must be compatible with operating culture of organization/society for effectiveness. This common agreement adds complexity to this issue because of two reasons: firstly, we must understand the organizational culture in order to adopt appropriate leadership style and secondly, there may be divergence of culture that require leadership with combination of styles like participative cum authoritative or participative cum situational. Realizing the importance of such divergent leadership style, Dr. Jai B.P. Sinha proposed a style called Nurturant Task Leader (NTL) fitting to the dominant work culture prevalent in most of the organizations in India. He published a paper titled "The Nurturant Task Leader" in *ASCI Journal of Management* in 1979 explaining this model in detail. The salient features of NTL are:

1. Two styles are in-built in NTL as the title suggests. *One is task-oriented,* i.e. leader structures his as well as that of his/her subordinates' roles clearly so that communications are explicit structured and task relevant. He/she initiates, guides and directs the subordinates to work hard so as to maintain the high level of productivity. Responsibilities are pinpointed and areas of decision-making are synchronized with them. The leader thus creates a climate of purposiveness and goal orientation. *The second is nurturance.* He/she cares for the subordinates, shows affection, takes personal interest in their well-being and above all, is committed to their growth. He/she makes them realize that they can grow up through task accomplishment and by cultivating better skills and job commitment. The leader's warmth helps create a climate of trust

and understanding where organizational processes, such as information sharing, decision making, goal setting, monitoring and controlling are graduated with the level of maturity and preparedness shown by subordinates.

2. Two experiments conducted on NTL in Indian organizations shown that NTL is a meaningful and effective cluster of leadership behaviours. This leadership style also proved to be more effective than participative and authoritarian styles. Though, there are some overlaps between NTL and other styles like participative, authoritarian, this is distinctly different from these. In other words, the behavioural characteristics of task orientation are not same as that of task orientation and nurturant is not similar to that of nurturance.

Managerial Implication

NTL model generated great interest among academicians as well as practitioners because of its realistic and down-to-earth approach. This was the first model that focused on a cluster of leadership behaviours instead of unidimensional behaviours seen in other leadership styles. The essence of the model is that there will be different people with different intellect and a mixed work culture in organization which inturn may require a mixed leadership. Finally, it is a significant learning to all the managers that they need to exhibit divergent leadership behaviours to motivate the subordinates. Surely, it is a practitioner's model of leadership.

THE ONE MINUTE MANAGER

Kenneth Blanchard and Spencer Johnson have developed the highly popular One Minute Manager model. This technique was popularized through their book published in 1983 titled *The One Minute Manager.* The book argues that managers are neither fundamentally democratic nor autocratic. Therefore, they are neither exclusively interested in people nor in results. Based on this powerful assumption, the authors advocate a balanced approach with the combination of both these worlds. Much of their book deals with the role of the manager as a teacher of employee or manager behaviour. The one minute goal setting, one minute praising and one minute reprimand are all aimed at providing psychologically effective ways of motivating people through positive reinforcements and information feedback. The One Minute Manager's Game Plan is illustrated in Figure 7.1.

Managerial Implication

The One Minute Manager model is highly pragmatic and has a balanced approach in itself. The model advocates both reward and punishment methods in motivating and leading the employees to achieve goals. It rightly emphasizes that it is the situation that prescribes what kind of leadership style is appropriate and therefore leadership effectiveness is not dependent upon the style alone but on style-situation combination. Further, the richness of the model lies in its practical tips and its simplicity in capturing the hard realities of complex nature. The model is useful to all the managers in enhancing their leadership effectiveness.

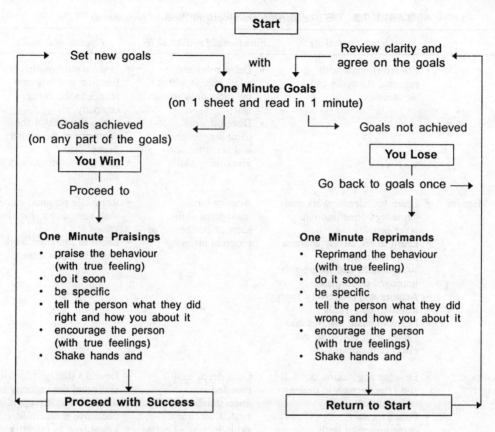

FIGURE 7.1 The one minute manager's "Game Plan".

GE's LEADERSHIP DEVELOPMENT PIPELINE

GE has an effective leadership strategy called Leadership Development Pipeline to groom managers in-house. This strategy distinguishes GE from other global corporations in terms of management development. This globally famous strategy consists of five important stages that transform an individual employee to an enterprise manager as indicated in Table 7.2. It typically starts equipping an employee (i) from managing oneself to managing others, (ii) from managing others to managing managers, (iii) to become a functional manager, (iv) to emerge as a general manager and (v) business manager. Each of these stages requires a manager to learn new skills, widen the perspective and learn to manage the things in new ways.

TABLE 7.2   GE's Leadership Development Pipeline

	Interpersonal skills	*Functional/Product skills*	*Operational skills*
Individual contributor	• Build effective communication and relationship skills	• Develop specific functional skills	• Synthesize personal values with organizational value system

TABLE 7.2   GE's Leadership Development Pipeline (*continued*)

	Interpersonal skills	Functional/Product skills	Operational skills
	• Effectively deal with personal strengths and weaknesses	• Learn roles and relationships within the functional/product unit • Develop work planning, program and performance assessment skills	• Understand how his/her function and business relates to the entire company • Grasp the role of the company in the global market place • Learn about customers and suppliers
New Manager	• Learn to delegate work and get things done through other people • Learn to effectively appraise the performance of subordinates and secure their improved performance • Acquire and effectively apply team-building skills • Learn to share insights and values with others so that effect is multiplied	• Acquire basic managerial skills, such as budgeting or program planning	• Reconcile personal values with company's shared values • Learn to integrate work of unit with related units
Experienced Manager	• Develop negotiation skills and effectiveness in dealing with conflicts • Gain executive communication skills required for broad-scale communications • Increase ability to deal with ambiguity, paradox and situations where there is not a right answer	• Gain deep, well-rounded understanding of all related functional skills in area of prime assignment	• Develop strategic thinking skills and the capacity to use both inductive and deductive problem-solving • Learn how to effectively implement organizational change • Understand difference between what is best for the customers and what is the easiest for the business • Maximize understanding of global business dynamics and inter-functional relationships
General Manager	• Gain capacity to deal with multiple issues of increasing complexity and ambiguity • Develop a recognition that he/she cannot and should not try to solve all problems personally • Build skill in framing problems for others to solve • Understand how to maximize contributions of individual, team and staff		• Refine broad perspective that extends to the well-being of the entire organization • Sharpen analytical and critical thinking skills for organizational problem solving • Play an active role in the development of the vision for his/her business

TABLE 7.2 GE's Leadership Development Pipeline (*continued*)

	Interpersonal skills	Functional/Product skills	Operational skills
	• Develop an understanding that asking for help is a sign of maturity rather than a weakness • Develop the sensitivity to respond to the needs of others based on limited stimulus or cues		
Business Leader	• Learn to effectively exercise power in making those decisions that only the leader can make • Develop projection and extrapolation skills to deal with situations where he/she has no firsthand knowledge. Develop sensitivity that motivate people to behave as they do		• Develop multifunctional integration skills to manage a business based on profit and loss • Develop and effectively articulate the vision for the business • Develop the capacity to conceive, not just adopt, change • Develop an effective understanding of the dynamics of the industry • Develop a balanced posture between leadership of the business and integration/cooperation among the functions or other business in the company • Develop the capacity to effectively manage community relations

This model is presented with detailed discussion in the book titled, *The Leadership Pipeline: How to Build the Leadership Powered Company* authored by the high powered leadership coaches Ram Charan, Steve Drotter and Jim Noel. All the three of them closely associated with this leadership programme while they were with GE's Crotonville (GE Leadership Institute).

Managerial Implication

Every organization should have its own customized leadership development programme to succeed in enterprise management. In the absence of such a programme, managers tend to learn and seek development through trial & error method which costs organizations dearly. It also reduces leadership and talent vacuum in the company apart from minimizing the dependency on outside expert help. Companies outside search for managers whenever there is an internal scarce will also decline. Further, managers groomed in a particular mode compatible with your company culture, technology and strategy will certainly have no substitutes outside.

ABBOTT LAB'S LEADERSHIP COMPETENCY MODEL

Most of the professionally managed organizations, particularly the global class have kicked off their own tailor made leadership development programmes. Among them, Abbott's leadership competency development model is the most systematically made and executed programme. Employees identified for leadership roles need to acquire six different competencies and they are given extensive training on these competencies using a variety of training tools. These six competencies are broken down into a number of skills. A brief description of this model is given here:

1. *Set vision and strategy.* Leaders must be able to set vision and define strategy for the company. For this to happen, they need to understand the global environment of their industry that include technology, customers, competitors, peers and resources. Based on this environmental scanning, they must build strategies for the company in short, medium and long terms.

2. *Build organization and inspire people.* This involves ability to (i) acquire and develop the talents, skills and abilities needed to achieve organizational goals, (ii) create a committed organization that acts with integrity, (iii) match organizational strengths with business opportunities and (iv) serve as a role model.

3. *Know the business.* This requires (i) understanding Abbott's customers, markets, business operations and emerging issues, (ii) continuously secure and evaluate relevant information, (iii) learn from and build on business experience to produce success and (iv) demonstrate a strong personal capacity for learning new aspects of the business.

4. *Drive for results.* The competency demands ability to (i) collaboratively set realistic, challenging, measurable goals and time-frames, (ii) set short term objectives and drive toward long term goals, (iii) support employees in terms of learning and resources and (iv) evaluate employees' performance in terms of target achievement.

5. *Make the difficult decisions.* This solicits developing skills to (i) demonstrate and willingness to make unpopular decisions, (ii) challenge status-quo, (iii) correctly and timely recognize crisis situations and take corrective action and (iv) make the difficult people decisions when necessary.

6. *Encourage open communication and knowledge sharing.* This deals with abilities such as (i) fostering a work environment of open communication and knowledge sharing, (ii) encouraging and inviting ideas, (iii) encouraging to express divergent views and (iv) proactively seek and give feedback, both critical and positive.

Managerial Implication

The above model helps practising managers in different ways. Firstly, it provides a practical framework of how and what a leadership development programme should consist of. Secondly, it drives home a major point that tailormade leadership development programme could be more beneficial and fulfilling in comparison to general leadership development programmes. HR managers can adopt this time-tested model in designing their own leadership programmes suiting to the requirement of their organizations.

SMITHKLINE BEECHAM'S 21 LEADERSHIP COMPETENCIES

The crux of developing a leadership programme depends upon the clarity, relevance, depth, coherence and comprehensiveness of the competency description. The drawback with most of the leadership development programmes is that either they are fragmented or too general in nature while others are just classroom based. Leadership development of this nature will not yield any results to the organization and in fact they contribute towards erosion of credibility of such programmes. Therefore, leadership trainers, managers and consultants must realize that developing a leadership development programme involves deep study of all the related issues, most importantly the competency description. This is highly critical activity. SmithKline Beecheam is one organization, which had developed twenty one leadership competencies based on indepth study for grooming their managers as world-class leaders. These are:

1. *Think strategically*—ability to identify the critical, high pay-off strategies and prioritize team efforts accordingly

2. *Innovate*—ability to generate new ideas and go beyond status-quo

3. *Champion of change*—ability to initiate and act as a catalyst of change

4. *Establish plans*—ability to develop common vision and plans for short, medium and long terms

5. *Manage execution*—ability to empower others, coordinate and monitor progress

6. *Influence others*—This includes assertiveness, capability to mobilize and gain commitment

7. *Drive for results*—This includes persistence, focusing and result oriented approach

8. *Improve systems and processes*—ability to identify, analyze and continuously improve the systems and processes to accomplish the work

9. *Commitment to quality*—ability to set standards in quality and oversees its implementation

10. *Focus on customer needs*—ability to continuously search for new ideas to delight the customers

11. *Foster enthusiasm and teamwork*—ability to build teams and set objectives flowing from that of organization's

12. *Reward and celebrate achievement*—ability to use rewards to inspire people and recognizing rightly the contributions of employees

13. *Attract and develop talent*—This involve dual capability of attracting high calibre employees and molding them to organizational needs

14. *Build relationships*—ability to create a conducive environment for people and maintains longlasting relationships

15. *Lead courageously*—ability to take unpopular decisions and lead the organization in difficult times

16. *Foster open communication*—ability to use right communication channels for right context and ensuring a smooth communication

17. *Act with integrity*—This involves demonstrating principled leadership and sound business ethics

18. *Use sound judgement*—ability to take timely decisions and even during uncertain conditions

19. *Convey information*—ability to get one's point across with all rationality, firmness and in a convincing manner

20. *Adapt and develop oneself*—ability to continuously learn, update and adapt oneself to the situational requirement

21. *Know the organization and the business*—This involves understanding the organization's business, vision, mission, technology, markets, global trends and developments that affect the business.

These 21 competencies in turn are classified into 6 dimensions such as: Innovation (1, 2, 3), Performance (4 to 7), Customer (8, 9, 10), People (11 to 14), Integrity (15 to 17) and Personal effectiveness (18 to 21).

Managerial Implication

The above model helps practising managers, particularly those involved in leadership development efforts significantly. Firstly, these 21 competencies provide a comprehensive perspective of competencies involved in leadership development. Secondly, these competencies are described in operational terms that enable managers to relate their organizational context and requirements. Especially, the characteristic indices used in developing 6 major competencies can be a valuable leadership lesson and guidance for all those interested to launch their own leadership development programmes of world standard.

MOTOROLA'S GOLD

All global giants not only have realized the importance of building able leadership internally but have also developed company-specific leadership development programmes. Among them, the critically acclaimed, well-conceived and implemented leadership programme is Motorola's Global Organizational Leadership Development Programme (GOLD). This is regarded as best-in-class successful leadership development initiative. The uniqueness of this programme is its deviation from traditional method of leadership development. Some of the world-respected experts are involved in design and implementation of this programme. Dr. Marguerite Foxon, senior performance improvement specialist at Motorola University is the lead designer of the GOLD programme. The programme consists of (i) a comprehensive set of leadership development assessment tools, (ii) technology to administer the tools on a global basis and (iii) highly focused and individualized development strategies. GOLD is developed based on the Motorola's strategic direction and the most pressing problems a manager would likely face.

The salient features of this model are:

1. Implementation of managerial assessment programme consisting web-based assessment integrator developed by Aon consulting group.

2. Emphasis on three critical dimensions: (i) global and transformational leadership, (ii) leading and managing change, (iii) internal culture change.

3. Application of action learning in the GOLD process. The business changes are designed to apply learning to on the job assignments and project works. Action learning projects are provided in detail.

4. Use of a data base model called GOLD miner. The GOLD miner database is both a database of GOLD alumni and a leadership development tracking system.

5. Adoption of a Multi-level evaluation method to assess the efficacy. The different types of evaluation include: (i) during and post-training evaluation, (ii) transfer evaluation and (iii) impact evaluation.

6. Collection, analysis and action on instant feedback of participants. During the currency of training sessions by each instructor, participants provide the feedback of strengths and weaknesses. This data is promptly used to make changes to gain real time benefits

Managerial Implication

Using GOLD strategy, Motorola has overcome its leadership crisis. This initiative also generated lot of interest among multinationals. Its success inspired many to launch similar initiatives in their companies. The model serves as a basis to HR managers or to whosoever intends to design and pursue the leadership development initiatives in their organizations. GOLD is the classic example of how leaders could be made. The secret behind its success is its globally administrable assessment techniques and multi-level evaluation of GOLD process that includes pre, present and post process evaluation measures.

SKILLED INCOMPETENCE OF LEADERS

The incidents of leaders suffering from incompetence due to inadequacy of certain skills are not uncommon in our organizations. But competent leaders do suffer despite their skills is a new perspective presented by Chris Argyris in his classic writing titled, "A Leadership Dilemma: Skilled Incompetence" published in *Business and Economics Review* in 1987. He argues that many times the skills leaders possess are factors that make them incompetent. Because they produce outcomes through their actions which are not intended to. For example:

1. Key leaders in an organization agree with their CEO that they must develop a vision and make some strategic decisions. They hold several meetings. Unfortunately, the meetings ended up in no agreement and no choice. They are a group of executives who are at the top; who respect each other; who are highly committed; and who agree that developing a viable vision and strategy is long overdue. Yet, whenever they meet, they repeatedly fail to create the vision and the strategy they desire. The reason is that all of them have strong egos. These egos are essential for leaders to be effective but the same are inhibitors because they are hurdles to make even functional compromises. This rigidity fuelled by ego prevents them from thinking about changing their behaviour, because it understandably makes little sense for them to undergo some kind of therapy. In other words, this may inhibit learning, while at the same time, it may over protect the executives. This is typical of skilled incompetence.

2. Many skilled executives act in a way that they believe will lead to productive consequences. They send mixed messages. They keep communicating. They

communicate in such a way that appears meaningful and fruitful but can be escaped when there is failure in its implementation. For example, communicating subordinates *be innovative and take risks, but be careful.* Though the receiver precisely understands its ambiguity, he or she will be discouraged to seek its interpretation by labelling the same as a sign of immaturity or inexperience. In order to send such mixed messages, a leader has to be skilled but tragedy is that it makes him/her incompetent.

Managerial Implication

HR managers must look for such instances and people with skilled incompetence in their organizations. They must play a facilitator role in highlighting such maladies, their adverse impact and generate awareness about need to handle it. They also must develop remedies and programmes to thwart such dysfunctional behaviour. If neglected, the skilled incompetence may become a norm of the organization and may spread to all levels across the organization. Therefore, watch for it!

Chapter 8

Team Management

In the knowledge-based society, tasks have become more interdependent than ever. Team working is the right strategy to execute these interdependent tasks. Team, though as old as any other HRM practice, the mixed results it delivered has become a potential deterrent for its widespread adoption in the organizational working and many managers are overcautious with the implemen-tation of team structures. However, experiences and research studies have consistently high-lighted that teams failed to deliver results wherever they are dealt wrongly, especially in their formation and development stage. Therefore, understanding these difficulties and mastering their solutions should be the primary responsibility of all HR professionals.

In order to equip them with such knowledge and skills, this chapter presents ten pragmatic classics. These classics offer valuable inputs such as: (i) how to build teams, (ii) how to manage transition to self-directed teams successfully, (iii) common problems teams face in their working, (iv) solutions to overcome such problems, (v) the characteristics of best teams, (vi) tips in team training, (vii) virtual teams working and (viii) best practices in team building etc.

TEN STEP MODEL TO BUILD TEAMS

Despite favourable evidence and successful track record of teams in practice, a few failures have dominated the option of using teams in organizations. Often, the reasons cited for a team's ineffectiveness are: (i) intra- and inter-team power dynamics, (ii) unequal knowledge/skill levels among team members, (iii) difficulties in setting off past practices, (iv) 'teething' problems during formation stage of teams and (v) difficulties in committing one's individuality for the team's achievements.

Some of these problems are formidable and realistic in nature. There is an effective training model, also called as 10 steps model that followed in GE for building teams and proven to overcome the team related problems. Paul Brauchle and David Wright who studied this model in action have reported it in their paper titled, "Training Work Teams" published in *Training and Development* in 1993. The salient features of this model (10 steps) are given in Table 8.1.

TABLE 8.1

Step	Methods of training	Summary
1.	Establish credibility	The trainers must first establish their knowledge and believability
2.	Allow ventilation	The trainers must have their anxieties and unresolved issues cleared before starting

TABLE 8.1 (*continued*)

Step	Methods of training	Summary
3.	Provide an orientation	The trainers should give specific verbal directions and provide clear expectations and models of behaviour
4.	Invest in the process	Early on, have the team identify its problems and concerns
5.	Set group goals	The trainees create, through consensus, their own mission statement and then set goals and specific activities and behaviours to accomplish these goals
6.	Facilitate the group process	The trainees are taught about how groups function, and are imparted techniques such as nominal grouping and paired comparison
7.	Establish intragroup procedures	This involves setting up a meeting format that might include reporting minutes, making announcements, discussing problems and issues, proposing solutions, taking action, and making new assignments
8.	Establish intergroup processes	Although the team is self-managed, leaders must be selected in order to interact with others, such as supervisors, managers and other teams
9.	Change the role of trainers	As the team becomes more experienced and empowered, the trainers take on a more passive role
10.	End the trainers' involvement	At this point, the team is on its own and is self-managing

Implementation of this model in GE resulted in formation of teams of dedicated people and increased productivity and contributed for harmonious relations at work place.

Managerial Implication

The cursory study of teams in organizations provides us with answer as to why teams succeed or fail and under what circumstances these happen. One striking thing that often surface is that teams will fail when adequate preparation in formation of teams is absent. Teams also fail when objectives are unclear. The 10-step model resolves both these issues in a highly pragmatic way. There is a high probability of success when a systematic approach like GE model is followed in preparing teams. Therefore, study, analyze and adopt the model for building teams in your organization.

FOUR STAGE MODEL OF GROUP DEVELOPMENT

Both formal and informal groups play important roles in functioning of organizations. In recent years the importance has further grown due to the interdependence of work and emphasis on teamwork. Therefore, understanding how groups form, develop, perform and wind up is helpful in many ways. B.W. Tuckman has presented a four stage model that explain group development in organizations in his paper titled "Developmental Sequences in Small Groups" published in *Psychological Bulletin* in 1965. These four stages are:

- Stage-I: *Forming.* This is an exploration stage. Members try to acquaint each other, share information, and explore commonalities. There will be uncertainty about the goal of the group, how to proceed, functioning of the group and what is appropriate and inappropriate for the group etc. There will also be some kind of leadership biddings and inquisitiveness to discover about the other person.

- Stage-II: *Storming*. The second stage is characterized by intragroup conflict. Every member tries to secure a position or a place in the group. Some try to lead and influence the group and as seen in the first stage, leadership battle also hots up. In this stage, they come out openly with their views and opinions on various issues that include roles of group members and group norms. At the end of this stage, there will be some amount of certainty and clarity about roles, issues and norms of group working.

- Stage-III: *Norming*. In this stage, group norms will be formed clearly and relationships among group members get solidified. There will be unity of purpose and binding of norms among members. Cohesiveness is the chief characteristic of the group here.

- Stage-IV: *Performing*. Group gets functional in this stage. Members perform roles agreed upon and that fit them. They put efforts to achieve the goals of the group as planned. They leverage each other's strengths and specializations to complete the task.

Managerial Implication

The author of the model also agree that groups do not necessarily develop in the fashion the model presented all the times and in all the situations. Groups may start developing from storming stage skipping forming stage or may jump from stage 1 to 3 likewise. However, this model is highly helpful to practising managers in gaining the perspective of group development and dynamics. The understanding of Tuckman's model makes manager's job easy in forming and cultivating the groups with success.

FIVE STAGE MODEL FOR TRANSITION TO SELF-DIRECTED TEAMS

It takes several months of sustained efforts to transform groups of employees into matured self-directed teams. The absolute commitment of management is a prerequisite element in this effort. Further, there will be stiff resistance from employees since the transformation to team working demands change in their working pattern and solicits new skills that include (i) technical, (ii) administrative and (iii) interpersonal skills. The transition to team working is an ongoing process and employees may have to undergo various phases of development before they become real team members. The self-managing team specialists, Jack Orsburn, Linda Moran, Ed. Musselwhite and John Zenger through years of their experience with teams mapped a five stage model for transition of groups into perfect self-directed teams in their book titled *Self-Directed Work Teams: The New American Challenge* published in 1990. These five stages are:

- Stage-I: *Start-up*. The dominant feature of start-up is intensive training for all involved. Team members learn the ABCs of communication and group dynamics, begin using administrative procedures, and expand their repertoire of technical skills. Supervisors who may see themselves as having the most to lose, also receive focused training and they must be encouraged to do their best to facilitate rather than control, the operational and decision making efforts of the teams.

- Stage-II: *State of confusion*. After the initial enthusiasm, a period of confusion is predictable, normal and perhaps necessary. With the supervisor fading as a clear authority figure, now teams often have difficulty in reaching cooperative decisions. Some teams fret about higher work standards or wait sullenly for hypothetical disasters. It is also the time for non-team members to express their opposition to team working openly and unions may spread adverse campaign.

- Stage-III: *Leader-centered teams.* Positive signs will appear if managers continue to demonstrate their faith in the ability of teams to manage themselves. Generally, one team member steps forward as the primary source of direction and information within each team. Now, the chief danger for teams at this stage is, becoming too reliant on its internal leader. So, to make sure everyone continues to learn and eventually exercise leadership skills, teams often rotate the leadership role or allow anyone to exercise leadership functions as needed.

- Stage-IV: *Tightly formed teams.* At this stage, teams manage their own scheduling, clearly express their needs, and meet challenging goals with limited resources. The significant phenomenon of teams in this stage is that they become extremely defensive if the organisation fails to meet their needs for information or resources. There will be inter-team conflicts and this results in enhancing productivity of teams as well as over zealous teams withholding information and assistance in order to undermine the efforts of other teams. At this point, managers must refocus the teams on cross team and organisation wide goals, often through councils of elected team members who review issues of mutual concern.

- Stage-V: *Self-directed teams.* After the fire storm of narrow loyalties comes the period of true self-direction. Mature teams develop a powerful commitment to achieving corporate and team goals, even if those goals require reconfiguration of the teams themselves. Teams have now learned to think for themselves about strategically vital information, so they need to understand the rationale behind important management decisions. Further, to maintain the competitive advantage of multilevel involvement, managers must continuously seek new ways to foster commitment, trust, and responsible involvement of team members. The system does not evolve into a perpetual motion machine. It must be constantly energized with training and information.

Managerial Implication

The model provides a practical glimpse of building self-directed teams. People who dealt with teams know that it is often a difficult and frustrating experience. However, the benefits teams offer relieves all these difficulties and tensions. An important aspect all of us must note is that successful teams are the outcome of persisting and enduring efforts of all: the managers, employees and facilitators of such teams. The failures are certain if anybody expects great results overnight or lacks in their commitment and conviction. Therefore, first question is whether your organization is willing to put that much of hard work through these five stages to reach the dream of self-directed team?

NUTS AND BOLTS MODEL FOR BUILDING SELF-MANAGED WORK TEAMS

Every manager and every organization wants to build self-managed work teams with a belief that they facilitate organizational effectiveness and some feel it is just the right thing to do since the successful organizations reported to have done the same. However, many of them are not quite clear to the extent (i) how to build these teams, (ii) under what conditions the teams can thrive and (iii) what these teams can offer in terms of organizational achievement. Therefore, managers must first create a clear mental map with regard to what, why and how of creating self-managed work teams in organizations. In this endeavour, Graham Wilson's eight essential steps that facilitate envisioning the future with teams illustrated in his famous book titled *Self Managed Team Working* published in 1995 will be immensely useful. These steps can work as nuts and bolts for building the teams, which organizations generally miss. These are:

1. *Extent.* The questions one has to answer include: (i) are there any areas that would not be suitable for SMWTs?, (ii) will the development occur equally on all sites? (iii) whether you need to add or cut manpower strength due to introduction of SMWTs? and (iv) what parts of the organization need to reorient to match the team working?

2. *Structure.* Here they include: (i) what kind of organizational structure is required for shifting to team based working?, (ii) are some functional areas likely to remain same? do certain customer groups demand sufficiently different services that the SMWT could operate autonomously?

3. *Activities.* You can identify a number of activities, which at present are carried out by a supervisor, foreman or manager and question how these can be handled by SMWTs. There may be some commercial constraints with existing customers, which require certain activities to be carried out by certain individuals.

4. *Reward and recognition.* Identify some of the changes which you think need to be made to the reward and recognition systems that you have in place. For example, you may have to give a greater incentive to the people involved in SMWTs in the form of short-term rewards which were not needed in the past.

5. *Product development.* Think about the product development process. What currently happens, and how do you think it will be affected by SMWTs? The evidence is that, once these teams become established, they have a great deal to contribute in the area of new product development.

6. *Training and development.* Think carefully of the skills you will need for SMWTs to be effective. You may feel that you have to launch a training process before SMWTs can be introduced. How to launch a training process? How many hours per employee? Who will provide the training? What will be the impact on budget? How to measure training utility? These are some important questions that need to be answered.

7. *Measures.* Try listing some of the success factors, which you will use to measure progress. How you will know that the SMWTs are succeeding?

8. *Social arrangements.* You are about to change the relationship between managers and other employees. One of the more tangible examples of an *us* and *them* culture is where frontline employees do not share social facilities with managers. Take an objective and look at your own organization. What sort of facilities does staff have? Who owns them? Who participate in them? Will any of these arrangements need changing or opening up?

Managerial Implication

The above eight steps are of hardcore practical tips to all those managers who intended to install self-managed work teams in their organizations. Wherever self-managed teams had failed, they failed only because of lack of proper preparation on the part of managers and certainly not due to the teams themselves. The preparation for shifting self-managed work teams involves very detailed, careful and incisive preparation. The above steps help managers as provocating guidelines to work on the relevant issues well in advance and this preparation facilitates success with SMWTs.

WHY TEAMS DON'T WORK: PROBLEMS, SYMPTOMS AND SOLUTIONS

People who know life in organization are also very familiar with the fact that anything that gives remarkable business results also poses remarkable challenges. Teams are no exception to it. Teams well conceived, developed and managed could provide organizations with real competitive advantage and put organizations in deep trouble if poorly organized. It is also a fact that all team-building efforts face formidable challenges at one stage or the other but it is the commitment and capability of the managers that make the teams to break through these hurdles of challenge. Harvey Robbins and Michael Finley developed a list of typical problems the teams encounter along with their symptoms and solutions based on their years of research on teams across the world and detailed them in their book titled *Why Teams Don't Work: What Went Wrong and How to Make it Right* published in 1997. These are briefly described in Table 8.2.

TABLE 8.2

Problem	Symptom	Solution
Mismatched needs	People with private agendas working at cross purposes	Get hidden agendas on the table by asking what people want, personally, from teaming
Confused goals, Cluttered objectives	People don't know what they're supposed to do or it makes no sense	Clarify the reason the team exists; define its purpose and expected outcomes
Unresolved roles	Team members are uncertain what their job is	Inform team members what is expected of them
Bad decision making	Teams may be making the right decisions, but the wrong way	Choose a decision making approach appropriate to each decision
Bad policies, Stupid procedures	Team is at the mercy of an employee handbook from hell	Throw away the book and start making sense
Personality conflicts	Team members do not get along	Learn what team members expect and want from one another, what they prefer, how they differ, start valuing and using differences
Bad leadership	Leadership is tentative, inconsistent, or stupid	The leader must learn to serve the team and keep its vision alive or leave leadership to someone else
Bleary vision	Leadership has foisted a bill of goods on the team	Get a better vision or go away

TABLE 8.2 (*continued*)

Problem	Symptom	Solution
Anti-team culture	The organization is not really committed to the idea of teams	Team for the right reasons or don't have team at all; never force people onto a team
Insufficient feedback and information	Performance is not being measured; team members are groping in the dark	Create system of free flow of useful information to and from all team members
Ill-conceived reward systems	People are being rewarded for wrong things	Design rewards that make teams feel safe doing their job; reward teaming as well as individuals behaviours
Lack of team trust	The team is not a team because members are unable to commit to it	Stop being untrustworthy, or disband or reform the team
Unwillingness to change	The team knows what to do but will not do it	Find out what the blockage is; use explosive or lubricant to clear it
The wrong tools	The team has been sent to do battle with a slingshot	Equip the team with the right tools for its tasks, or allow freedom to be creative

Managerial Implication

The above description of problems and solutions equips practising managers with valuable knowledge and tools. Firstly, it enables the team managers and facilitators to anticipate the kind of problems teams, team members and organizations could face. Therefore, team initiators in organizations need not worry when they come across such situations. In fact, they can equip themselves to face them without fear, or could initiate proactive measures to avert them. Secondly, the solutions help managers to build counter strategies to manage the challenges.

TEN PRINCIPLES OF GREAT GROUPS

Often, we forget that great achievements were possible only because of group effectiveness and sum of their performance. We tend to believe and ascribe the exaggerated credits to individuals that create an image of super human beings out of them. The fact, remain is that in the past, present and possibly in the future, individual entities can not equal the group performance and achievement. It has been seen that whenever leadership succeeded, it was largely due to quality and commitment of the group he/she was leading than the effectiveness of that person alone. But thats what makes groups so great. All great groups have something in common. The intellectual visionary Professor Warren Bennis, who studied the groups working in great depths, reported that all great groups observe 10 principles and apply them as well to their larger organizations. These are:

1. *At the heart of every great group is a shared dream.* All great groups believe that they are on a mission from God, that they can change the world, make a dent in the universe

2. *They manage conflict by abandoning individual egos in the pursuit of the dream.* Conflicts are natural when diverse people work together. This is resolved by reminding people of the mission

3. *They are protected from the suits.* All great groups seem to have disdain for their corporate overseers and all are protected from them by a leader—not necessarily the leader who defines the dream

4. *They have a real or invented enemy.* Even the most noble mission can be helped by an onerous opponent. Most organizations have an implicit mission to destroy an adversary, and that is often more motivating than their explicit mission

5. *They view themselves as winning underdogs.* World-changing groups do not regard the mainstream as the sacred Ganges. The sense of operating on the fringes gives them a don't-count-me-out scrappiness that feeds their obsession

6. *Members pay a personal price.* Membership in a great group is not a day job; it is a night and day job. Emotional and family disturbances are typical when a project ends

7. *Great groups make strong leaders.* On the one hand, they are all non-hierarchical, open and very egalitarian. Yet they all have strong leaders. You cannot have a great leader without a great group and vice versa

8. *Great groups are the product of meticulous recruiting.* They can recruit right people and place them on right jobs, and get the right constellations and configurations within the group

9. *Great groups are usually young.* Great groups are young in chronological age. Great groups don't know what's supposed to be impossible. That gives them the ability to do the impossible

10. *Real artists ship.* In the end, great groups have to produce a tangible outcome external to themselves. Most dissolve after the product is delivered; but without something to show for their efforts, the most talented assemblage becomes little more than a social club or a therapy group.

Managerial Implication

The above ten principles were not created out of pure academic work, nor are they conceptual. The ten principles came out of insightful observations of Prof. Bennis while studying the groups at world class organizations like Apple Computer, Xerox's Palo Alto Research Centre etc. in action. HR managers with the collaboration of line managers must make concerted efforts to build teams in the line of above ten principles. It may be a difficult task for some organizations but valuable returns can accrue only out of such efforts.

SEVEN BEST PRACTICES OF VIRTUAL TEAMS

The concept of team has undergone a revolutionary change with the advent of virtual teaming. The credit for popularizing the use of virtual teams goes to two leading management consultants namely Jon Katzenbach and Douglas Smith whose publications include *The Wisdom of Teams* and the latest *The Discipline of Teams*. They had shown how people working in different countries, having different cultural and technical settings and with different skill profiles can collaborate to build and innovate products with least physical dislocation. In the process, they redefined the teamwork as something beyond engendering a feeling of togetherness and a supportive emotional mechanism to a collaborative effort to create a new wisdom. Through the years of research, practice and consultancy, they have indicated seven practices that fuels virtual teams to excel. These are:

1. *Convene a face to face meeting early on.* Get your group members together physically to establish group performance purpose and goals, practical working approach, ground rules, apart from getting to know each other

2. *Make conscious choices about disciplines.* Divide tasks and goals into two buckets: individual versus collective work products. If most results imply collective work products, apply the team discipline and individual effort if it can be done by a single person

3. *Match member skills and perspectives to collective work products.* Assign task and leadership roles in ways that take full advantage of the different skills, experiences and perspectives in the group

4. *Hold face-to-face sessions as often as needed.* Convene face-to-face meetings strictly on need base, such as to share critical information or to solve problems.

5. *Consciously shift and share leadership roles.* Virtual work requires more leadership attention. Group should self-consciously divide up and assign different leadership roles. There were always be roles of facilitator, note keeper, and discussion leader.

6. *Pick and practice groupware features together.* It is wise for all members to participate in choosing the groupware to be used. It is also critical for members to immediately put them in practice.

7. *Agree on your own netiquette.* Virtual teams must self-consciously discuss and choose how they expect to apply technology to their advantage. The more explicit you can be about your netiquette, the more likely it is that your electronic networking will enable rather than confuse the virtual interactions.

Managerial Implication

With the increased geographical spread of operations, every company one day or the other will have to introduce virtual teams. The advantages with such kind of teaming may includes (i) speed of innovations/project execution/problem solving, (ii) assimilation of technical brilliance, (iii) decreased cost of team working and (iv) opportunity to involve people from across the globe. HR managers must note a point that virtual teams are relevant to companies even working in the same city/location and not necessarily to only a globalized company.

TEN COMMANDMENTS OF TEAM LEADERSHIP

Teams are omnipresent, at least in knowledge driven organizations. Team effectiveness depends on quite a few elements. Among them, very important is team leadership. In fact, the success of team working goes to a considerable extent to its leader's behaviour. If it so, how a team leader should conduct the team business? Team specialist, Kenneth Hultman prescribed 10 commandments adherence to which assures effective team management in his paper tiled "It's A Team Effort" published in *Training and Development* in 1998. These are:

1. *Don't stray from your mission and vision.* Mission and vision are crucial to team

effectiveness. Teams can lose sight of the big picture and get lost in details as pressure increases to get results. When that happens, it's important to remind team members of their mission and vision

2. *Don't allow self-interest to prevail over mutual interest.* A team can outperform individuals working alone, but only if members suspend self-interest in favour of mutual interest. Some people have trouble working in teams because they're unwilling to share responsibility or unable to adjust to interdependence environment. One way a leader can deal with that is to make teamwork a criterion for satisfactory performance

3. *Don't tolerate unacceptable behaviour.* Behaviour is so crucial to team success or failure that a willingness to abide by agreed upon values and norms should be a qualification for membership. A leader who champions positive behaviour gains respect; a leader who ignores negative behaviour loses it

4. *Don't allow fear to control team behaviour.* Fear operates as an invisible barrier between people and keeps them from developing effective work relationships. A leader can help team members neutralize their fear by championing such norms as honouring confidentiality, encouraging risk taking, agreeing to disagree without taking it personally and treating each other with respect

5. *Don't allow cliques to control team dynamics.* Cliques tend to compete with each other and exhibit self-interest over mutual interest. A team member should inform team members that cooperation is expected. A leader should convey that identifying and resolving a clique difference is non negotiable

6. *Don't shy away from conflict.* A leader shouldn't be afraid of conflict as cohesiveness cannot emerge without it. A team must learn that it can handle conflict, otherwise the members will never fully trust each other. Rather than avoid conflict, team members should resolve or manage it

7. *Don't accept lack of trust as an excuse.* When trust issue surface, the leader should insist that team members face them head-on and never accept mistrust as a reason for lack of cooperation. It's much easier to build and maintain trust than to lose and try to rebuild it

8. *Don't let people to play it safe.* Even if a team establishes a norm for risk taking initially but they may gradually revert to old style. Typically, thus happens when people get caught up in work demands, and it is safer to be less open. To maintain more openness, a team leader must model risk taking and reward risk takers

9. *Don't be stingy with information.* Sharing relevant and timely information should be high on any list of team norms. As a rule of thumb, it's usually safer to share too much information than too little

10. *Don't neglect process in a rush to get results.* When under pressure, people tend to forget team norms and use methods they think will get fast results. To prevent this, a leader must remind the team of its norms and stress the importance of abiding by them.

Managerial Implication

Achieving team effectiveness certainly demands a quality team leadership. This quality leadership cannot just happen like that but emerges only as a result of good preparation of employees as team leaders. The above ten commandments can be drawn as a curriculum for team leadership training. Apart from formal training, regular audits must be conducted to assess the team leadership facilitation sourcing the ten commandments as basic parameters.

QUALITY CIRCLES

Quality circle is a form of voluntary participation of employees in decision-making, particularly performance related. A quality circle is a small group consisting of 10 to 12 members who meet voluntarily once in a week to discuss work related issues focusing on improvement. In these meetings not only they identify areas of development, but also their solutions and implementation. Quality circles, though reported to have been invented in United States, became popular in Japan. The Japanese successful experience with quality circles has drawn the attention of many organizations worldwide and most of them have adopted them at their work places. However, the experience of these organizations is a mix of success and failure. Though, quality circles ideally should be successful always given employees capabilities and knowledge to solve day to day shop floor problems, these are not free from failures because of various problems. Two specialists namely Edward Lawler and Susan Mohrman presented the anatomy of quality circles in an authentic way in their paper titled, "Quality Circles After The Fad" published in *Harvard Business Review* in 1985. They identified the phases in formation of quality circles, the activities that each phase comprise and threats to quality circle that emerge at each stage as illustrated in Table 8.3.

TABLE 8.3

Phase	Activity	Destructive forces
1. Start-up	• Publicize • Obtain funds and volunteers • Training	• Low volunteer rate • Inadequate funding • Inability to learn group process and problem solving skills
2. Initial problem solving	• Identify and solve problems	• Disagreement on problems • Lack of knowledge of problems
3. Approval of initial suggestions	• Present and have initial suggestions accepted	• Resistance by staff members and middle management • Poor presentation and suggestions because of limited knowledge
4. Implementation	• Relevant groups act on suggestions	• Prohibitive costs • Resistance by groups that must be implemented
5. Expansion of problem solving	• Form new groups • Old groups continue	• Member–non-member conflict • Raised aspirations • Lack of problems • Expense of parallel organization • Savings not realized • Rewards wanted
6. Decline	• Fewer groups meet	• Cynicism about programme • Burnout

Managerial Implication

Quality circles, if pursued systematically and with perseverance, will not only succeed as a participatory mechanism but also as a formidable problem solving mechanism. HR managers, intending to adopt quality circles in their organizations, must observe the six-phase model presented above and need to be cautious of destructive forces. In any case, adopting quality circle is much easier in comparison to its functional continuance. Undoubtedly, quality circles offer number of benefits if pursued with determination. But do not adopt them for the sake of goodwill or merely for the sake of it.

TIPS AND GUIDELINES ON TEAM TRAINING

Training teams to function efficiently and effectively is a prerequisite in building a team oriented organization. Training teams is often a complex exercise because it involves cross functional training that include technical, behavioural, decision-making, leadership communication. Eduardo Salas et al., provided a comprehensive framework containing ten valuable tips and several guidelines on team training in their paper titled "What We Know about Designing and Delivering Team Training: Tips and Guidelines". These are illustrated in Table 8.4.

TABLE 8.4

Tips	Guidelines
1. It takes more than technical skill to make an effective team.	• Training should foster both individual and team skills. • Team members' knowledge should reach a threshold level before they can go on to acquire teamwork skills. • During team training, individuals should be made aware of the relationship between (1) individual development and team performance and (2) team performance and individual preparation and accomplishment.
2. A complex set of interrelated behaviours, cognitions, and attitudes underlie effective teamwork.	• Team members should learn teamwork skills, such as situation awareness, communication, team leadership, adaptability, and compensatory behaviour. • Team members should learn each other's roles and develop realistic expectations of task performance. • Team members should be made aware of the importance of clear concise communication, including requesting clarification if information is ambiguous. • During team training, members should be urged to make verbal gestures of support to one another. • Team members need motivational guidance; factors that may hinder motivation should be highlighted.
3. All teams are not created equal and therefore instructional strategies may vary.	• Training for transportable competencies must be done at the individual level. • To learn team-contingent or context-driven competencies, teams must receive feedback that facilitates formation of shared expectations of task performance. • To learn task-contingent or context-driven competencies, teams need to be trained as close to the actual environment as possible. • To train task-contingent competencies, simulations of the task environment will be useful, as will cross-training and passive demonstration.

TABLE 8.4 *(continued)*

Tips	*Guidelines*
4. The power of team-based task analysis (behavioural, cognitive) should not be underestimated.	• Begin with a traditional task analysis. • Use subject matter experts and source documents to identify the tasks that need to be coordinated. • Rate tasks that have been deemed to require coordination or interaction. • Begin to articulate the conditions, events, or situations in which coordinated tasks occur. • Identify the competencies needed for coordinated tasks.
5. Training should be designed to facilitate information presentation, demonstration of learned behaviours, guided practice, and constructive feedback.	• A climate of learning may be fostered if participation is encouraged in an uncritical environment. • Where feasible, hands-on guided practice should be provided. • During training, difficult, but achievable goals should be set. • Models and demonstrations of desired behaviours should be provided. • Feedback should be timely, focused on the task (not the person), and constructive. • Advance organizers should be used when possible. • Prepractice briefs help promote shared expectations about training. • Training should include varied practice situations and events to increase transfer and team adaptability.
6. Opportunities for guided, hands-on practice should be built into training.	• Scenarios of different difficulty levels should be used throughout the training program; problems should not have easy solutions or only one answer. • Scenarios should allow members to take different courses of action. • Scenarios should allow participants to exhibit desired behaviours at several times. • Scenarios should be developed with goals for the specific knowledge, behaviours, and attitudes to be exhibited; they should provide opportunities to practice important teamwork competencies. • Events should elicit expected actions to measure the desired skill. • When developing scenarios, small details should be included, such as tools and documentation that would be used in real operations and constraints that would occur in actual operational settings. • Role-plays should provide practice and feedback of specific behaviours; they should be semi-structured. • Each participant should have a role in the role-play. • Guidelines for running the role-play should be provided.
7. The prepractice environment has an effect on trainees.	• Advance organizers may be used before training to help participants develop a basic structure for the information they will learn in the practice environment. • Preparatory information may be given before training to set participants' expectations about the events to occur and their consequences. • The trainer may use prepractice briefs to clarify team performance expectations and set team member roles and responsibilities. This serves to develop shared knowledge and increase coordination. • Participants tend to have higher motivation to learn when mastery goals, rather than performance goals, are set.
8. Training can be delivered through various proven strategies.	• Team coordination training should be used to help team members learn to employ the resources of the entire team effectively, especially in stressful situations.

TABLE 8.4 (*continued*)

Tips	*Guidelines*
	• Team coordination training can be delivered through task simulation, principles, guidelines, information, and demonstration of effective and ineffective behaviours. All methods should be accompanied by feedback. • Cross training should be used when exposure to and practice with other teammates' tasks, roles, and responsibilities is needed. • Cross training can be delivered through lectures, role-plays, or multimedia. • Team self-correction training uses lectures, demonstration, practice, and feedback to teach teams how to debrief. • Event-based training uses trigger events embedded into scenarios to structure team training in complex environments where decision-making and coordination skills need to be practised. The events are based on training objectives.
9. Timely feedback is critical, to allow team members to adjust their knowledge before incorrect behaviours become deeply ingrained.	• Both process and outcome feedback should be delivered. • Feedback should be clear, concise, and constructive (focusing on the task, not the person). • Checklists and benchmarks aid in providing feedback. • Feedback must be given on all important aspects of team functioning. • Feedback should be based on training objectives. • Before practising, the relationship between teamwork processes and the outcomes that will be used as a basis for feedback should be clarified. • Team self-correction techniques can be used as a tool for providing feedback to the team; and peer involvement is important.
10. Team performance measurement is a critical part of a successful team training system.	• Measurement tools should provide trainers with information about the achievement of training objectives. • Observation of team members is inevitable. • Performance should be measured at several points as the team matures. • Measurement should be tied back to team training objectives and debriefings. • Measurement should be done at the team and individual levels. • Shared knowledge should be measured. • Measurement must be diagnostic; both process and outcome measures should be collected. • Team process measures determine how team achieves its objectives; outcome measures determine the effectiveness of the team as a whole in meeting its objectives.

Managerial Implication

The above tips and guidelines contain in them a number of practical suggestions. These are useful to all those involved in team management. HR managers and training specialists can use these tips in their team training programmes. They can also use these inputs to develop a systematic team-training module.

Chapter 9

Employee Communication, Involvement and Empowerment Management

Soft HRM issues such as communication, involvement and empowerment have been dominating the modern people's management since sometime. Many companies and their managers across the globe have realized that real employee commitment could be obtained only through making all sections of employees as partners in organizational functioning and management. This realization gave fillip to introduce a wide range of models to institutionalize the communication, involvement and empowerment practices. Here also, like anywhere else, the models built, developed and implemented on sound fundamentals have succeeded in delivering, great results to the companies in terms of productivity, bottomline and strategic advantage to the organizations. These practices failed to contribute anything worthwhile when pushed in organizations without a clear agenda, purpose and structure.

In the age of outsourcing of pay-roll type functions, HR managers must focus on these issues and attain related skills. Twelve classics in this chapter covers issues such as: (i) basics, (ii) techniques, (iii) models and (iv) best practices in employee communication, involvement and empowerment practices.

SIX-STEP MODEL FOR HR COMMUNICATION

Effectiveness of HRM activities and programmes are dependent upon good communication practice to a large extent. It has been amply demonstrated that communication gaps resulted in failures of some of HR programmes in implementation than due to the deficiencies of these programmes themselves. When there is a miscommunication or no communication or inadequate communi-cation, even a programme that is designed to deliver positive outcomes to employees can back-fire and may simply fail to materialize. Therefore, organizations should develop a communi-cation model that can be catalyst for HR programmes. Such a model must possess six essential features as described below:

- Step-I: *Assess communication needs.* To begin with, we must conduct a systematic study to understand the communication needs of individual employees, groups,

179

departments, situations and organization. Techniques like employee survey, analysis of critical organizational incidents, analysis of various media resources/tools, etc. can be employed in such needs assessment.

- Step-II: *Establish communication goals.* After all, communication is a means to an end. Therefore, clearly identify what should be the goals/objectives of communication. For example, fostering interpersonal relationships in the organization, thereby enhancing the awareness levels of employees on organization related issues can be objectives of a communication policy.

- Step-III: *Translate communication goals into action plans.* It involves identifying target groups, selecting right media tools for right situations, training on written and oral communication skills, monthly communication planner consisting of specific activities, communication bulletins, web-based communication, and informal gatherings.

- Step-IV: *Link communication programmes with critical organizational programmes.* The effectiveness of communication practice can be rightly demonstrated during critical events. For example, during mergers, downsizing or any organizational change programme needs critical support of communication management.

- Step-V: *Define communication limitations.* The law of limitation applies to communication too. Excessive communication may produce counter productive results. Therefore, we must be clear in what is functional communication and dysfunctional communication. In other words, subjects that should be kept confidential from all/ limited communication in terms of people and content must be clearly identified.

- Step-VI: *Evaluation of communication practices.* Communication practices in use must be regularly evaluated to assess their efficacy and limitations. This helps in improving the system in real time. The evaluation methodology and frequency of such assessment must be clearly set.

Managerial Implication

Communication practice is more important to HR manager on account of two major reasons. Firstly, they are responsible for putting in place an effective organizational communication practice. Secondly, such communication is essential for them to communicate their own policies, programmes and actions. Despite its criticality, very few organizations have clearly spelled out policy or model for implementation of communication. The above-described model may be useful to HR managers intending to draft an HR communication programme.

FIVE MODELS OF COMMUNICATION

Communication is a system that can be a bane or boon to organizations. Many factors such as employee grievances, disappointments, interpersonal conflicts, intergroup rivalries, differences between management and their employees and ultimately lack of trust and eroding organizational commitment are attributable to poor management of communication. Communication as the name suggests very sensitive too. There is a problem with every side of it: over communication, no communication, under communication, poor communication—all are potential enough to create misconceptions in organizations. On the other hand, if systematically and aptly managed, communication can be a force of formidable integration. The success with communication can be attained using right model of communication for right context. The models used in practice for communications can be classified into five according D. Fisher who described them in his book titled *Commentaries in Organizations* published in 1993. These are:

1. *One-way model.* This is characterized by speeches, lectures, presentations, written directives, office memos etc. This is often a one-way communication and do not allow any feedback instantly. This is effective for clearly communicating official messages and one's point of view without obstruction. The limitation is that its effectiveness depends upon the receivers' competence to understand the message.

2. *Interaction model.* As the title suggests, it allows simultaneous communication like messenger on the Internet. In other words, it enables both transmission and exchange of messages. This is most effective when the situation demands exchange of views and requires instant feedback. The limitation of the model is that unlike one way communication, persons involved should be physically available at the same time and there is a danger that each individual may feel that he/she has not communicated fully their point of view.

3. *Two-person relationship model.* This model suggests that same issue need to be communicated differently to different persons. For example, a manager communicates same issue to colleagues in a friendly style and to a subordinate in an authoritative way. It implies that our communication is affected by perceptions of equity too. An effective communication is one that reckons these organizational relationships apart from the content of communication.

4. *Communication-in-context model.* This suggests that an effective communication is one which considers (i) the organizational environment, (ii) organizational culture, (iii) understanding of group characteristics to whom the communication is targeted and (iv) communication subject while shaping and delivering the communication. This model is apt for organizational level communication process.

5. *Strategic model.* This model comprises of all the groups: employees, suppliers, and customers. It advocates that objective of every communication in the organization must be to generate goodwill and positive image. Therefore, even a simple one-to-one communication also should not be taken casually since it is potential enough to cause damage to reputation of organization. This objective of goodwill automatically ensures a perfect communication practice.

Managerial Implication

The above models provide the basic impetus for effective communication in organizations. These models have two major managerial implications. Firstly, it helps in creating our communication policy in the organization with the help of five models. For this purpose, managers need to identify the situations in which each of these models fit in. Secondly, it emphasizes that, a combination of methods should be used for communication because a single approach or method falls short in keeping communication system in a perfect shape.

SEVEN PRINCIPLES OF EFFECTIVE LISTENING

Active listening is the most critical element in effective communication practice. The listening can solve many problems and offer many contributions. Listening can enhance the learning opportunities of managers and at the same time can make other person feel adequate. Every manager intending to be effective must spend at least 40 to 50 per cent of the time in listening. However, listening is difficult than speaking. The effective listening could be achieved by following some fundamental principles. Robert Denhardt, Janet Vinzant Denhardt and Maria Aristigueta in their book titled *Managing Human Behaviour* published in 2002 proposed seven essential principles in effective listening as given below:

1. *Have a reason or purpose for listening.* You must be motivated to listen so as to listen most effectively. Having a reason or purpose to listen increases your motivation to listen well. One must be motivated to listen; it does not just happen. Think carefully about why it is important that you listen effectively in a particular situation.

2. *Suspend judgement initially.* Communication can be improved by avoiding our natural tendency to evaluate. We should try to listen with empathetic understanding, that is, understanding with a person rather than about the person. This means seeing the expressed idea and attitude from the other person's point of view, sensing how it feels to the other person, and achieving his or her frame of reference about the subject being discussed.

3. *Resist distractions.* There are many things that can distract us as we try to communicate with others, but those distractions can be resisted. This principle is especially important as people from different cultures and even different countries come together in work situations. Even if every one speaks English, there can be variations in accents and figures of speech that make some speech difficult to follow. In effect, hearing an unfamiliar accent becomes a distraction. Concentrating on what is being said will help to overcome these problems. Therefore, concentration is the key.

4. *Wait before responding.* There is a strong tendency to respond to someone's statement before he or she is finished, especially if you believe that you already have received the gist of the person's message. When you are overly eager to contribute to a conversation, you become so excited about your own anticipated contribution that you turnoff the other person. The response principle suggests that you wait for an appropriate opportunity to respond.

5. *Rephrase what you listen to in your own words.* We occasionally take time to restate or paraphrase what you understand the other person has said before making your own contribution. By restating the other person's comments without evaluation, you almost have to enter into the person's frame of reference and to understand the context of his or her comments.

6. *Seek the important themes.* The principle suggests that listening for the main idea in message is more important than listening for specific facts. Understanding the major themes of the message gives you a framework for organizing the facts, thereby making the facts themselves easier to remember.

7. *Use the thinking-speaking differential.* People think much faster than they speak.

Although the rates vary by region, in an average, people speak at a rate of about 150 words per minute. But they think at a rate of about 500 words a minute, more than three times faster than they speak. This difference can offer a temptation to do things that interfere with effective listening such as day dreaming, thinking about something completely apart from the conversation, and practising your response in advance. But it also can provide an opportunity to listen more effectively as this time can be utilized for reflecting on what the other person is saying.

Managerial Implication

Listening is one of the most influential factor in managerial effectiveness. This can be used to show concern and importance towards employees and their views and can be used as a motivator. With the growing adoption of team working, employee involvement and empowerment initiatives, training on effective listening and building these skills is utmost important. HR managers must accord priority for this.

THIRTEEN BARRIERS TO EFFECTIVE COMMUNICATION

The barriers to effective communication are many and it appears the list is almost endless. Most of these barriers do not block the communication in an organization completely but they damage the quality of communication. The barrier may be due to a manager's reluctance to see other's point of view or junior employees' hesitation to communicate openly or organizational pressure to brush certain things under carpet. All these barriers cause enormous loss to the organization in terms of trust, commitment, dependability, and ultimately productivity. Therefore, HR managers must make conscious efforts to remove communication barriers as much as possible. In order to do this, first they need to know the kind of communication barriers that exist. Dalmer Fisher listed thirteen varieties of barriers studying 130 individual barriers of communication in his book titled *Communication in Organisations* published in 1998. These are:

1. *Perceptual selectivity.* The fact that people can take in and understand only so much information at one time

2. *Evaluating things and people as good or bad.* A tendency that can easily place others on the defensive

3. *Implicit assumptions.* Beliefs the communicator holds without being fully aware of them and without having thought them through

4. *Language differences.* The fact that the same words can mean different things to different people

5. *Inadequate receiving.* The tendency to send so many messages that a communicator devotes inadequate time and energy to listening to the other person

6. *Excessive niceness.* Reluctance to express negative thoughts or feelings for fear of damaging the relationship

7. *Lack of feedback.* Anything that keeps the sender away from learning whether the other has received, acknowledged, and understood the message

8. *Loss or distortion of information.* Changes in meaning brought about through serial

communication, involving transmission of messages through one or more intermediate persons (up or down the organization's "chain of command," for example)

9. *Failure to consult.* Tendency to avoid the input of persons who will be affected by, or who are capable of improving, a decision

10. *Geographic factors.* The distance between corporate headquarters and domestic or overseas divisions

11. *Task specialization.* Differences in jargon, training, and work focus that impair organization members' understanding of one another

12. *Status, power, and authority differences.* Social factors within an organization that lead to mistrust between its members and groups

13. *Pressure.* Misunderstanding and conflict resulting from elements such as adaptation to technological changes, demands for increased productivity, and competition for rewards within the organization.

Managerial Implication

Communication system can make or mar the health of HR system in organizations. There is hardly any HR system that includes training, compensation, industrial relations, and career planning performance management, retirement schemes that do not need support of communication system. Therefore, HR managers must take and make communication as central activity. Ensuring barrier free communication must be the fundamental function. The above list help to understand the nature of communication barriers and draw suitable remedial measures to overcome them.

TRANSACTIONAL ANALYSIS

Transactional Analysis is a technique of social psychology that seeks to understand the interactions of people in order to improve the quality of communication. According to this, each person is made up of three ego states as described here. Each ego state denotes a state of mind that has related patterns of behaviour.

1. *Parent.* This is a state of Dos and Don'ts—a set of feelings, attitudes and behaviour patterns which resemble those of parental figure. Typically embodied by phrases and attitudes such as, you should not, you must, that is wrong, never, always, etc. This is the result of a person's conditioning that takes place under the influence of parents, teachers, relatives and neighbours during childhood.

2. *Child.* This ego state represents intuition, creativity, spontaneous drive and enjoyment. The behaviour patterns, attitudes and feelings are relics of the person's own childhood.

3. *Adult.* It is an ego state of abilities that include thinking, analyzing, developing solutions and applying. Adult is characterized by an autonomous feelings, attitudes and behaviour patterns which are adapted to the current reality. We keep our adult and child states under control through the adult state.

When we communicate we are doing so from one of our own alter ego states—our parent, adult or child. Effectiveness of communication is contingent upon state of transaction. If the transaction is crossed, there will be a problem between sender and receiver. The communication will be ineffective. Therefore, communication must be complementary. This can happen only when stimulus is parent to child; response must be child to parent.

A person trained in Transactional Analysis will be able to recognize (i) what ego states people are transacting from, (ii) the transactional sequences that people engage as they interact with each other and (iii) to facilitate effective communication and interaction between persons and groups.

Eric Berne developed this technique in 1957. He presented it for the first time in a conference of American Group Psychotherapy Association of Los Angeles, a year after his case was rejected for conferring the title of Psychoanalyst by San Francisco Psychoanalytic Institute. Later, he published several books that include *Transactional Analysis in Psychotherapy* in 1961, *Games People Play* in 1964 and *What Do You Say After You Say Hello?*, in 1970.

Managerial Implication

A great deal of misunderstanding in personal and professional life happens due to uncomplimentary communications. Therefore, understanding of Transactional Technique helps people to improve their functioning. It also provides opportunity for self-realization and frees us from dysfunctional effects of the behaviour. People cause great pain to themselves and to others by certain habitual unhealthy psychological manoeuvres, which can be unlearned through application of this technique. In organizations, it helps to improve employee (internal) and client (external) relationships.

JOHARI'S WINDOW

If there is one model that can provide you the complete understanding of interpersonal process and communication that is Johari window. Joseph Luft and Hari Ingham are the architects of this most popular technique who presented it for the first time in 1969 in their book titled *Of Human Interaction*. The technique also titled as Johari window taking first two letters of Joseph Luft and four letters from Hari Ingham. The model consist of four cells as indicated below:

- *Cell 1.* It is known as *arena* of communication. In this stage, information is commonly held and simultaneously known to you as well as to others. However, the effectiveness of arena is contingent upon how wide is your arena. This can be widened through two techniques. Firstly, expose yourself completely enabling others to understand you fully. Secondly, solicit reciprocity in feedback in terms of feelings, opinions and values.

- *Cell 2.* It is labelled as *blind spot*. Here, information is not known to self but known to others. In other words, other people know about you something that you do not know yourself. The other people who know that something will never tell you unless you actively solicit in the form of feedback. Often, a person in cell 2 tends to discount the feedback of others because it has no confirmation from self-knowledge. Therefore, one has to be very conscious of this fact. Sensitivity training can help to some extent in reducing the size of blind spot.

- *Cell 3.* It is also known as *Façade*. This is characterized by a dimension that information is not known to others but known to self: means other people do not know something about you. Persons use this in order to protect themselves from something, fearing or apprehending that divulgence of this information may cause loss to the self. This has the potential to create mistrust apart from its own benefits

- *Cell 4.* It is termed as *unknown*, a kind of unconscious state. In this state, information is neither known to self nor to others. It means you do not know something about yourself and others also do not know that something.

Managerial Implication

This model has two chief implications for managerial action. Firstly, it can be used to generate awareness that we all operate from four cells. The knowledge of such fact can contribute to introspection or self-scrutiny among employees. Secondly, using this technique the dominant style of employees can be mapped. Based on the results, efforts could be made to develop a functional Johari window for managers to achieve good interpersonal relationships and communication.

MODEL FOR HIGH INVOLVEMENT WORK ORGANIZATION

During the current decade, the focus on involvement is shifted from individual employee involvement to group involvement and to organization wide involvement. In the competitive environment, ever changing markets, technologies have made organizations to believe that HR is the only a dependable resource to succeed. In the quest of realizing that belief, a few organizations found that HR simply cannot be a dependable resource unless it is highly involved HR. To transform HR as highly involved HR, organizations also realized that they need to create high involvement work organization. Creating high involvement organizations is easier said than done. Organizations, which created high involvement work organization successfully, can provide us with some learnings that can serve as model to organizations, which are planning to start. Edward E. Lawler III who studied a number of organizations published a paper titled "The New Plant Revolution" in *Organizational Dynamics* in 1978. The author found unique HR characteristics with effective work organizations. These are:

1. *Employee selection.* In contrast to the traditional way of HR departments screening, testing and selecting among applicants for the jobs, high involvement organizations followed a dual strategy of involving line managers in selection process and also counselling applicant to make a valid decision about taking the job.

2. *Job design.* In high involvement work organizations, employees provided with jobs that are challenging, motivating and satisfying. In some cases it is done through individually based job enrichment approaches that emphasize personal responsibility for a whole piece of meaningful work.

3. *Creation of autonomous work groups.* The use of teams and autonomous work groups are very frequently used in high involvement work culture. Most of the teams are self-managed ones and they are given responsibility for a clearly defined work. They are also given sufficient freedom and authority.

4. *Employment security.*   High involvement organizations are publicly committed for no lay offs. This stand generates a sense of security among employees, which in turn result in greater employee involvement.

5. *Pay system.*   Most high involvement organizations have taken a different stand in determining the pay, i.e. fixed pay based on individual employee skills rather than following job evaluation techniques.

6. *Emphasis on development.*   All high involvement work organizations placed heavy emphasis on training, career development and personal growth of employees.

7. *Flat structures.*   Few hierarchical levels and elimination of intermediate levels and absence of supervisory level are common with high involvement work organizations.

8. *Shared culture.*   Decisions are arrived at with consultations and participation of all employees in the organization. The participatory issues ranged from operational to strategic level.

Managerial Implication

The above described eight characteristics make a difference between an ordinary organization and high involvement work organization. Studies found that high involvement work culture contributes to (i) increased number of innovations, (ii) competency building, (iii) enhanced problem solving capabilities, (iv) low employee turnover and (v) fast decision making. It is also important to note that in high involvement work organizations, all these characteristics are integrated into a grand HR strategy. Therefore, organizations intending to join the bandwagon of high work involvement organizations must carefully evolve the plan, and implement it in an integrated manner as indicated above.

TEN-STEP MODEL FOR EMPLOYEE INVOLVEMENT

Employee involvement appeared in theory as well as in practice ever since management shaped as a discipline and profession, of course in different forms that include, employee participation, co-determination, self-managing teams, quality circles, project teams etc. Whatever may be the form, employee involvement mechanism drew extreme arguments. There are academicians and practitioners who say that no benefit worth noting can be gained through this form of management and still there are others who believe it can do wonders. However, careful analysis of all these experiences and models would reveal an important lesson that employee involvement is certainly beneficial but not in all occasions and for all purposes. For example, it is the most appropriate mechanism when (i) the solution presupposes multidisciplinary skills, (ii) to balance confrontations/conflicts, (iii) to build consensus and (iv) to provide opportunities for development of employees. This is most inappropriate when (i) one person has greater expertise than others, (ii) the subject is part of someone's regular assignment and (iii) when the solution to the problem is known.

Experiences in this regard point out that quite a number of employee involvement efforts fail even when it is the most desirable form of management in that particular situation due to misplaced expectations of management and wrong implementation or inadequate understanding of the subject. Professor R.M. Kanter of Harvard Business School prescribed ten lessons for organization that want success with employee involvement in her remarkable book titled *The Change Masters* published in 1983. These are:

1. Start small and with local issues
2. Neither promise nor expect too much
3. Allow people to define for themselves the issues they want to discuss (including managers as team members) and to opt out of those they wish to avoid
4. Involve parties whose power might be at stake (middle managers, unions, and so forth), and give them important, rewarded roles in the new system
5. Provide education on both the skills of participation/decision-making and the issues to be discussed
6. Maintain leadership. Be explicit about fixed items and constraints on decisions
7. Make sure minority views are heard; be wary of group pressure
8. Keep it time bound and manageable
9. Provide rewards and feedback, the tangible signs that participation mattered
10. Expect participative teams to wax and wane; they supplement, rather than replace, the hierarchy or routine structure.

Managerial Implication

The above described ten guidelines help managers immensely in their efforts to leverage employee involvement schemes. The model also offers two valuable insights: Firstly, managers must analyze the appropriateness of using involvement management based on the nature of problem and its utility rather than with an intention to gain goodwill. Secondly, the involvement practice must be pursued in consonance with above ten steps. Most importantly, employees must be trained and prepared adequately prior to their participation in involvement forums.

FORD'S EMPLOYEE INVOLVEMENT MODEL

Employee involvement pays rich dividends in terms of employee and organizational effectiveness when implemented with commitment and conviction. The same programme when adopted for the sake of goodwill or with lesser degree of commitment can create confusion and disappointment. Ford's employee involvement implementation model is considered as most pragmatic and systematic intervention that brought many benefits and laurels to that company. Ford follows eight steps in execution of this programme. These are:

1. *Local management-trade union agreement.* This was considered essential for positive organizational change and the involvement of employees at every level
2. *Local joint employee involvement steering committee.* A local joint group was formed which meet regularly. The members were also given training on effective group process soon after their inclusion in this committee
3. *Briefing employees on employee involvement.* Steering committee members conduct these briefing sessions. These sessions are conducted in small groups to facilitate discussion
4. *Selection and appointment of an employee involvement coordinator.* Coordinator is appointed by joint steering committee; internal to the site selected from interested applicants. The coordinator's role is to support and later to train problem-solving groups and to provide a link between them and the rest of the organization

5. *Information gathering and diagnosis.* A number of techniques are used in data collection and diagnosis that include: (i) interviews with sample of workforce, managers and trade union representatives' dealings with their perceptions of the site, (ii) interviews conducted by the third party consultant and (iii) data fed to coordinating committee and then to workforce

6. *Training.* Training is conducted in two phases. In the first phase, awareness workshops of two days' duration for mixed groups of middle management and union leader exploring employee involvement in depth are conducted. Skill training workshops for problem solving work groups are conducted in the second phase

7. *Problem solving group launches.* These groups are launched at all levels of the organization involving all the employees

8. *Monitoring and support of groups.* This process included coordinators and consultants meeting with problem solving groups and continued training and coaching; leadership and facilitation.

Managerial Implication

The eight-step strategy of Ford drives certain valuable points. Firstly, managers must realize that the implementation of employee involvement calls for detailed preparation and action plans. The intervention tends to yield no breakthrough results for knee jerk kind of implementation. Secondly, management must question itself whether it is prepared for complete delegation for decision making since the core objective of employee involvement is nothing but allowing employees to decide their own role and perform. Thirdly, employee involvement as above is drawn to infuse the teamwork and as a joint process of management. The above model is of great practical value to all those organizations that intended to follow suit. However, before jumping into this bandwagon, managers must answer the key question of what they intended to achieve through the employee involvement and must develop an implementation plan like that of Ford.

THREE-STAGE MODEL FOR EMPOWERMENT

Empowerment is one practice that can be realized only through a systematic plan, persistence and commitment of management as well as employees. There are hardly handful of organizations that had implemented empowerment with these principles. Hence, failures are more common with empowerment rather than success. This is mainly because of managers' misconception that empowerment can happen with few days of work and like one time action. John Nicholls suggested a three stage model that help to build a sustainable empowerment programme in organizations in his paper titled "Getting Empowerment into Perspective: a Three-stage Training Framework" published in *Empowerment in Organisations* in 1995. These are:

1. Stage-I: *Get the basics rightfully using current capability.* The idea, in the first stage, would be to empower people to the fullest extent of their current capability, within the scope of their current job/task. Perhaps, a bottom-up, training-based approach might work better, setting more modest objectives and getting the basics right first, before going onto the big picture. In the first stage, we are looking at empowerment through

delegation in the current job/task to make optimum use of current capability. Managers who achieve this could be called enablers.

2. Stage-II: *Stretch people beyond their current capability to fulfil their full potential.* The second stage of empowerment must surely be to grow people beyond their current capability so they may achieve their full potential. This occurs when enablers act as coaches to stretch people by delegation and empowerment slightly beyond their current limits. The coaching process must include the following:

   • Devoting time to show people how to perform tasks that are beyond their current repertoire.

   • Having alertness for opportunities to delegate a real task that will use the capability that is being developed. This task should be relatively simple and clear cut; not take too long; have a clear, easily measured outcome; have a high probability of successful achievement.

   • Having identified a task, do a good job of delegating it: take time to prepare before making the assignment.

   • During implementation, avoid temptation to over control. Do not insist that people do things in exactly the way you would do yourself.

   • When the task is successfully completed, offer congratulations, praise and recognition.

   • Sometime later, invite people to review their own performance and work with them to draw out the lessons for the future.

3. Stage-III: *Widen/Deepen empowerment by creating commitment throughout the organization.* In stages, one and two, the focus has been on individuals who are empowered by their managers. When this is accomplished, there is a firm and practical base, which makes it feasible to look at the third and broadest implementation of empowerment. The foundation should be laid for a change of attitude and behaviour in the organization as a whole. As people are involved in wider activity, well beyond the confines of their particular job/task, their broader understanding and growing range of activity transforms their capability. It is at this stage that managers begin to realize that by letting go of authoritarian power they gain the power to energize people-achieving results beyond expectations.

Managerial Implication

The author argues that empowerment is not a one shot game but a dynamic process that involves three stages. This framework can help all those managers committed to real empowerment initiative in their organizations. Before launching such a programme, they must question themselves and substantiate why they want to have an empowerment programme in their organizations and what objectives it is supposed to achieve. If answers are convincing, they can go head with a programme consisting comprehensive plan like the above described one.

EMPOWERMENT vs DISEMPOWERMENT

Most of the employees in most of the organizations are victims of disempowerment. Managers could not achieve what they intended to due to their inability to give up control. Organizational commitment remained low despite many HRD related initiatives thus launched because all those ultimately centered around making employees submissive and disempowered. Study after study and live experiences in organizations proved beyond doubt that empowerment is not a fad but a reality for motivation of employees and a potential source to integrate them with organization. In order to understand the power of empowerment, it may be appropriate to focus on the disempowerment as much as on empowerment. Two empowerment specialists, Mike Van Oudtshoorn of Saket Lynd and Laurie Thomas of Brunel University distinguished the characteristics associated with empowerment and disempowerment in their paper titled "A Management Synopsis of Empowerment" published in *Training for Quality* in 1995. These characteristics are illustrated in Table 9.1.

TABLE 9.1

Associated with empowerment	Associated with disempowerment
• Accepting of responsibility	• Avoiding taking responsibility
• Being active	• Being passive
• Boldness	• Timidity
• Creative	• Conventional
• Energetic	• Lethargic
• Enjoys life	• Gets little joy out of life
• Happy	• Depressed and miserable
• Healthy	• Many health problems
• Imaginative	• Dull and unimaginative
• Independent	• Dependent
• Individualistic	• Conforming
• Innovative	• Sticks to routines
• Interesting	• Dull and boring
• Motivated	• Unmotivated
• Prepared to take risks	• Reluctant to take risks
• Observant	• Unobservant
• Satisfied with job	• Frustrated in job
• Sensitive to subtleties	• Not sensitive to subtleties
• Uses full potential as a human being	• Uses only a fraction of potential
• Uses intelligence to the full	• Does not use intelligence to the full

Managerial Implication

With the growing knowledge about work, widespread use of teams, soaring significance of quality and customer satisfaction, managers have no choice but to give up control, and empower employees through a systematic coaching and enabling practices. Further, the new generation of employees is more concerned about freedom to work and more likely to be motivated by higher initiatives such as quality of assignment and scope for contribution and variety in tasks. Therefore, organizations have to find the way through which employees are provided with these opportunities and facilities. Empowerment is a prime tool for this purpose. However, planning and implementing empowerment is a challenging task. Therefore, a progressive model should be developed involving all the employees and their commitment is a pre requisite. HR managers must spend their quality time to dispel the disempowered characteristics as indicated above for organizational excellence. However, do not start just for the sake of goodwill or as the thing in the town or as a flavour of the month.

UNSUCCESSFUL EMPOWERMENT

The number of failures with empowerment attempts is much more in comparison to its success rate. This is mainly because of two prime reasons: firstly, this is due to the halfhearted attempts of management in implementation of empowerment. Secondly, it takes longer time than expected to institutionalize empowerment culture because the authority structures in the organization are existing ever since the concept of industry came in. Linda Honold, president of Empowerment Systems, USA vividly described the failure experiences in her paper titled "A Review of the Literature on Employee Empowerment" published in *Empowerment in Organizations* in 1997. These are briefly presented here:

1. Employee empowerment is impossible in practice because empowerment is incompatible with strong leadership and is an efficient way to control an organization. For example, a company touted for its empowerment practices for a long time, concluded that empowerment appears to be an attractive and sometimes successful approach but only for medium sized ambitions.

2. A case study entitled 'The empowerment effort that came undone' describes a situation where the president of a company empowered a team to deal with declining sales. The effort fell apart on presenting their recommendations to the company's management team; the solutions were criticized as being unworkable. It was found that employees did not have the authority to make anything 'happen'; boundaries were not clearly defined. Too much was expected too fast without ensuring that everyone in the company knew what empowerment was about.

3. Another study conducted in 1995 found that, unless the culture of an organization is appropriate, employee empowerment efforts are doomed to fail. The study led to the conclusion that, empowerment is not for every organization. It should be undertaken only when it fits an internal or external need and when the people and the systems are willing to make changes. This willingness can be determined by looking at the issues of control and power, trust and inclusion, and risk-taking.

4. If employee empowerment is successful, unions become virtually superfluous, as their role of mediating between employees and management is no longer needed. The other view is that, employee empowerment is nothing more than a new form of exploitation, taxing people's minds as well as their hands while providing them with no real control of their work. These employees seem to define empowerment as having production employees taking on responsibility previously performed by the supervisor or by a skilled tradesperson. This is considered as incomplete empowerment as there is no authority or capacity to mobilize resources to get anything done.

5. The other school of thought equate employee empowerment to a management by stress approach that pushes people and systems to the breaking point by increasingly forcing workers to do more with less.

6. In a case study of automobile industry, it was found that empowerment was working, but only to a point. Workers get control over doing things like stopping the

production line over quality issues and cross training, yet the work that they do is standardized and controlled by the management. Responsibilities that were transferred to employees were things like ability to hand out paychecks on payday. They were more symbolic than substantive.

Managerial Implication

The essence of these failures is that empowerment as a concept and model is successful but not successful in its implementation. This is because of lack of adequate efforts in implementation. It is common across the organization that they go ahead with the implementation without preparing proper ground like altering the management systems particularly the power equilibrium and without augmenting the enabling work culture. Further, empowerment is either left unaddressed or disbanded, the moment signs of resistance and complexities are encountered. Therefore, managers must realize that implementing empowerment calls for organization wide revolution and if pursued religiously can deliver unparallel results.

Chapter 10

Intelligence and Motivational Management

The basis for most of the HRM practices lies in two critical disciplines—intelligence management and motivational management. Intelligence management has implications for many practices that include recruitment, performance evaluations, training and development. Motivational management has answers for questions related to employee's performance, rewards and recognitions, work and personal life, work culture and achievement levels.

Therefore, HR professionals need to possess strong fundamental knowledge in these twin areas in order to manage the related HRM functions effectively. On the other hand, the knowledge of these areas could also lead the practitioners to develop tailor made HR practices to meet the organization specific demands with sound principles derived from these basic sciences. Keeping this objective in view, the present chapter deals with basic as well as modern trends in intelligence and motivational management. Eighteen classics are included here to capture these issues in a manner that help and enable HR practitioners in their mission to achieve intelligent and motivated enterprises.

CORPORATE IQ

Many organizations even the modern ones seem to follow the traditional method of data keeping or information management that dents the organizational abilities and consequently its intelligence. It is a common experience that we seek the help of people who earlier handled the assignment when we do not know where to search for and get the information/papers/files/maps/documents in the organization. In this process, we also end up reinventing the wheel. Depending on a few individuals or leaving the crucial organizational knowledge to be carried in the heads of two/three managers will have serious implications for the organizations. Therefore, creation of a systematic knowledge base or knowledge management is of paramount importance. A systematic knowledge base enhances the corporate IQ, argues Bill Gates, CEO of Microsoft in his latest book titled *Business @ The Speed of Thought*. Corporate IQ is a measure of how easily your company can share information broadly and of how well people within your organization can build on each other's ideas. Corporate IQ involves sharing both history and current knowledge. This in turns helps organizations in many areas. For example:

1. A consumer information system that was developed in 1996 and used widely by all

employees in Coke has resulted in smarter staffs who focus on anticipating the market rather than reacting to it.

2. Information systems at Yamanouci pharmaceuticals and Microsoft have contributed for speedy customer service. For example, Yamanouci sales staff can immediately answer half the questions that come in from doctors or pharmacists using an information system called PRINCE (Product Information Centre Supporting System).

3. People want to improve their knowledge and skills but may not have a systematic way or information to learn from. A systematically delivered information/knowledge would enable people to learn at their own pace and online information facilitates them to learn without being off from the office.

4. A well-equipped information system can sharpen the product development capabilities of people. For example, Nabisco has created leading edge development processes that have produced some of the most popular snack food brands in the world using information technology devices. Once a project is done, all the details are kept in this information system that works as a corporate brain. Employees who want to develop a product can access all the past breakthroughs and their processes by tapping this corporate brain.

Managerial Implication

HR managers have an influential role in raising corporate IQ in their organizations. They must establish a culture of information sharing and impress upon the top management and CEO the need of creating a systematic knowledge system. They also must design and implement a concomitant reward system that promotes organizational knowledge creation. An initiative must be taken to formulate the strategy and working plans for an organization specific knowledge management method that facilitates speedy customer service, product development, speedy decision making and real empowerment of employees. In a nutshell, a system that raises the organizational intelligence.

FLYNN EFFECT

James R. Flynn, a political Scientist at the University of Otego, New Zealand discovered that IQ scores for different populations over the past six decades increased from one generation to another generation for all the countries. Intelligence scores are rising but the author is certain that we are not getting any smarter. This phenomenon is now called as Flynn Effect. James Flynn reported and summarized his study of IQ rise in fourteen nations in the book titled *Encyclopaedia of Human Intelligence* published in 1994.

Study reveals that, average scores on intelligence tests have been rising in a progressive manner. Flynn established with the support of a number of studies that the subjects achieved higher scores on the older version of a test. The results appeared to have been same for all major tests, all age groups and in every industrialized society. It is felt that these gains are too rapid to result from genetic changes. There evidently are substantial environmental influences. Flynn who puzzled himself with these results says that, compared to the previous generation, the number of people who score high enough to be classified as Genius have increased more than 20 times. This means that we should now be witnessing a cultural and technological renaissance too great to be overlooked. Therefore, he suggests that what has risen is not intelligence itself but some kind of abstract problem solving ability. Factors such as increased sophistication, better nutrition, more schooling, alert child rearing practices, technology driven changes and highly visualized environments might have contributed for increase in IQ scores.

Managerial Implication

Findings of study are useful to business organizations and other institutes involved in design and conduct of competitive and selection tests. The lesson is that selection tests should be re-modelled and re-standardized from their existing shape. People in recruitment function know that candidates' ability to handle recruitment tests is going up due to the familiarity with the selection instruments, increased techniques and coaching back-ups. The serious issue here is that they are not substantially different from previous test takers in terms of real capabilities despite increase in score profiles. This can have adverse implication for quality of recruitments. Hence, HR managers must work on re-modelling of selection tests/procedures at regular intervals.

FLUID AND CRYSTALLIZED INTELLIGENCE MODEL

Fluid intelligence is an ability to learn new information or new ways to deal with new situation whereas crystallized intelligence is an ability to use familiar things to deal with familiar situations. Raymond Bernard Cattell proposed this model in 1963 in his insightful paper titled "Theory of Fluid and Crystallised Intelligence: A Critical Experiment" published in the *Journal of Educational Psychology*. Cattell in association with J.L. Horn further strengthened the model in 1966 and published the same in the *Journal of Educational Psychology* titled "Refinement and Test of the Theory of Fluid and Crystallised Intelligence". The salient features of these intelligences are:

1. Fluid intelligence is thought to be primarily innate in nature and is related to all types of problem solving.
2. Fluid intelligence is relatively formless and appears independent of experience and education.
3. Fluid intelligence ability dimensions include: reasoning and problem solving, induction, deduction, figure classification, analyses of figures and matrices. These basic processes flow into various other intellectual activities.
4. Crystallized intelligence is a learned ability to process information, to find relationships, make judgements, analyze problems, verbal comprehension, numerical abilities and ability to apply leanings in practical life.
5. Crystallized intelligence also believed to be culturally based since it is mostly applied to acquired abilities in a formal way, i.e. through schools and colleges.

In combination, both types of intelligence cover most of the learning tasks. Fluid and crystallized intelligence are mutually complimentary. For example some situations like surgery can be managed only through exercising both the intelligences in combination. In some situations like housekeeping either of the cluster is sufficient.

Managerial Implication

The model helps managers in two ways. Firstly, it facilitates to profile the employees in reference to these twin clusters of intelligence. Based on the results, appropriate measures could be initiated to strengthen the crystallized ability of employees since learning of this is possible at any age unlike fluid intelligence, which reaches its maturity in adolescence. Crystallized intelligence is a dominant factor in performance differences among employees and also fluctuations in the same employee over a period of time. Further, proper understanding and application of crystallized intelligence strategies are imperative for managers not only for their benefit but also to chart an effective course of employee training for better problem solving abilities.

MULTIPLE INTELLIGENCE MODEL

Is intelligence a single faculty or a combination of factors or independent intellectual faculties? is the question raised, researched and answered with irrefutable evidence by Dr Howard Gardner, Professor of Cognition and Education at Harvard Graduate School of Education. He introduced a new definition and theory of intelligence known as Multiple Intelligence in his book titled "Frames of Mind" published in 1983. He challenged the traditional view of intelligence as a unitary capacity that can be adequately measured by Intelligence Quotient tests. Instead, his Multiple Intelligence model defined intelligence as an ability to solve problems or create products that are valued at least one culture. According to Gardner, there are eight autonomous intellectual capacities that individuals apply in problem solving and create products. These are:

1. Linguistic intelligence involving syntax, phonology, semantics, pragmatics
2. Musical intelligence involving pitch, rhythm
3. Logical Mathematical intelligence involving numbers, categorization, relation
4. Spatial intelligence involving accurate mental visualization, mental transformation of images
5. Intrapersonal intelligence involving awareness of one's own body, control of one's own feelings, emotions, goals, motivation
6. Interpersonal intelligence involving awareness of other's feelings, emotions, goals, motivation
7. Naturalistic intelligence involving recognition and classification of objects in the environment
8. Body Kinesthetic involving control in handling objects

Gardner made an interesting observation in this context that, it becomes necessary to say, once and for all, that there can never be, a single irrefutable and universally accepted list of human intelligence.

Managerial Implication

Theory of Multiple Intelligence stands apart for its insights and utility to the practice of HRM. The foremost is it established that intelligence is multiple and not single as believed till the birth of this model. Secondly, it provided an exhaustive and rational classification of human intelligence, which becomes handy in recruitment and other employee assessments. Thirdly, this model proved that every person possess dynamic intelligences and deserve opportunities to nurture the multiple intelligence profile. This inference alone has wide implications for HR development practices in organizations. Fourthly, all human intelligence are dynamic implying that intelligence faculties can be sharpened regardless of the age factor.

THREE FACES OF INTELLECT MODEL

Three Faces of Intellect also called, as Structure of Intellect (SI) is a theory of human intelligence that was developed by Dr. J.P. Guilford at the University of Southern Carolina. He proposed this model for first time in the journal *American Psychologist* in 1950 in a publication titled, Creativity and later published a book in 1967 on this, titled The Nature of Human Intelligence. As the title suggests, the model views intelligence in three dimensions. These are:

1. *Processes*—basically deals with what a person does and consists of five operations such as (i) cognition, (ii) memory, (iii) divergent production, (iv) convergent production and (v) evaluation

2. *Contents*—basically deals with the nature of the materials upon which operations are carried out and includes five kind of contents such as (i) visual, (ii) auditory, (iii) symbolic, (iv) semantic and (v) behaviour.

3. *Products*—basically deals with the forms in which information is processed that include six products such as (i) units, (ii) classes, (iii) relations, (iv) systems, (v) transformations and (vi) implications.

Each of the components of three dimensions described above is an independent intelligence factor. Guilford again researched and developed a wide variety of psychometric tests approximately numbering 150 to measure each of these components. Many psychologists and educational scientists also developed instruments that measure three dimensions of intellectual model. However, these researchers including Guilford admitted that administering these multiple number of instruments, analyzing and mapping intelligence profile of a person is quite an imposing and overbearing exercise.

Managerial Implication

The significant utilities of this model even to current generation organizations are two fold. Firstly, the psychometric tests based on three face of intellect model can be used individually, i.e. to analyze the specific ability and also to map of general ability profile by administering all the tests in combination. Therefore, these are useful for selection decisions of all types of positions that include operational/clerical, managerial/administrative. Secondly, the results obtained by administering these tests can be relied upon to determine training (skill upgradation) plans of individuals and groups against collective aggregate results.

TRIARCHIC MODEL OF HUMAN INTELLIGENCE

Robert J. Sternberg, IBM Professor of Psychology and Education at Yale University is the author of Triarchic theory who brought new insights through his well researched book titled, *Beyond IQ: A Triarchic Theory of Human Intelligence*, published in 1985. The Triarchic theory of human intelligence consists of three sub-theories. These are:

1. A componential sub-theory that relates intelligence to the internal world of the individual. Componential sub-theory includes (i) Metacomponents (monitoring and evaluating a problem), (ii) Performance components (encoding, inferring and applying) and (iii) Knowledge acquisition components (learning new facts or concepts)
2. A contextual sub-theory that focuses on intelligent behaviour including adaptation, selection and shaping of one's environment
3. An experiential sub-theory that focuses on the role of experience in intelligent behaviour.

A complete explanation of intelligence entails the interaction of these three sub-theories. The Triarchic theory though is a general theory of intelligence has implications for skill training which include training

1. intellectual performance socio-culturally relevant to the individual
2. to provide links between the training and real-world behaviour
3. to provide explicit instruction in strategies for coping with novel tasks/situations.
4. to provide explicitly in both executive and non-executive information processing and interactions between the two
5. actively encourage individuals to manifest their differences in strategies and styles.

Managerial Implication

A key contribution of this model is application of intelligence theories (otherwise abstract to corporate context) particularly in terms of design and implementation of training and management development programmes. Based on Triarchic model, intelligence profile of an organization and its HR could be mapped. Action plans can be drawn based on the findings and analysis to build a more balanced intelligence mix. A standard instrument namely Sternberg Multidimensional Abilities Test may be useful to organizations intending to map the intelligence profile. Sternberg says that real life is where intelligence operates and not in the classroom.

TWO-FACTOR MODEL OF INTELLIGENCE

Charles Edward Spearman, a British Psychologist who being a student published his seminal work for the first time in 1904 titled "General Intelligence: Objectively Determined and Measured" now known as two-factor theory of intelligence in *American Journal of Psychology*. He speculated that all intelligence functioning was underpinned by an overall mental ability accompanied by specific abilities for different mental tasks. According to two-factor theory, there are two factors in intelligence. One is called as general intelligence (*g* factor), which is present in a whole range of mental abilities and the other as specific factor of intelligence (*s* factor), which is involved in narrow and single mental ability tests. The performance of any intellectual act requires some combination of *g* (problem solving ability-reasoning and logic) which is available to an individual to the same degree for all intellectual acts and of *s* (e.g. dance/sport/computation) which is specific to that act with varied strength from one act to another. A near cent per cent accurate prediction is possible in *g* factor. For example, a person will give same performance level on different tasks of *g*. Prediction of performance on tasks related *s* factor are less accurate. However, the most important information to have about a person's intelligence ability is an estimate of g factor. Spearman concluded that a g factor was the engine that drives the performance of any person. He also established beyond doubt that g and s factors compliment each other. The widely used statistical procedure, we know, as factor analysis was operationalized for the first time through this theory.

Managerial Implication

An important lesson to be learned from this theory is that there are broadly two spheres of intelligence—general intelligence and specific intelligence. To any organization, both these are important. But g factor assumes more importance in managerial roles and s factor for operational roles. Another important revelation that can help while recruiting and assessing people is that, once performance of a person on a g type task is measured, it could serve as an indicator for his/her general abilities. Therefore, a standard method may be adopted for this. Obviously, there need to be different tests for measuring specific abilities to handle specialized tasks. It is also advisable to have clearly defined training programmes to enhance general and specific intelligence of people in organizations.

LAWS OF THORNDIKE

Edward Lee Thorndike, Professor of Psychology and Education at Harvard University spent his life exploring and proposing path breaking theories in the fields of Learning and Intelligence. Thorndike came up with a model that consisted of three primary laws in his book titled *Educational Psychology: The Psychology of Learning* in 1913 and later on with a detailed description in the book titled *The Fundamentals of Learning* in 1932. These are popularly known as Thorndike's Effect. These laws are:

1. *Law of Effect.* Responses to a situation that are followed by a rewarding state of affairs will be strengthened and become habitual responses to that situation. In other words: (i) responses to a situation that are followed by satisfaction are strengthened and (ii) responses that are followed by discomfort are weakened.

2. *Law of Readiness.* A series of responses (stimulus-response) can be chained together to satisfy a goal, which will result in annoyance if blocked. For example, linking incentives to performance.

3. *Law of Exercise.* Connections become strengthened with practice and weakened when practice is discontinued. For example, (i) stimulus-response connections that are repeated are strengthened and (ii) stimulus-response connections that are not used are weakened.

Intelligence is a function of the number of connections learned according to Thorndike. He classified intelligence into three dimensions:

1. Abstract intelligence that deals with verbal and mathematical connections
2. Social intelligence that deals with the ability to maintain interpersonal relationships successfully
3. Mechanical intelligence that deals with the ability to understand relationships among objects and how the physical world works.

Managerial Implication

Thorndike's laws are basic tools that can be effectively used in design and application of reward, training and development functions. For example, in order to motivate meaningful work behaviour in organizations, Law of Effect is to be followed. It means a clearly defined reward and punishment system should be put into place. In similar fashion, Laws of Readiness and Exercise must be formed as a basis in training efforts. Reward and training systems that are made in consonance with these laws help organizations to realize value for efforts. Further, the three-dimensional classification of intelligence has practical wisdom for managers. We need to put efforts to understand the intelligence type of employees in order to develop and utilize their talents fitting to the demands of jobs.

PRIMARY MENTAL ABILITIES

L.L. Thurstone, Professor of Psychometry while he was at the University of Chicago introduced the theory of Primary Mental Abilities. He presented the said model with support of various studies in the books titled *Primary Mental Abilities* and *Multifactor Analysis* published in 1938 and 1947 respectively. Thurstone disagreed with the notion of general intelligence, a univariate view encompassing general intelligence. Instead, he asserted that a multidimensional view of intellect is appropriate. Each individual has his/her strengths and weaknesses that can be measured. His theory identified seven primary mental abilities as indicated here:

1. Word fluency that include words in special contexts
2. Verbal comprehension that include verbal reasoning, reading comprehension
3. Number ability (Arithmetic comprehension)
4. Spatial visualization that include the ability to mentally manipulate and visualize geometric relations
5. Associative memory (ability to make random paired associations that require rote memory
6. General reasoning ability (ability in finding rules in test items)
7. Perceptual speed (ability of finding or in recognizing particular items in a perceptual field).

He successfully tested the intercorrelations among these seven primary abilities and found a *g* factor or commonly known as general intelligence factor. He also used new and improved methods of multifactor analysis to prove the interaction among these primary abilities. Later, L.L. Thurstone in conjunction with his wife T.G. Thurstone, also Professor of Psychometry at University of North Carolina had developed a number of tests that yield a profile of the individual's performance on each of the ability tests, rather than general intelligence that yield a single score.

Managerial Implication

Thurstone's ability tests are widely used in industrial organizations to map the intelligence profile of people. The model of primary abilities has been adapted in various aptitude tests too. Probably, Thurstone's framework is the oldest framework that proposed intelligence as multi-variate and provided well-defined factors for assessment. These factors known as primary mental abilities are still highly useful and work as a basic tool in management of human intelligence in organizations. Understanding of this model of intelligence is also essential to the people who deal with design and implementation of aptitude tests that include HR managers.

NATURE-NURTURE CONTROVERSY

Nature-Nurture controversy is as old as history of Psychology. There is more than a clinching evidence in favour of an argument that nature (heredity) determines our intelligence, abilities and in general our behaviour. On the other hand, the proponents of nurture principle cite prolific source and internationally regarded multidisciplinary research that support their point of view that it is the environment that determines the behaviour code of human beings. Let us examine both the perspectives in order to understand the anatomy of human behaviour:

Studies that support nature argument are:

1. In a study known as Colorado Adoption Project, researchers found that kids raised by their biological parents tend to be similar to their parents in intellectual ability and certain personality traits, but that adopted children have little in common with the people who raise them.
2. DNA scientists through their studies established that 70 per cent of intelligence is determined by heredity, i.e. the genetic factor. Various other gene studies also tentatively linked specific genes to traits such as inhibitions, anger, happiness, achievement drive and the like.
3. In other studies, it has been observed that certain human behavioural characteristics tend to run in families implying that heredity determines the human psyche also.

Studies that support the nurture argument are:

1. John Watson, Father of Behaviourism wrote

   give me a dozen healthy infants, well formed, and my own specified world to bring them up in and I will guarantee to take any one at random and train him to behave any type of specialist I might select: doctor, lawyer, artist, merchant-chief and yes even beggar-man and thief regardless of his talent, penchants, tendencies, abilities, vocations and race of his ancestors.

2. In a research study of University of Maryland it was found that environment remains potent determinant of behaviour.

Managerial Implication

Both these arguments are important to managers to understand human behaviour at work place. One more perspective of the issue is that both nature and nurture are complimentary in the sense that any one of them cannot be hold responsible for all the behaviour. Behaviour is an outcome of interaction between both. Whatever may be the strength of these arguments, it is clear that the behaviour of employees at work place is consequence of the environment provided to them. Hence, creating right environment is the primary responsibility of managers.

STANFORD-BINET IQ

The Stanford-Binet test was the first widely administered method of gauging human intelligence. This test is the American adoption of the original French Binet-Simon intelligence test. The predominantly verbal test is scaled in order of difficulty and used to find a person's intelligence quotient. The test is scored in terms of intelligence quotient, a concept first suggested by German Psychologist William Stern and adopted by Lewis Terman, a Psychologist at Stanford University in the Stanford-Binet scale in 1916. The intelligence quotient (IQ) was originally computed as the ratio of a person's mental age to his chronological (physical) age multiplied by 100. The Stanford-Binet scale tests intelligence across four areas: verbal reasoning, quantitative reasoning, abstract/visual reasoning and short-term memory. These four areas are in turn covered by 15 subtests which include: vocabulary, comprehension, verbal absurdities, pattern analysis, matrices, paper folding and cutting, copying, quantitative measures, number series, equation building, memory for sentences, memory for digits, memory for objects and bead memory.

The fourth edition of Stanford-Binet Intelligence test released in 1986 designed by Robert Thorndike, Elizabeth Hagers and Jerom Sattler, is currently in practice. This revised version is much larger in scope in terms of testing items. According to this tool, the classification of IQ is shown as in Table 10.1.

TABLE 10.1

120–140	Very superior intelligence
110–120	Superior intelligence
90–110	Average intelligence
80–90	Dullness
70–80	Border line deficiency
69–below	Definite feeble-minded

Managerial Implication

Understanding of Stanford-Binet is important to all those involved in aptitude testing. Almost all the general selection tests being employed across the globe such as G-MAT are based on this scale. It also helps in designing purpose specific tests in organizations. The Stanfords-Binet test has many benefits and very few limitations. The benefit is that the test is highly reliable, time tested and well standardized. The test allows the administrator to have close personal contact with the subjects that allow gaining some important and pertinent information. Further, the test can be administered on all types of employees and on all age groups. This universal applicability is also found to be its potential problem. It is logical to conclude that it will be impossible to have a test that can be equally made useful to all types of employees and age groups. However, as a general aptitude test, certainly it has universal appeal and can yield useful data.

EMOTIONAL INTELLIGENCE FRAMEWORK

It is how we handle ourselves that determine our success in the organization rather our technical/functional expertise alone. This people call it being practical, matured, down to earth or shrewd.

Some experienced people might have realized the value of it but not many. Daniel Goleman proved the value of such practicality with his path breaking research and developed a comprehensive framework called Emotional Intelligence Framework. Probably, this is one work that shaken the entire community of intelligence, psychology and management disciplines worldwide in the last decade. Goleman supported by comprehensive evidence illustrated that emotional intelligence is twice important than rational intelligence (intelligence quotient) to succeed in life that include career in organizations. His research points out that IQ alone at best leaves 75 per cent of job success unexplained. In other words, it does not determine who succeeds and who fails. On the other hand, low EQ can make even top specialists in their own area as stupid. Goleman argue that emotional intelligence leads to outstanding performance at work. The emotional intelligence can be learned at any stage of life. It comprises five major dimensions and twenty-five emotional competencies as presented below:

Personal Competence

These competencies determine how we manage ourselves. This comprises three dimensions:

1. *Self-awareness.* Knowing one's internal states, preferences, resources, and intuitions. This include (i) emotional awareness, (ii) accurate self-assessment, (iii) self-confidence

2. *Self-regulation.* Managing one's internal states, impulses, and resources. This consists (i) self-control, (ii) trustworthiness, (iii) conscientiousness, (iv) adaptability, (v) innovation

3. *Motivation.* Emotional tendencies that guide or facilitate reaching goals. It consists of (i) achievement drive, (ii) commitment, (iii) initiative, (iv) optimism.

Social Competence

These competencies determine how we handle relationships. This comprises of two dimensions mentioned below:

1. *Empathy.* Awareness of other's feelings, needs and concerns. This consists of (i) understanding others, (ii) developing others, (iii) service orientation, (iv) leveraging diversity and (v) political awareness

2. *Social skills.* Adeptness at inducing desirable responses in others. It includes: (i) influence, (ii) communication, (iii) conflict management, (iv) leadership, (v) change catalyst, (vi) building bonds, (vii) collaboration and cooperation, (viii) team capabilities.

Managerial Implication

Building emotional competence can solve many of the problems in organizations and improves performance significantly. We come across managers not succeeding as expected not because of their lack of skill/competence in their field but their incompetence to influence people, to take decisions, to assess the situation and inability to behave in an emotionally controlled manner. On the other side, we also see people thriving despite very moderate skill/competence in their field but with lots of pursuing and people leading capabilities. Therefore, emotional intelligence is important than of technical skill/competence building measures. Unfortunately, there is more focus on developing people on technologies/sciences and least concern is shown to impart emotional competence. The fact is that, with rapid changes in environment and consequential uncertainties, emotionally intelligent managers are more important than mere technologists/ functional specialists. Hence, HR managers must accord special focus on training managers on emotional competence.

HIERARCHY OF NEEDS

Hierarchy of needs is one theory that not only enabled us to understand the motivational behaviour of human beings but also helped in designing of various reward and punishment strategies that can be helpful in obtaining the desired behaviour at work place. Abraham Maslow, a legend in clinical psychology propounded this theory for the first time in his paper tilted "A Theory of Human Motivation" published in *Psychological Review* in 1943. He proposed the need structure of human beings in a hierarchy starting from lowest needs to highest needs in an ascending order. The premise of this ascending hierarchy is once a lower level need is fulfilled, a person will be driven to fulfil the next higher level need. Once a need is fulfilled, it will lose the power of motivating the behaviour and only the next higher level need can do it. The hierarchy of needs is:

1. *Physiological needs.* It is the most basic level in the hierarchy. Fulfilment of this level is sought to sustain the human life itself. The needs include, food, water, clothing, sleep, sexual satisfaction and shelter. Maslow hypothesized that until these basic needs are fulfilled, other needs will not motivate people.

2. *Security needs.* It seeks certainty of fulfilment of the physiological needs on a long run. In other words, seeking free from fear of loosing food, water, clothing, shelter and emotional hazards.

3. *Social needs.* This is a need of seeking affection, love, recognition, acceptance, belongingness etc. It is natural that human being as part of the society seeks to identify with other people or a group of people.

4. *Self-esteem.* This is a need manifested by a behaviour seeking holding oneself in esteem by self as well as others. This is a logical extension of social need where human beings limit to seeking belongingness and acceptance. This also has correspondence to achievement motivation.

5. *Self-actualization.* This is the highest need in the order. It is realizing completely, within oneself, what he or she is capable of. It is an inner motivation to accomplish something uncommon.

Managerial Implication

This theory has significantly contributed to the management of HR. Undoubtedly, it is fundamental and first step for anyone intended to understand the motivational behaviour. Though it is not the last step and conclusive, but one of the comprehensive frameworks that can help HR professionals in design and implementation of various monetary and non-monetary rewards. Despite of its clear message, unfortunately some organizations are yet to realize the diverse human needs. They limit themselves to providing opportunities to fulfil the lower level needs of physiological, security and social needs. They must focus on creating avenues for fulfilling the higher level needs like self-esteem and actualization by providing challenging and quality tasks.

HYGIENE-MOTIVATOR FACTORS

The two-factor model of motivation has direct relevance to motivational behaviour at work. This has been extensively used to explain the job satisfaction and its relationship with productivity. Psychologist Frederick Herzberg, and his associates based on extensive research had proposed two factors that explain motivation in their book titled *The Motivation to Work* published in 1959. The salient features of these factors are:

1. The first is an extrinsic motivator called hygiene or maintenance factor consisting such things as company policy, administration, and supervision, working conditions, interpersonal relations, salary, status, job security and personal life. These are something to do with the quantity aspect of it. In other words, the non-fulfilment of these can demotivate a person but the fulfilment will not lead to any motivational behaviour. What Herzberg called them as dissatisfiers and not motivators.

2. The second called as motivators are related to job content and an intrinsic motivator. These include quality things such as: achievement, recognition, challenging work, advancement, and growth in the job. Non-fulfilment of these factors dissatisfies persons and fulfilment leads to satisfaction unlike hygienic factors.

Herzberg himself and many others tested the application of this model in practice. The studies found support to the premise that motivators are important for job satisfaction and consequential productivity enhancement. The factors leading to job satisfaction are separate and distinct from those that lead to job dissatisfaction. The managers who seek to eliminate factors that create job dissatisfaction can bring about peace, but not necessarily motivation. In other words, they are only placating the employees instead of motivating them.

Managerial Implication

Most of the organizations and HR managers just limit themselves in taking care of maintenance or hygiene factors such as pay, allowances, benefits, designations, welfare and physical working conditions. As the two-factor theory of motivation clearly establishes, these actions can only assure of no dissatisfaction. They need to create opportunities in the form of enriching jobs, providing challenging assignments, broader responsibilities and roles, opportunities for professional growth and advancement to motivate the employees that bring satisfaction to employees. Slackness in taking care of motivators can lead to employees seeking only fulfilment of hygienic factors and skipping motivators. This behavioural pattern can affect performance and organizational success adversely. Therefore, HR managers must focus on motivators for building a real motivated work environment.

VALENCE-EXPECTANCY MODEL

It is motivational theory that pronounces that people will be motivated to do particular thing in a particular way because they expect that such action lead to achieve something they value. In other words, the effort one put in to achieve something is equivalent to the value he or she assigns to that thing. This model known as valence-expectancy theory of motivation has rightly highlighted the complexities in motivational behaviour in contrast to the simplification of other theories like hierarchy of needs and two-factor theory of motivation. The theory was propounded by V.H. Vroom in his book titled *Work and Motivation* in 1964. Vroom's work generated widespread interest and it continued to be much talked about theory in the subject of motivation. It is a calculative psychological model which put forwarded that the ultimate goal of motivational behaviour is to maximize the pleasure and minimize the pain in life. There are three important elements in this model as explained here:

- First is *valence*, meaning the strength of an individual's preference for a particular outcome. For example, the valence is zero if you are indifferent to a particular outcome and it is negative valence if you don't like that outcome. In other words, your own efforts will be zero if you are indifferent to your promotion in the organization. If your valence (value) to promotion is high, you tend to put lot of efforts and perform well to achieve this.
- Second is *expectancy*, which means probability. This is your hope that certain actions on your part will lead to the outcome you desire. For example, you expect that performing well on your job will lead to achieving fast promotion.
- Third is *instrumentality*, referring to first level and second level outcomes. For example, in the expectation of promotion, you perform exceedingly well. Here, exceedingly well performance is the first outcome, and promotion is the second outcome. Typically, the first level outcome will lead to second level outcome.

Managerial Implication

This modern model of motivation has some significant and pertinent lessons to offer to managers particularly to HR managers. The first lesson is, we need to appreciate that motivational behaviour of human beings is dynamic and complex. In other words, the things motivate a person, may not motivate others. Therefore, they differ in their efforts to achieve that outcome. Hence, regarding an employee incompetent is a simplified reaction because his or her zero valence to the outcome (reward) is the factor responsible for non-performance. The second lesson is expectancy, i.e. belief of employees that particular action will lead to the desired outcome will be dependent upon the organizational norm. For example, if there is no direct connection between performance and promotion, your employees will not expect that superior performance will lead to their promotions. Therefore, HR managers must create proper organizational norms that form a basis for expectancy behaviour of employees. The third lesson is to remember that employees differ in their valence to outcomes. Therefore, try to understand the differences in valence of employees to motivate them through proper second level outcome.

THREE-PHASE GOAL SETTING MODEL

The essence of HRM practices is how to convert HR potential into performance. This is often a complex question. Because how to do and what should be done to realize the performance in organizations was not clear. Edwin Locke and Gary Latham provided basic answer to this question in the form of goal setting theory in 1960s and detailed it in their book titled *Goal Setting: A Motivational Technique That Works,* published in 1984. The goal setting theory occupied centre stage in performance management practices that include Management By Objectives (MBO). The chief premise of this theory is that performance of people can be enhanced substantially by setting challenging and clearly defined goals. There are many advantages with goal setting process that include: (i) employees will be clear about what and how much they should perform, (ii) it captures the attention of employees on the tasks they need to perform, (iii) it allows to develop action plans, (iv) serves as a reminder, (v) provides a kind of quantification of tasks, (vi) gives clarity and perspective to employees about their roles etc.

But how to set goals? The three phases described below help in setting goals:

- Phase-I: *Set appropriate goals.* This is a vital phase. The goals to be established for each employee must be specific, challenging, quantifiable, and clear. Challenging tasks means the goals thus assigned must be moderately difficult for the employee to achieve but should not be either impossible or beyond the person's capacity. The impossibility leads to counter productive results. Therefore, managers must have a clear understanding of the employees' capacity to perform.

- Phase-II: *Secure goal acceptance from employees.* There are many methods in this. One is employees must be clearly explained their goals and rationale behind them. The second and most ideal method is seeking participation of employees during goal setting process itself. Third is rewards must be clearly tied to the achievement of the set goals.

- Phase-III: *Provide support and feedback to employees.* Support refers to extending training and other developmental facilities to employees to acquire the related skills for achieving the set goals. Employees must also be given continuous feedback about their performance and progress. This serves as a reinforcer as well as to alter the course of action.

Managerial Implication

Goal setting, though four-decade-old theory has great relevance to today's organizations. A number of organizations still manage employees without assigning clear goals. There is overwhelming evidence to the effect that goal allocation enhances employees' performance and organizational effectiveness. It also helps employees with a clear career objective. Despite awareness, some organizations hesitate to take up goal setting exercise because of its complexity and lack of tools to implement it. Adopting three phases as described above, can minimize the complexity and tools can be developed either internally or by seeking the help of external expert. HR managers must take lead to make a beginning.

DRIVE-REDUCTION MODEL

It is a model that explains learning and motivational behaviour. The model centred on a cardinal principle that body wants to stay in a homeostatic environment. For example, hunger disturbs the equilibrium, we immediately indulge in eating in order to reduce the drive of hunger. This process of reducing the drive like hunger through eating is called drive-reduction. In a similar way, motivation and learning takes place according to Clark Leonard Hull, Professor of

Psychology at Wale, who proposed the much acclaimed Drive-Reduction model in his book titled, *Principles of Behaviour* published in 1943. Drive is a condition that exists when the body feels a biological deficiency. The goal of all motivated behaviour is the reduction or alleviation of a drive state.

Habit tends to form when a relationship between a drive and the objective of reduction is established. It is like the relationship between hunger drive and eating. This relationship would be strengthened since eating fulfils the drive and brings back balance. Over a period of time, this strengthened relationship contributes for reduction method (eating) itself becoming a drive/motivating factor. Drive reduction is a necessary condition for learning. If a stimulus leads to a response and if it satisfies a need, the stimulus-response bond is strengthened. However, this model does not explain all motivated and learning behaviours, particularly those of non-homeostatic behaviour. Non-homeostatic models point out that drives can be present even in the absence of a physiological need. Latent learning (putting efforts even on the face of failures means no reduction of drive instantly) is an example of this non-homeostasis behaviour.

Managerial Implication

Understanding of this basic model helps in design of reward and training tools. There are two learnings, which are relevant to HR managers. Firstly, they need to grasp the drive structure of their employees. Secondly, provide environment in terms of work/performance opportunities to reduce these drives. A high performance work culture could be build through this process of defining a relationship between macro HR drives and organizational reduction mechanisms. These macro HR drives could be money, personal and professional growth, freedom and meaningful, work etc. which could be handled through organization wide mechanisms such as pay, career opportunities, skill and competence enhancement openings, various recognition schemes, etc. Hull's Drive-Reduction model if applied, undoubtedly can produce meaningful, performance oriented and productive organizational behaviour.

ACHIEVEMENT NEED

This is a need represented by characteristics such as competing, solving complex problems, taking calculated risk, seeking immediate feedback on their performance, determination to break standards and occupying with task performance all the time. In brief, it is the behaviour to excel. High achievers differentiate themselves from others by their desire to do things better. Neither they like to take chance nor do gambling. Rather, they carefully plan, evaluate all options and undertake when probability of success is nearly fifty per cent. They tend to avoid assignments or tasks that are generally known to be easy to perform. David McClelland, a Psychologist at Harvard University and his associates conducted quite a few studies on the achievement need, which is also known as *n Ach*. McClelland presented his findings together with a detailed discussion on this motivation in his book titled *The Achieving Society* published in 1961. Incidentally, he conducted many studies in India, particularly in the states of Rajasthan and Andhra Pradesh studying the achievement need in many small entrepreneurs and businessmen.

He found in his studies that there is a positive correlation between achievement need in population of a country and state of its development. In other words, a nation which has a large population with achievement need will develop economically much faster in comparison to a nation where achievement need of people is moderate or minimal. The case may be similar with business organizations. Therefore, an argument is that development could be achieved by enhancing the achievement need of people. The achievement need though is formed at early stages of life, it can be taught with reasonable success in adults, according to McClelland. Such a training to trigger achievement motivation should focus on (i) Training people to behave in a manner that of high achievers, (ii) Exposing groups to emotionally experience each other's success and failure (like Mahabharat and other War stories), (iii) Enhancing self-awareness among people and (iv) Stimulating people to set formidable goals but carefully planned and achievable with existing capabilities.

Managerial Implication

Achievement training offers many benefits to organizations and therefore, efforts should be made to design and conduct these programmes. Apart from training, organizational culture must be set in such a way that everybody is motivated to realize his/her best. Studies in the past had conclusively established the positive effects of achievement building efforts in organizations. Managers in various countries who attended training programmes were reported of receiving more promotions, made more money and expanded their businesses. It also appears that, achievement need exists dormant in most of the people and such drive can be stimulated with training supplemented by right organizational practices.

Chapter 11

Creativity and Decision-making Management

HR practitioners are increasingly under pressure on two counts: One is to build systems in order to tap the creative talents of its employees and second is to impart in managers the decision-making skills. These are two critical areas that determine survival, existence and success of companies. However, these are also too difficult to manage given their complexity, intricacy and sophistication. It is complex because the industrial era prepared people to mostly execute routine tasks and nothing much left to either decide or apply creative talents. Therefore, HR system in most of the organizations also has been tuned themselves to this reality. The emergence of information revolution has changed these basic rules and now companies look toward HR practitioners to devise and implement methods to transform every employee capable of innovating and deciding on own.

Hence, the job of HR managers in contemporary times presupposes adequate knowledge and skills in these areas. This chapter consisting fifteen classics is devoted to present a few techniques, practices and methods in building creative talents and decision making skills in people in organizations. In the process, efforts are also made to include the traps of ineffective creative management such as myths of creativity and ineffective decision making like managerial powerlessness.

TEN MYTHS AND TRUTHS OF CORPORATE CREATIVITY

Creativity assumed new importance in the competitive era. Now more than before, companies need to innovate and this innovation rate has to be faster. In order to build a work environment that is creative oriented, companies followed different methods and some of them are successful and some not. Creativity gurus, Alan Robinson and Sam Stern, based on years of experience illustrated ten common mistakes that companies make in their quest for creativity and suggested remedies to overcome them in their book titled *Corporate Creativity: How Innovation and Improvement Actually Happens* published in 1997. These are briefly presented here:

- *Myth-1.* Large, bureaucratic companies can't be as creative as small, entrepreneurial ones

- *Truth.* A company's creative potential increases rapidly with size. The larger the company, the more likely the elements of a potentially creative act are within that company. But it's less likely that those elements can be brought together without help

- *Myth-2.* Companies can get more creativity by rewarding it
- *Truth.* When it comes to creativity, rewards and incentives can do more harm than good
- *Myth-3.* If a company wants more creativity, it should encourage employees to take more risks
- *Truth.* Though some creative acts involve risk, most require caution, care, and good judgement
- *Myth-4.* The best way for a company to promote creativity is to identify its most creative people and give them the backing they need
- *Truth.* Most creative acts are unanticipated by management and come from where they are least expected
- *Myth-5.* A creative company has procedures to match a creator with a champion—someone with clout who can help push an idea through the system to completion
- *Truth.* Once a champion is needed, the system has already failed. Instead of trying to overcome barriers to creativity, a company should remove them so champions are no longer needed
- *Myth-6.* Creativity can't be managed
- *Truth.* Once companies realize how creativity occurs, they can take specific, practical actions that will dramatically improve their creative performance
- *Myth-7.* A person's age, intelligence, and expertise are the best indicators of how creative he or she will be
- *Truth.* What is known about how those characteristics relate to creativity reinforces the no-preconceptions principle that it can't be known in advance who will be involved in a creative act or what that act will be
- *Myth-8.* Teaching employees such problem solving approaches as brainstorming will make them more creative
- *Truth.* There is no recipe for creativity. In practice, even brainstorming has a poor track record for delivering useful creativity
- *Myth-9.* There is little or no room for creativity in companies with highly standardized operations, procedures and policies
- *Truth.* All work has nonroutine aspects. Even the most standardized work places are alive with opportunities for creativity, as long as such aspects are not overlooked
- *Myth-10.* Because most creative acts are the result of chance, there's little a company can do to promote them
- *Truth.* When it comes to creativity, serendipity, not chance, is what really counts. There is much that companies can do to promote that.

Managerial Implication

The above ten myths and their solutions were drawn from study of business organizations by the authors. Therefore, these have immense practical value. Every organization endeavouring to promote creativity must check the respective positions in the light of ten myths. The truths will be of great use for initiating managerial actions to achieve the objective of effective creativity management.

3M HR PRACTICES FOR INNOVATION MANAGEMENT

The objective of 3M is to become the most innovative company in the world. Accordingly, the people management practices followed in 3M are oriented toward encouraging innovative behaviour and culture in that organization. Adam Brand of 3M in the paper titled "Knowledge Management and Innovation at 3M" published in *Journal of Knowledge Management* in 1998 highlights fourteen HRM practices their company follow for institutionalizing the innovative work behaviour. These are:

1. *Tradition.* 3M encourages a sense of tradition. Lifetime employment and promotion from within are important traditional 3M policies—the average service at 3M is decades and employee turnover is low

2. *Continuity.* Senior people have worked in or visited many different countries. They have a personal connection with a wide variety of people and that makes knowledge transfer, using electronic communication, across different cultural boundaries effective

3. *Loyalty overtime.* Some companies, worried about long term pension responsibilities and the need for head count flexibility, employ people on short-term contracts. 3M believe these practices deter innovation capabilities. It believes that employees' loyalty is important for innovation and that comes only from long-term employment

4. *Tolerance for mistakes.* Long-term commitment at 3M also allows for mistakes to be tolerated. For example, 3M's ceramic business began as a result of mistakes in the development of a new abrasive grit.

5. *Story telling.* Top managers who joined the company when they were young and who have absorbed the company's traditions and stories, re-tell those stories to reinforce the values and atmosphere that encourage innovation.

6. *Vision.* For a company to be successful in innovation, 3M argues that it needs vision; what it want to be, a knowledge of where the world is going, an understanding of its core competencies and freedom of its employees to achieve the goals

7. *Top management involvement.* At 3M knowledge management does not just bubble up from middle management; top management see it as one of their major duties to encourage knowledge linkages

8. *Flat organization.* 3M wants to be swiftly adaptive and it knows that the best adaptive systems are the ones, which are self-organizing. The company has been compared with a nickel and dime stories many times over. Rather than a hierarchy, it is a collection of networks

9. *Cross divisional cooperation.* Top management's long-term support for innovation is important to prevent groups becoming turfy, that is, people protecting their own patch and keeping out possible new ideas. At 3M top management's long-term commitment to innovation encourages cross divisional cooperation

10. *Coping with chaos.* The path of innovation rarely runs smoothly, especially where technology is the driver. Innovation in its early stages is a loose activity and can follow

a chaotic path. Top management must make allowances and not move too fast to judge, assess and audit projects. Pulling up a tender plant to see it still alive kills it

11. *Recruiting and keeping the right people.* If innovation is to be furthered, it is important that right people, who fit the culture, are recruited in the first place. 3M found the ideal people are those who want to start things rather than inherit business

12. *15 per cent rule.* An important support for innovation is signalled by 3M's 15 per cent rule, which states that 3M people can spend 15 per cent of their time working on innovative ideas of their own choice

13. *Grants.* Technical people can apply for 3M Genesis grants to buy equipment to assist them in the development of 15 per cent of their ideas or they can use these grants to the temporary labour

14. *Recognition programmes.* 3M also sees that certain inventors known and recognized across the company through articles and presentations. As a result 3M people tend to know more about the heroes of innovation than they do about senior management. There also a number of award programmes to recognize innovation.

Managerial Implication

The HR practices followed in 3M can be benchmarks for all those companies intending to promote innovation. More than technology, it is the HR management practices and philosophy that built innovation culture in the organization. Therefore, it can offer quite a good number of lessons to all knowledge driven organizations. It will be worth for HR managers to study these practices in order to analyze their own.

MOZART EFFECT

Mozart Effect is a system that deals with transformational power of music in enhancing the productive behaviour of people. In Mozart Effect, there are more than two dozen specific, easy to follow exercises to help you to raise your spatial IQ, sound away pain, boost creativity and make your spirits raising. The term Mozart Effect is believed to have been originated from the work of a team consisting Dr. Francis Raucher, Dr. Gordon Shaw and their colleagues at University of California. Don Campbell, a free lancing consultant who also did a great deal of work published a book titled *Mozart Effect* in 1997. The book provides formidable evidence of the influence of particular sounds, tones and rhythms on mental performance and spiritual outlook. It shows how music can be used to improve memory and learning, boost productivity, sooth jingled nerves, strengthen endurance, unlock creative impulses, sound away pain and heal the body from a host of ailments.

Research findings of many studies conducted across the globe highlight that music is not just an entertainment but a formidable discipline that can offer multiple opportunities to build physical and mental health of employees. The findings include the following:

1. A study conducted in 1994 found that listening to composition of Mozart increased scores on one of the tests of Stanford-Binet scale of intelligence

2. Research in Neuroscience found that attending to music increases brain creativity. Music structure facilitates cognitive processing in the brain

3. Campbell studies found that music affects perceptions and can alter the behaviour. It can stimulate mental growth and spark creativity
4. Research studies conducted in Japan supports a view that listening to music can improve the ability to perform complex tasks of spatial reasoning.

Managerial Implication

The above content is self-explanatory in its implications to practice in organizations. Despite familiarity with benefits of music at work place, many managers are yet to provide such a facility in their organizations. It is certainly a cost effective option that can help organizations and employees to derive numerous tangible benefits. Implementing music may not be as easy as it seems since one has to confront with number of factors like type, time, volume, sound of music etc. However, now a scientific and integrated model in the form of Mozart Effect is available to organizations, which if implemented, can reap rich dividends apart from supplementing their HRD efforts.

NEURO-LINGUISTIC PROGRAMMING (NLP)

NLP provides well-defined knowledge on how verbal and non-verbal communications affect the human brain. As such it presents an opportunity to not only communicate better with others, but also imparts know-how to gain more control over what we considered to be automatic function of our own neurology. It is important to note here that NLP is neither a diagnostic tool nor a therapy. It is simply an educational tool learned through experiential mode. The word Neuro refers to an understanding of the brain and its functioning. Linguistic relates to the communication aspects, both verbal and non-verbal, of our information processing. Programming is the behavioural and thinking patterns that we all go through. There is relationship between perceptions, thinking and behaviour that is neuro-linguistic in nature. The relationship is operating all the time and it can be studied by exploring a person's internal or subjective experience.

How NLP is actually done or practised is often a question that is posed. NLP is not based on any theory. It is based on building models (generally referred to as human modelling) with the help of information gathered from questioning a person in a systematic manner. NLP practitioners use techniques of transformational grammar, general semantics, observing cues people give that indicate very specific kind of thought process that include eye movements, certain gestures, breathing patterns, voice tone changes etc. For example, you want to create a model of 'a skilled software programmer' through using NLP. First step in this process is identifying a known skilled software engineer. Second step is you will start questioning him what he/she does? Why they do it? What works and what doesn't work? And so on. This questioning using with combination of NLP techniques such as thought process, observable behaviour, semantics, cues etc., makes it possible to build a human model of a software engineer that he/she is not aware of. There are number of models and associated techniques that are used as a part of NLP. These include (i) Sensory acuity and physiology, (ii) Meta model, (iii) Representational systems, (iv) Milton model, (v) Eye accessing cues, (vi) Submodalities, and (vii) Meta programs.

Richard Bandler, then a post-graduate student at University of Santa Cruz, and John Grinder, Professor at the same university, developed this technique in 1970. The original works in the field of NLP are books authored by Richard Bandler and John Grinder titled (i) The Structure of

Magic (A book about language and therapy), (ii) The Structure of Magic-II (A book about communication and change) published in 1975 and 1976 respectively, (iii) Patterns of The Hypnotic Techniques of Milton Erickson published in 1975.

Managerial Implication

NLP is widely used for multiple purposes such as to enhance learning capabilities, creativity and of course communication. The efficacy of some of the models is well established in enhancing the effectiveness of individuals through greater understanding of their cognitive structures. But it is also seen that experience of no two individuals is similar with NLP interventions and therefore their view of its utility. However, NLP has proved to be successful with skilled workers in enhancing quality of their thinking pattern. There are very few NLP practitioners who are well conversant with all the models and techniques and competent to use the technique in a scientific manner. Therefore, organizations intending to derive the benefit of NLP application must make a proper assessment of all the related issues including the quality of trainer.

MIND MAPPING

Mind Mapping is a technique that facilitates fast learning and agile memory of things learned. Recent research also found its potential for stimulating creativity and strengthening the ability to organize thought process. Tony Buzan, Chairperson of Brain Foundation, USA is the originator of this technique who published a book titled *The Mind Map Book* in 1993 followed by several other publications on the subject. There are two prime techniques in Mind Mapping:

1. Technique of using symbols, colours, images, dimensions, tree analysis in imparting ideas/taking notes instead of linear text method. For example, generally we read all the contents in text formats like books and try to remember in the same fashion. If the same is presented in the form of pictures or symbols or shapes or icons, it will be much easier for the brain to receive and store.
2. Technique of using each alphabet in a word to generate discussion and build ideas around it. For example, A stands for Apple P stands for Pineapple and another P for Pumpkin and the like. The identification of related words goes on which will be used to build a theme or an idea around it.

There are many independent techniques in mind mapping to serve a specific purpose like creative and report writing, reading, visual memory, meeting notes, speeches, restructuring of ideas, originality, etc. These techniques are (i) Mnemonic mind map technique, (ii) Computer mind map technique, (iii) Hierarchy based mind map, (iv) Association based mind map (v) Creative thinking mind maps, (vi) The mind map organic study technique, (vii) Knowledge mind map technique etc.

Several business organizations are reportedly using this technique in the areas of training, idea generation/sharing, and to improve productivity. For example, British petroleum and Digital Equipment extensively use mind mapping in their training programmes. A study found that, Boeing Aircraft engineers who usually take few years to learn some complex aeronautical engineering aspects have taken only few weeks to master the subject with the aid of mind mapping techniques. It resulted in saving of $10 million to the company. Philips Lighting of Netherlands reported that mind mapping usage had helped them in sharing of ideas in the company quickly and clearly. Other companies experimenting with this technique include Hyundai motors and a number of software companies.

Managerial Implication

The use of mind mapping techniques certainly benefit the organizations and their people to learn and innovate new ways of handling work. Firstly, well trained persons and right equipment are a prerequisite for implementing mind mapping in organizations. Secondly, this should be applied in a phased manner, may be starting with training function. Thirdly, customized mind mapping packages/programmes should be developed for a clearly defined purpose. For example, specific images, icons, tree pictorial graphs etc. need to be developed to teach strategic management topic to managers in an organization. Mind mapping can benefit organizations and its people when adequate preparations are made and implemented in a systematic manner.

SYNECTICS

Synectics is a creative stimulating technique that helps small groups to create new structures and new ideas/forms by bringing together disconnected elements. Its main tools are analogies and metaphors. It helps breaking the existing mindsets and is based on following premises:

1. Creative output increases when people become aware of the psychological processes that control their behaviour
2. The emotional component of creative behaviour is more important than the intellectual component; the irrational is more important than the intellectual component
3. The emotional and irrational components must be understood and used as precision tools in order to increase creative output

The following steps are adopted in synectics technique to enhance a group's creative abilities in problem solving:

- Step-I: A manager or someone facing the problem (problem owner) provide the description of the problem
- Step-II: Group members generate large number of spring boards (alternatives/ideas/solutions)
- Step-III: Group members led by problem owner selects one spring board that appears potential
- Step-IV: Group members generate more ideas on chosen spring board with a focused approach
- Step-V: Group members deliberate on each of these sub-ideas to understand their linkages with problem
- Step-VI: *Itemized response.* Each group member gives his/her response on suitability of a particular solution over others
- Step-VII: *Recycle or end.* The exercise ends if the solution is acceptable to problem owner or it again starts from Step-III if not acceptable.

Studies found that Synectics helps individuals in three ways: (i) it encourages the ability to live with complexity and apparent contradictions, (ii) it stimulates creative thinking and (iii) it mobilizes both sides of the brain.

This technique was developed by William Gordon in 1961 and presented in his book titled "Synectics" and further expanded by Nolan in 1989 in the book titled *The Innovator's Handbook*. Gordon believes that creativity can be enhanced and taught through the use of Synectics and argues that working in groups can serve to encourage creativity rather than inhibit it. He points out that putting three people in a room doesn't mean tripping their effect. You have to do more than putting the people in the same space to make them do what they are capable of doing.

Managerial Implication

Synectics is a highly valuable tool for organizations where innovation, research and development are fundamental for success. Much of the success of this kind will be contingent upon a deep understanding of the technique by the facilitator, and commitment of group members. The procedure involved is cumbersome but worth for the benefits it offers. However, this technique must be employed when the solutions and ideas are needed for a problem of high intensity and complexity. Further, the consistent practice of it strengthens the person in dealing with uncertainties and contradictions.

BRAINSTORMING

Brainstorming is a conference technique by which a group attempts to find a solution for a specific problem by amassing all the ideas spontaneously by its members. Alex F. Osborn is the father of this technique who detailed it in his book titled *Applied Imagination* published in 1963. The technique is widely used to generate solutions/alternatives to a problem and create ideas for development such as products, services, processes etc. The following steps are involved in a brainstorming exercise:

1. Assembling of a group of members
2. Presenting a problem or an issue to members
3. Encouraging them to propose solutions
4. Consolidating all the proposals/solutions
5. Evaluating these proposals/solutions to identify the appropriate ones.

However, conducting brainstorming session and deriving real benefits from such sessions is often a difficult task. The following rules should be followed while conducting brainstorming for beneficial results:

1. The leader who facilitates the session must be objective and friendly, and present the problem or subject for brainstorming clearly
2. The focus must be on quantity of ideas rather than quality at this juncture
3. Judgements or critical comments on the proposal of a member by others should be discouraged
4. All should be encouraged to present their ideas
5. The group members for the session must be drawn from multidisciplines
6. Members must be invited to build on ideas of other members
7. Mutual respect should be maintained and every one should believe that every member has the potential to contribute

Ever since this technique came into existence, many developments have been added to its original form that include:

1. An individual-oriented brainstorming in which a single person is provided with a statement of problem to propose the solutions or ideas (encouraging an individual to brainstorm himself/herself)
2. A mixed brainstorming method in which (i) initially individuals are encouraged to write down their ideas, (ii) all individual ideas are consolidated and (iii) members are assembled to discuss on consolidated ideas
3. A computer aided brainstorming in which programming is inbuilt that engages an individual in brainstorming

Managerial Implication

Brainstorming is a highly useful technique in realizing the creative potential of human beings. With the introduction of new methods such as computer-aided brainstorming, the application of technique has become less cumbersome. A cursory observation of the studies reveals that brainstorming did not yield expected results only when the process had been handled improperly. Brainstorming is a cost-effective method to generate ideas and solutions particularly to complex and abstract problems. The method can produce wonders once the members' inhibitions are expelled. This has great relevance to the organizations particularly in the context of increasing business value of innovations.

SOMATIC MARKERS

Somatic markers, a term used by Dr. Antonio Damasio, a Neurologist at University of Iowa means gut feelings. In life, whether professional or personal, we make critical decisions out of gut feeling and not depending upon any data or rationality. People acquire these gut feelings from their past experience. The somatic marker is a kind of automatic alarm that alerts us and drives us to choose a course of action over others. When people lack somatic markers in them, they make dispassionate decisions that will be disastrous in their outcomes. But they are perfectly capable of defending these decisions with pros and cons and can describe under what circumstance such a decision was arrived on with all rationality. What they miss in their decision-making is passion that cannot be substituted with data and rationality. These types of people immerse themselves with minute details to the extent they tend to overlook the essential features/central issue of a problem. Dr. Daniel Goleman in his book titled *Emotional Intelligence* rightly highlights the power of gut feeling (intuition) in decision-making through many examples:

1. In a study of 3000 top executives, it was found that intuition plays an influential role in reaching their decisions.
2. Bjorn Johansson, head of a Zurich executive search firm specializing in placing top level executives states that the business is intuition from A to Z. First you have to assess a company's chemistry-size up the CEO, his personal qualities and expectations, the tone he sets, and the resulting culture of the corporation you have to understand how the management team works, how they deal with each other. That's what you might call a smell to every corporation, a distinctive quality you can see.

3. Nalini Ambady and Rosenthal in their study of Harvard students found that people could sense intuitively in the first thirty seconds of an encounter with basic impression they will have about the other person after fifteen minutes-or half a year.

4. In a study of credit managers at Citibank, it was found that managers who took successful decisions in terms of credit worthiness are those who seldom consulted the data and background information. Their decisions were derived from gut feeling and taken in first few minutes.

Managerial Implication

In an uncertain environment as most of the businesses and managers are in, the role of intuition in decision-making is unbounded. Passionless decision-making is as good as computer data processing. Unfortunately, machines cannot deal with situations that are new and programming of which is yet to be done. The case is the same with managers who rely upon data excessively for decision-making. We need to remember that data that is available are mostly of the past. The past data undermines the reality. Secondly, too much consideration of data blurs the emotional side of the problem. When data are scarce, one needs to take a leap in dark. Therefore, managers need to be encouraged to use their intuitive competence.

MANAGERIAL POWERLESSNESS

Powerlessness is a bigger problem than use of power arbitrarily among managers in most of organizations for two broad reasons: firstly, organizational factors that inhibit exercise of power for which it is meant for, and secondly incompetence of managers to exercise powers. Rosabeth Moss Kanter, professor at Harvard Business School authored a classic paper in this context titled "Power Failure in Management Circuits" published in *Harvard Business Review* in 1979. She says, powerful leaders are more likely to delegate, to reward talent and to build a team that places subordinates in significant positions. Powerlessness in contrast, tends to breed bossiness rather than true leadership. In large organizations at least, it is powerlessness that often creates ineffective, desultory management and petty, dictatorial rule-minded management styles.

The specific factors that can be responsible for powerlessness are:

1. *Incompetence.* Most of the managers are not trained enough in how to exercise power and when to exercise power. The paradox is regardless of its usage, every manager in organizations solicit powers. As someone said, power is what people say they want until they get it. What most people truly want is the aura of power because the burdens of power are so overwhelming, and few can handle them with both style and grace.

2. *Organizational inhibitors.* Despite formal delegation, a number of practices or operating culture in organization discourage managers to exercise their powers which include (i) a practice of appraising seniors before decisions are taken, (ii) too many rules/procedures in carrying out a task, (iii) excessive interference of officers in hierarchy, (iv) surveillance over the decisions taken in the name of audit, (v) little or no involvement in policy/key decision-making and only responsible for implementation, (vi) ineffective organizational communication, (vii) distrust in the organization, (viii) lack of rewards for initiative, (ix) discouragement to risk taking and (x) routine jobs.

Managerial Implication

Organizations must encourage their managers to effectively use the existing delegated powers instead of starting any fresh empowerment programmes. Establishing an enabled work culture is more important than just paper-based delegation of powers. There will be no use of such executive powers in which people are sceptical. Powerlessness in an organization is directly proportionate to fewer decisions its managers take in a day. Therefore, two actions will assume importance in this context. Firstly, a culture of recognizing decision-making/risk-taking must be nurtured in a conscious manner. Secondly, managers who are victims of helplessness should be trained in decision-making and confidence must be built in them.

BOUNDED RATIONALITY

Herbert Simon, Nobel prize laureate and professor of Psychology and Computer Science at Carnegie Mellon University proposed the concept of bounded rationality in 1957. He discussed vividly and expanded it further in his book titled, *Models of Bounded Rationality* published in 1983. Bounded rationality means whatever decisions managers make are limited in their rationality and not absolutely rational because of two reasons.

1. *Firstly*, managers can never have all the information required or all alternatives on any issue or situation to arrive at decisions of unlimited rationality. Available information and alternatives will not be exhaustive. Their decisions will be based on limited information and alternatives. Therefore, decisions are bounded in rationality.
2. *Secondly*, managers are not competent enough in absolute and infinite terms because of human mind limitation to deal with all the information and alternatives, as most of them are complex. Hence, complex information is translated into a simplistic model by capturing the essential features from problems and not taking all the features into account. Based on these, managers take decisions.

How does this bounded rationality happen in organizational life? Let us find out

1. We make efforts to collect all the relevant information and alternatives to handle an assignment or when encountered with a problem. In reality, sometimes, we do not get all the relevant information and all the alternatives. Despite this lack of complete information, we take decisions because they ought to be. This incomplete information-based on which the decision is taken, is bounded in its rationality.
2. In other times, the volume of information and number of alternatives available to an issue/problem become unmanageable. In these circumstances, we try to reduce the number of alternatives or complexity of problem to the level that can be handled or understood. Simon calls this phenomenon as *satisficing model*. Decision taken in this mode is limited in its rationality because the decision arrived at is in considers few alternatives or facts.

Managerial Implication

Bounded rationality is all pervasive and there would be no organization or manager. However, they may differ in intensity. Variety in the way problems are solved would be minimal when decision makers are struck with this syndrome. They look for precedents and maintain status quo in decision making methods. This attitude beyond a point may cost organizational problem solving capabilities. Further, managers may miss some unique ways of solving problems because of this. Therefore, managers' ability to generate and evaluate alternatives must be enhanced for lasting benefits.

GROUPTHINK

Groupthink is a mode of thinking that group consensus overrides realistic appraisal of a problem. Groupthink is a disease that attacks many groups. We see many times that, persons who hold a different view/perspective from that of majority are under pressure to suppress or withhold their views. This is known as Groupthink. Irving Janis is the author of Groupthink model who published a book on it titled, *Victims of Groupthink* in 1972. The symptoms of Groupthink are:

1. *Unanimity illusions.* If some members of a group tend to go with views of other members in spite of having a different view. This is called as unanimity illusion. They do not like to hurt each other or differ for fear that it may disturb the consensus mode. Silence of a member is regarded as support to the view that is presented.

2. *Rationalization.* Members rationalize their decisions in all the circumstances. The assumptions that are conflicting with group consensus will be undermined.

3. *Direct and subtle pressures.* Members exert subtle pressure on each other to toe the line of their thinking. Sometimes, direct pressures are also applied through sarcastic remarks and mockery. Deviation from the shared views is considered as disloyalty to the group.

4. *Underestimation.* Members of a group tend to underestimate the strength of others. They believe that their capabilities are supreme and nobody can defeat them.

5. *Isolation.* Groups tend to distance themselves from external environment. Therefore, opinions which are inconsistent with their groups internal beliefs get rejected.

6. *Mind guards.* Those members who have doubts or hold differing points of view seek to avoid deviating from what appears to be group consensus by keeping silent about misgivings and even minimizing to themselves the importance of their doubts.

Managerial implication

The phenomenon of Groupthink has serious implications for business organizations because organizations follow some kind of group decision-making method. If not formal groups, a kind of coterie exists around decision-makers who influence decision-making in organizations. Groupthink can lead to a number of irrational decisions. Therefore, efforts should be made to avoid pitfalls of group decision-making or groupthink. Historical failures such as Pearl Harbour attack, Vietnam fiasco, and Challenger explosion are attributed to Groupthink disease. Factors such as homogeneity of group, insulation of group, a consensus seeking tendency, absence of methodical process, etc. are responsible for Groupthink. Hence, Organizations must see that these faults are removed. Functional deviant behaviour must be encouraged and instead of a large group, small groups may be opted for offering solutions, which can be reviewed by a large group.

DELPHI TECHNIQUE

This is a group decision-making technique that does not require group members to physically meet and interact with each other. Though it is a complex method, it is used widely across all business and non-business organizations on account of its ability to facilitate forecasting decisions with high degree of success. C.N. Dalki and his associates have developed this technique in 1950 while working for Rand Corporation. The essence of this technique boils down to the following:

1. Group members will be identified to solve a potential problem.
2. A well structured questionnaire covering all the features and possible alternatives will be circulated among all such identified members
3. Group members will be given a reasonable time to evaluate the information provided in the questionnaire and offer their recommendations/solutions. The identity of such members will be kept confidential and actions will be taken that no member will come into contact with other member on the issue.
4. All the recommended solutions will be compiled and forwarded to all group members seeking their recommendations afresh on the problem.
5. This review of consolidated views/solutions/predictions will be circulated number of times till the solution framework emerges clearly.

The uniqueness of this decision-making process is keeping members identity confidential that helps in avoiding group influence or influence of any one individual over the others. This method provides for objective decision-making process. However, this is suitable only where the time allowed to solve a problem is of a reasonably long duration.

Managerial Implication

This technique is highly useful when the nature of problems is very complex. The number of such complex problems an organization has to encounter is progressively growing in the competitive environment. Further, the wide geographical spread of organizations and their operations seek a method that permits participation of people in decision-making without dislocation from their work places. Delphi technique can meet this requirement and still can produce the best decisions. Empirical studies conducted on the efficacy of the technique proved that even average people could offer intelligent solutions and predictions while participating in a Delphi type group decision-making.

NOMINAL GROUP TECHNIQUE

It is a group decision-making method. With the increasing use of team working, the need for group based decision-making and problem solving has gone up significantly. Nominal group technique is a complete functional mechanism that encourages people to discuss threadbare on the subject problem and restricts any other discussion not pertaining to the subject and any other interpersonal matters. The following steps are usually prescribed and followed in this method:

1. Group members assemble at pre decided venue
2. Problem will be either orally presented or given in a written text

3. Members will be requested to understand and carefully study the problem
4. Members will be requested to write down their ideas on a paper with all the reasons/ justification/logic/reasoning
5. Each member of the group will present his/her ideas
6. All the ideas so presented will be displayed on a clip board
7. All members participate evaluating each view/option so displayed
8. Members at this stage will be advised to rank these options in order or keep in ranking by assigning numerical values
9. The final decision will be arrived based on highest aggregate marks of an option

The advantage of this method is, it allows group members to meet freely but restricts discussion only on the subject problem. Further, this technique also encourages open discussion on each of the options to evaluate its appropriateness in an objective manner. Each member will get adequate time and freedom to carefully scrutinize the problem without influence of other group members. By this, all the members will also have the satisfaction of active participation in decision-making. This method acquired the title of nominal because it doesn't allow discussion other than on identified task. This restriction of discussion to only on identified problem can be of disadvantage sometimes since the solution for the problem may lie in interpersonal affairs or on periphery of the problem.

Managerial Implication

This technique provides for systematic group decision-making. Nominal group technique is very useful to present generation organization since most of the problems they face are inter-disciplinary in nature and involves group decisions. There is adequate evidence that this type of group decision-making generates good ideas, evaluates the options objectively and leads to right decisions. Particularly, it's a method of allowing discussion consequent upon presentation of problem and conceptualization of individual ideas found to be effective.

PARETO PRINCIPLE

Pareto Principle, also known as 80:20 ratio has been developed by Vilfredo Pareto, an Italian-Swiss socio-economist who is referred to as *the father of social systems approach to organization and management*. During 1906, on study of Italian people, he made an observation that 20 per cent of the people owned 80 per cent of their country's accumulated wealth whereas 80 per cent of people owned 20 per cent of the wealth. The principle was extended to different situations in the following years. Joseph Juran, a quality management specialist was the first to apply this concept to the industrial environment. Pareto principle is applicable to a variety of situations. For example:

1. 80 per cent of problems are created by 20 per cent of people and 20 per cent of problems by 80 per cent of people
2. 80 per cent of people read 20 per cent of newspaper and 20 per cent of people read 80 per cent of newspaper
3. 80 per cent of efforts result in 20 per cent of production and 20 per cent of efforts in 80 per cent of production

4. 80 per cent of time spent on 20 per cent of things and 20 per cent of time on 80 per cent of things

5. 80 per cent of roads used by 20 per cent of commuters and 20 per cent by 80 per cent of commuters

6. 80 per cent of decisions come from 20 per cent of time spent in a meeting and 20 per cent of decisions in 80 per cent of time

Managerial Implication

80:20 ratio principle if managed can reap substantial benefits to organizations. Studies have proved that consistent application of Pareto principle dramatically improves productivity. For example by applying Pareto principle, time management can be improved in considerable terms. You know that, you will be spending 80 per cent of time on 20 per cent of issues, therefore focus on those issues for optimization. Research findings of many studies have clearly established that about 80 per cent of problems in organizations are related to HRM and 20 per cent to technology/equipment. Therefore, it doesn't make any sense in having 80 per cent of people with tech skills and 20 per cent of people with social skills. In nutshell, Pareto effect drives managers to be focused because they know 20 per cent of 100 is crucial.

GESTALT PSYCHOLOGY

Max Wertheimer was the founder of Gestalt Psychology who published a book titled, *A Source Book of Gestalt Psychology* published in 1938. The central theme of this faculty is that one must interpret elements as part of larger structures rather than as independent atoms, which combine to form larger units. In other words, we must learn to see and understand things in an integrated perspective rather than in a piece meal fashion. For example, a man is not only a part of his field but is also one among other men. When a group of people work together it rarely occurs that they constitute a mere sum of independent sum of egos. Instead, the functioning of their organization becomes their mutual concern and each employee is a meaningful part of the whole. Why most of us perceive things in parts instead of their wholeness? This is because of following factors:

1. *Proximity*—elements tend to be grouped together according to their nearness

2. *Similarity*—items similar in some respect tend to be grouped together

3. *Closure*—items are grouped together if they have similar entity

4. *Simplicity*—items will be organized into simple figures

Gestalt principle is not only a technique that promotes wholeness but also a more encompassing science that asserts interaction of the individual and the situation in the sense of a dynamic field that determines experience and behaviour. Connections among psychological contents are more readily and more permanently created on the basis of substantive concrete relationships rather than by sheer repetition and reinforcement.

Managerial Implication

Gestalt Psychology is a problem solving technique. It helps managers to understand the underlying assumptions of issues, situations and behaviours. These insights enable them to conceive and apply integrated solutions to the problems. We know that many of the problems organizations face are repetitive in nature. It means that problems are resolved for the time being; therefore they reappear at either regular or irregular intervals. This situation arises since we look at the things in parts (single function perspective) or simply rely upon external symptoms and derives solutions. Gestalt training promotes an integrated problem solving approach in managers among other behavioural benefits.

Chapter *12*

Self-Management

In a dynamic and uncertain environment, employees must be trained to be capable of managing their professional and personal life in a systematic manner. The self-management skill is a key factor in ensuring a stress-free, fruitful and enjoyable working. Studies highlight that majority of employees fail to achieve what they intended to achieve in life, not because of their lack of technical skills but due to poor management of self. The inaptitude of employees in managing self could have devastating effects on their lives and ultimately on the survival and success of companies. Therefore, this is one area that HR practitioners need to address on priority basis. This goes well with a popular saying that, train how to fish instead of offering a fish everyday. Instead of offering individual solutions, HR practitioners must equip employees with self-management skills.

This chapter focuses on self-management skills, techniques and models. A total of seven classics present a novel and new perspective in managing the self, that mainly touches you as a person, your time, psychic, physiology, family, peace, life goals, work life etc.

TWELVE-STEP SELF-MANAGEMENT MODEL

Each one of us has goals—be it career-related or personal or professional. However, all of us may not be successful in achieving these goals. The difference between successful and unsuccessful people is determined by their self-management skills. In other words, successful people are those who could achieve their goals and unsuccessful are the ones' who couldn't. The other differences between successful and unsuccessful people are indicated in Table 12.1.

TABLE 12.1

Successful people	*Unsuccessful people*
• Set goals	• Do not set goals
• Resolve to pay the price in advance	• Refuse to pay the price
• Focus and concentrate on goals	• Focus and concentrate on television, sports news, alcohol and drugs
• Expect good things to happen	• Expect bad things to happen
• Think they are incharge of their own lives	• Think their lives are controlled by forces outside themselves
• Forces on successes	• Forces on failures
• Visualize perfect outcomes	• Visualize disasters
• Mentally rehearse success	• Mentally rehearse failures

TABLE 12.1   *(continued)*

Successful people	Unsuccessful people
• Emotionalize perfect outcomes	• Emotionalize disasters
• Make good positive affirmations	• Make bad negative affirmations
• Do not suffer from self-limiting beliefs	• Suffer from self-limiting beliefs
• Continue to learn and grow	• Have stopped learning and growing
• Talk challenge/opportunity	• Talk problems and threats
• Do not use victim language	• Use victim language
• Accept that change is inevitable	• Fear and fight change
• Understand that there is a reason for everything	• Believe in luck and accidents
• Accept responsibility for themselves	• Blame others
• Manage their time well	• Manage their time badly
• Read non-fiction books, go on courses, and listen to tapes	• Don't read, never go on courses, never listen to tapes
• Spend time with their mastermind alliance	• Spend their time with people going nowhere
• Forgive and forget	• Bear grudges
• Have high self-esteem	• Have low self-esteem
• Have high self-concept level of health, income, etc.	• Have low self-concept levels of health, income, etc.
• Make the necessary efforts	• Do not make the necessary efforts
• Take action	• Procrastinate
• Set priorities	• Focus on the unimportant
• Accept that it takes 20 years to be successful	• Want everything now, without effort
• Are proactive, make things happen, do it now	• Are reactive, wait and see what happens, do it later
• Make plans	• Don't make plans
• Are full of energy, well-informed, unselfish, generous, patient, fair-minded, self-effacing	• Are lazy, ill-informed, selfish, greedy, impatient, ruthless and vain
• Use deadlines	• Will get round to it one day
• Use the expression "I am"	• Use the expressions "I wish" and "I'll try"
• Are excited and enthusiastic	• Have no enthusiasm, can't be bothered
• Use their time well	• Always use time as an excuse
• Make lists	• Put it at the back of their minds
• Ask for help	• Refuse to ask for help
• Are flexible, adaptive	• Are inflexible, won't change
• Question beliefs, assumptions	• Hang on to their beliefs, stick to same assumptions
• Carry out action plans to completion	• Don't finish what little they start
• Separate the situation from the person	• Take everything personally
• Listen to others	• Justify the status quo

Why some people are successful in achieving their goals and others are not? This is mainly due to the attitude, determination and lack of understanding in how to go about achieving the goal. The self management gurus' Richard Dobbins and Barrie Pettman in their mind boggling paper titled "Self-Development: The Nine Basic Skills for Business Success" published in *The Journal of Management Development* in 1997 have prescribed 12 steps that enable people to set, plan and achieve goals. These are:

1. Make a decision that you desire to achieve the goal
2. Believe that you will achieve the goal
3. Write down your goal on paper

4. Be honest with yourself
5. Analyze your present position
6. Use deadlines
7. Identify the rocks that stand in your way
8. Identify the skills you will need
9. Identify those people from whom you will need cooperation
10. Make a complete business plan
11. Visualize the perfect outcome, emotionalize how terrific you will feel when the outcome is achieved and make the necessary affirmations consistent with achieving the goal
12. Determine to back your plan with patience and persistence

Managerial Implication

In a changing world of work and given growing preference for flexible work schedules, involvement and empowerment measures, all employees need to acquire self-management skills and HR managers must facilitate imparting these skills to them. All the modern management practices may not deliver desired results if employees of the organization lack self-management skills. Therefore, self-directed work practices should start with equipping the employees with self-management skills. In this effort, the above model will be of great value to the managers.

ART OF LIVING

There are two techniques in this school of thought. One is called as *Sudershan Kriya* and the other as *Vipassana Meditation*.

1. *Sudershan Kriya*, a healing breathing method patented by Sri Sri Ravi Shankar who discovered it in 1982 is the founder of Art of Living Foundation that has centers in 110 countries. This is the most popular among meditation techniques. Sudarshan Kriya is translated as like this: *su* for right, *darshan* for vision and *kriya* for purifying action. This technique is taught through two courses. The first one is a basic course. This is a 22-hour, six-day interactive session of breathing, yoga exercises and meditation. The second is an advanced course of five days duration. The course lays emphasis on meditation and silence, apparently to achieve a higher self-awareness.

2. *Vipassana*, which means to see things as they are, is one of India's most ancient technique of meditation. Goutama Buddha rediscovered it more than 2500 years back. Vipassana is a way of self-transformation through self-observation. It focuses on the deep interconnection between mind and body, which can be experienced directly by disciplined attention to the physical sensations. The technique is taught through a 10-day residential course during which participants learn the basics of the method and practice sufficiently to experience its beneficial results. The entire practice is a mental training to develop a healthy mind. There are three steps in Vipassana meditation training. Firstly, one must abstain from any action: physical or vocal, which disturbs the peace and harmony of others. The next step is to develop some mastery over the wild mind by training it to remain fixed on a single object: the breath. The third step is purifying the mind of defilements by developing insight into one's own nature.

Managerial Implication

There is adequate research evidence that practice of the above described techniques leads to a positive mind and frees the body from stress and anxiety. Many corporate organizations in India and abroad have exposed their employees to this technique through formal management development programmes. Sudershan Kriya and Vipassana Meditation are integrated techniques, which teaches a healthy way of life. This may be right medicine for many attitudinal problems in organizations. It is worth trying these techniques, which certainly strengthen efforts of organizations in evolving a salutary work culture.

TRANSCENDENTAL MEDITATION TECHNIQUE

Maharshi Mahesh Yogi introduced Transcendental Meditation as a principal technique of Maharshi Effect. Robert Roth who published a book titled *Maharshi Mahesh Yogi's Transcendental Meditation* asserts that, TM is much more than an idea—it is a powerful proven technology to unfold our most precious natural resource—the human mind. The process of this technique has its theoretical basis in principles of Physics, which describe how coherent influences combine to create a transition to greater orderliness. The Maharshi Effect is described as a powerful, scientifically measurable influence of increasing harmony and positivity.

TM technique is a simple, natural, effortless procedure practised for 15–20 minutes in the morning and evening, while sitting comfortably with the eyes closed. During this sitting, the individual's senses settles down and experiences a unique state of restful alertness. As the body gets absolutely relaxed, the mind transcends all mental activity to experience the simplest form of awareness and Transcendental Consciousness is open to itself. This is the self-referral state of consciousness. The experience of Transcendental Consciousness develops the individual's latent creative potential while dissolving accumulated stress and fatigue through the deep rest gained during the practice. This experience enlivens the individual's creativity, dynamism, orderliness, and organizing power, which result in increasing effectiveness and success in daily life. A person has to follow seven steps to learn the TM technique as indicated below in Table 12.2.

TABLE 12.2

Step 1	Introductory Lecture	A vision of all possibilities through the TM programme	90 Minutes
Step 2	Preparatory Lecture	The mechanics and origin of the TM technique	90 Minutes
Step 3	Personal Interview	Interview with a qualified teacher of the TM programme	10 Minutes
Step 4	Personal Instruction	Learning the TM technique	120 Minutes
Step 5	Verification and Validation of Experiences	Verifying the correctness of the practice and further instruction	120 minutes
Step 6	Verification and Validation of Experiences	Understanding the mechanics of the TM technique from personal experiences	120 Minutes
Step 7	Verification and Validation of Experiences	Understanding the mechanics of the development of higher states of consciousness	120 Minutes

Managerial Implication

Competitive environment of organizations coupled with ever changing methods of work are subjecting the employees of all classes to stress and anxiety. These maladies further lead to increased employee fatigue, loss of focus, creativity, and problem solving capabilities and declined work performance. Therefore, a programme like TM can help organizations not only to counter these ills but also to create a natural semblance in organizations. Numerous research studies conducted in various countries on the efficacy of TM prove that it benefits all areas of an individual's life: mind, body, behaviour and environment.

STEREOTYPING

A stereotype is a widely held generalization about a group of people or attributing the generalized characteristics to an individual merely because he or she may be member of the group. According to Richard Steers and Stewart Black, stereotyping is a process in which attributes are assigned to people solely on the basis of their class or category. It is particularly likely to occur when one meets new people, since very little is known about the person that time. On the basis of a few prominent characteristics such as sex, race, religion, caste, nativity or age we tend to place people into a few general categories. We ascribe a series of traits to them based upon the attributes of the category in which we have put them. This most of us do in our daily life in understanding or misunderstanding people like attributing certain characteristics to south Indians or Punjabis or Biharis likewise. Generally, there are three types of stereotypes that could be seen in organizations. These are concerned with age, race and gender. Two psychologists Rosen and Jerdee, had conducted a study using few students as subjects on stereotyping of age factor. Their inferences are that these students found all older employees to be people who (a) are more resistant to organizational change, (b) show minimum interest in learning new things (c) have inadequate capability in acquiring new knowledge, (d) are less innovative and (e) have low capability in facing uncertainty. This study amply illustrates the stereotyping among students about older people. There is also a view that stereotyping may be, to some extent, based upon the fact.

Managerial Implication

Stereotyping though benefits in understanding the groups in an easier manner could also lead us to make wrong judgements which lead managers to take wrong decisions. Therefore, they need to be conscious of this. One needs to be open in judging others before understanding the generalized attributes. Have a check on stereotyping for quality decisions. Therefore, HR managers must make efforts to minimize stereotyping among the employees to the maximum extent possible. This has assumed greater importance during the contemporary times since most of old time stereotypes have become irrelevant in gauging anything with changing times and generation.

ALEXANDER TECHNIQUE

Alexander Technique is a century old practice that helps (i) to understand our unnatural and improper physical movements that harms physiological and psychological health and

(ii) facilitates to reconstruct the habit of natural physical movements. In other words, human beings are usually born with an overall fundamental pattern of coordination programmed into their nervous systems. This primary pattern works efficiently and easily with the human structure. Unfortunately, as they grow, they tend to develop wrong habits. For example, a year old baby sits upright naturally. However, when grown up, the adult learns to slouch into supposedly relaxed sitting posture. Similarly, we form habits which are destructive and that destroys overall mental and physical coordination of the body. Maladaptive habits have been found to alter general sensory feedback. They also alter perceptions and concomitant feelings. They cause back pains, chronic fatigue, and stiff neck, fixed movements, migraine, restricted breathing and other chronic ailments.

Alexander Technique a unique method developed by F. Matthias Alexander in 1890, restores balance, posture and freedom of movement. It inculcates self-management through a constructive control of habit and reaction. The technique achieves this by establishing a good foundation for movement—what Alexander calls *The Primary Control.* The Alexander Technique teacher takes the student through basic movements giving gentle hands-on guidance. This neither involves exercises nor any physiotherapy methods. Instead of looking at the body as a set of separate parts, this technique guides a student through movement, observing and working with whole pattern of coordination, which includes tension and postural patterns. The student actively participates in this process, learning to apply his own intelligence to effectively change habits. Two of the major Alexander Technique professional organizations are: The American Society for the Alexander Technique (AmSAT) and the British based Society of Teachers of the Alexander Technique (STAT). A number of books are published on the technique that include a book containing original writings of F.M. Alexander titled *The Essential Writings of Alexander* edited by Edward Meisel published in 1989.

Managerial Implication

Working in modern organizations is fraught with many constraints like sitting/standing/browsing computer screen for long hours. This working pattern coupled with improper physical postures and wrong movements will certainly cause health hazards. Problems such as chronic pains will have adverse implications to the emotional health of employees. Therefore, organizations must focus on the management of cultivating right habits of physical postures and movements. Alexander Technique is the practical version of Ergonomics for application in business organizations. This technique can help to build occupation-specific physical work pattern/habits in organizations.

PREMACK PRINCIPLE

Dr. David Premack, Emeritus Professor at University of Pennsylvania propounded this principle in 1962. Premack asserts that contingent access to high frequency behaviour serves as a reinforcer for the performance of the low frequency behaviour. It means performing desirable behaviour can be used as a positive reinforcement for performing less desirable behaviour.

The principle brought a new insight in the motivational and learning management, i.e. just look at what an organism does as what is important and not concern yourself with determining what is reinforcer. An example of the experiments conducted in this context may make it easy to understand this phenomenon. Imagine training a rat to eat and drink—say in order to get food and water, needs to press a lever first. The rat follows the sequence of pressing lever-eating food—drinking water in this order. Having been engaged in this behaviour of eating-drinking-pressing in this order it spends more time on eating and drinking, and minimal time in pressing lever. However, once eating becomes contingent upon lever pressing, the frequency of lever pressing becomes much more. Premack explains that, the rat is engaged in a less desired behaviour, lever pressing to get the opportunity of getting engaged in a more desired behaviour of eating and drinking. By looking at it this way, a reinforcer event is simply one that is more probable than the one upon which it is contingent. Much of our behaviour can be viewed in this way—we work (less desirable activity) in order to do things that we enjoy.

Managerial Implication

Premack principle serves as a self-management tool. Most of us have a tendency to engage and spend time on tasks which we like and either avoid it or spend very little time on tasks which we don't enjoy. Tasks which we do not enjoy might be more important than the enjoyable 'ones' to the organization, and also many times for the individuals. Therefore, one needs to keep a list of tasks to be performed in a day and arrange then in a hierarchy in consonance with their importance or coupling each unenjoyable task with an enjoyable task. This will help in achieving high productive behaviour. Like this, you can control your own behaviour or other's behaviour by using this principle. For this, you need to understand the reinforcement hierarchy of the person(s) to be controlled. Then, you must be able to make items high on that hierarchy depending upon the performance of items low on the hierarchy. This is like offering ice cream to a child contingent upon completing homework.

ZEIGARNIK EFFECT

A tendency to remember incomplete task than the one completed, and the reluctance to work on a task before completion of ongoing activity is called as *Zeigarnik Effect*. We come across many incidents and people with this experience. Overstretched meetings, too much occupied with same task even with the pressure other tasks, habitual inability to break for lunch, etc. are commonly observable examples of this effect.

Russian Psychologist Bluma Zeigarnik discovered this effect in 1927. As put forwarded by her, once you struggled with a given piece of information trying to remember it, in interacting, a question and trying to decide which is the best answer, that piece of material is embedded more effectively in your memory. The Zeigarnik Effect is generally referred to as the principle that any task that is interrupted will be recalled better than a task that the individual is permitted to complete. Fulfilment is defined in terms of the individual's own sense of satisfaction; it is not simply completion of a task but the satisfactory completion of it in terms of the goals of the person working on it. However, this is commonly present in all the people but degree differs. This will assume as a managerial problem when an executive falls victim of Zeigarnik Effect, i.e. inability of the executive to focus on multiple assignments simultaneously since he/she tends to get bogged down with one incomplete task.

Managerial implication

A good number of managers has fallen a victim to Zeigarnik Effect. A Manager's role demands that he should have ability to plan and carry out various activities simultaneously. These actions are intended to optimize the use of resources. Most of the tasks are interdependent in organizations which presupposes acting on multiple tasks in a given time framework. For example, any project management operations demand working on multiple tasks. Therefore, managers need to be trained on handling simultaneous assignments, and their capabilities in coping with a number of incomplete tasks (progressing tasks) must be enhanced. Working and thinking on a single incomplete task at a time, at the best could be a characteristic of an assistant or a technician.

Chapter 13
Selected Classics in OB and OD

Knowing the basic concepts, techniques and practices of organizational behaviour and organization development helps HRM practitioners immensely. The focus is also fast moving from a kind of maintenance role of HR issues to a more advanced and new-fashioned organizational behaviour and organization development oriented issues. Therefore, HR practitioners not only need to be aware of these issues but also they must be well versed in analysis, design and implementation of various behavioural and development centered interventions.

However, it is not possible here to present all such concepts, tools and techniques of organizational behaviour and organization development since they are wholistic and comprehensive disciplines in themselves. As such, this chapter confines itself in presenting a few issues which HR practitioners ought to know and which help them in their daily working. Fifteen different issues are dealt with here such as (i) personal values, (ii) behavioural models focusing on individuals like self-efficacy, locus of control, cognitive dissonance, (iii) OD implementation models, (iv) action learning, (v) consultancy skills and (vi) future search conference etc.

FIVE-STEP ORGANIZATIONAL BEHAVIOUR MODIFICATION MODEL

Contribution of organizational behaviour models in effective management of HR in organizations is profound. The recent literature has accorded focus on how to convert potential of HR into performance for greater realization of human capabilities and resource optimization to organizations. Organizational Behaviour Modification Model developed by Fred Luthans and Robert Kreitner is a comprehensive approach that aids performance improvement through five steps. These are:

- **Step-I:** *Identification of performance behaviours.* The goal of this first step is identifying the critical behaviours that account for outstanding performance in the organization. Many organizations face HR behavioural problems that adversely affect the performance of employees and consequently organizational effectiveness. These 'good' and 'bad' organizational behaviours could be identified through two methods: One method is direct observation of the person by an expert while performing the job to determine critical behaviour and the other method is use of behavioural audits.

- Step-II: *Measurement of the behaviour.* Baseline measures are developed at this stage. These measures determine how often the identified critical behaviours occur in existing conditions. Taking into account this frequency data of critical behaviours, operational measures will be developed to gauge the employees' performance.

- Step-III: *Functional analysis of the behaviour.* This is the A-B-C analysis of critical behaviours identified in step-I. Here, A means antecedents, B means behaviour and C, consequences of the behaviour. In other words, analysis will be done to find as of why an individual performs in a particular way, what causes that behaviour and what will be the consequence of that behaviour in terms of outcome to the individual.

- Step-IV: *Development of an intervention strategy.* Based on above three steps, a strategy will be developed to encourage the functional behaviour and discourage the dysfunctional behaviour. Popular techniques such as positive reinforcement and a punishment-positive reinforcement will be employed in this process.

- Step-V: *Evaluation to ensure performance improvement.* In simple terms, this is an exercise to understand the efficacy of intervention strategy adopted to build performance-oriented behaviour in the employees. The evaluation will be carried out at four levels: reaction, learning, behavioural change and performance improvement.

Managerial Implication

The above model helps HR managers in two ways. Firstly, it provides a systematic framework of how behavioural management can be utilized to identify the critical performance behaviours in the organization. Secondly, it also offers the basic mechanisms to build the performance behaviour through reinforcement technique. This fundamental behavioural modification knowledge also enables HR managers to examine the effectiveness of current HR system applying this model.

ATTRIBUTION THEORY

Fritz Heider, professor of Psychology at Kansas University is the father of attribution theory. This behavioural model has been presented in a comprehensive manner in his book titled, *The Psychology of Interpersonal Relations* published in 1958. Social psychologists like Edward Jones and Harold Kelly had further strengthened the concept of attribution through their works, respective works *Correspondent Inference Theory* and *ANOVA Model*.

In simple terms, this is a theory about how people generate causes to any outcome. For example, an employee who fails to achieve promotion (outcome) in his/her organization will search for causes of failure to understand why it happened. The individual may attribute the same to organizational politics, irrationality in procedures, bias on the part of evaluation committee etc. This is called as external attribution. The same is called internal attribution, if the individual thinks that failure is due to his/her mistakes such as insufficient preparation, under-performance, lack of skill etc. When people make an internal attribution for their actions, it appears that they also change their attitudes and beliefs about themselves. Therefore, the key to change is internal attribution. In contrast, external attribution can undermine an existing habit. Further, under achievers tend to attribute to external, and achievers to internal. People generally focus on the following factors when making attributions:

1. *Distinctiveness information.* It is called 'low distinctiveness' if an individual behaves in the same manner in all situations and 'high distinctiveness' if this individual does not.

2. *Consensus information.* These are of two types—'low consensus' means, others do not behave in the same manner in this situation and 'high consensus', if others behave in the same manner in this situation.

3. *Consistency information.* An individual repeatedly acts in the same way in similar situations.

Combination of (a) Low distinctiveness, (b) Low consensus and (c) High consistency causes the internal attribution whereas, (a) High distinctiveness, (b) High consensus and (c) High consistency causes the external attribution.

Managerial Implication

The attribution model has profound influence over motivational and learning behaviour of employees in organizations. Hence, proper understanding of attribution patterns in organizations is of paramount importance for design of reward, promotion and training efforts. Though external attribution behaviour may not always be undesirable, it could discourage the efforts of behavioural changes. Internal attribution behaviour is crucial for organizations, which are HR driven.

PERCEPTUAL CONSISTENCY

This concept implies that we strive to be consistent in our perceptions, perception of people, their behaviours and situations. This is guided by our consistency in attitudes, beliefs and values, and also coherence among them. Prof R. Abelson and other Psychologists named this phenomenon as cognitive consistency and dealt the subject extensively in their book titled, *Theories of Cognitive Consistency: A Source Book* published in 1968. Cognitive consistency suggests that people will try and maintain consistency among their beliefs and make changes, i.e. accept or reject. For example, a strict vegetarian finds it difficult to recognize advantages of non-vegetarian food and the case is same with connoisseurs of non-vegetarian. The fact is that both these food habits have their own merits and demerits. But people refuse to see benefits in others food habit because that is inconsistent with what they believe. It seems likely that people's attitudes all cohere, in other words, they all fit together without contradicting one another. They do not contradict one another because they derive from some underlying core system of values. In organizations, not only individuals but also groups themselves maintain this perceptual consistency by filtering the facts/data that is inconsistent with the group's beliefs, irrespective of the factual position. For example, trade union members tend to have a fixed perception about management, and this fixed perception lead them to interpret every act of management in a grudging manner, regardless of its utility to its own community.

Managerial Implication

The issue of perceptual consistency among managers and employees is a critical issue in any change management programme. Change management often involves change of attitudes and many times contradicting to what we believed for years. It is difficult to bring change in attitude and concomitant perceptions because some of them were acquired at an early age and deep-rooted. Further, each of the perception is correlated with others in the whole scheme of perceptional world and therefore likely to be difficult to change in piecemeal. But the silver line is that it won't be impossible to bring change if organizations could put persistent efforts in redefining people's core attitude profile in an integrated perspective. Perceptual consistency also contributes in discouraging managers to carefully evaluate all the alternatives before a decision is taken. They tend to be convinced with a particular dimension of a problem solving method instead of seeking a holistic approach. Therefore, sensitivisation of managers with this tendency is important.

COGNITIVE DISSONANCE THEORY

Cognitive dissonance theory developed by Leon Festinger is concerned with the incompatibility a person experiences between his/her attitude and behaviour or perceived differences between two or more attitudes. For example:

1. An employee is likely to experience cognitive dissonance when asked to praise boss whom he/she dislikes most.
2. A person invited to speak on integrity and honesty would feel uncomfortable if he/she were corrupt himself/herself.
3. Likewise, a person who is believer of non-violence will experience dissonance if made to defend the country in a war situation.

All of us experience this behavioural discomfort in our daily personal and professional life. Festinger, who proposed the said model in his book titled, *A Theory of Cognitive Dissonance* published in 1957 state that any form of inconsistency is uncomfortable and that individuals will attempt to reduce the dissonance, and hence the discomfort. Therefore, individuals will seek a stable state where there is minimum of dissonance. A person who has dissonant cognitions is said to be in a psychological state of dissonance, which is experienced as unpleasant psychological tension. Research indicates that people tend to handle dissonance without much difficulty at work in comparison to home because organization provides them rewards. These rewards rationalizes the behaviour, leads to conciliation between belief and behaviour and reduces the tension inherent in dissonance. When dissonance is minimized, the consistency in behaviour will increase.

Managerial Implication

The theory of cognitive dissonance has an important role in recruitment, reward management and building a performance-oriented culture. Persons recruited with a set of beliefs/attitudes that suit the demands of job will experience no dissonance, resulting in enhanced commitment and productivity. When the employees are required to take decisions or perform certain things that do not go well with their attitudes, they need to be induced with rewards to reduce the degree of dissonance and concomitant tension. However, HR managers must ensure placing people with compatible attitude and value system that suit the demands of the position/assignment because inducing with rewards to perform a function that is in conflict with their attitude is only a temporary remedy.

IMMATURITY–MATURITY CONTINUUM

Chris Argyris, the renowned Organizational Behaviourist proposed a seminal model popularly known as Immaturity–Maturity continuum in his book titled *Personality and Organization* published in 1957. The core of this model is that individuals as infants *move from a state of immaturity* characterized by (i) passiveness, (ii) in dependence, (iii) behaving in limited ways, (iv) erratic shallow interests, (v) short-term perspective, (vi) subordinate position and (vii) lack of awareness of self, to a state of maturity (adult) characterized by (i) activeness, (ii) independence, (iii) capability to behave in different ways, (iv) deeper and stronger interests, (v) long-term perspective, (vi) equal or superordinate position and (vii) awareness of and control over self. The graphical representation of the model is illustrated here as Figure 13.1

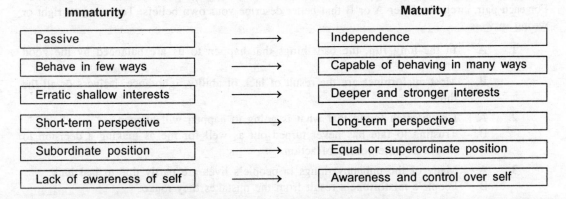

FIGURE 13.1 Immaturity–Maturity continuum.

Organizational environment and practices determine how an individual behaves. Depending upon this environment, employees' behaviour in organizations moves from one side to the other side of continuum. For example, in a closed organizational culture, employees tend to exhibit the behaviour of immaturity regardless of their actual state in the continuum as shown in the diagram. When the degree of maturity of employees does not match with organizational practices, a conflicting situation will arise. For example, less freedom, less control over work, routine assignments, excessive supervision are the features of immaturity. Employees with a degree of maturity face conflict, frustration and anxiety when subjected to these practices. Argyris called this as basic ingruity between organization and individual, which has drastic impact on performance of employees.

Managerial Implication

Two critical implications of this model to managerial practice are: (i) organizational practices and structure should be evolved keeping in view the maturity continuum that all adults are capable of behaving in a matured way and (ii) the fit between individual personality characteristics and organizational practices is paramount for optimal employee performance on the job. Therefore, efforts must be made to ensure this fit as much as possible to minimize dysfunctional effects.

LOCUS OF CONTROL

Locus of control is a personality attitude. There are two kinds of locus of control: (i) internal locus of control and (ii) external locus of control. People with internal locus of control are those who believe that they are masters of their destiny and they are only responsible for what they are now. People with external locus of control believe that their lives are controlled by external forces. A scale to measure the locus of control has been developed by Julian Rotter in the year 1966. This self-assessment tool is given below:

Self-Assessment of Locus of Control

Instructions.   This lists several pairs of statements concerning the possible causes of behaviour. For each pair, circle the letter A or B that better describe your own beliefs. There are no right or wrong answers.

1. A.   In the long run, the bad things that happen to us are balanced by the good ones.
   B.   Most misfortunes are the result of lack of ability, ignorance, laziness or all the three.

2. A.   I have often found that what is going to happen will happen.
   B.   Trusting to fate has never turned out as well for me as making a decision to take a definite course of action.

3. A.   Many of the unhappy things in people's lives are partly due to bad luck.
   B.   People's misfortune's result from the mistakes they make.

4. A.   Without the right breaks one cannot be an effective leader.
   B.   Capable people who fail to become leaders have not taken advantage of their opportunities.

5. A.   Many times I feel I have little influence over the things that happen to me.
   B.   It is impossible for me to believe that chance or luck plays an important role in my life.

6. A.   Most people don't realize the extent to which their lives are controlled by accidental happenings.
   B.   There really is no such thing as luck.

7. A.   Unfortunately, an individual's worth often passes unrecognized no matter how hard he tries.
   B.   In the long run, people get the respect they deserve.

After completing the questionnaire, score it by assigning a O to any A you have selected and 1 to any B. Then add up your total score, and compare it to the below indicated norm:

- An external locus of control: 1–3
- A balanced locus of control: 4–5
- An internal locus of control: 5–7

Managerial Implication

Understanding locus of control profile of managers' help primarily in two ways. First, suitable measures can be taken up to enhance the internal locus of control of managers because managers cannot manage unless they believe that they can influence the things. Secondly, this data therein help to place managers to suitable positions. Further, HR managers must keep track of managers' locus of control; otherwise excessive external locus can put the whole organization on defence.

SELF-EFFICACY

Self-efficacy is the belief in one's capabilities to organize and execute the sources of action required to manage prospective situations. In other words, it is the confidence of an individual in performing a task or handling a situation. For example, a person with high self-efficacy is highly confident of achieving a given target and a person with low self-efficacy is not confident and highly doubtful of his ability to achieve. Albert Bandura introduced this concept in 1977 in his seminal publication titled "Self-efficacy: Toward a Unifying Theory of Behavioural Change" in the journal *Psychological Review*. After nearly two decades of its origin, he published a book in 1997 titled *Self-efficacy: The Exercise of Control*. Bandura illustrated a view of human behaviour in which the beliefs that people have about themselves are key elements in the exercise of control and personal agency and in which individuals are viewed both as products and as producers of their own environment and of their social system.

How is this self-efficacy formed? It appears that the following four factors contribute for it.

1. *Mastery experience.* It is the self-interpretation of a person's experience as success or as failure. Actions interpreted as successful help to create self-efficacy on that issue and those interpreted as failure lead to low self-efficacy.

2. *Vicarious experience.* It is the effect of others' beliefs on your capabilities to perform a given responsibility or assignment. When persons are uncertain of their abilities they tend to be more susceptible to this.

3. *Verbal persuasions.* It is the judgements others provide to you on your behaviour of approaching a problem or solving it. Effective persuasions are those, which are persistent. These should not be confused with kneejerk reactions.

4. *Physical state.* These include anxiety, stress, arousal and fatigue. Mood states also determine the state of self-efficacy.

The outcomes of self-efficacy are: (i) it influences the choice people make, (ii) determines how much effort people will expend in an activity, (iii) determines how long they will preserve confronting obstacles and (iv) determines how resilient they will prove in the face of failures.

Managerial Implication

Self-efficacy has serious implications to career management and allocation of assignments to HR in organizations. It is well established in the self-efficacy research on the employees in corporate sector that, people in many instances underestimate their capabilities because of lack of belief in themselves in performing an assignment. The reality may be that they are quite capable of handling those assignments. Organizations are bound to perform sub-optimal when its employees undervalue their competence. Low self-efficacy also leads to wrong career choices. Hence, efforts should be made to objectively assess the employees' forte. In this effort, the above described four sources of self-efficacy will be useful in understanding how people form beliefs about their competence.

PERSONAL VALUES

Values are fundamental to human life, as well as to organizational effectiveness. The values play a key role in shaping an organization as a class apart from other organizations. In the contemporary management research and practice, values are regarded as cardinal to organizational functioning and given a prominent place. There are two types of values according to Rokeach M. These are: (i) Instrumental values and (ii) Terminal values as indicated below. The author vividly describes these values in the book *The Nature of Human Values* published in 1973. A person could assess himself/herself against these values and map the personal value profile.

Instrumental values

1. Ambitious (hard working, aspiring)
2. Self-controlled (restrained, self-disciplined)
3. Responsible (dependable, reliable)
4. Capable (competent, effective)
5. Clean (neat, tidy)
6. Broadminded (open-minded)
7. Cheerful (light-hearted, joyful)
8. Courageous (standing up for your beliefs)
9. Forgiving (willing to pardon others)
10. Helpful (working for the welfare of others)
11. Honest (sincere, truthful)
12. Imaginative (daring, creative)
13. Independent (self-reliant, self-sufficient)
14. Intellectual (intelligent, reflective)
15. Logical (consistent, rational)
16. Loving (affectionate, tender)
17. Obedient (dutiful, respectful)
18. Polite (courteous, well-mannered)

Terminal values

1. A comfortable life (a prosperous life)
2. An exciting life (a stimulating, active life)
3. A sense of accomplishment (lasting contribution)
4. A world of peace (free of war and conflict)
5. A world of beauty (beauty of nature and the arts)
6. Equality (brotherhood, equal opportunity to all)
7. Family security (taking care of loved ones)
8. Freedom (independence, free choice)

9. Happiness (contentedness)
10. Inner harmony (freedom from inner conflict)
11. Matured love (sexual and spiritual intimacy)
12. National security (protection from attack)
13. Pleasure (an enjoyable, leisurely life)
14. Salvation (saved, eternal life)
15. Self-respect (self-esteem)
16. Social recognition (respect, admiration)
17. True friendship (close companionship)
18. Wisdom (a mature understanding of life)

These are also called as Rokeach value survey variables. Managers can profile the employees' value system using this technique.

Managerial Implication

In an ultimate perspective, HR manager's objective shall be to build the compatible value system among the employees. Employees as well as organization will be successful when there is harmony between the values system of the organization and its employees. Organization will be rendered ineffective when there is conflict in the values of employees and that of the organization. Therefore, it is the primary responsibility of HR managers to understand the required value system in the organization and cultivate it in the organization. In this endeavour, the above described framework helps in a significant way.

RECIPROCAL DETERMINISM

Reciprocal Determinism is nothing but the process of mutual influence and interaction between individual and environment. The great Psychologist Albert Bandura who conceived the model, has described it in his book *Social Learning Theory* published in 1977. Bandura holds that human functioning is moulded by the reciprocal interaction of behaviour and personal factors including cognition, and environmental events. In other words, individual affects the environment and environment affects the individual and this interaction goes onto result in learning. The important issue here is who influences whom in a given situation? Whether it is environment or individual? The answer is, it depends on which factor is strongest at that moment. In organizational life too, we see people influencing the environment through their decisions that are referred as unconventional or revolutionary and we also see individuals being influenced by the environment to be conformists. Within the limits, we can choose to behave in a way that influences our environment, which then helps shape our future behaviour. Every individual tries to influence the environment, of course with varied degrees of perseverance. Continuation of these attempts of influencing their environment would be dependent upon the success or failure they experience. Typically, success leads to further attempts to influence environment and failure contributes for being influenced by the environment.

This model has contributed in understanding learning as an interactive process. It also recognized a vital aspect that an individual could control the environment as much as the environment controls the individual. Reciprocal Determinism is a departure from the past models and theories, which believed that environment alone, influence and determine the individual and his/her learning. The past models also implied that individual have got no control over the environ-ment and therefore an individual cannot choose his/her way. This model has a significant place in Organizational Behaviour literature as it altered in the direction of Psychology.

Managerial Implication

Individuals in organizations could make efforts in influencing their environment instead of being status-quoists all the time in order to (i) bring change, (ii) emerge as leaders and (iii) learn new paradigms. HR Departments must channelize ways and motivate people in influencing environment instead of encouraging brute loyalty to existing systems.

NINE-STEP IMPLEMENTATION MODEL FOR OD INTERVENTIONS

Studies point out that some OD intervention fail to deliver expected results because of inadequacy in implementation rather than the worthiness or suitability of such interventions. This inadequacy arises when the models adopted for implementation are not comprehensive or the sequence followed are unnatural. Therefore, organizations must appreciate that implementation of OD intervention is twice a challenging task than that of planning for it. A systematic implementation model must consist of following steps:

- Step-I: *Preliminary diagnosis.*   The first act of an OD programme must be carrying out a preliminary analysis with the support of few internal resource persons. This helps to assess the organizational problems at perceptual as well as ground level.

- Step-II: *Hiring of OD services.*   OD being a highly specialized field, organizations must seek the help of an external OD consultant. The services of able and competent OD consultant must be drawn based on the type of OD intervention being thought of, and on verification of track record of such consultants.

- Step-III: *OD awareness programme.*   With the assistance of external OD consultant, half or one day awareness programmes should be conducted to familiarize all the employees likely to be affected about OD interventions at general level.

- Step-IV: *Formation of core OD team.*   A high level committee consisting all stakeholders such top managers, departmental heads and union office bearers must be constituted who will foresee the OD implementation.

- Step-V: *Formation of subcommittees.*   A suitable number of sub-committees with cross representation need to be formed to take lead participation in design and implementation of OD intervention.

- Step-VI: *OD workshops.*   Specially designed workshops shall be conducted to equip the selective personnel at step-IV and V as resource persons. These workshops also must help to infuse team working and problem solving skills.

- Step-VII: *Confrontation meetings.*   An interactive session comprising all the employees will be organized to identify the organizational problems together with their possible solutions. The meeting also will be used to assign the responsibility of implementing these solutions to specified groups.

- Step-VIII: *Implementation phase.* Groups not only initiate the implementation of agreed solutions but also enlist the support and participation of all the employees. In brief, they create conditions for employees owning the OD intervention.
- Step-IX: *Evaluation.* The evaluation, though a continuous process, a full-fledged assessment will be carried out with the help of experts to understand the utility of OD intervention and its efficacy.

Managerial Implication

Well done is better than well said. This is the essence of this nine-step OD implementation model. Unfortunately, top managers think that their responsibility ends with selection of an external OD consultant. They need to note that, this is just a beginning in a systematic OD effort. External OD consultant cannot progress without active involvement of internal staff. This model implies that not only they need to involve but also carefully oversee its implementation on continuous basis. HR managers can draw these steps as action plans since they ought to play a dominant role in any OD intervention.

ORGANIZATION DEVELOPMENT TECHNIQUES

Organization development technique is a planned intervention intended to bring a change in the organization to enhance its effectiveness. Organization development interventions are intended to equip and strengthen organizational abilities in diagnosis and problem solving. Wendell French and Cecil Bell Jr have classified organization development interventions into thirteen families in their book titled, *Organization Development: Behavioural Science Interventions for Organization Improvement* published in 1983. These are illustrated below:

1. *Diagnostic activities.* Fact-finding activities, designed to ascertain the state of the system, the status of a problem. Data collection methods such as interviews, questionnaires, and meetings are commonly used.
2. *Team building activities.* Activities designed to enhance the effective operation of system teams.
3. *Intergroup activities.* Activities designed to improve effectiveness of interdependent groups.
4. *Survey feedback activities.* Activities involving analyzing data produced by a survey and designing action plans based on these data.
5. *Education and training activities.* Activities designed to improve skills, abilities, and knowledge of individuals. Here are many approaches, which include T-Group, sensitivity training, lecturing, experiential workshops.
6. *Techno structural or structural activities.* Activities designed to improve the effectiveness of the technical or structural inputs and constraints affecting individuals or groups. Examples would include interventions involving job enrichment, matrix structures, and management by objectives.
7. *Process consultation activities.* Activities on the part of consultant that help managers to understand and act on human processes in organizations. This includes teaching

skills in diagnosing and managing communication, leadership, cooperation and conflict and other aspects of interpersonal functioning.

8. *Grid organization development activities.* Activities developed by Robert Blake and Jane Mouton, constituting a six-phase change model involving the entire organization. The phases include upgrading leadership skills, team improvement activities, intergroup relations, corporate planning, development of implementation tactics, and evaluation of change and future directions.

9. *Third-party peace making activities.* Activities designed to manage conflict between two parties, conducted by some third party, mostly by a skilled consultant.

10. *Coaching and counselling activities.* Activities that entail working with individuals to enable them better to define learning goals, learn how others see their behaviour, explore alternative behaviours and learn new behaviours.

11. *Life and career planning activities.* Activities that help individuals to identify life and career objectives, capabilities, area of strength and deficiency and strategies for achieving objectives.

12. *Planning and goal setting activities.* Activities that include theory and experience in planning and goal-setting. They may be conducted at individual, group or organizational level.

13. *Strategic management activities.* Activities that help key policy makers identify their organization's basic mission and goals; ascertain environmental demands, threats and opportunities.

Managerial Implication

Organization development interventions, if implemented will contribute for organizational effectiveness and improving the quality of work life of employees. HR managers must identify one or more (combination) organization development intervention(s) that are needed to build robust diagnosis and problem solving competence in individuals, groups and at organizational level. Also they should acquire the requisite skills to perform the role of internal OD consultant since OD is an integral part of HRM.

FIVE-STEP MODEL FOR ACTION LEARNING

In an ever-changing environment, learning in organizations should take place continuously and the gap between such learning and its implementation must be narrowed down to zero. Such a fast learning, reflection and its adoption in practice could be possible only through group process. This group process (learning together by employees) through problem solving is called *Action Learning*. Reg Revans is the architect of action learning method who authored several papers and books on this that include *Action Learning: New Techniques for Management* published in 1980. The chief characteristics of action learning are: (i) learning is voluntary, (ii) learning is as important as finding solution to the problem, (iii) learning take place while finding solution to a problem and (iv) action learning is a social process in which a group of people join together to find a solution.

There are five basic elements in action learning as described below:

1. *Problem.* The nature of problem must be clear to participants. All participants involved in solving the problem must be concerned with it in their working in the organization.

2. *Group.* Generally, there will be four to six persons who work together to solve the problem. The group members (participants) must have commitment to solve the problem and possess competence to deal with it but they need not be specialists.

3. *Client.* This refers to the person/department/organization owning the problem.

4. *Group adviser.* This person acts as facilitator whose job include ensuring group cohesiveness, open communication, and interpersonal communication among the members

5. *Process.* This involves observation of the problem, alternatives generation, analysis, action, evaluation, modification/choosing another alternative etc.

The 5-step model described below can be helpful for effective implementation of action learning in organizations:

- Step-I: *Orientation.* The participants of action learning must be given an orientation programme about problem solving methods, action learning process and its philosophy and small group working. This prepares them for effective participation in action learning event.

- Step-II: *Personality assessment.* Participants must be assessed on learning and personality styles. The feedback should be provided to them based on the results and their interpretation. The relevance of such results to the process of action learning may also be explained.

- Step-III: *Orientation to group adviser.* The person selected as group adviser, however experienced he may be in action learning process, must be exposed to facilitation techniques afresh every time. This helps the person to update himself/herself

- Step-IV: *Power politics.* Power, influence, politics among group members can be functional to a small extent and dysfunctional to a large extent. Therefore, the possible occurrence of group dynamics must be anticipated and remedial measures should be initiated in the first meeting of the group.

- Step-V: *Documentation.* All preparatory activities, developments in group process, learning of group members, observations of group adviser, experiences of each member and solution generated and applied must be documented.

Managerial Implication

Action learning is highly beneficial in solving non-technical problems like enhancing the team work, increasing the learning capabilities of employees, and improving problem solving capabilities, interpersonal skills etc. However, this is not free from challenges. It is often time-consuming activity and may not be cost effective in some cases. The political and emotional process among group members must be dealt with carefully; otherwise this may create more problem than the subject problem itself. On the other hand, if properly implemented, it can be a powerful learning and problem solving method.

SEVEN-STEP CONFRONTATION MEETING

It has been the experience with many organizations that there will be some kind of confusion and miscommunication/inadequate communication whenever a change programme is initiated or organization is under stress due to either internal or external reasons. In order to overcome this problem, managers also had tried various means like talking to employees and analyzing the issue with the participation of selective executives. All these actions could not help much in accurately assessing what all the employees feel or organizational stance is. Richard Beckhard has developed a technique popularly known as *Confrontation Meeting* that taps all resources from employees and channelizes them in a purposeful direction through an action play. He authored a paper presenting case examples titled "The Confrontation Meeting" published in *HBR* in 1967.

The experience with confrontation meeting in organizations shows that it is appropriate where: (i) there is a need for the total management group to examine its own workings, (ii) very limited time is available for the activity, (iii) top management wishes to improve the conditions quickly, (iv) there is enough cohesion in the top team to ensure follow-up, (v) there is real commitment to resolving the issues on the part of top management and (vi) the organization is experiencing, or has recently experienced, some major change. There are seven steps in confrontation meeting process as discussed below:

- Step-I: *Climate setting.* Top management communicates with the group of executives/managers the goals of the meeting and shares the background. Top management also assures that there will be no negative fallout to anybody's confrontation. Encourages open discussion. This phase takes about 45 minutes.

- Step-II: *Information collection.* The group is divided into sub groups, each group comprising 8 members with heterogeneous representation. These groups will be given a task (i) to think as an individual what his/her goals and needs are, (ii) think as a person concerned with total organization: what are the obstacles, demotivators, poor procedures, unclear goals are there and the poor attitudes that exist in the organization. Each group will make a presentation on these. The exercise takes 60 minutes.

- Step-III: *Information sharing.* The group presentations will be consolidated and classified into a few meaningful groups. These will be circulated among all the members. This exercise also takes about 60 minutes.

- Step-IV: *Priority setting and group action planning.* The total group will be sub-divided into units representing homogeneity like all manufacturing as one group, sales as other group likewise. These sub-groups need to (i) discuss the problems and issues which affect its area, (ii) identify the issues/problems to which the top management should give its attention and (iii) decide how to communicate the results of the session to their subordinates. The session takes 75 minutes.

- Step-V: *Organization action planning.* Each sub-group shares briefly its action plans and reports the commitment. The top management reacts to the list of issues and makes its commitment. It may need 100 to 120 minutes.

- Step-VI: *Immediate follow up by top team.* Top management team meets and finalizes the action plans with timeframe, and reports back to confrontation meeting group. It may take 100 minutes to 200 minutes.

- Step-VII: *Progress review.* Follow up with total management group 30 to 45 days later.

Managerial Implication

The implementation of confrontation meeting technique provides top management with valuable information and also action plans and commitment of key resource persons in the organization. Many times the information is quite revealing and act as eye opener to senior managers. This is useful particularly in organizations where the environment is closed and goody-goody. HR managers can equip managers with this technique with a realistic perspective of the organization.

CONSULTING SKILLS

Peter Block, who is well known for his outstanding contribution to the development of human side of management discipline published a book in 1981 titled, *Flawless Consulting: A Guide to Getting Your Expertise Used.* The book deals with consultation approach and skills required to become an able and competent consultant in a systematic perspective. According to him, there are following three important skill groups that a consultant must master. This is shown here as Table 13.1.

TABLE 13.1

Technical skills	Interpersonal skills	Consulting skills
Specific to your discipline	*Apply to all situations*	*Requirement of each consulting phase*
• Engineering	• Assertiveness	**Contracting**
• Project Management	• Supportiveness	• Negotiating Wants
• Planning	• Confrontation	• Coping with mixed motivation
• Marketing	• Listening	• Dealing with concerns about exposure and loss of control
• Manufacturing	• Management style	• Doing triangular and rectangular contracting
• Personnel	• Group process	**Diagnosis**
• Finance		• Surfacing layers of analysis
• Systems Analysis		• Dealing with political climate
		• Resisting the urge for complete data
		• Seeing the interview as an intervention
		Feedback
		• Funnelling data
		• Identifying and working with different forms of resistance
		• Presenting personal and organizational data
		Decision
		• Running group meetings
		• Focusing on here and now choices
		• Not making it personal

Consultants must use these skills in appropriate and judicious manner. They also must bear in mind that problem solving in a consultation process is a joint effort of managers in the organization and the consultant.

Managerial Implication

The consultation skills are extremely important for HR managers because most of the time they are expected to play the role of internal consultant in organization. Therefore, in addition to a deep knowledge in their own field of HRM, they must possess inter-personal and consultation skills required at different phases as illustrated above. Familiarization, especially with diagnostic, analytical and problem solving mechanisms, is of utmost importance. Further, HR managers must equip themselves with a right mix of skills, generally interdisciplinary in order to facilitate group and team meetings in a smooth manner.

FUTURE SEARCH CONFERENCE

Future search conference is a technique (i) that brings together 70 to 90 people in one room or hundreds of people in parallel rooms in order to, (ii) propose a series of alternative scenarios of the future vision of an organization they themselves are willing to make happen based on, (iii) examination of past and present of the organization. Marvin Weisbord is the chief architect of this technique who presented it in a detailed fashion in the book titled *Future Search: An Action Guide to Finding Common Ground in Organizations and Communities* published in 2000.

Future search has been derived from well-researched theories on the conditions under which groups will cooperate. The methodology for the meetings were designed based on well-established theories and tested principles in many cultures for years. Business organizations such as Bank of America, Sony Electronics, World Bank, Johnson & Johnson, Cogna International, Haworth Inc, Advanta Corporation, Canadian Imperial Bank of Commerce etc., which used Future Search Conference technique have reported to have gained the following advantages:

1. Creation of a vision and strategic direction
2. Contributed to build organizational unity after a merger or restructuring
3. Improved performance of the whole
4. Supported quality, productivity and safety plans
5. Created key partnerships and alliances
6. Developed community partnerships
7. Accelerated existing plans and strategies

The structure of Future Search Conference that is generally followed is as indicated below:

Day	Subject
Day-1: Afternoon	• *Focus on the past.* People make timelines of key events in the world, their own lives, and in the history of the future search topic. Small groups tell stories about each timeline and the implications of their stories for the work they have come to do
	• *Focus on present, external trends.* The whole group makes a mind map of trends affecting them now and identifies those trends most important for their topic
Day-2: Morning	• Stakeholder groups describe what they are doing now about trends and what they want to do in the future
	• *Focus on present.* Stakeholder groups report what they are proud of and the way they are dealing with the future search topic

Day-2: Afternoon	• *Ideal future scenarios.* Diverse groups put themselves into the future and describe their preferred future as if it has already been accomplished
	• *Identify common ground.* Diverse groups post themes they believe are common ground for everyone
Day-3: Morning and early afternoon	• *Confirm common ground.* Whole group dialogues to agree on common ground
	• *Action planning.* Volunteers sign up to implement action plans

Managerial Implication

Future Search Conference technique is a valuable technique, particularly for the purpose of building vision and mission for the company. The implementation of the technique also helps (i) to build strong cohesive group in the organization, (ii) integrate people capabilities for a common purpose and (iii) facilitates employees to involve themselves in future setting of the company. This is probably the only technique that can allow all your employees regardless of the number to participate in the event with high task focus. Further, its methodological rigour and systematic structure makes the technique reliable and dependable.

Chapter *14*

Organizational Learning and Knowledge Management

Both, foregoing and forthcoming decades in the practice of HRM belongs to two systems: Organizational Learning and Knowledge Management. With the advent of information technology and increased emphasis on smart ways of doing things and avoiding reinventing the wheel, both these systems received attention worldwide. It has become a nightmare even to some of the internationally renowned experts to track the developments in this area. In the recent past, there is no system or practice in organizational history that generated so much of interest, research studies and practical models that these two have created.

HR practitioners have a distinct role to play in each of these systems because they are more to do with software (people) than hardware of these disciplines. This chapter comprised of seventeen classics is presented illustrating key models, practices, tools and techniques in Organizational Learning and Knowledge Management systems. Reading of these classics helps practitioners to be fully aware of a wide range of issues and practices in this area and enable them to adopt some of them into their organizational life.

ORGANIZATIONAL LEARNING SYSTEMS

An organization learning system is a tool that facilitates acquisition, communication and interpretation of organizationally relevant knowledge for use in decision-making. They are rooted in organizational practices. Every organization tends to practice a learning system that equips its employees with knowledge of work and create organizational capabilities. The difference will be some organizations adopt an organizational learning system after careful thought and analysis while others may adopt it in an undefined way initiated by individuals and independent groups and still others may not be conscious that some kind of learning system is operating in their organizations, may be haphazardly. A systematically chosen appropriate learning system contributes for creating strong organizational capabilities. In contrast, haphazard and undefined systems debilitate the capabilities. Professor Paul Shrivastava of New York University conducted a study of organizational learning systems in 32 business organizations in 1983. This study led to identify six different types of organizational learning systems. These are:

1. *The one-man institution system.* This is a system in which a single person controls and coordinates all the information in the organization. Knowledge, perceptions,

252

biases, strengths and weaknesses of this person becomes the organization's knowledge, strengths and weaknesses. This typically happens in an autocratic and closed organization.

2. *Mythological learning system.* This is a story exchange based system. Here, people exchange mythical stories about how things happen in the organization and stories about various organizational aspects (memos, circulars, policies, decisions etc.). These stories contribute to perform a task in a particular way, make some as corporate heroes and some situations as wars and some places as battlegrounds.

3. *Information sharing system.* Some organizations promote inquisitiveness and curiosity culture. This system encourages sharing of information through word of mouth. People seek information directly and indirectly related to their work. The information collected through this method will be used for decision-making. This is a suitable system for organizations in newspaper industry, consultancy, and stock management companies.

4. *Participative learning system.* This is institutionalized through use of committees, project teams, small groups, working groups, task teams etc. for decision-making. Organizational learning occurs through these committees. This system provides for open trust, democratic oriented work culture. This is appropriate to knowledge driven companies.

5. *Formal management system.* Management Information System (MIS), budgetary systems, and project management system, strategic management system, corporate planning etc., forms this system. Standard formats and procedures will be used to collect, analyze and interpret the information. This will be made available to organizational members for decision-making and is the most popular method among the learning systems and is useful to large organizations.

6. *Bureaucratic learning system.* It is an inflexible system where strict formats and procedures are laid down. Information is available only to designated persons. The information passage will be impersonal and specific guidelines of confidentiality will also exist. As the title suggests, it exists in public sector and government departments.

Managerial Implication

HR managers must work in collaboration with line managers to identify the appropriate learning system for the organization. The identification may be done keeping in view, the nature of organization, HR quality, nature of information that need to flow in the organization for decision-making etc. All organizations definitely require a systematically defined learning system. Such a system not only helps to strengthen individual and organizational problem solving capabilities but also promotes organizational commitment and citizenship behaviour.

4 'I' MODEL OF ORGANIZATIONAL LEARNING

There are many models explaining how learning takes place in organizations: some of them are very abstract while some deal it at a macro level. One model that has practical relevance and insight to managers is 4 'I' model of organizational learning that explains how learning takes place at individual, group and organizational level. Mary Crossan, Henry Lane and Roderick White of Richard Ivey School of Business are authors of this model who proposed it in their paper titled "An Organizational Learning Framework: From Intuition To Institution" published in *Academy of Management Review* in 1999.

The 4 'I' framework of organizational learning contains four related processes: intuiting, interpreting, integrating and institutionalizing occuring over three levels—individual, group and organization. Intuiting and interpreting occur at individual level, interpreting and integrating occur at group level and institutionalizing occurs at the organizational level. These four processes are explained below:

1. *Intuiting.* Intuiting is a process of pattern recognition. For example, to become a chess grand master one must play a lot of chess, reflect on past experiences and learn about great plays. An interesting thing to be noted is that what once required conscious, deliberate, and explicit thought, no longer does now. What once would have taken much deliberation and planning becomes the obvious thing to do. What has been learnt becomes tacit knowledge. Intuition is the beginning of new learning.

2. *Interpreting.* Intuiting focuses on the subconscious process of developing insights whereas interpreting begins picking up the conscious elements of the individual learning process. Interpreting involves individuals developing cognitive maps of the intuitions and sharing these maps with groups. Groups will have interpretive capacity that develops a common meaning and language to these intuitions of individuals.

3. *Integrating.* As the interpretive process moves beyond the individual and becomes embedded within the workgroup, it becomes integrative. This integration take place through various forms that include (i) dialogue among and between individuals, (ii) shared practices and conversations and (iii) story telling. The information gathered through these forms becomes the repository of wisdom and a part of the collective memory.

4. *Institutionalizing.* The integrated learning of groups—some of them and not necessarily all of them—will become part of systems, structures, strategy, routines, and prescribed practices of the organization. This is what institutionalization of learning process means. The institutionalization mechanism is a means for organizations to leverage the learning of individual members.

Managerial Implication

The above model provides a perspective of how intuition of individuals can be transformed into organizational learning. It is not to say that all individual intuitions become part of organizational knowledge repository. In fact most of them, do not. This is because it is not an automatic process. Managers must devise methods and implement them in order to tap the individual learning resource into organizational learning. When managers fail to create avenues for this, it may result in widening the gap between the knowledge level of organization and its employees. This dysfunctional gap can be a potential source for conflict.

FIFTH DISCIPLINE

The credit for popularizing the concept and practice of organizational learning goes to the strategist of the century, Peter M. Senge. He brilliantly operationalized the concept of organizational learning through five disciplines in his book titled *The Fifth Discipline: The Art and Practice of The Learning Organization* published in 1990. According to him, organizational learning capabilities can be built through institutionalizing five disciples, which are explained below:

1. *Systems thinking.* It involves (i) seeing interrelationship rather than linear cause-effect change and (ii) seeing processes of change rather than snapshots. We tend to focus on the parts rather than seeing the whole, and fail to see organization as a dynamic process. We tend to look to actions that produce improvements in a relatively short timespan. However, when viewed in systems terms, short-term improvements often involves very significant long-term costs. For example, cutting down costs on training of employees can bring quick savings but can cause the shortage of skill base that will in turn damage the long-term viability of the company. Thus, a better appreciation of systems will lead to more appropriate action. System archetypes, learning labs and simulations help people think in a holistic manner and change the organizational systems, in tune, with changing environment.

2. *Personal mastery.* Personal mastery as most of the people believe is not what you possess but a life long process. This is self-knowledge about one's ignorance, incompetence and growth areas. People with a high level of personal mastery live in a continual learning mode. This encompasses (i) developing personal vision, (ii) learning to uncover tacit and hidden assumptions and (iii) capability for realistic assessment of current reality.

3. *Mental models.* The discipline of mental models starts with (i) turning the mirror inward, (ii) learning to unearth internal pictures of the world and (iii) bringing them to the surface and hold them rigorously to scrutiny. It also includes the ability to carry on meaningful conversations that balance inquiry and advocacy, where people expose their own thinking effectively and make that thinking open to the influence of others. Fostering openness, distributing business responsibility far more widely, and facilitating people to learn new skills and orientations are the methods for developing mental models.

4. *Building shared vision.* The practice of shared vision involves the skills of unearthing shared pictures of the future that foster genuine commitment and enrolment rather than compliance. Visions spread because of a reinforcing process. Increased clarity, enthusiasm and commitment rub off on others in the organization. When there is a genuine vision, people excel and learn, not because they are told to but because they want to.

5. *Team learning.* This is a discipline of group interaction. Through techniques like dialogue and skilful discussion, teams transform their collective thinking, learning to mobilize their energies and actions to achieve common goals, and drawing forth an intelligence and ability greater than the sum of individual members' talents. It has three dimensions: (i) developing the ability of the team to think insightfully about complex issues, (ii) learning to act innovatively in a coordinated manner and (iii) fostering learning in other teams in the organizations.

Managerial Implication

It is a complete philosophy of managing organizations than a simple technique or tool. It requires complete revolution on the part of organization and involves systemic transformation. Organizations who intend to succeed in knowledge era have no option but to pursue five disciplines. What requires in its implementation is (i) commitment of all sections of employees, (ii) knowledge of five disciplines, (iii) persistent efforts, (iv) resource allocation and (v) sacrifice of old habits and patience for gaining benefits.

TEN ORGANIZATIONAL LEARNING TOOLS

By the end of last century, it was acknowledged without dispute that organizational learning is a potential source to achieve competitive advantage. However, the problem that bothers organizations considerably is how to pursue and implement organizational learning. In the process, organizations have created many tools. Robert Fulmer, Philip Gibbs and Bernard Keys brilliantly consolidated these tools and explained them in their paper titled "The Second Generation Learning Organizations: New Tools for Sustaining Competitive Advantage" published in *Organizational Dynamics* in 1998. These tools are:

1. *Maintenance tools.* These include (i) employee suggestion systems, (ii) self-directed work teams, (iii) statistical process control, a specific tool associated with total quality management and (iv) benchmarking (studying the best practices from outside organizations and adopting them).

2. *Crossover tools.* These encompass: (i) transferring innovations for diffusing the successful methodology of one group throughout the organization, (ii) business process reengineering, a high-impact tool used to create substantial and discontinuous changes, (iii) task forces to deal with specific problems.

3. *Utility tools.* These are basically three types: (i) customer surveys, (ii) external advisory groups or consultants who help organizations in addressing specific problems and (iii) content analysis, a sophisticated tool used in creating the future.

4. *Anticipatory tools.* These are: (i) decentralized strategic planning, (ii) scenario analysis, (iii) joint ventures/strategic alliances, (iv) external management development efforts and (v) impact analysis techniques.

5. *Dialogue.* This is a process of collective thinking and inquiry, a process for transforming the quality of conversation and in particular, the thinking beneath it. It enables a group to reach a higher level of consciousness and creativity through the creation of shared meanings and common thinking processes.

6. *Scenario planning.* Scenario planning involves thinking through strategic alternatives—not just one alternative for the future. These strategic alternatives are assembled from wide ranging role players and a breadth of data and information, to form alternative stories about the company.

7. *The merlin exercise.* The merlin exercise is a combination of free form simulation and scenario planning. The concept is based on a whimsical account by T.H. White about how Merlin meets the future king Arthur and knows how to set a table and prepare a meal for the guest. This exercise begins by asking participants to project themselves into some future period.

8. *Action learning.* Action learning involves asking participants to organize or work in teams and attack real problems. In the process of resolving a real challenge, they acquire and use new skills, tools or concepts.

9. *Practice fields.* Teams in the practice fields study complex case and game backgrounds and industry environments, accept starting positions with defined resources, and play out strategy implementation over several simulated years of operation. Used appropriately, practice fields can assist in providing big picture learning, encourage experimentation without the high risk incurred in real organizations, promote understanding of systems theory and dynamic interdependencies and promote futuristic planning

10. *Knowledge management and mapping.* Much of the knowledge capital possessed by an organization is not readily and widely available. Knowledge management is a process for identifying what knowledge is needed within an organization what gaps exist, and what skills are required to solve a problem or complete a project.

Managerial Implication

The above description helps managers in two ways: Firstly, it provides precise information on various first and second generation organizational tools that facilitate in institutionalizing organizational learning. Secondly, every organization is already using some of these tools like suggestion schemes or strategic planning may be for a specific purpose. These can be integrated with organizational learning strategy and their utility can be leveraged. Managers also can select some of the above-indicated tools in their efforts of organizational learning since these had come from practice.

SINGLE LOOP AND DOUBLE LOOP LEARNING

Chris Argyris is the originator of these seminal models of organizational learning called single loop and double loop learning who presented them in his paper titled "Organizational Learning and Management" published in *Accounting, Organizations and Society* in 1977. According to him organizations learn in two ways: in a single loop or in double loop. These are explained here:

Single loop learning

When the error detected and corrected permits the organization to carry on its present policies or achieve its present objectives, then the error-and-correction process is single loop learning. In other words, Single loop learning occurs when problems are solved by changing actions or strategies for achieving a desired result without changing the underlying theory or assumptions about those actions. The following examples may clarify its meaning in more detailed manner:

1. Single loop learning is like a thermostat that learns when it is too hot or too cold and turns the heat on or off. The thermostat can perform this task because it can receive information (the temperature of the room) and take corrective action

2. Learning occurs when an organization achieves what it intends, and, there is a match between its decisions for action and the actuality of outcome

3. Assigned or chosen goals, values, plans and rules are operationalized rather than questioned. Single loop learning allows for incremental change within a given framework

4. The overwhelming amount of learning done in organizations is single loop because it is designed to identify and correct errors so that the job gets done and the action remains within stated policy guidelines. The massive technology of management information systems, quality control systems and audits are designed for single loop learning.

Double loop learning

Questioning the governing variables and subjecting them to critical scrutiny is called double loop learning. In other words, double loop learning occurs when problems are solved by changing the fundamental values and assumptions of the theory as well as strategy and actions. Such learning may then lead to an alteration in the governing variables and thus, a shift in the way in which strategies and consequences are framed. The following examples may clarify further:

1. Questioning the underlying assumption behind a phenomenon in order to achieve transformational changes
2. Learning through errors, means learning occurs when a mismatch between intentions and outcomes is identified and corrected, and, mismatch is turned into a match
3. Double loop learning occurs when error is detected and corrected in ways that involve the modification of an organization's underlying norms, policies and objectives

Managerial Implication

Our organizations are mainly built on single loop learning principle. This approach, though appropriate for many of the activities in organization, can cause many disadvantages. For example, single loop learning in organizations discourages people to question, to experiment, innovate and bring transformational changes. The need of the hour for organizations is to be innovative, question and change the basic premises. However, managers who are used to single loop learning, i.e. only used to learning through success and by being conformists feel utterly inadequate to act in a transformational way. Further, when single loop learning methods fail to deliver results (which eventually happens), managers will become defensive, screen out criticism and put the blame on others. Therefore, top management and HR managers must make conscious efforts to encourage and nurture the culture of double loop learning in organizations in order to innovate, develop and succeed in competitive environment.

KOLB'S EXPERIENTIAL LEARNING CYCLE

Kolb's learning cycle is at the core of experiential learning theory. Professor David A. Kolb author of this learning cycle illustrated it with a detailed discussion in his book titled *Experiential Learning: Experiences as The Source of Learning and Development* published in 1984. This is a model that best accommodates two aspects of learning: know-how and know-why. Kolb's learning cycle consists four elements as depicted in the following figure:

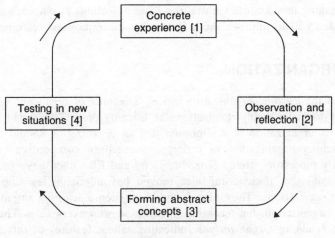

FIGURE 14.1

This is also called as Lewinian experiential learning model since Kolb's learning cycle captures Kurt Lewin's idea of experiential learning. As Lewin describes, a person continually cycles through a process of having a concrete experience, making observations and reflections on that experience, forming abstract concepts and generalizations based on those reflections, and testing those ideas in a new situation, which leads to another concrete experience. In other words, the experiential learning involves four steps as described here:

1. *Concrete experience.* Learning cycle can begin at any of the above four points and it should really be approached as a continuous spiral. However, it is suggested that the learning process often begins with a person carrying out a particular action and then seeing the effect of the action in this situation

2. *Observation and reflection.* The second step is to understand these effects in the particular instance so that if the same action is taken in a different circumstance it would be possible to anticipate what would follow that action

3. *Forming abstract concepts and generalizations.* The third step would be understanding the general principle under which the particular instance falls. Generalizing may involve actions over a range of circumstances to gain experience beyond the particular instance and suggest the general principle.

4. *Testing implications of abstract concepts and generalizations.* The fourth step in this model is, applying the generalized concepts into action.

Managerial Implication

All the four steps are required for effective learning. However, managers have to encourage employees to move beyond step two, i.e. forming abstract concepts and testing them in new situations. Most of the organizations lack mechanisms in utilizing the observations and reflections of employees. This model is also relevant in training of employees. For example, unless it is understood where the trainees stand in these four learning levels, it will be difficult to draw appropriate learning strategy. Therefore, HR managers must use this model to gain three benefits of (i) managing new knowledge drafting from reflections of employees, (ii) testing them in new situations and (iii) to improve the effectiveness of employees' learning.

TEACHING ORGANIZATION

Since the advent of the learning organization model, a number of organizations have spent huge amounts of money to make their organizations as learning ones. The recent studies show that becoming a learning organization is a minimum that an organization should do to survive and need to be a teaching organization in order to succeed in competitive environment. Two Michigan University professors named Noel M. Tichy and Eli Cohen have found in their study of winning companies that these companies moved beyond being learning organizations to become teaching organizations. They also found that when a learning organization comes up against a teaching organization, the teaching organization won every time. They have published a paper titled *The Teaching Organizations* indicating salient features of this study in *Training and Development* journal in 1998. The central point of this paper is all leaders in an organization must be dedicated teachers.

A teaching organization is one, which constantly focuses on developing its HR to transform them as high quality leaders in their fields. There is neither a single blue print nor a standard model that can be adopted to make an organization as teaching organization. However, all teaching organizations follow some common strategies. These are:

1. *Developing leaders as a core competency.* Most companies view their competitive strengths in terms of the ability to devise smart strategies and efficiently deliver the goods and services that customers want. Teaching organizations view it differently. They start with the premises that people devise the strategies and implement the execution. Therefore, they focus on developing people as much as developing strategies.

2. *Teachable points of view.* Teaching organizations not only develop leaders with clear views, ideas and values but also encourage them to pass these on to others. It is not enough to have experienced leaders in learning organization. Leaders in teaching organization draw appropriate lessons from their experience and make their tacit knowledge explicit.

3. *Institutionalized methods of teaching on a wide scale.* In a teaching organization, the leadership development is a continuous process and all the employees are covered. This is in contrast to non-teaching organization where leadership development is either a haphazard effort or restricted to a handful of high potential employees.

Managerial Implication

Transforming an organization into a teaching organization is a mammoth task. More than the dedication of physical resources, it is the commitment of the HR across the organization that determines the success of this approach. For HR managers, it is the greatest opportunity to evolve at careers based on competence rather than usual traditional and hierarchical oriented structures. Apart from this, HR managers have a dominant role in creating right structures, operating culture and channelization of energies in institutionalization of teaching organization.

POLAROID'S REFLECTION WORKBOOK

Photographic products manufacturer Polaroid used an innovative technique called *Reflective Workbook* that facilitates their employees to learn on daily basis in a systematic manner. The workbook is designed to be used independently or with one other by persons who act as a learning coach. An interactive small group process has also been used to help users get used to writing in the workbook and share their learning with others. The reflection workbook developed by Polaroid contains three essential tools:

1. *The learning journal.* This provides the information on innovations, practices and developments regarding particular equipment in a detailed manner. This also includes how the present way of, developing or manufacturing or doing a particular thing in Polaroid has been found to be right.

2. *The learning log.* Each employee is given a preformatted learning log—a diary kind of thing in which employees are expected to record their suggestions how the existing practice can be improved upon with supporting instances on a daily basis. The report must also include how the proposed method of doing/development can benefit the organizational process.

3. *The learning conversation.* This encourages employees to present and share their random thoughts and learning statements with their colleagues. This exercise, called community reflection who takes around 90 minutes. Participants who are introduced to the process, agree to a set of ground rules. They spend 20 minutes reflecting themselves, using the learning journal, the learning log or both. During this individual reflection time, participants are asked to think and write about their learning. For the next fifty minutes, a facilitator leads the group through a process, which allows participants to share their individual learning. This exercise ends with a brief surfaced as a result of the process.

Polaroid managers report that the tools have brought to the surface a large amount of personal learning, which would otherwise have gone unrecognized. The other benefits include:

1. Managers found that both the individual and group reflection time created a sense of fellowship. The act of revealing learning—from both positive and negative experiences—created a sense of trust and friendship which had not previously existed.

2. They indicated that the learning conversation provided a much-needed chance to slow down and reflect quietly on what had been learned. This proved to be a relief from the rapid and continuous assault of new learning which is a regular part of their learning.

3. In addition to the personal insights and lessons which were shared, dilemmas and questions emerged which were explored in the later training activities.

Managerial Implication

It is a hard truth that real learning happens while working. This learning can be systematically converted into a knowledge base when managed properly. The knowledge base can fuel the innovation and development in organizations. This is what exactly Polaroid understood and achieved through the method of reflection. It is a wonderful experience that Polaroid could structure an event like reflection which most of the manager believe as impossible. The real learning comes from methods like this wherein every employee has an opportunity to learn and contribute. Certainly, this experience can be a great lesson to many managers and to many organizations.

MODEL ILLUSTRATING KNOWLEDGE WORK vs TRADITIONAL WORK

HR practices, processes and methods that are appropriate for traditional work will not be suitable to knowledge work. The challenges of dealing with knowledge work include: (i) how to attract knowledge workers—a scarce resource and what talent sourcing techniques shall be used, (ii) how to develop, nurture and motivate knowledge workers, (iii) what type of reward strategy shall be adopted, (iv) how to assess the performance/output of knowledge workers, (v) how to build career and competency systems that are apt for knowledge workers and (vi) what kind of organizational structure shall be drawn. In order to decide on these issues, we must understand the nature of knowledge work and how it is different from traditional industrial work. Charles Despres and Jean-Marie Hiltrop of The International Institute for Management Development, Switzerland have defined these differences of knowledge and traditional forms of work in their paper titled "Human Resource Management in the Knowledge Age: Current Practice and Perspectives on the Future" published in *Employee Relations* in 1995. These differences are illustrated in Table 14.1

TABLE 14.1

HRM dimension	Knowledge work	Traditional work
Employee's career formation	External to the organization through years of education and socialization	Internal to the organization through training, development, rules and prescriptive career schemes
Employee's loyalty	To professions, networks and peers	To the organization and its career systems
Skill/knowledge sets	Specialized and deep, but often with diffuse peripheral focuses	Narrow and often functional
Locus of work	In groups and projects	Around individuals
Focus of work	Customers, problems, issues	Tasks, objectives, performance
Skill obsolescence	Rapid	Gradual
Activity/feedback cycles	Lengthy from a business perspective	Primary and of an immediate nature
Performance measures	Process effectiveness Potentially great, but often erratic	Task deliverables Little (as planned), but regular and dependable
Impact on company success	A few major contributions of strategic and long-term importance	Many small contributions that support the master plan
Organizational structure	Hierarchic, mechanistic, atomic	Holographic, organic, overlapping
Control of work	Vested in the supervisory process	Vested in the individuals

TABLE 14.1 (continued)

HRM dimension	Knowledge work	Traditional work
Managerial functions	Functions	Processes
Authority/power	Hierarchical position, command and control	Professional influence, communication
Control of work outcomes	Remains with central management	Negotiated between supervisors and groups of knowledge workers

Managerial Implication

A different HRM policy and practice framework is required to manage knowledge workers effectively. This is because knowledge work deals with more intangible, uncertain and complex problems than industrial work. Therefore, attracting, developing and retaining HR in such an environment is a challenging task for HR managers. The first step in developing knowledge work compatible to HR practice is understanding the form of knowledge work. The above framework helps managers in gaining an insight into this issue. The HR policies centred around standardization, specialization, synchronization, hierarchies, and optimization of industrial era are not only unsuitable to knowledge work but also can work as a great stumbling block in managing people.

TEN PRINCIPLES OF KNOWLEDGE MANAGEMENT

Knowledge management is an evolving field and most of the organizations have started managing it in their own way. However, one common dominant understanding is that knowledge management is something to do with technology and tools. This is only partially true. There are many issues, particularly managerial practices that organizations must understand for systematic management of knowledge assets. The KM expert, Thomas Davenport, co-author of the famous book *Working Knowledge* classifies KM issues into ten practices such as the following:

1. *Knowledge management is expensive.* Knowledge is an asset, but its effective management requires investment of other assets. There are many knowledge management activities requiring investment of money or labour and include: (i) knowledge capturing of, i.e. creation of documents and moving documents onto the computer systems, (ii) adding value to knowledge through editing, packaging and pruning, (iii) developing knowledge categorization approaches and categorizing new contributions to knowledge, (iv) developing information technology infrastructures and applications for the distribution of knowledge and (v) educating employees on the creation, sharing and use of knowledge.

2. *Effective management of knowledge requires hybrid solutions of people and technology.* Firms wishing to effectively manage knowledge today need both, fine human labour and computers. This is because humans are very good at certain types of activities, and computers at others.

3. *Knowledge management is highly political.* Knowledge is power and knowledge

management is a highly political undertaking. Knowledge is associated with money, success and also with lobbying, intrigue and backroom deals.

4. *Knowledge management requires knowledge managers.* Knowledge won't be well managed until some group within a firm has clear responsibility for the job. Among the tasks that such a group might perform are collecting and categorizing knowledge, establishing a knowledge-oriented technology infrastructure, and monitoring the use of knowledge.

5. *Knowledge management benefits more from maps than models, more from markets than from hierarchies.* Mapping organizational knowledge is the single activity most likely to yield better access and it is better than a hypothetical model. Letting the market work means that knowledge managers try to make knowledge as attractive and accessible as possible.

6. *Sharing and using knowledge are often unnatural acts.* Generally, people do not tend to share knowledge because of fear of losing advantage over others. Sharing has become an unnatural act or almost extinct. Sharing must be encouraged consciously.

7. *Knowledge management means improving knowledge work processes.* Knowledge is generated, used and shared intensively in a few specific knowledge work processes. The specific processes vary from industry to industry, but they includes market research, product design and development. If real improvements are to be made in knowledge management, improvements must be made in these key business processes.

8. *Knowledge access is only the beginning.* More active involvement with knowledge can be achieved through summarizing and reporting to others. Mere access is just a beginning.

9. *Knowledge management never ends.* Knowledge managers may feel that if they could get their organization's knowledge under control, their work would be done. However, the tasks of knowledge management are never ending.

10. *Knowledge management requires a knowledge contract.* Few firms have policies to deal with this issue. Many organizations have held employee knowledge—at least that developed between nine and five to be the property of the corporation. If knowledge becomes a more valuable resource in organizations, we can expect to see more attention to the legalities of knowledge management.

Managerial Implication

These principles present a pragmatic perspective of knowledge management practice in organizations. It is of great relevance to not only to knowledge officers but also to almost all the managers. Understanding of these principles helps managers in many ways that include (i) design and implementation of knowledge management policies and (ii) crafting the overall KM theme and canvas for adoption across the organization.

TWELVE-STEP MODEL FOR IMPLEMENTATION OF KNOWLEDGE MANAGEMENT

Knowledge management has emerged as an essential strategy in effective management of organizations. Unlike most managers tend to believe, knowledge management is not a tool that is applicable only to new economy organizations like software consultancy, and financial, research and development organizations but pervading and equally relevant to the traditional companies like manufacturing and process organizations. It is a fact that knowledge management received wide attention and appreciation in new economy organizations. Probably, wide adoption in new economy organizations might have given an impression that knowledge management got nothing much to do with traditional companies. The fact remains is the organizations that want to (i) leverage its expertise, (ii) intended to create synergy and (iii) committed to transform organizations as adoptable to prerecognized reality must pursue knowledge management strategy. A common characteristic with most of the organizations is that some organizations embracing knowledge management philosophy and some yet to seek this are not quite clear on how to go about in implementing knowledge management strategy. In order to resolve this dilemma, three knowledge management experts—Atefeh Sadri McCampbell, Linda Moorhead Clare and Scott Howard Gitters of Maryland conducted a study of knowledge management practice in organizations like Microsoft, Ernst & Young, and Hewlett Packard and prescribed the following twelve-step model for implementation of knowledge management strategy in their paper titled "Knowledge Management: The New Challenge for the 21st Century" published in the *Journal of Knowledge Management* in 1999. These steps are summarized here as Table 14.2.

TABLE 14.2

Step 1	Form powerful coalition	Senior management support
Step 2	Communicate vision	Incorporate the message into daily company activities
Step 3	Establish teams	Create needs assessment team and sub teams
Step 4	Analyze needs	Conduct needs assessment
Step 5	Identify and acquire knowledge	Determine tacit knowledge, collect internal knowledge
Step 6	Design technological structure	Warehouse knowledge, both internal and external
Step 7	Maintenance of technology	Conduct needs assessment update meeting
Step 8	Re-test	Run system test
Step 9	Training of knowledge workers	Conduct company-wide training programs on use of knowledge management tools
Step 10	Roll-out use of knowledge management practices	Initiate use of intranet developed data repositories
Step 11	Track usage	Creation of management reports
Step 12	Systems go live	Initiate use of external knowledge management data repositories
On-going	Measure quality and productivity	Refine reporting techniques
On-going	Measure performance of knowledge management practices	Track return on investment
On-going	Conduct needs assessment meetings	Communicate performance levels and continual improvement opportunities

Managerial Implication

The authors had developed the above-mentioned twelve-step implementation model based on their study of existing practices in world-class companies combined with their years of study on the subject. The model will be useful to all the organizations that intended to create a knowledge management system. Organizations, which are already progressing in this direction, can use this model to compare their plan and effect changes if required.

TEN SHIFTS IN KNOWLEDGE MANAGEMENT

Knowledge management that has been considered by many as a passing fad has now emerged as the hardcore reality. For example, a survey conducted by KPMG reveals that only two per cent of thousands of managers surveyed believe that it is just a fad, whereas ninety eight per cent believe it as a fact. David Skyrme, the Knowledge Management guru, observes that in just two to three years knowledge management has come a long way. He believed that beneath the knowledge management fad lie substantive management practices, and predicted ten major shifts in knowledge management that will take place soon in his paper titled "Fact or Fad? Ten Shifts in Knowledge Management" published in *Knowledge Management Review* in 1998.

1. *From a dimension of other discipline to a discipline in its own right.* It will be a subject of degree courses and a profession distinct from information management. Watch out for the first faculty of knowledge management.

2. *From strategic initiative to routine practice.* The chief knowledge officer of the future will embrace some of the functions of today's HR managers and chief information officers.

3. *From inward focus on knowledge processes to external focus on knowledge businesses.* Companies will identify how their knowledge assets can be recombined to create new knowledge-based businesses. For example, an engineering/manufacturing company might create an engineering consultancy business; many computer manufactures have shifted their focus to IT services.

4. *From best practices to breakthrough practices.* Rather than improve incrementally, companies should strive for factor ten improvements in key areas, like time to market and functionality per unit cost. Those looking for five or ten per cent gains through process improvement will be left behind those looking for factor of ten or twenty gains.

5. *From knowledge codification and databases to tradable knowledge assets.* Many companies are now realizing the opportunities from trading their databases, e.g. fleet car managers are now trading privileged information on car reliability with co-partners.

6. *From knowledge processes to knowledge objects.* Just as computer applications are going object oriented, so will be the application of knowledge. We will package knowledge as objects (that might include an information record, a multimedia clip, and access to a person) that can be manipulated and transmitted in different ways. There will be knowledge markets for them—precursors e.g. for intellectual property design, rights already exist.

7. *From knowledge maps to knowledge navigators/agents.* Maps are static representations of objects, and without extensive real-time map-making capability (which could

happen in the future). We need other ways to find existing and emerging knowledge. These will be human brokers (people with know-where and know-who) and intelligent software agents.

8. *From knowledge centres to knowledge networks.* Although aggregating knowledge and knowledgeable people at knowledge centres gives critical mass, a more effective model may well be the local nodes of expertise interconnected through human and computer networks i.e. the virtual knowledge center.

9. *From knowledge communities to knowledge markets.* Communities are emerging that provide an effective vehicle for knowledge exchange. But as knowledge acquires value, and becomes 'productized' as objects these communities will develop payment mechanisms and other trappings of a market place. The phrase "a penny for your thoughts" will have real meaning—people will have microchips embedded under their skin will handle knowledge transfer and micropayments under directives from the human brain!

10. *From knowledge management to knowledge innovation.* Knowledge management is in a transition phase to something more fundamental. Knowledge management implies custodianship and managing what you know—innovation is creating something new and better, and that surely must be the ambition of all existing knowledge managers.

Managerial Implication

The above description presents the scenario of knowledge management in immediate future in an authentic and convincing fashion. The knowledge of these trends is important to both knowledge officers and HR managers. The practitioners already steering their HRM practices towards knowledge work environment must consider the above predicted/happening shifts. The other practitioners who are yet to realize the reality of knowledge work must wake up to this scenario and should control the damage through swift actions.

KNOWLEDGE MANAGEMENT TOOLS

Technology is the backbone for knowledge management initiatives in the organizations. There are many tools that managers use in creating knowledge base and knowledge functioning. KM technology expert Hoffmann Ingo identified eleven basic KM tools and described their utility in his paper titled *Knowledge Management Tools* published in the book titled Knowledge Management Best Practices in Europe. These are found in Table 14.3.

TABLE 14.3

Tool	Utility
Intranet Technology	Intranets and Extranets are technologies that can be used to build a knowledge management system. The unified surface and access to various sources of information make this technology perfect for the distribution of knowledge throughout a company.
Groupware	Groupware is a further substantial technology that is used for knowledge management systems. Groupware offers a platform for communication within a firm and for cooperation between employees.

TABLE 14.3   (continued)

Tool	Utility
Electronic document management	Documents are a central means of storing and spreading knowledge. Procedures for using and maintaining such documents, such as a check whether an update is overdue can be easily implemented for knowledge management systems.
Information retrieval tools	Information retrieval offers a solution to tasks from text searches to the automatic categorization and summation of documents. Advanced search algorithms use thesauri and text mining to discover contexts that could not be found with wimple queries. Semantically text analysis can also be implemented.
Workflow management system	The business processes of a company contain a large part of knowledge. In addition, the integration of knowledge management into business processes is an important factor for success.
Data analysis	Pattern recognition and classification and forecasting are the techniques used for data analysis. Data analysis is a possible method for generating new knowledge.
Data warehousing	A modern database is where data and information is stored. Connections that are not readily apparent can be uncovered with the use of data mining and OLAP. These techniques are part of data analysis.
Agent technology	Software agents based on the essentials of artificial intelligence enable the user to independently search for information according to a personal profile and to use various sources and other agents.
Help desks	Help desks are an important application area for case-based reasoning technology based on individual cases. Case knowledge can be quickly put into use in this way.
Machine learning	This technology from the field of artificial intelligence allows new knowledge to be generated automatically. In addition, processes can be automatically optimized with time with little necessity for human intervention.
Computer based training	This technology is used to pass on knowledge to colleagues. The spread of implicit knowledge is possible with multimedia applications.

Managerial Implication

The above list provides the basic information about various knowledge management tools that are available and being used. Managers must understand the utility and purpose of each tool before deciding on which tool to adopt in their organizations. The adoption of tools must be considered after due examination of their suitability to the organizational context. HR managers can be benefited if they know the background and classification of various tools.

IBM'S COMMUNITIES OF PRACTICE

Communities of practice are the chief means to build and leverage knowledge management assets in organizations. IBM is one organization that was highly successful in using communities of practice, according to P. Gongla and C.R. Rizzuto who dealt these issues at length in their paper titled "Evolving Communities of Practice: IBM Service Experience" published in *Knowledge Management* in 2001. By 2001, there were over 60 knowledge network communities operating in IBM globally. All of these knowledge network communities were formed through the following described five stages facilitated by knowledge management programme specialists.

1. *Potential stage.* A community just starting to form. It is in a prebirth stage, but a nucleus begins. This nucleus is made up of individuals with something in common related to their work or interest, but the individuals have not yet discovered fully what the commonality is or how far it extends. At this potential stage, connection is the fundamental function. Individuals who form the nucleus must be able to locate one another, then communicate and form relationships. A small nucleus of individuals is enough to start the process and prepare for movement to the next stage.

2. *Building stage.* At the building stage, both context creation and memory are fundamental functions. The core members of the community create things together, building a common understanding of what the community is and what it is not, why it is forming, and how it will function. The community then remembers those things, putting them to use over time. Through this process it begins a shared history. The core group of individuals building the community begins to recognize what it means to be a member of the community and can then, in turn, recognize and reach out to others—potential community members who should belong.

3. *Engaged stage.* A community actually operates with a common purpose. It functions on a sustainable basis. The structure and processes designed in the previous stage are put into action. The community grows in size and complexity. Access to one another as community members and access to what the group knows are key functions. At this stage, the community really begins building its capability to leverage its explicit and tacit knowledge.

4. *Active stage.* A community reflects, analyzes and really starts to understand, define and assess the value of what it is doing and what it is contributing to its membership and to the organization. The community further extends its membership and builds relationships to other communities. Collaboration that occurs on multiple planes is the fundamental function at the active stage. Community members further collaborate to assess the value of what the community is doing and to publicize that value to the larger organization. Collaboration promotes an understanding throughout the larger organization of the need for and distinct benefit from the community's knowledge and work.

5. *Adaptive stage.* A community has moved to a level where it senses and responds to external conditions. It can adjust continuously to create knowledge and to establish the new structures and processes it needs for leveraging its knowledge effectively and to influence and potentially redefine its environment. At this stage, the community innovates and generates, creating significant new business objects—new solutions, new offerings, new methods, new processes and new groups.

Managerial Implication

In order to institutionalize knowledge management practices, communities of practice are essential. Now there is irrefutable evidence that these communities are not only useful in handling intellectual capital, explicit and tacit knowledge in organization but they also promote highly productive work environment, build relationships and collaboration. This proved to be the most effective method to spread knowledge and culture in the most cost effective manner. In order to reap such benefits, organizations should have true communities of practice. IBM case can provide many useful hints for this purpose.

FOUR PROCESSES IN KNOWLEDGE MANAGEMENT

Though many organizations and their managers have realized that management of knowledge or building knowledge management systems is key to survival and success, they are not quite clear about the processes that help to achieve this. The help came from A.D. Marwick of Thomas Watson Research Centre who illustrated that knowledge takes place through four processes as described below in his paper titled "Knowledge Management Technology" published in *IBM Systems Journal* in 2001.

1. *Socialization* (*tacit to tacit*).   Socialization includes shared information and communication of tacit knowledge between people, e.g. in meetings. Knowledge sharing is often done without ever producing explicit knowledge and, to be the most effective, should take place between people who have a common culture and can work together effectively. Thus tacit knowledge sharing is connected to ideas of communities and collaboration. A typical activity in which tacit knowledge sharing can take place is a team meeting during which experiences are described and discussed.

2. *Externalization* (*tacit to explicit*).   By its nature, tacit knowledge is difficult to convert into explicit knowledge. Through conceptualization, elicitation, and ultimately articulation, typically in collaboration with others, some proportion of a person's tacit knowledge may be captured in explicit form. Typical activities in which the conversion takes place are in dialogue among team members, in responding to questions, or through relating stories.

3. *Combination* (*explicit to explicit*).   Explicit knowledge can be shared in meetings via documents, e-mails etc., or through education and training. The use of technology to manage and search collections of explicit knowledge is well established. However, there is a further opportunity to foster knowledge creation, namely to enrich the collected information in some way, such as by reconfiguring it, so that it is more usable. An example is to use text classification to assign documents automatically to a subject schema. A typical activity here might be to put a document into a shared database.

4. *Internalization* (*explicit to tacit*).   In order to act on information, individuals have to understand and internalize it, which involves creating their own tacit knowledge. By reading documents, they can to some extent re-experience what others have previously learned. By reading documents from many sources, they have the opportunity to create new knowledge by combining their existing tacit knowledge with the knowledge of others. However, this process is becoming more challenging because individuals have to deal with every larger amounts of information. A typical activity would be to read and study documents from a number of different databases.

Managerial Implication

The four processes as given above clearly captures the means of knowledge building in organizations. The classification and description helps managers to decide their strategy for knowledge building. Managers can chose techniques to build knowledge systems in each of these process areas. All the four processes are required to be used and institutionalized for effective knowledge management. Therefore, a clear understanding of these processes is a must for all managers whosoever intended to drive knowledge systems.

FIVE TYPES OF KNOWLEDGE TRANSFER

Understanding types of knowledge transfer is essential to all those involved in knowledge management and HRM. This enables to create pertinent knowledge systems in organizations for facilitating effective transfer of knowledge from one group, one place, one setting, one context to another group, place, setting and context. How this knowledge transfer takes place is certainly a potential question to many including KM professionals. KM guru, Nancy Dixon on a study of several organizations and their knowledge transfer systems, identified and classified five types of knowledge transfer in her book titled *Common Knowledge* published in 2000. These are given in Table 14.4.

TABLE 14.4

	Serial transfer	*Near transfer*	*Far transfer*	*Strategic transfer*	*Expert transfer*
Definition	The knowledge a team has gained from doing its task in one setting is transferred to a different setting	Explicit knowledge a team has gained from doing eloquent and repeated task is reused by other teams doing very similar work	Tacit knowledge a team has gained from doing a non-routine task is made available to other teams doing similar work in another part of the organization	The collective knowledge of the organization is needed to accomplish a strategic task that occurs infrequently but is critical to the whole organization	A team facing a technical question beyond the scope of its own knowledge seeks the expertise of others in the organization
Similarity of task and context	The receiving team (which is also the source team) does a similar task in a new context	The receiving team does a task similar to that of the source team and in a similar context	The receiving team does a task similar to that of the source team but in a different context	The receiving team does a task that impacts the whole organization in a context different from that of the source team	The receiving team does a different task from that of the source team, but in a similar context
Nature of the task	Frequent and nonroutine	Frequent and routine	Frequent and nonroutine	Infrequent and nonroutine	Infrequent and routine

TABLE 14.4 *(continued)*

	Serial transfer	*Near transfer*	*Far transfer*	*Strategic transfer*	*Expert transfer*
Type of knowledge	Tacit and explicit	Explicit	Tacit	Tacit and explicit	Explicit
Design guidelines	• Meetings are held regularly • Meetings are brief • Everyone involved in the action participates in the meeting • There are no recriminations • Reports are not forwarded • Meetings are facilitated locally	• Knowledge is disseminated electronically • Electronic dissemination is supplemented by personal interaction • Users specify the content and format • Knowledge is pushed • A limited number of items are pushed • There is compliance with choice • Usage and business goals are monitored • Brief descriptions are adequate • The database is targeted	• Exchange is reciprocal • Source team knowledge is translated • People carry the knowledge across the organization • Process is given a recognizable name	• Knowledge needed is identified by senior-level managers • Knowledge specialists collect and interpret the knowledge • Collection occurs in real time rather than retrospectively • Focus is on the end user • Multiple voices are synthesized	• Electronic forums are segmented by topic • Electronic forums are monitored and supported • Differing levels of participation are encouraged • Knowledge is pulled
Example	A power generator replacement team replaces a generator in a chemical plant. The team uses that knowledge when replacing a generator in a refinery	A team in an Atlanta auto plant figures out how to install brakes in ten seconds. A team in Chicago uses that knowledge to reduce its time by fifteen seconds	Peers travel to assist a team dealing with a unique oil exploration size. The collaboration provides new approaches	A company acquires ABC; six months later another team in a different location uses what was learned with ABC to acquire DFG	Technician e-mails the network asking how to increase the brightness on out-of-data monitors. Seven experts provide answers

Managerial Implication

The above classification and description of task, context and guidelines help KM professionals in building relevant knowledge transfer systems in a formal manner. This knowledge is critical to HR managers working in knowledge driven companies since the transfer of knowledge is more of a human act than technological initiative. HR managers, therefore, must grasp clearly the KM transfer systems and augment with appropriate HR practices.

MODEL FOR KNOWLEDGE OFFICER'S ROLE

With the growing presence of knowledge based organizations, the necessity of officers to manage the knowledge also peaking up. Already a sizable number of people are employed and performing the roles of knowledge officers. However, the role of knowledge officer is not clear, except that they are supposed to manage knowledge in the organization. Further, most of the knowledge management officers are basically HR managers. They tend to perform this role as an extension of HR function in the absence of clear definition of knowledge officer's competency profile. Therefore, the immediate need is to understand the essential and desirable competencies that are required to perform the role of knowledge officer. Bob Guns, management consultant at Coopers & Lybrand, based on his survey of twenty-five knowledge driven organizations, identified the competency profile of knowledge officer and described them in detail in the paper titled "The Chief Knowledge Officer's Role: Challenges and Competencies" published in the journal of *Knowledge Management* in 1998.

According to the said survey, knowledge officers encounter formidable challenges in order to convert knowledge into profit by leveraging the corporation's intellectual assets. These are: (i) setting knowledge management priorities, (ii) getting a knowledge (best practices) database up and running, (iii) gaining commitment of business leaders to support better a learning environment, (iv) transforming a centre for shared intelligence into that of intelligence provocateurs, (v) putting in place a process for managing intellectual assets, (vi) obtaining customer satisfaction information from customers in near real time and (vii) globalizing knowledge management.

In order to perform the role of knowledge officer effectively and manage the above-indicated challenges, the following competencies are imperative:

1. *Passionate and visionary leadership.* They should have a vision to shape the institution as learning organization and must have the leadership qualities to materialize this vision.

2. *Business acumen.* Knowledge officer needs to be grounded in the business of the business. Business acumen means being familiar with financial levers, what kinds of strategies will impact those levers, and how to implement those strategies.

3. *Strategic thinking skills.* Strategic thinking skills are something fundamentally required since their role involve setting up strategies and systems to effectively leverage intellectual capital.

4. *Champion of change.* The field is new. The position is new. Knowledge officer is responsible to stir changes in support of learning organization. He/she must be champion of change to perform this role.

5. *Collaborative skills.* The ability to interact with people across major functions and geographic reach of the business is fundamental to their success in this position.

6. *Integrative skills.* They need to work on different subjects that include: (i) legal/technical: patents, copyrights, licensing, (ii) corporate librarian: use of World Wide

Web databases, (iii) information technology: electronic performance support systems and (iv) training and development: multimedia delivery of learning. This variety demands the knowledge officers to possess integrative skills.

Managerial Implication

It is high time to recognize that the role of knowledge officer is central to any knowledge driven organization. We must remember that merely recognizing the importance of role is not enough. It must be translated into action by putting a competent person in charge of such a function. The competence, here, in reference to the above model of knowledge officer. It will be difficult to source a person with all these competencies because of scarcity of such manpower. Therefore, efforts must be made to develop the persons internally whosoever has the basic aptitude to perform the role effectively.

Chapter 15
Organizational Management

In order to succeed in practice, HR practitioners should possess adequate knowledge of business related matters. This is because of three broad reasons: firstly, HR managers have to play a more strategic role in the coming years in comparison to operational or mere implementation role. Secondly, HR strategy and practices should be sharply aligned and integrated with business planning and corporate strategy. In other words, HRM policy and practice is dependent on business management and environment. Thirdly, there is an increasing realization that HR shall be utilized as a strategic edge. All these reasons demand that HR professionals must be well versed with business aspect of companies.

In order to equip HR practitioners with such knowledge, twenty classics are included in this chapter to provide the vital inputs of organizational management. These classics mainly focus on (i) patterns of successful companies, (ii) best practices and traits of excellent companies, (iii) basics of business environment, (iv) experiences and lessons from winning companies, (v) model for strategy making and implementation, (vi) organizational structures and popular models and (vii) organization wide strategies like quality, equity, rationality etc.

FOURTEEN KEY PRINCIPLES OF 'BEST IN CLASS' PERFORMING FIRMS

It is well established in study after study that all high performing companies follow certain fundamental principles that keep them in good stead. The absence of these principles may answer why some companies fail to perform well despite all advantages. Firms without principles tend to move in circles and lose direction and purpose. Of course, all firms think they have and follow certain principles explicitly or implicitly. The difference is, there must be clarity and coherence among these principles. Danny Samson and David Challis on a comprehensive study of best in class performing firms identified fourteen principles that these companies follow and presented them in their book titled *Patterns of Excellence* published in 1999. These are described in Table 15.1.

TABLE 15.1

1. Alignment	There is good alignment of employee behaviour with stated company values and direction at all levels of the organization
2. Distributed leadership	Individuals and work teams are assigned, and accept, responsibility for operational decision making and performance improvement

TABLE 15.1   (*continued*)

3. Integration of effort	The organization is focused on value creation and process management, not functional needs and hierarchies
4. Out front	The business proactively strives to lead the pack in all industry standards and practices; safety, customer service, product and process design, environmental design, etc.
5. Up front	All employees demonstrate integrity and openness in all areas of work and dealings with others. Relationships are highly valued
6. Resourcing the medium term	The business is able to balance effectively short term operational and medium term development and growth issues and requirements
7. Time based	Time is developed as a critical organizational value. The business practices the principles of time based competition
8. Embracing change	All employees demonstrate a willingness to embrace and accept change as an essential part of doing business. The organization excels at implementing new ideas
9. Learning focus	All employees demonstrate a willingness to develop skills and knowledge and are involved on a learning/development programme
10. Discipline	The organization invests in policies, procedures and standards and applies a strong systems perspective in everything it does
11. Measurement and reporting	The business measures and reports to all employees the financial and nonfinancial performance information needed to drive improvement
12. Customer value	All employees understand the set of order winners and actively strive to enhance customer value creation
13. Capabilities creation	Business and organizational capabilities are defined and prioritized and drive critical development and investment decisions
14. Micro to macro	All employees know how their particular activities and individual efforts contribute to the big picture of business success.

Managerial Implication

It is essential that top management must introspect on continuous basis the principles they implement in their firms. HR managers must help top managers in this process. The above list since emerged from top class firms can be helpful as benchmarks for comparison. Therefore, managers can make a critical examination of their principles, and reason out their utility. Organizations can refer the above fourteen principles.

TWELVE-STEP MODEL FOR GLOBAL SUCCESS

In a borderless economy, organizations are mandated to globalize their business strategy for success. It is a daunting task for the organizations to evolve a globally oriented strategy that ensures success. Based on face-to-face interviews with CEOs of more than 75 companies in 28 countries and a survey of 1000 senior executives around the world, Robert Rosen and Patricia Digh, Washington based researchers and consultants have presented a blue print for creating a global success in their book titled *Global Literacies: Lessons on Business Leadership and National Cultures* published in 2000. The book that has been selected as best business book by *Fortune* magazine and prescribes twelve steps as briefly described in Table 15.2.

TABLE 15.2

Steps	Actions
1. Create a global vision and values	1. Develop a vision for becoming a world-class organization 2. Globalize you learning vision and values 3. Build a global point of view
2. Build a global roadmap	1. Chart a global roadmap for the organization's learning future 2. Teach the global context of the business 3. Tailor the roadmap for local adaptation
3. Execute a global enterprise strategy	1. Cultivate a global learning philosophy 2. Initiate an integrative global enterprise strategy 3. Invite input from senior executives, operating units, prospective learners, and outside experts
4. Create global leadership competencies	1. Assess global literacy capability worldwide 2. Globalize and localize leadership competencies 3. Require global literacy skills of executives, managers and employees
5. Develop globally literate executive teams	1. Cultivate psychological, business and cultural intelligence 2. Foster cross cultural executive communication 3. Teach executive teams about global context, competencies and problem solving techniques
6. Cultivate global leaders at all levels	1. Make international functioning a part of the company's bloodstream 2. Foster cross business and cross cultural work assignments 3. Develop global coaching and mentoring networks
7. Globalize your management routines	1. Identify universal global management tasks 2. Determine what is global and mandatory and what is local and discretionary 3. Ensure that global leaders model global management tasks
8. Create a global-local business culture	1. Globalize-localize HR policies and systems 2. Create a global information infrastructure 3. Develop a global communication system
9. Foster multitalented, cross cultural teams	1. Foster virtual, multicultural teams 2. Develop global business action teams 3. Create global learning communities of practice
10. Deliver enterprise-wide tools and processes	1. Create enterprise-wide multidimensional learning tools (assessments, laboratories, e-learning, action learning) 2. Foster global collaborative learning technologies (web based, distance, satellite, multimedia) 3. Build a global learning infrastructure learning portal, virtual campus, partner networks)
11. Create global knowledge banks	1. Teach global collaborative competencies to management teams 2. Develop a global knowledge bank of stories and best practices 3. Develop a global knowledge management community
12. Build global-local centres of excellence	1. Develop a global benchmarking process 2. Develop local centres of innovation and excellence around the world 3. Develop global metrics and standards for performance and excellence

Managerial Implication

These twelve steps mainly encompass HR-related actions implying a greater responsibility to its managers. Creating global leaders, setting global learning mechanisms, infusing global culture, shaping global teams etc. are the few that catapult HR managers to the centre stage. In other words, shaping an organization as a successful global entity is contingent upon its success in creating world-class HR practices that enable to embrace global business strategy.

EIGHTEEN PARADOXES OF BUSINESS ENVIRONMENT

Understanding organization's internal and external environment has become fundamental to effective functioning of HR managers in the current decade. This is because the impact, contribution and value of HR practices are contingent upon how well these are compati-ble with organizational environments. Creation and implementation of compatible measures is often a complex exercise to many and HR managers are no exception. The compatibility doesn't come by adopting measures/solutions that appear comparable to the environment but by contrast. This statement holds valid if we agree with Tom Peters who suggest unconventional methods to manage paradoxical business environment in his book of forty-five change management prescriptions titled *Thriving On Chaos* published in 1987. The 18 paradoxes of business environment are:

1. More stable employment is necessary to deal with less stability in the environment
2. More competition requires more co-operation
3. More productivity will come through more people—not fewer
4. Success will stem from more love of the product and less attachment to it
5. We must be wary of the economies of the scale but create more complex alliances
6. More de-integration goes hand-in-hand with more re-integration
7. Big yields low cost can and must rapidly give way to small yields low cost
8. More productivity ensues from having fewer suppliers
9. The more a market seems commodity like, the more of adding small increments of value pay-offs
10. More products (with shorter production runs) does not mean lower quality
11. High quality yields lower costs
12. Higher quality comes with fewer inspectors
13. Accelerating the success rate comes only from accelerating the failure rate
14. Tighter control can be achieved through more decentralization
15. Tighter adherence to policy is accomplished when less time is spent in the office
16. Strategic planning exercises led by staffs are being supplanted by strategic capability building led by the line
17. More appropriate measurement is achieved with fewer measures
18. Success will come to those who love chaos and constant change, not those who attempt to eliminate it.

Managerial Implication

There are two important learnings for HR managers from these 18 paradoxes. Firstly, we must realize that the traditional way of viewing and treating the problems with conventional solutions will not work any longer. The conventional problem solving/solutions were successful in the past for decades, these will be failures in today's environment and may become blunders tomorrow if continued. Secondly, only paradoxical perspectives can generate appropriate solutions to problems of chaotic environment. Therefore, HR managers must encourage unconventional managerial styles in a consistent way. They must build a work culture that is tolerant of chaos and paradoxes.

EIGHT COMMON TRAITS OF EXCELLENT COMPANIES

It appears that approaches may be different, but all successful companies follow same principles to attain their objectives. This is what Tom Peters and Robert Waterman has to say based on their study of sixty two high performing (excellent) companies representing cross section of American companies like high technology, consumer goods, general industrial service, project management and resource based. These two researchers summarized eight traits that all these excellent companies possessed in their book titled *In Search of Excellence* published in 1982. These eight traits are:

1. *Simple structure and lean staff.* The excellent companies maintained a simple organizational structure. They do not prefer complex structures like matrix, tentative teams and project structures. They employ relatively few people.

2. *Close to the customer.* These companies put all efforts to be close to customers, consider customer wishes as orders and delightment of customers as the ultimate goal.

3. *Productivity through people.* Employees are seen as the key resource of the organization. This is emphasized in involvement programmes and through activities designed to reinforce in employees the importance of their contribution to the success of their organization. They leave no stone unturned to impress upon their employees that organizational success and personal success of employees are same.

4. *Autonomy and entrepreneurship.* Employees are given total control over their work and encouraged to innovate and develop the products and services. Organization is broken down into meaningful units and given freedom with proportionate responsibility.

5. *Simultaneous loose and simultaneous tight emphasis.* The basic ground rule applicable to all the employees is that they must wholeheartedly respect core values of the company. Employees who adhere to them are given considerable freedom and their mistakes are tolerated.

6. *Stick to manageable.* Excellent companies tend to stay neither small nor big and they stay close like well-knitted family. They do not fall into the trap of becoming big diversified conglomerate company.

7. *A bias for action.* These companies are highly action-oriented and do not idle themselves in search of solutions. They do not engage in excessive analysis of a problem or allowing committees and other bureaucratic manifestations of a large organization to cause delays.

8. *Hands-on and value driven.* Senior executives lead the company by example. They promote a strong corporate culture and continuously obtain feedback by keeping in close touch with core business activities.

Managerial Implication

The very fact that all successful companies behave in a particular manner establish that this is the way companies which intend to be successful must behave. The above eight traits of excellent companies could serve as benchmarks for the rest of the industry. Managers must pay a serious thought to it and reflect upon their own organizational functioning and organizational management principles. HR managers must spread awareness of the need for companies to move from an inward and production focused organizations to customer-oriented companies. The key learning of this study is be firm on the ground while encouraging experimentation.

TEN GREAT LESSONS FROM WINNING COMPANIES

It is worthwhile to study the companies, that are regarded as successful and innovative, in order to learn a few lessons and pick up essential threads. However, it may not be as easy as it appears to study these companies because of two reasons. Firstly, choosing and identifying the companies for study involves a comprehensive exercise and secondly, the parameters on which the study shall be based also calls for a detailed study of all the managerial issues/dimensions. Companies, though eager to learn the lessons from this successful lot, refrain because of these difficulties. Their job has been made easy by James Pilditch who did extensive study of companies and is credited with many internationally regarded awards, listed ten lessons that other companies can learn from winning companies in his book titled *Winning Ways: How Companies Create the Products We all Want to Buy* published in 1992. These ten lessons are:

1. *Care about products.* Winning companies care about their products far more than most others do. The boards of many other companies are far more concerned with finance and short-term profit.

2. *Be obsessive about customers.* They have teams committed to studying not only the customer needs now, but future life style trends.

3. *Integrate design.* They see design as only one aspect of developing new products. In the leading companies design is an integral part of a multidisciplinary approach to product development.

4. *Break down the walls.* Most of the companies are organized by function: engineering, marketing, finance etc. Winning companies have largely broken down these walls. They have multidisciplinary teams drawn from all these departments.

5. *Concentrate on design.* Winning companies give designers and the multidisciplinary design team a much more central place in the company than in most other companies.

6. *Have a product strategy.* This may be dual; both to improve incrementally all the time and to take larger, and more innovative leaps.

7. *Chase technology.* Many buy in all they can. But note that they say competitive advantage is not achieved by technology but by how you relate it to the needs of the customer.

8. *Co-operate with your suppliers.* Most of these companies are developing long-term relationships with their suppliers. Their choice is based on quality and reliability rather than on low cost. They design components together, and see themselves as partners in growth.

9. *Demand quality.* The winning companies design quality in, rather than inspects faults.

10. *Commitment.* A characteristic of all winning companies is excellent communication across the company and all through it.

Managerial Implication

It is one of the most practical, cost effective and natural ways to learn things from organizations, which mastered them. This is the objective of above description. The ten lessons will be of immense practical value to managers. These lessons have manifold uses. For example, they can be used (i) to build organizational mission statements and objectives, (ii) to adopt them with right modifications to match your organizational need, (iii) to draw inspiration etc. These ten lessons may be the highway for your organization to become a winning company.

BEST PRACTICES OF THIRD WAVE COMPANIES

It is more than imperative for the companies to be just with the changing times. Companies that put resistance to these changes or are incapable to adopt themselves would render them irrelevant and may eventually disappear from the scene. The change always brings new set of code, new set of practices and new set of behavioural pattern. The current trend is termed as third wave. The companies belonging to this wave have built distinct practices that made them successful and adroit. Companies, which still are in the grip of second wave, can come out by adopting the third wave practices. The future technology specialist Martin Weisbord in his critically acclaimed paper titled "Toward Third Wave: Managing and Consulting" published in *Organizational Dynamics* in 1987 identified four principal best practices of third wave companies. These are:

1. *Assess the potential for action.* Instead of diagnosing the gaps, third wave companies search for conditions under which it can progress. This leads these companies away from problem lists toward an assessment of leadership, business opportunities and sources of energy. In other words, this practice involves three conditions. Firstly, the committed leadership, which is, ready for risk taking and searches for alternatives than unilateral actions. Secondly, it look for good business opportunities which include mergers, acquisitions, reorganizations, declining markets, overhead crises, new technologies etc. Thirdly, it solicits energized people who are driven by passion.

2. *Get the whole system in the room.* The third wave companies employ many ways to achieve one objective: getting whole system together. They promote system thinking, integrated working, interdisciplinary teams engagement and promote a culture in which every goal is treated as every body's goal. For example, in the merger that created Sovran bank, the largest financial institution in Virginia, the operations departments used an interlocking chain of team development conferences, starting with three executives from each bank culminating in a mass meeting of several hundred people. People planned their own roles and divided up work, an exercise many believed was impossible. The companies which reported similar experience are: McCormack & Dodge, Bethlehem Steel etc.

3. *Focus on the future.* Visioning is the other name for it. The third wave companies are

more obsessed with future than the present. They use many techniques to envision the future that include running a group of employees through a visioning training session, effectively using customer and suppliers expectations. The resources they use prominently in building vision are: committed leadership, business opportunities and energized HR. In precise, they get feed forward from their imagination, which is qualitatively different experience from feedback on past behaviour.

4. *Structure tasks that people can do for themselves.* The third wave companies create structures that make it possible for people to learn, focus on the future and action for themselves. They organize task focused working conferences to acquire the tools of future mapping. They employ sophisticated performance management systems to make work meaningful, build competencies, build potential and convert this potential into performance.

Managerial Implication

These four practices of third wave companies are hardcore managerial action plans in themselves. Two important learnings these practices offer are: Firstly, we need to note that these are very progressive and future oriented and all the four practices have this futuristic theme in-built in themselves. Secondly, companies that are intended to succeed in this competitive era must switch over to third wave practices in all the areas, i.e. in policies, practices and processes. The other practical prescription is, these practices should not be adopted in piecemeal and should not be mixed with second wave practices in order to obtain greater impact.

MODEL FOR BUSINESS EXCELLENCE

HR managers must understand the basic principles that enable organizations to attain business excellence. Knowledge of these principles helps them to perform the strategic role in organizations apart from orienting HR strategy to be central to such excellence. Stephen George based on the review of current management thinking and through the best practices of world class organizations had proposed a model comprising eight basic principles that equip the organizations to achieve business excellence in his pathbreaking book titled *Uncommon Sense: Creating Business Excellence in your Organization* published in 1997. These eight basics are described here:

1. *Lead by serving.* To excel, organizations must be flatter, faster, and more flexible with high quality processes, products and services. That can happen only with fewer layers of management and with employees who are completely engaged in improving quality, reducing cycle times and meeting customer requirements. This cannot happen when you lead by command. This can happen only through facilitating that include teaching, coaching, supporting, listening, and designing.

2. *Focus through shared vision.* A shared vision has three qualities that make it an ideal focal point for an organization: (i) it reflects a sense of the organization that people in the organization support; (ii) it states what the organization is working toward, giving its members a guide by which they can validate actions and decisions, and (iii) it focuses all decisions and actions in one direction, i.e. producing a

collective strength of purpose that makes it possible for an organization to be fast, flat, flexible and focused.

3. *Engage employees.*   Engaging employees is about respect, trust and responsibility. In organizations where employees are guided by a shared vision, people are engaged in interpreting that vision when they complete a task, make a decision or initiate an improvement.

4. *Know your customers.*   An organization exists to serve customers. To do that effectively, it must know exactly what its customers requirement, and it cannot know that intuitively or by assumption. It can know only by asking customers often and in different ways, by verifying requirements at every opportunity, and by seeking requirements that the customer has difficulty in articulating.

5. *Organize to optimize.*   Fast, flat and flexible suggest the need for new thinking about organizational design. Hierarchies are well suited to serve managers, leaders and owners but they are not designed to serve customers. Unless an organization commits to serving customers first, it will endanger its source of revenues and dim its prospects of long-term success.

6. *Think process.*   Process thinking is imperative supports many of the basics of business excellence. It engages employees who work the process in improving it, and focuses on the customers of the process. It demands management by fact. In contrast, functional thinking helps managers control what their people are doing, often at the expense of speed and quality.

7. *Manage by fact.*   Managing by fact means identifying exactly what your customers require. It means creating a system of measures that best represents the factors that lead to improving performance. It means collecting and graphing the data at every reasonable opportunity.

8. *Align through planning.*   Strategic planning is a means of translating a shared vision into measurable objectives for the organization, work units and individuals. It involves key employees, customers and suppliers in a process that considers a broad range of issues—customer, supplier, competitive, organizational, financial, technological etc. The strategies and plans that come out of this process are translated into key business drivers, requirements, and measures that are used to align the efforts of everyone in the organization.

Managerial Implication

This is great wisdom of business excellence filtered into the form of eight basic principles. Mastering these eight can put HR managers in a good stead to gain the status of strategic player. These eight principles are drawn from the volumes of management literature and by observing successful behaviour of world-class organizations. Therefore, it is relevant to all managers who are determined to steer their organizations into top class.

FIVE PRINCIPLES OF STRATEGY FOCUSED ORGANIZATIONS

The working pattern and approach of strategy-focused organizations worldwide are found to be similar. These organizations use Balanced Scorecard approach to build a new kind of management system in order to be at the long odds against successful strategy execution. The architects of Balanced Scorecard, Robert Kaplan and David Norton based on their extensive study of strategy focused organizations found that each of these organization approached the challenges of achievement in different ways, at different paces, and in different sequences but all of them followed five common principles at work. They presented these five principles in their book titled *The Strategy Focused Organization: How Balanced Scorecard Companies Thrive in the New Business Environment* published in 2001. These principles are briefly described here:

1. *Translate the strategy to operational terms.* The strategy-focused organizations translate their strategy into the logical architecture of a strategy map and Balanced Scorecard and by so doing this they create a common and understandable point of reference for all their units and employees. Strategy maps and Balanced Scorecards address the shortcomings of the industrial age's tangible asset measurement systems. The measurement linkages of cause and effect relationships in strategy maps show how the intangible assets are transformed into tangible (financial) outcomes. The scorecard's use of quantitative but non-financial measures such as cycle time, market share, innovation, satisfaction, and competencies allows the value creating process to be described and measured rather than inferred.

2. *Align the organization to the strategy.* Organizations are traditionally designed around functional specialties such as finance, manufacturing, marketing, sales, engineering and purchasing. Each function has its own body of knowledge, language, and culture. Functional silos arise and become a major barrier to strategy implementation, as most organizations have great difficulty communicating and coordinating across these specialty functions. Strategy focused organizations, however break this barrier. Executives replace formal reporting structures with strategic themes and priorities that enable a consistent message and a consistent set of priorities. Often, ad hoc organizations emerge to focus on scorecard strategic themes.

3. *Make strategy everyone's everyday job.* Strategy focused organizations encourage all employees to understand the strategy and conduct their day to day business in a way that contributes to the success of that strategy. This is not top down direction. This is top down communication. Individuals far from corporate and regional headquarters are the ones who will find ways of doing business that will contribute to achieving the organization's strategic objectives. To understand the strategy, employees have to learn about customer segmentation, variable costing, and database marketing. Instead of assuming that the workforce was incapable of understanding these ideas, the strategy focused organizations made concerted efforts to educate employees at all levels of the organization about these key strategic components.

4. *Make strategy a continual process.* Much like a navigator guiding a vessel on a long journey always sensing the shifting winds and currents and adapting the course, the executives of the strategy-focused organizations used the ideas and knowledge generated by their organization to constantly finetune their strategies. Instead of being an annual event, strategy becomes a continual process.

5. *Mobilize change through executive leadership.* Strategy requires change from virtually every part of the organization. Strategy requires teamwork to coordinate these changes. Strategy implementation requires continual attention and focus on the change

initiatives and performance against the targeted outcomes. The strategy-focused organizations nurture energetic leadership who use every opportunity to achieve breakthrough performance.

Managerial Implication

The understanding of strategy and Balanced Scorecard methodology is very important to all managers. It is particularly very essential to HR managers on account of two reasons: firstly, it is due to the growing importance of HR role in achieving organizational strategy and secondly, it is the HR function that enable organization to travel successfully through the strategy execution process. Therefore, HR managers must pay special attention in grasping the pertinent issues of strategy. The above-described five principles provide a crisp and authoritative description of strategy that help quick understanding of strategy in action.

TEN REALITIES IN STRATEGY MAKING

One factor that contributed for organizations' survival and growth on the face of ruthless competition and uncertain business environment is 'strategy'. Of course, by now, there is hardly any organization that is without a corporate planning department meant for strategy making. The important point here is that mere creation of exclusive department and other resources will not guarantee a good strategy because the approach and input that goes into strategy making is more important. Gary Hammel, the strategy guru, in his paper titled *Strategy as Revolution* published in the book titled seeing differently (1997) described 10 realities in strategy making. These are:

1. *Strategic planning is not strategic.* In vast majority of companies, strategic planning is a calender driven ritual, not an exploration of the potential for revolution. More important than strategic planning is its implementation and this implementation is not a routine procedure—it is a quest.

2. *Strategy making must be subversive.* Rule makers and rule takers are the industry. Rule breakers set out to redefine the industry, to invent the new by challenging the old.

3. *The bottleneck is at the top of the bottle.* In most companies, strategic orthodoxy has some very powerful defenders: senior managers. If you're a senior executive, ask yourself: Has a decade or two of experience made you more willing or less willing to challenge the industry's conventions? Have I become more curious or less curious about what is happening beyond the traditional boundaries of my industry?

4. *Revolutionaries exist in every company.* There are revolutionaries in your company too. You will find people straining against the bit of industrial orthodoxy. If you don't let the revolutionaries challenge the company from within, they will eventually challenge from outside.

5. *Change is not the problem, engagement is.* All too often, when senior managers talk about change, they are talking about change inducing fear, because internally they resist change.

6. *Strategy making must be democratic.* The capacity to think creatively about strategy is distributed widely in an enterprise. People in organizations deserve a larger say in strategy making. The capacity for strategic innovation increases proportionately with each mile you move away from the headquarter.

7. *Anyone can be a strategy activist.* Activists are not anarchists. Their goal is not to tear down but to reform. People who care about their organization don't wait for permission to act. When planning has supplanted strategizing, and when more energy is being devoted to protecting the past than to creating the future, activists must step forward.

8. *Perspective is worth fifty IQ points.* Without enlightenment, there can be no revolution. To discover opportunities for industry revolution, one must look at the world, through a new lens. A view of the corporation as a bundle of core competencies rather than a collection of business units, and discontinuities as levers of change rather than threats to the status quo is the new perspective.

9. *Top down and bottom up are not the alternatives.* To achieve diversity of perspective and utility of purpose, the strategy making process must involve a deep diagonal slice of the organization. Bringing the top and bottom together in the creation of strategy will help bypass the usually painful and laborious process whereby a lowly employee champions an idea up the chain of command.

10. *You can't see the end from the beginning.* Though it is impossible to see the end from the beginning, an open ended and inclusive process of strategy creation substantially lessens the challenge of implementation.

Managerial Implication

The author using his extensive consultancy experience with world-class organization combined with critical examination of strategy making process in a number of organizations had proposed the above ten realities. These will be widely useful in strategy making; both macro and micro. HR managers must equip the senior managers of the organizations with these realistic factors. Further, the approach emphasized in strategy making is involvement and participation of people in strategy formulation. Therefore, HR managers have responsibility to build a system through which this participation can be made possible and effective.

GOLD AND GARBAGE IN MANAGEMENT THEORIES

James Lee, a sociologist published an insightful book in the year 1980 titled *The Gold and the Garbage in Management Theories and Prescriptions.* The pros and cons of many management theories, particularly those related to Organizational Behaviour are dealt with in this book in a comprehensive and incisive manner. Lee states that much of what has been sold as theory by behaviourists is untested and advocative. The critical observations of the author include the following:

1. Behaviourists such as Abraham Maslow, Frederick Herzberg and Douglas McGregor believed the key to productivity was essentially motivation of the non-remunerative variety. In dealing with professional people, they may be probably partially right. In dealing with a worker-putting nut B on bolt C, however, they may be, well, wrong.

2. Self-actualization—the highest level needed in hierarchy of motivation model of Abraham Maslow appears ambiguous and therefore difficult to refute or support. There is no adequate empirical evidence in the espousal of every individual seeking the fulfilment of self-actualization need.

3. Frederick Herzberg's theory of dual motivation lacks the evidence and strength of being acknowledged as a general or universal theory of motivation. In fact, many findings contradict the hygienic-motivator model of motivation.

4. The path-goal finding theory proposed by Vroom also has its share of deficiencies. The assumption of human behaviour of seeking pleasure and avoiding pain on which this theory is based is highly philosophical.

5. It is generally believed that there is direct relationship between job satisfaction and performance. The fact however is that there is no proven relationship between these two. Evidence in this context include (i) continuous record of low or negative co-relation between the two variables, (ii) employees' and unions' continued demands, not for love and care, but for wage and fringe benefits and (iii) failures in human relations training of supervisors to replicate the alleged advantages of the Hawthorne experimental supervisory style.

6. There is a common belief that group work is superior to individual work. In reality, groups not necessarily perform better than individuals. Groups do not necessarily solve problems better nor make better decisions than individuals.

7. McGregor's X and Y assumptions are not theories at all as claimed by him but a philosophy because there is no evidence of these assumptions guiding managers at work.

8. Non-linear systems—probably the most extensive effort to embrace the organizational behaviour theories appears to have been a documented failure.

Managerial Implication

Understanding behavioural theories and models helps not only in widening the perspective of managers but also managing HR in a scientific manner. Do remember that there is gold as well as garbage in these theories and prescriptions. The rider is, understand the essence of these and build your own models in tune with your organizational reality.

MODELS OF ORGANIZATION

In order to understand and design organizational structure, we must have the basic knowledge of organizational models. Organizations adopt a particular model to manage its activities. In practice, these are hierarchical structures, flat structures, strategic business units, matrix structures etc. Organizational structure can influence the type of policy, delegation of powers, work practices etc. an organization is likely to follow. Therefore, organizational model play an important role. The legends of organizational change and structure, Larry Greiner and Virginia Schein classified organizational structures into three and detailed them in their book titled *Power and Organizational Development* published in 1988. These models are:

1. *Rational/Bureaucratic Model.* This model emphasizes rationally structured systems, built on division of labour and job specialization. Authority is top down, and utilizes formal communication channels. It comprises of usually vertical, and well-defined policies and procedures. Organizational goals are clearly specified to direct efforts of employees toward greater efficiency. Formal systems and policies are used to provide control, predictability and stability. Upward power in this model is generally seen as

disruptive and non-legitimate. Sideways power receives virtually no consideration in this model, since vertical authority is the prescribed decision-making channel; integration occurs only at the apex of the pyramid.

2. *Collegial/Consensus Model.* This model places emphasis on interpersonal and small group behaviour in organizations. Rules, policies and procedures are relaxed or even disbanded in order to enhance interaction and participation in decision making. The need for direction and control is replaced by teamwork in the spirit of all for one, one for all. Individual contributions are highly valued, within the focus on collaboration and integration. Upward power is seen as legitimate and encouraged in this model. A flat organizational structure, appropriate to a professional group, reflects the high priority given to upward power. Further, in this model, downward power is barely tolerated, and then only in limited situations in which peer pressure proves ineffective.

3. *Pluralistic/Political Model.* This model sees organizations as composed of differing interest groups. Each group pursues its own goals; sometimes on selfish grounds but often for well-intended reason based on its view of what is best for the organization as a whole. Conflict is viewed as inevitable and a normal part of the way things get done. Political behaviour results when an attempt to influence is countered by another interested group. The pluralistic model allows for all forms of power expression. Those desiring to fulfil their work related objectives truly everywhere and naturally use power. Sideways power is recognized as a necessary and frequently exercised component of managerial effectiveness. Groups across the organization must compete for scarce resources, and they are horizontally dependent on one another to perform their jobs on schedule.

Managerial Implication

Everything in organizations appears like a jigsaw puzzle when the underlying principles are not understood. The above models are intended to clear those principles. This knowledge is particularly important for HR managers. When you understand the model your organization has adopted, it will be clear to you how the relationships are built, power is delegated, practices are formed and policies are made. This knowledge also helps when to engineer any change in the organization. One more important implication for practice is that, there is no perfect model and the perfection comes only on its appropriate adoption suiting to organization's vision and mission.

MECHANISTIC AND ORGANIC SYSTEMS

Structure is like the nervous system of an organization. It plays a critical role in management of a variety of functions. Every organization adopts a particular structure that facilitates its functioning. Logically, structure flows from strategy of organization. For example, organizations that choose aggressive and dynamic working opt for a flexible and loose structure where as organization in stable environment tend to have mechanistic structure. There are organizations that embrace contingency structure. Therefore, understanding of organizational structures is one of the important educations to managers. Tom Burns and G.M. Stalker, two renowned experts, classified organizational structure in to two: Mechanistic and Organic systems in their path-breaking book titled *The Management of Innovation* published in 1961. Each one of them will have distinct characteristics as indicated below.

Mechanistic structure

1. A high degree of task differentiation and specialization is practised. Division of labour and specialization of work are the chief characteristics. Every individual will be confined to his work only.
2. A high degree of reliance on hierarchy for decisions, communication and coordination.
3. A tendency for top management controlling all the activities.
4. A high degree of emphasis on dyadic relationship and vertical interactions. The subordinates' activities are subject to instructions of seniors.
5. Insistence on loyalty to organization as well as to superiors.
6. A tendency to value internal knowledge, skills based on local knowledge than general competency based on external exposure and macro knowledge.

Organic structures

1. Broadly defined jobs and roles. A continuous review of skills and expertise in the organization. Emphasis is placed on utilizing the knowledge of everybody in solving the problem.
2. Reliance on the network model in the place of hierarchy for decisions, controls and communication. This network comprises of people with expertise and commitment.
3. A tendency to keep organizational communication open and extensive. The communication pattern will be vertical, horizontal as well as formal and informal.
4. A greater emphasis on commitment to organizational objectives and success rather than sheer loyalty and obedience to leadership.
5. A tendency to value knowledge and expertise that is considered appropriate and macro than local and narrow based.

Managerial Implication

Understanding organizations will be contingent upon understanding their structures. The knowledge of mechanistic and organic structures helps managers many ways in practice. Firstly, it enables them to choose a particular type of organizational structure that suits their organization. Secondly, managerial systems, delegation of powers, other policies and practices will have to originate from the structure. There must be harmony between structure and managerial systems failing which conflicts are bound to arise. These conflicts can weaken the organizational functioning. Therefore, knowledge of structures makes the job of managers easy in attaining this harmony through compatible systems.

NEUROTIC ORGANIZATIONAL STYLES

Like human beings, organizations are also susceptible to erratic behaviour. This arises when leadership is erratic and behaves in irrational manner, which percolate down in the entire organization, and this irrationality assumes as an organizational norm. This erratic organizational norm reflects in its strategy, structure, organizational climate, decision-making, managerial style, customer service etc. For example, there are five neurotic types such as dramatic, depressive, paranoid, compulsive and schizoid in human beings as described in psychiatric literature. Based on these, two organizational psychologists namely Kets de Vries and Miller D. proposed five organizational styles that are neurotic, in their paper titled "The Neurotic Organization" published in *Psychology Today* in 1984. These are:

1. *Dramatic.* These are hyperactive, impulsive, dramatically venturesome and dangerously uninhibited. The structure of the dramatic organization is usually far too primitive. Too much power is concentrated in the chief and other top-level executives who meddle even with routine operating matters. The decision makers live in a world of hunches, intuition and impressions rather than facts.

2. *Depressive.* These organizations are conservative, lack confidence and insulate themselves from external environment. Red tapism, procrastination, ineffectiveness, obesity are its characteristics. The activities are very routine, bureaucratic and rule bound which make them inactive. Though there are formal powers vested to its executives, most of them feel powerless and helpless due to voluminous rules and long hierarchy. These organizations are not quite aware of their strengths and weaknesses, and are generally aimless in their approach.

3. *Paranoid.* Suspicion is the key characteristic of this type. They are suspicious about customers, about competitors, about technology, about regulations and in general about their environments. They create many systems, communication sharing and consultative mechanisms, carry out frequent assessments, audits, and change of organizational strategy. They try to change their colour in tune with outside environment than having any internal consistency.

4. *Compulsive.* This type is tradition- and custom-oriented. Adherence to procedures, hierarchy, routines, and conformity are its traits. Generally these are large-sized organizations. Despite its outdated and unsuitable procedure and systems, these organizations prefer to continue the same and fear to change them. The ability to face uncertainty is almost zero and its leaders very formal, hierarchical and power oriented.

5. *Schizoid.* These organizations are harmful to themselves. The individual goals of CEOs dominate that of the organization. Middle level executives indulge in political games. Organization lack any strategy and lives in daydreaming. There is mutual respect among its employees and most of the decisions and actions are arbitrary. They prefer secrets, confidential documents and closed meetings. Audit reports are used to settle the score among executives.

Managerial Implication

The understanding of this typology helps to analyze and identify the style of your organization. It also helps to check whether that style is beneficial or harmful to your kind of organization. The knowledge of organizational styles is particularly important to HR managers because it answers many of their questions and provides a wider perspective. HR managers must be conscious of these neurotic styles and are responsible to see that organizations do not exceed their limits to be clearly categorized into one of these styles.

BUREAUCRACY

German intellectual namely Max Weber proposed the theory of bureaucracy in 1940s and authored a book on this concept that was translated into English with the title *Bureaucracy Theory* published in 1946. He built this framework based upon his observations of Church, Government and military functioning. This provided a rich perspective in understanding a form of organizing, which became popularly known and widely referred as bureaucracy. Weber is one who regarded bureaucracy as synonymous with efficiency and air efficient way of conducting administration. He believes that it is superior to any other form of organization in terms of precision, stability and stringency of discipline. Bureaucracy aptly suits to the modern organizations since they are not run by their owners but by their managers. The bureaucratic characteristics of an organization are:

1. The principle of fixed and official jurisdictional areas, which are generally ordered by rule, i.e. by laws or administrative regulations.
2. The principles of office hierarchy and levels of graded authority mean a firmly ordered system of superior-subordinate system in which there is a supervision of the lower officials by higher officials.
3. Management of office is based upon written documents (files).
4. Management of the office follows general rules, which are more or less stable, and exhaustive.
5. The office is managed by an official who has received necessary training.
6. The office works in specified timings and only official work carries out during this scheduled time.
7. The bureaucratic official is appointed in a clearly defined designation by a senior bureaucratic official, generally for long years.
8. The official receives the regular pecuniary compensation of a normally fixed salary and age-old security provided by person.
9. The official is set for a career within the hierarchical order of public service.

Managerial Implication

Bureaucracy though attained more unpopularity than popularity in the recent years has still greater wisdom to offer to modern managers and organizations. Bureaucracy system failure is more on account of ineffective implementation of the principles than this system itself. The ambiguities in procedures, overlapping in functional or locational jurisdictions are makings of managers in deviation from basis tenants of Bureaucracy model. This model helped governments, business organizations and other institutes for decades together in organizing the work. These principles and thorough understanding of them is essential for all those who are in the business of running organizations and managing HR.

THE RATIONAL MODEL

Tom Peters and Robert Waterman in their book titled *In Search of Excellence*, published in 1982 brought out the significant limitations with the popularly practised management approach for what they labelled as *The Rational Model*. Central to this discussion is the The Rational Model, which is basically a numerical/quantitative oriented management tool, misses a lot and falls short of certain crucial points. It does not

1. tell what the excellent companies have apparently learned
2. teach how to love the customers
3. recognize the rock-bottom importance of making the average Joe a hero and a consistent winner
4. show how strongly workers can identify with the work they do if we give them a little say so
5. tell why self-generated quality control is so much more effective than inspector-generated quality control
6. tell to nourish product champions like the first buds in springtime
7. allow in-house product competition
8. command that companies over spend on quality, overkill on customer service and make products that last and work

Further, the authors state that much of the conventional business rationality seems to drive the engine of business and simply it does not explain most of what makes the excellent companies work. The shortcomings include the following:

1. The enumerative, analytical component has an in-built conservative bias. Cost reduction becomes the top priority and revenue enhancement takes a back seat.
2. The exclusively analytic approach run wild leads to an abstract, heartless philosophy.
3. To be narrowly rational is often to be negative.
4. Today's version of rationality does not value experimentation and abhors mistakes.
5. The rational model causes us to denigrate the importance of values.
6. There is little place in the rationalist world for internal competition .

Managerial Implication

Companies need to be cautious of adverse impact that over-practice of the rational approach to management could create to the bottom-line. The curricula of most of the management programmes, which excessively focus on the pros of The Rational Model, need to be redesigned in order to provide a holistic perspective.

EQUITY MODEL

The equity model refers to the perception of fairness. In other words, the confidence of an employee over the management that he or she will be given impartial, unbiased and equal treatment in all the activities. Though the equity model has been in circulation since very long, the credit for popularizing it in an organizational context is given to J. Stacy Adams who published a paper titled *Inequity in Social Exchanges* in 1965. The inequity arises due to many reasons that include under rewarding or over rewarding a performance or inconsistently rewarding or punishing behaviour etc. For example, a manager was promoted to a higher level as a reward for executing a project within the time schedule and budget. The other manager who had given similar performance was not elevated. This not only results in frustration in the person who was not promoted but also raises doubts in the mind of the person elevated earlier. In sum, it creates inequity. The principle of equity in this model is dependent upon comparison of persons among themselves in terms of resources allocated to them and how their outcomes are treated. There are four types of comparisons that employees use:

1. *Self-inside*—to an employee's own experiences inside the organization
2. *Self-outside*—an employee's experiences outside the organization
3. *Others-inside*—other individuals or group of persons inside the organization
4. *Others-outside*—other individuals or group of persons outside the organization

There are two important aspects in the model. The first is employees do perceive even over rewarding as inequity and they prefer proportionate reward to their performance. Secondly, a person who perceives inequity will put efforts to alter the position through various means. For example, he may change his/her way of performance or activities or quit the job.

Managerial Implication

This model offers very relevant and valuable knowledge to HR managers. More than half of employee problems in organizations arise out of perception of inequity among the employees. Therefore, while rewarding or punishing an employee's performance, managers need to consider its implications to the common perception. Further, we should not confuse the equity model with some kind of socialistic perspective. Both are entirely different. Equity model advocates a consistent and equitable treatment in all the aspects of HRM. If failed, high pay leads to turnovers, incentives to low-level performances and promotions to demoralize workforce. However, ensuring equity is the toughest job. Once Sigmund Freud stated that the best form of equity could be achieved only in depriving everybody equally, because awarding equally is always difficult in practice.

McKINSEY 7-S FRAMEWORK

Tom Peters, Robert Waterman Jr., and J.R. Philips advocated that any intelligent approach to organizing had to encompass and treat as interdependent, at least seven variables: Structure, Strategy, Systems, Style, Staff, Skills and Shared Values in their paper titled "Structure is not Organization" published in *Business Horizons* in 1980. This integrated model is generally known as Mckinsey 7-S Framework. These seven variables are briefly described here in Table 15.3.

TABLE 15.3

1. Style	Management/staff interpersonal	It comprises two chief elements: (i) management style and (ii) organizational culture
2. Staff	HR Management	This includes methods of talent sourcing, HRD, shaping basic values and managing careers of employees
3. Skills	Current and future requirements	The way the company make efforts to build distinctive competencies to meet not only the present but to surpass the future requirements

TABLE 15.3 (*continued*)

4. Shared vision	Shared values/ culture	This involves setting basic framework, defining fundamental ideas around which a business is built
5. Strategy	Direction of the organization	Actions a company contemplates and plans; both in response to changes in the external environment of organization as well as to stir changes in the environment
6. Structure	Organizational flow	A coordinating mechanism/tool that facilitates the implementation of strategy and enables the internal processes to move efficiently
7. Systems	Procedures, processes and communications	Formal do's and don'ts and informal shared methods that facilitate organizational functioning

The salient features of this model are:

1. The first four variables are classified as soft and the rest as hard. The architects of this model state that, in retrospect what our framework has really done is to remind the world of professional managers that soft is hard. And all that stuff managers have been dismissing for so long as intractable, irrational, intuitive, informal in an organization can be managed. However, managers need to take into account all the seven factors for organizational success.
2. The relative importance of each of the factor may vary over time.
3. Impacting any *s* will cause stress on the other *ss*.
4. All the seven factors shall be dealt with in an integrated manner and kept in harmony in any change of programme. If dealt in coherent manner, these factors can become a powerful vehicle for successful change. However, when dealt in disintegrated manner they can cause each of these factors function for cross-purposes.

Managerial Implication

The model offers profound wisdom to all managers and particularly to HR managers since it has brought the importance of soft issues into focus. The model is highly pragmatic and established to be a valuable tool in managing change processes effectively. Further, the model presents a commonsensical framework that enables managers around the globe to understand the anatomy of organization very well and without much effort. The model helps HR managers in managing all kinds of change programmes.

REENGINEERING MANAGEMENT

The essence of reengineering lies in discontinuous thinking in order to bring changes in many areas of the organizational functioning. In other words, a strategy to start afresh everything that is connected with organizational processes such as the way business is conducted, job designs, organizational structure, management systems and integrating them tightly. This model of reengineering was developed on the following premises:

1. Our business processes and structures are outmoded and obsolete: our work structures and processes did not keep pace with the changes in technology, demographics and business objectives.
2. We cannot achieve breakthroughs in performance by cutting fat or automating existing process. Rather, we must challenge old assumptions and shed the old rules that made the business underperform in the first place.
3. Conventional process structures are fragmented and piecemeal, and they lack the integration to maintain quality and service.

Reengineering model is built around the following principles:

1. *Organize around outcomes.* A job shall be designed keeping in view the outcome or objective of that job in organization instead of around a single task.
2. *Have those who use the output of the process perform the process.* Too much of specialization in carrying out a task should be discontinued. As much as possible, one department must be made responsible for all the processes involved in completing the task instead of distributing it among many departments.
3. *Subsume information processing work into the real work that produces the information.* Organizations create separate departments to collect, process and analyze the information. With the advent of computers and its availability makes these departments an unnecessary burden. Therefore, they must be closed down and this responsibility should be decentralized to every department.
4. *Treat geographically dispersed resources as though they were centralized.* Organizations must encourage use of databases, telecommunications, electronic networks and standardized systems to create economies of scale.
5. *Link parallel activities instead of integrating their results.* This principle advocates that activities during in progress must be coordinated, instead of integrating them at the final stage like assembling the finished parts.
6. *Put the decision point where the work is performed, and build control into the process.* Organizations must stop empowering who actually does not perform the tasks at shop floor. Instead empower who are directly handling the work.

Reengineering is a tremendous effort that mandates changes in many areas of the work in line with above principles. Michael Hammer and James Champy are the architects of this model. They presented it supported by live examples in their publications that include books titled, *Reengineering Corporation* and *Reengineering Management*, published in 1992 and 1995 respectively and a paper titled "Reengineering Work" published in *Harvard Business Review* in 1990.

Managerial Implication

Reengineering has been implemented in many organizations across the globe. There was a mixed reaction to its success. Some organizations reported stupendous results and others moderate whereas a few landed in confusion. The failures are mostly attributable to a poor change in management especially human side of it. The model is revolutionary in its approach and philosophy. Therefore, organizations undertaking reengineering without proper study, and systematic implementation plan are likely to face many problems, in particular resistance that may overtake the execution. So think sincerely before applying.

Z THEORY

William G. Ouchi is the author of the famous theory Z. He had published a book titled *Theory Z: How American Business can meet the Japanese Challenge*. A detailed comparison and contrast has been made between American and Japanese styles of management in the book. Ouchi called the organizations that are generally known for developing the talents and techniques internally to manage well as type Z companies. The characteristics of this Z model are briefly described in Table 15.4.

TABLE 15.4

HRM dimension	American model	Japanese model	Z model
1. Employment with a firm	Usually short-term; contract-based; lay-offs and retrenchments are common	Usually long-term; Lifetime employment in most of the large firms. Lay-offs and retrenchments are uncommon	Neither short nor lifelong but long-term employment; objective is to create a dedicated permanent workforce
2. Career upgradations	Accelerated promotions; employees who do not receive rapid promotions usually quit and seek employment elsewhere	Stagnated promotions; very slow and conservative. Promotions are given only on serving for years	Slow promotions; more emphasis is on upgradation of skills and competence rather than hierarchical elevations
3. Career paths	Very focused, specialized and micro; employees tend to spend their entire career in one discipline/function	Very general and macro. Employees are rotated across all the functions and objective is to provide an overall perspective	General and oriented to give a feel of entire organization and its operations
4. Decision-making	Powers are vested with individual managers and generally centralized	Powers are vested with groups/teams	Fluid; teams are empowered to take decisions based on consensus and active participation of group members
5. Control	Very explicit; people know exactly what to control and how to do it	Very implicit and informal; people rely heavily on trust and goodwill	More attention to informal control procedures coupled with explicit performance measures
6. Responsibility	Individual centric; every employee is given clearly defined responsibilities	Group centric; all group members are equally responsible for a defined activity/function	Individual oriented
7. Concern for the personnel	Work life is taken care of; personal life is considered completely personal	A holistic concern for employees life is accorded; Concern is shown equally to an employee's professional, social and personal life	Organization is concerned with total life of an employee that include work and family life

Managerial Implication

The dominant characteristics of the above three models—American, Japanese and Z, provide three different approaches in managing HR in organizations. The American model and Japanese model represent two extreme sides in every aspect of HRM starting from recruitment to separation where as Z model is poised between these two. William Ouchi, the author of Z model tried to assimilate the characteristic of both the models, mainly leaning towards Japanese model. Z model fits well with cross-cultural organizations that mainly include multinationals. However, in practice, every organization need to implement a model or approach depending on its overall internal and external organizational environment and culture. In the process, the above three perspectives equips the HR managers with the valuable input.

QUALITY MANAGEMENT

Creating customer-oriented organization has become the dominant theme in the competitive era. Quality-centered approach is considered as pivotal instrument in achieving this customer orientation from the traditional inward looking approach. Within quality management, there are three main approaches propounded by the three stalwarts, i.e. ten quality principles of Joseph M. Juran, fourteen principles of W. Edwards Deming and fourteen quality principles of Philip Crosby. These are illustrated in Table 15.5.

TABLE 15.5

Juran's 10 principles	Deming's 14 principles	Crosby's 14 principles
1. Build awareness of the need for quality and an opportunity for improvement 2. Set goals for improvement 3. Organize to achieve goals 4. Provide training 5. Carry out projects to solve problems 6. Report progress 7. Give recognition 8. Communicate results 9. Keep score 10. Maintain momentum	1. Create constancy for the purpose of improvement of product and service. Allocate resources to provide for long-term needs with a view to becoming competitive 2. Adopt the new philosophy. We are in a new economic age. We can no longer live with mistakes and defects. 3. Eliminate dependence on mass inspection. Quality must be built into the product. Quality must be the foundation on which the organization is built. 4. Eliminate awarding business based on price alone. Instead minimize total cost. Move toward a singular supplier for any one item, on a long-term relationship of loyalty and trust. 5. Improve constantly the system of production and service to improve quality and productivity, thus constantly decreasing costs. What is good enough for today is not good enough for tomorrow. 6. Institute training on the job. 7. Institute leadership. The aim of supervision would be to help people and machines do a better job. Supervision of management is in need of overhaul, as well as supervision of production workers. 8. Drive out fear. Create a climate in which everyone may work effectively for the company. 9. Break down barriers between departments. People in research, design, sales and production must work as a team to tackle problems encountered with the product or service.	1. Make it clear the management is committed to quality. 2. Form quality improvement teams with senior representatives from each department. 3. Determine where current and potential quality problems lie. 4. Evaluate the cost of quality and explain its use as a management tool. 5. Raise the quality awareness and personal concern of all employees. 6. Take actions to correct problems identified through previous steps.

TABLE 15.5 (*continued*)

Juran's 10 principles	Deming's 14 principles	Crosby's 14 principles
	10. Eliminate slogans and exhortations and targets for the workforce asking for zero defects and new levels of productivity. Such exhortations only create adversarial relationship, as the bulk of the causes of low quality and low productivity belong to the system and thus lie beyond the power of the workforce.	7. Establish a committee for the zero defects programme.
	11. Eliminate work standards (quotas). Eliminate management by numbers and numerical goals.	8. Train supervisors to carry out their part of the quality improvement programme.
	12. Eliminate barriers to pride of workmanship. This implies, inter-alia, abolition of the annual or merit rating and of management by objectives. The responsibility of supervisors must be changed from sheer numbers to quality.	9. Hold a 'zero defects day' to let all employees realize there has been a change.
	13. Institute a vigorous programme of education and self-improvement. Workers should be educated to use tools and techniques of quality as well as develop new methods of working in teams.	10. Encourage individuals to establish improvement goals for themselves and their groups.
	14. Take action to accomplish transformation. The transformation is everybody's job.	11. Encourage employees to communicate to management the obstacles they face in attaining their improvement goals.
		12. Recognize and appreciate those who participate.
		13. Establish quality councils to communicate on a regular basis.
		14. Do it all over again to emphasize that the quality improvement programme never ends.

Managerial Implication

The principles of these three quality gurus form the essence of quality management. The rest of quality science in fact is built around these principles. Therefore, understanding of these is a must for all managers in organization. This is particularly so since all types of organizations have some or other quality initiatives being implemented. HR managers need to accord special attention towards the quality principles because more than ninety per cent of quality management involves management of people.

Chapter 16

Culture Management

It is a well-established fact that culture has profound influence on individual, group and organizational performance. Culture, a soft aspect, is considered to be hard in its management. This is because of many reasons: firstly, it is not easy to describe and explain the dimensions, operational aspects, structure, shape and ingredients of culture. For example, we come across statement such as, a particular organization has very good culture but when we ask what exactly it means, explanation becomes very difficult. This is due to the fact that culture is more an issue of experience and entrenched in the feelings of people than the properties of a physical object. But still it has a powerful presence and place in management of organizations. Secondly, it is often difficult to replicate or adopt a particular culture unless we understand the philosophy and overall objective of it. Thirdly, appropriateness of a culture model is dependent upon the organization's internal and external environment. Fourthly, culture can be nurtured only through sustained efforts and perseverance and it often takes years.

However difficult the culture issue may be, the effectiveness of HRM practice is depends upon it. Therefore, HR practitioners have no choice but to tackle it with professionalism. In this backdrop, the present chapter presents seven pragmatic classics to provide the micro, macro perspective of culture management laced with practical tips, tactics, approaches and models.

MODEL LINKING ORGANIZATIONAL CULTURE AND ORGANIZATIONAL PERFORMANCE

The relationship, contribution and impact of organizational culture over organizational performance is well established. Study after study have clearly highlighted that a salutary organizational culture helps organizations to enhance its financial performance. The culture specialist, Joseph Champoux illustrated these studies together with how performance oriented organizational culture is to be created, in his book titled *Organisational behaviour: Essential Tenets for a New Millennium* published in 2000. These issues are briefly discussed in the following points:

1. Organizations with cultures featuring well-dispersed, participatory decision making had higher returns on investment and sales than those not as well dispersed. The differences in financial performance became even greater over time.

2. Organizations with cultures that had well organized and adaptable work procedures and presented clear goals to employees outperformed organizations that did not. These

cultural characteristics were strong predictors of long-term financial performance than short-term performance.

3. A strong, widely dispersed culture helps high risk organizations. People in these cultures perform with a collective mind, a cognitive interdependence that helps them know how to act and how others will act.

4. Organizations with social responsibility as an espoused value were higher on a composite index of financial performance than organizations emphasizing the state of the economy.

5. Within accounting organizations with cultures emphasizing accuracy of work, predictability, and risk taking, poor performing employees quit at a higher rate than high performing employees. No difference existed in the rate of quitting in organizations with cultures valuing collaboration and teamwork.

6. Culture characteristics of widely shared values and a value of adaptability correlated well with performance in later years in eleven life insurance companies.

The performance oriented organizational culture can be created through the following three methods:

1. *Creating organizational culture.* It is a deliberate effort to build a specific type of organizational culture. It happens when an entrepreneur forms an organization to pursue a vision or when managers of an existing organization form a new operating unit. The new culture needs an ideology that is understandable, convincing and widely discussed. The ideology is a key tool for getting commitment from members of the organization to the vision.

2. *Maintaining organizational culture.* Culture maintenance requires managers to be aware of what organizational culture is and how it manifests itself in their organizations. It requires knowing the existing organizational culture's artefacts, values and ideologies. A way by which managers can become familiar with their culture is by doing a culture diagnosis. Culture maintenance also requires managers to carefully examine any new practices for consistency with their culture's ideology.

3. *Changing organizational culture.* It requires breaking from some features of the old culture and creating new features. The size and depth of the change will vary depending on the degree of difference between the desired new cultures and the old. Successfully managing the change process requires managers to attend several issues. One is choosing the proper time for change. Managers should know the roots of their organization's culture and maintain some continuity with the past by keeping elements that are valued widely in the organization. Further, managers must not assume that everyone in the organization will share their view of the need to change.

Managerial Implication

Despite abundance of awareness about the importance of culture, most of the organizations tend to leave it to manage itself. The result of this attitude is evident in organizations performance. Therefore, managers must realize that in line with the changing business demands, they need to either build or change the culture or else it should be maintained on a continuous basis. The above content helps to emphasize the importance of culture and methods to achieve performance-oriented culture.

TWELVE TYPES OF CORPORATE CULTURE

Understanding the classification or what researches call as taxonomy of culture is important to all in the business of HRM on account of two reasons. Firstly, the knowledge of types of corporate culture gives us a macro perspective and secondly we can identify the organizations in reference to these types in a meaningful way. In turn, this helps us to decide the course of action on a variety of HR related issues including deciding what type of corporate culture is appropriate to one's organization. Adrian Furnham, professor at University College, London and Barrie Gunter, Fellow of the same college have presented a classification of corporate culture in their book titled *Corporate Assessment* published in 1993. These are:

1. *A humanistic-helpful culture.* Organizations are managed in a participative, consultative and mutually supportive manner.

2. *An affiliative culture.* Interpersonal relationships are given high priority.

3. *An approval culture.* Agreement, consensus seeking, conflict avoidance dominate this type of organizations.

4. *A conventional culture.* These are conservative, bureaucratic and traditional organizations. Conformity and adherence are valued.

5. *A dependent culture.* Centralization, formal roles and seeking instructions from seniors all the time for all the activities are the traits of this culture.

6. *An avoidance culture.* Punishing mistakes and no reward to good work characterize this type of organizations.

7. *An oppositional culture.* Awarding negativism and being critical is the virtue in these organizations. Here members criticize each other's decisions.

8. *A power culture.* Using positional power, hierarchical orientation, arbitrariness and subjectivity prevail in the organizations of this culture.

9. *A competitive culture.* Employees are rewarded for exceeding targets, outperforming others and this culture promotes win-lose situations.

10. *A perfectionist culture.* Perseverance, perfection, hard work are valued here and avoiding mistakes is the hallmark of this type.

11. *An achievement culture.* It is characterized by success, achieving targets/ accomplishing their own goals and pursuing standards of excellence.

12. *A self-actualization culture.* Creativity, research, and development, quality emphasis behaviour is valued in this culture.

Managerial Implication

HR managers must identify the dominant culture that is existent in their organizations and should analyze whether that is appropriate, given the organizational history. For example, a self-actualization oriented culture will be conducive to the working of a research organization. However due to certain reasons it may be in the trap of a power culture orientation. In such circumstances HR managers must generate awareness and advise chief executives the need to set right culture in the organization. The misfit of culture is a common problem with most of the organizations. This is because organizations continued to operate with old culture despite change in its technology, products, employees and customers. Therefore, responsibility of setting right corporate culture rests with HR managers.

FOUR PRACTICAL APPROACHES TO CULTURAL CHANGE

The biggest challenge managements encounter in organizations is effecting cultural change. There is plausible evidence that even the best of the plans with best of the intentions fail to yield expected results. This is due to pitfalls in the approach adopted in driving the change. Therefore, organizations must critically examine various options and choose an approach over others in managing cultural change. The culture expert, S. Bate classified the cultural change approaches into four that organizations follow and presented them in an interesting manner in his book titled *Strategies for Cultural Change* published in 1995. These are summarized in Table 16.1.

TABLE 16.1

Approach	Characteristics	It can	But it usually
1. Aggressive	• Rapid change • Dismantles traditional values • New culture is non-complex • Top down monitored • Detailed plans/actions	• Lead to a strong, integrated culture • Suit a situation where there is a simple source of authority	• Mobilizes dissent • Is politically naïve • Lacks skills, breadth of support leads to crisis of change
2. Conciliative	• Reasonable, quiet • Slow grafting onto new values • Deals with means, not ends • Collusion, not confrontation • Continuous development • Based on power and control	• Lead to a common sense welcoming of the new culture • Disarm opposition	• Loses sight of its radical intent • Gets seduced back to status quo
3. Corrosive	• Uses informal network • Unseen manipulation • High participation • Act first, legitimise later • Planned and programmed	• Lead to genuine and large-scale change initiated by small-scale network	• Is used to defend existing order and oppose change initiators
4. Indoctrinative	• Explicit learning process • Socializing • Unified, logical framework • Advocates one world view	• Lead to wide scale changes at an informational, technical level	• Does not succeed in bringing about fundamental cultural change

Managerial Implication

Managers who are exposed or involved in managing cultural change in organizations know that many times the gap between plans and implementation of culture is so wide that it frustrates even the most positive minded. In other cases, the delivered results are disfavourably disproportionate to the efforts and cost incurred. This is precisely due to excessive attention paid on cultural plans and inadequate consideration of approach strategy. The above classification helps practitioners to gain a broad perspective of approaches that are available to them. HR managers must advocate a suitable approach for implementation of cultural change based on the type of cultural change planned and organizational environment.

HOFSTEDE'S MODEL OF CULTURE DIMENSIONS

Geert H. Hofstede, a Dutch researcher conducted a classic study that received international recognition while he was with IBM as Psychologist. He collected data from a massive one lakh and sixteen thousand employees working in seventy countries on their attitudes and work related behaviour. All these employees were working for IBM and its subsidiaries. The data were collected during the period from 1967 to 1973. Based on this data, he developed a model that identifies four primary dimensions that differentiate culture. Understanding these dimensions and their variations among different countries assumed greater significance in the globalized scenario. The cultural dimensions are:

1. *Power distance.* These are two types. High power distance means high tolerance to unequal power distribution and members of an institution/organization grants unlimited power to an individual. Low power distance means low tolerance to unequal power distribution. In high power distance countries the leaders tend to be autocratic and paternalistic. Subordinates also fear of boss and his unlimited power is viewed as natural. In low power distance countries, bosses tend to use democratic methods and subordinates do not hesitate to challenge the bosses. India was found to be high power distance society.

2. *Individualism-collectivism.* Individualism refers to valuing one's own freedom, and interests and taking care of own family. Here people are motivated by personal challenges and rewards. Collectivism relates to loyalty to one's own group and is characterized by social framework. Here, people derive pride and satisfaction by merging their identity and achievements with their group. Collectivism was found to be the dominant characteristic of India.

3. *Uncertainty avoidance.* Strong uncertainty avoidance means, tendency to perceive uncertain things/situations/ambiguity as threats. Such societies/organizations try to avoid these uncertainties through voluminous rules, a stable career, rejecting the deviant ideas etc. Weak uncertainty avoidance refers to people feeling less threatened by unknown. Here there will be less rules and minimal rigidity in the systems. India was identified as weak uncertainty avoidance country.

4. *Masculinity-femininity.* Masculinity refers to materialistic things like money and assertiveness. For example, in masculine countries, people seek higher advancements in career, more rewards and accomplishments. Femininity is characterized by value to relationships, security, cooperation, long term standing with an organization etc. India was found to be masculine society.

   Dr. Hofstede Geert who is respected worldwide for his seminal work on culture has authored several books. The culture dimensions model is presented in his book titled, *Culture's Consequences: International Differences in Work-Related Values,* published in 1980.

Managerial Implication

Basis for effective HRM lies in culture understanding. Culture understanding is paramount in designing culture compatible HR policies and their administration. This has occupied centre stage since trade across the borders is on the rise and employing people from different counties has become common. International businesses that are ill informed about the culture and associated practices of other countries are unlikely to succeed, particularly in the area of HRM. Organizations, when adopting the models and approaches of other countries, must consider their suitability in the light of cultural dimensions.

MODEL ILLUSTRATING PROGRESSIVE vs STATIC CULTURES

Understanding the role of culture and its influence over HR is central to the job of HR managers. The solution to many of the problems; whether small or big, micro or macro and simple or complex could be traced to the culture dimension. Further, understanding the type of culture that exist in organizations or societies can provide vital clue why a particular kind of working pattern or work behaviour prevail in organizations. Lawrence Harrison and Samuel Huntington classified the culture into two types: Progressive and Static, each represented by ten different values, attitudes and mind sets and presented them in their book titled *Culture Matters: How Values Shape Human Progress* published in 2000. These are:

1. *Time orientation.* Progressive cultures emphasize the future; static cultures emphasize the present or past. Future orientation implies a progressive worldview—influence over one's destiny, rewards in this life to virtue, positive-sum economics.
2. Work is central to good life in progressive cultures but is a burden in static cultures. In the former, work structures daily life; diligence, creativity, and achievement are rewarded not only financially but also with satisfaction and self-respect.
3. Frugality is the mother of investment; and financial security, in progressive cultures is a threat to the "egalitarian" status quo in static cultures, which often have a zero-sum worldview.
4. Education is the key to progress in progressive cultures but is of marginal importance except for the elites in static cultures.
5. Merit is central to advancement in progressive cultures; connections and family are what that count in static cultures.
6. In progressive cultures, the radius of identification and trust extends beyond the family to the broader society. In static cultures, the family circumscribes community. Societies with a narrow radius of identification and trust are more prone to corruption, tax evasion, and nepotism, and they are less likely to engage in philanthropy.
7. The ethical code tends to be more rigorous in progressive cultures. Every advanced democracy (except Belgium, Taiwan, Italy, and South Korea) appears among the twenty-five least corrupt countries on transparency International's Corruption Perceptions Index. Chile and Botswana are the only Third World countries that appear among the top twenty-five.
8. Justice and fair play are universal impersonal expectations in progressive cultures. In static cultures, justice, like personal advancement, is often a function of who you know or how much you can pay.

9. Authority tends toward dispersion and horizontality in progressive cultures, toward concentration and verticality in static cultures.

10. The influence of religious institution on civic life is small in progressive cultures; its influence is often substantial in static cultures. Heterodoxy and dissent are encouraged in the former, orthodoxy and conformity in the latter.

Managerial Implication

The above ten factors provide a macro perspective of culture from which practising managers can draw a number of lessons. The above description of progressive and static cultures characteristics mainly serve to understand the whole spectrum of culture. These ten characteristics enable managers to analyze the differences between organizations existing in different societal values. These macro culture characteristics have implications for policy and practice of all HR functions. Probably, knowledge of these basic differences in cultural values can make managers to match the HRM with the dominant culture type.

RENAISSANCE MODEL OF CULTURE CHANGE

Success of any organizational change programme lies in effective management of culture. There is overwhelming evidence pointing out that introduction of quite a few technical systems have failed because of organization's failure to align the culture rather than technology per se. Many organizations and their managers have realized this fact. But the puzzle is how to align or transform the culture in consonance with organizational change strategy or programme at ground level. A HR consultancy based in America developed a culture change model using leadership and training strategies to successfully manage the culture transition following the merger of Glaxo and The Wellcome Foundation to form Glaxo Wellcome in 1995. This model helped to infuse a proactive, accountable, commitment oriented and unified organizational culture replacing the divergent culture of two organizations. The significant features of this model now known as Renaissance four phase approach to culture change are:

- Phase-I: *Development of master plan.* Studying the kind of environment that presently exists in organization and defining what kind of environment aspired are the two critical activates in this phase. Based on this study, a strong plan should be developed outlining the broad objectives.

- Phase-II: *Change intervention.* This is a detailed exercise involving operational strategy finalization. As a logical sequence to the first phase, here a process of identifying various change programmes will be identified. This process also includes identifying various constraints that are likely emerge during the implementation of the change programmes so planned.

- Phase-III: *Leadership, skill and tool development.* Firstly, organizing a large scale change effort requires a critical mass of influential players, beginning with top management. In order to achieve this, a suitable number of managers will be trained on change management skills especially in the context of organization who will perform the role of key resource persons/change agents. Secondly, skill and tool approach will be applied wherein workshops and clinics are conducted to bring changes in the employees' attitudes, behaviour and practices.

- Phase-IV: *Systemic behavioural integration.* The critical challenge in this phase is to align developed behaviour patterns and practices with the new vision, values and master change plan of the organization. It is a systemic behavioural integration that helps to sustain positive shifts. The integration process allows existing organizational systems to be changed or replaced so that they reinforce desired behaviours.

Managerial Implication

Renaissance model has the potential to serve as a standard in design and implementation of culture change initiative in organizations. This is a practical model because it had arisen out of Glaxo Wellcome organizational change need and evaluation reports established that the model was successful in infusing a unified salutary organizational culture. This model also contributed to solve merger related HR problems in a smooth manner. The Glaxo experience has some insightful learning to offer to HR managers.

AT&T MODEL OF CULTURE MANAGEMENT

Culture management is a critical managerial function in any change or restructuring programme. In fact, much of the success of these change programmes is contingent upon the cultural aspects that include HR policies, practices and process and leadership style. Many of the restructuring programmes do not succeed due to failure to integrate the cultural measures within the grand strategy. AT&T culture management, particularly in the context of its take over of Bell operations, and the way it had brought cultural assimilation, is internationally lauded. Tunstall Brooke who studied this culture management of AT&T from close quarters analyzed it in his paper titled "Culture Transition at AT&T" published in *Sloan Management Review* in 1983. The salient features of this culture management are:

1. *Set the example.* Cultural changes cannot be delegated to the employee information staff. They must begin at the top of the organization with the chief executive officer and have the support of his/her inner circle of top officers. For example, several years before the process of divestiture began at AT&T, chairman Charles Brown began to set the stage for cultural change in a speech before the commercial club in Chicago. This experience proved that the chief executive officer whose behaviour is consistent with the norms and values he or she has articulated for the company has an enormous head start.

2. *Revamp the system of management.* Even the influence of leadership, of course, has its limits, particularly in large corporations where the principal management is far removed from day to day middle and lower management functions. Cultural norms must be reoriented by changing the system of management—the many management processes, the organizational structure, and the management style that drive the corporation. AT&T adopted a practice of clearly communicating the pattern of values and behaviours it wants to achieve by changing reward systems, reorienting resource allocation processes, restructuring the organization and establishing its new identity.

3. *Articulate the value system explicitly.* It is critically important to communicate all employees in specific terms precisely what the corporate value system is, especially in

periods of change. At AT&T, a clearly recast document, 'A Statement of Policy', set forth the corporation's evolving goals.

4. *Gear training to support cultural values.* The other mechanism for effecting change in the corporate culture is management training that is explicitly geared to modify behaviour in support of new corporate values. The Bell advanced management programme launched by AT&T, a developmental experience for high performance fourth and fifth level managers of the business, exemplifies such training. Its components include business strategy formulation and implementation, financial challenges, strategic marketing and the management of change.

5. *Revise recruiting aims and methods.* Potential problems of culture clash can be avoided by making certain that the individual value systems, personalities and educational backgrounds of younger managers coming aboard are in harmony with the corporation's aims. AT&T has a long history of recruiting and developing managers for a regulated milieu. This process tended to produce company men, i.e. employees who are dedicated to the business, who equate their personal success with the corporation's long-term development, and who have exceptional managerial skills.

6. *Modify the symbols.* At AT&T for example, the loss of the Bell name and logo was a serious one. However, Chairman of AT&T saw this as an opportunity to reinforce the AT&T image both internally and externally. The chairman impressed upon all the employees that by continuing to use AT&T as a trade name, the corporation can capitalize on its long-standing reputation throughout the world.

Managerial Implication

Culture must be reshaped, adapted and reoriented whenever there is a restructuring or a major change. Culture, well articulated and managed in tune with organizational demands can facilitate organizational effectiveness. However, managing culture is easier said than done given its complexities. This is because the management of culture involves many aspects and some of them are multivariate. It is always easy to gain insights through the experience of other organizations. In this context, the AT&T case will be of a practical use. Managers handling culture issues have many important practical tips in this.

Chapter 17

Change Management

Change management is one of the permanent and commonly handled functions in all organizations and a common function to all managers regardless of their functional affiliation. Success of most of the organizations and managers is proportional to how best they can adopt or manage the changes. Individuals as well as organizations may have to ready for downslide if they resist or fail to manage change. HR practitioners have no choice but to clearly understand the change related issues that include people related change, systems related change, structure related change and environmental change. This is because each of these changes will have direct implications and consequences for policy and practice of HRM.

In consonance with this, the current chapter presents fourteen classics on change management. These classics focus on a variety of issues within the change management that include: (i) models in design and implementation of change programmes, (ii) Obstacles in execution of change interventions, (iii) models in managing change resistance, (iv) transition management, (v) critical points in change management and (vi) change agent's role in conceptualization, execution, and appraisal of change strategy.

MODEL OF ORGANIZATION CHANGE

Change Management, an issue once confined to people and organizations that were branded as radical has become something fundamental to all. The concept of change also underwent drastic change from its earlier shape: change that is viewed in micro perspective, i.e. fragmented change, often limited to one or two functions/activities to a macro perspective, i.e. organization-wide change affecting structure, systems, processes. This was because of realization that fragmented changes are seldom effective. Professor Lary Greiner of Harvard Business School who deeply studied the organization change patterns avers that successful organization change programmes pass through a six phases change process, and, absence of it contributes for less successful changes. He presented this model in the classic book titled *Organizational Change and Development* published in 1970. These six phases are:

1. *Pressure and Arousal.* Two types of pressures organizations face pressures that arise from two sources: One type is external that include lower sales, lower turnover, lower stock value and losses, and the second type is internal such as low employee morale, low productivity, trade union pressure, interdepartmental conflicts etc. These factors pressurize top management to seek organizational change.

2. *Intervention and Reorientation.* The pressures described above triggers change of leadership at top. Generally, an outsider who possesses skills to manage crisis is likely to occupy the leadership role. This person is likely to reorient the power structure in the organization at the beginning.

3. *Diagnosis and Recognition.* The new leader will start collecting the information relating to all the aspects of organizational functioning. This person also engages a dialogue with all sections of employees to seek first handed information (sharing experience). It also helps to induce an idea that top management is trying to bring changes. These actions help to diagnose and recognize the root causes for poor performance.

4. *Intervention and Commitment.* Here, search for best solutions to solve the recognized problems start. All employees are involved to participate in this effort. This involvement breeds participative culture (shared power) in the organization and leads to greater organizational commitment.

5. *Experimentation and Search.* All solutions thus offered would be evaluated and finalized for implementation in a phased manner again with the involvement of employees (shared power). The implementation starts with pilot study to gauge their efficacy.

6. *Reinforcement and Acceptance.* An audit will be carried out to check pay-off of such intervention. The interventions of change established as contributors of performance garner organization-wide acceptance to its continuance and positive changes create a reinforcement effect.

Managerial Implication

Greiner's six phases change model helps managers to understand the scientific process of change management. A change programme that follows this pattern will be successful in its attempts. The central issue in this model is shared power. It means all employees should be involved in identification, analysis and applying the solutions as a part of change management. In such a context, HR managers have an important role to play. At least in four out of six phases as illustrated above, human side of change management takes a lion share in change management effort.

EIGHT PHASES CHANGE MODEL

Sometimes, it appears that organizations that have not attempted the organizational change efforts are better off than those who attempted. This is because failures have dominated the success in organizations. For example, more than half of the organizations who had tried with reengineering, TQM, learning organization etc. had reported the dissatisfactory outcomes. These failures are attributable to organizational inability to implement the change programmes systematically than due the deficiencies of the models. Therefore, understanding the mistakes organizations make in any change programme thus assumes importance. Professor John Kotter of Harvard Business School addressed these issues in an insightful manner in his book titled *Leading Change* published in 1996. In this book, he points out eight common errors in organizational change efforts. These are: (i) allowing too much complacency, (ii) failing to create a sufficiently powerful guiding coalition, (iii) under communicating the vision, (iv) permitting obstacles to block the vision, (v) failure to create short-term wins, (vi) declaring victory too soon and (vii) neglecting to anchor changes firmly in the corporate culture.

Prof. Kotter prescribes a change management model comprising eight phases that guides organizations in their effort to change without committing the above-described common errors. These are:

1. *Establish a sense of urgency.* Executives underestimate how hard it can be to drive people out of their comfort zones. They talk about change begins with some people noticing vulnerability in the organization. The threat of losing ground in some way sparks these people into action, and they in turn try to communicate that sense of urgency to others.

2. *Form a powerful guiding coalition.* The need in this phase is to gather a large enough initial core believers. This initial group should be pretty powerful. Regardless the size of your organization, the guiding coalition for change needs to have 3–5 people leading the effort.

3. *Create a vision.* A vision helps clarify the direction in which an organization needs to move. Successful transformation rests on a picture of the future that is relatively easy to communicate, and applies to customers, stockholders and employees.

4. *Communicate the vision.* The bottom line is that a transformation effort will fail unless most of the members understand.

5. *Empower others to act on the vision.* Free key people from existing responsi-bilities so they can concentrate on the new effort. In short, remove any obstacles there may be to getting on with the change.

6. *Plan for and create short-term wins.* Since, real transformation takes time, the loss of momentum and the onset of disappointment are real factors. In successful transfor-mation, leaders actively plan and achieve some short-term gains which people will be able to see and celebrate.

7. *Consolidate improvements and keep the momentum for change moving.* Do not declare victory too soon, until changes sink deeply. Leaders of change must go into the process believing that their efforts will take years

8. *Institutionalize the new approaches.* Until new behaviours are rooted firmly in social norms and shared values, they are subject to degradations as soon as the pressure for change is removed.

Managerial Implication

This model helps in drafting your own implementation strategy of change. The knowledge of eight-phase model is imperative to HR managers since all organizations are either planning or implementing some kind of change programmes. Most of the issues are HR related in the organizational change efforts and therefore, it is the commitment and professionalism of HR professionals that guarantee the success.

TWELVE-STEP MODEL FOR ORGANIZATIONAL CHANGE AND RENEWAL

Even the best of intentions can not help an organizational change and renewal effort unless a systematic model is followed. However, it is also a fact that, finding or developing a foolproof plan and executing it is the toughest of managerial jobs. There will be many questions to be asked and there will be many issues to which no answers will be available. Still managements should take a leap in dark. This may be true to some extent but still the harder truth is that the portion of this darkness can be minimized to a large extent with a carefully articulated strategy. In articulation of such an effort, twelve critical factors identified by the management experts, Patrica Felkins, B.J. Chakiris and Kenneth Chakiris based on their benchmarking study of organizational change and renewal will be of immense value. They proposed these successful factors, which can work as a practical change model in their book titled *Change Management: A Model for Effective Organisational Performance* published in 1993. These factors are:

1. Involve senior executives in identifying vision, values, and critical success factors for benchmarking, so that priorities become known for each business unit and or function.
2. Establish an advisory council of representatives of senior executives including chairperson, chief executive officer, and chief operating officer for guidance, ownership to provide a test-development climate, and to establish accountability. In a nonprofit agency, this could include the board members, executive committee chairs, and senior staff.
3. Clarify role responsibilities for each function so that resources and support are given to the effort.
4. Create an executive-development strategy that fits the business so that ownership, involvement, and commitment are given to the benchmarking change effort.
5. Focus efforts on determining the critical success factors for achieving the strategic business plan in order to focus developmental efforts on those criteria that result in the greatest pay-off for the business.
6. Do not expect too much too soon, and understand the impact of change process on culture, roles, structure, and work practices.
7. Provide awareness of the competitive threat so that a rationale for change and innovation is obvious.
8. Learn from others and find ways to transfer that learning to other parts of the business. Move beyond the "not-invented-here" syndrome and integrate outside resources.
9. Start in friendly areas where success can be achieved and support gained for test development.
10. Take adequate time to plan and involve key people in determining change requirements.
11. Communicate the idea that change is an ongoing process, not just a program.
12. Integrate the directed and nondirected elements of change.

Managerial Implication

The above twelve factors were drawn from the varied and rich experience of authors in handling the organizational change and renewal programmes. They are in fact benchmarked as parameters for successful change management. Hence, these can be considered as fundamental rules of change management in action. Therefore, change managers that include HR managers can adopt them as thumb rules while developing a change management strategy for their organization. It is strongly believed that, adherence to these twelve steps can assure success with change management programmes.

TEN COMMANDMENTS MODEL FOR EXECUTING CHANGE

Executing of any change programme is often double the amount of work and challenges than that of developing a change strategy. Even the finest of change strategy fall flat when implementation plan is not free from pitfalls. As someone said, the proof of pudding is in its eating. Similarly, the reality of change is in its execution and not in its idea. The change management experts Rosabeth Moss Kanter, Barry Stern and Todd Jick, based on their vast experience in dealing with change strategy implementation, had prescribed ten commandments that facilitate effective execution of change in organizations in their best selling book titled *The Challenge of Organisational Change: How Companies Experience and Leaders guide it* published in 1992. These are:

1. *Analyze the organization and its need for change.* Leaders must understand how the proposed changes will affect various parts of the organization and its people in order to craft an effective implementation plan.

2. *Create a shared vision and common direction.* One of the first steps in engineering change is to unite an organization behind a central vision.

3. *Separate from the past.* It is difficult for an organization to embrace a new vision of the future until it has isolated the structures and routines that no longer work and has vowed to move beyond them.

4. *Create a sense of urgency.* Convincing an organization that change is necessary isn't that difficult when a company is teetering on the edge of bankruptcy. But when the need for action is not generally understood, a change leader should generate a sense of urgency.

5. *Support a strong leader.* An organization should not undertake something as challenging as large-scale change without a leader to guide, drive and inspire.

6. *Line up political sponsorship.* Leadership alone cannot bring about large-scale change. There should be a coalition building. This coalition building should include both power sources—the holders of important resources necessary to make the change work and stakeholders who stand to gain or lose from the change.

7. *Craft an implementation plan.* The change plan is a road map for the change effort specifying from where the first meeting should be held, to the date when the company hopes to achieve its change goal.

8. *Develop enabling structures.* Enabling structures designed to facilitate and spotlight change range from the practical, such as setting up pilot tests, offsite workshops, training programmes, and new reward systems, to the symbolic such as changing the organization's name or physically rearranging space.

9. *Communicate, involve people and be honest.* Full involvement, communication and

disclosure are not called for in every change situation but these approaches can be potent tools for overcoming resistance and giving employees a personal stake in the outcome of a transformation.

10. *Reinforce and institutionalize.* Throughout the pursuit of change, managers and leaders should make it a top priority to prove their commitment to the transformation process, reward risk taking and incorporate new behaviours into the day-to-day operations of the organization.

Managerial Implication

The above Ten Commandments are immensely useful to all those involved in the change management in organizations. Managers must draft implementation plans in consonance with these commandments and adherence to these can guarantee the success. These have come from people involved in change strategy execution in a number of world class companies and their learning over the decades have culminated into these. Therefore, managers can adopt them as a working checklist in their efforts of change execution.

FIVE POTENTIAL OBSTACLES OF CHANGE

Change management calls for a change in its managers in terms of their approach, beliefs, behaviours, attitude and in their expectations from that of traditional, static, hierarchical and formal set-up to that of dynamic, informal and team-based. Managers, who intend to manage the change, particularly change of large-scale, need to prepare themselves to encounter quite a few potential obstacles. James Belasco in his eye-opening book titled *Teaching the Elephant to Dance* published in 1990, has presented five major and common obstacles managers face in the change management situation. These are:

1. *It always takes longer.* People learn slowly and forget easily. It takes a long time to change—usually a lot longer than expected. It's hard to change habits that have been established for years. The larger your organization is the longer it will take. Take a long-term perspective because it will take that long. Stick with it over the long term. But your people need short-term validation that your vision works. They need to see a continuous stream of short-term progress produced by the use of your vision.

2. *Exaggerated expectations, everyone wants everything, now.* Turn people on and they get turned on! Deliver some progress, and people want lots of progress immediately. And they look to you to deliver that progress. Generally, employees look for heroes to believe in, to follow, and to imitate. They expect heroes to be perfect, to handle every situation with aplomb. They carefully examine his every action to be certain that it meets impossibly high standards. Unfortunately mankind is not perfect. It will make mistakes. It's bound to happen.

3. *Carping sceptics.* There are professional sceptics in every organization. Unfortunately, you can't ignore these sceptics. Of course, they point out significant obstacles that you've overlooked. Furthermore, a large number of employees hear them. They are often loud and persistent in their carping negative comments.

4. *Procrastination.* Vision involves the intangibilities of running a company such as

consumer attitudes and employee motivations. They deal in uncomfortable and difficult areas, and they are all too easily postponed. Vision supporting activities are all too easily postponed. They are difficult to do and often are viewed as not part of the individual's real job.

5. *Imperfection.* Prepare yourself for failure—at least some of the time. A vision does not guarantee perfection. You will make mistakes. Your people will make mistakes. There will be backsliding from time to time. Expect it, anticipate it, and accept because it will happen.

Managerial Implication

No manager can ever expect to be successful in managing change without facing formidable challenges. In fact, the success depends on abilities of managers in handling these challenges. Managers can handle these challenges/obstacles in the most effective manner when they are expected to happen. Therefore, managers must commence any change management effort with anticipation of obstacles to prepare themselves to deal with them. In this process, the above-illustrated five obstacles may constitute the list of your obstacles.

HR MODEL TO MANAGE CHALLENGES OF CHANGE

Any organization that attempts transformational change will have to encounter many challenges. The success or failure of change efforts lies in handling these challenges. HR professionals have a central role in this scenario. Studies in the past point out that many of failures in change management efforts were due to failure of human factors rather than technology, finance, legal factors etc. Richard Beckhard listed the following challenges that an organization must be prepared to meet when a transformational change is attempted, in his insightful paper *A model for the Executive Management of Transformational Change* published in 1989 in which HR managers have a pivotal role:

1. Reaching an appropriate balance between managing the change and managing the stability of the organization.
2. Ensuring appropriate use of special roles, temporary systems, study groups, consultants and transition teams.
3. Continually evaluating both the total effort and its individual parts in terms of planning improvement.
4. Establishing and maintaining continuity of leadership during the change process.
5. Appropriately allocating rewards (and punishments) consistent with the priority of the change effort.
6. Ensuring adequate information flow among various parts of the organization.
7. Constantly monitoring the system to ensure that people know what is happening during the change, understand their roles in the process, and comprehend the total effort rather than isolated elements of it.

Managerial Implication

The operational role of HR managers in ensuring above arrangements include the following:

1. To see that a clear written description of change is prepared. Such a description must include basic organizational character, policies, and values.
2. To explain to the executive managers that the transformation will not occur unless people are feeling so much pain in the present situation that they are motivated to change.
3. To gather views of all employees through the means of participation, surveys and interviews and use them to gain commitment to change initiatives.
4. To discourage quick-fix solutions and help managers to develop a clear strategy to manage challenges of change (for example: employees resistance).
5. To pinpoint the kinds of awareness, education required and providing such education through various training programmes.
6. To assist in assessing people's orientations toward risk, fostering risk taking behaviour and developing an appropriate reward system.
7. To help by stressing the importance of communication, by suggesting appropriate ways to communicate and by recommending, setting up and coaching in communication.

McKINSEY vs MOVEMENT MODELS OF CHANGE

For decades now, the McKinsey model of change is regarded as most appropriate for engineering the major restructuring and change programs in organizations. This model is basically drawn with the objective of profit and wealth maximization. There is also a large-scale evidence of sustained success obtained through this model of change. However, the turnaround guru Pradip Khandwalla argues that this model has its own structural disadvantages and can only provide limited benefits to organizations. He alternatively proposed a model of change called Movement Model of Change in his well researched paper titled "'McKinsey vs. Movement Management: The Two Modes of Major Change" in the book titled *Designing and Developing Organisations for Tomorrow* published in 2001. The salient features of both the models on selective parameters are described in Table 17.1.

TABLE 17.1

Parameter	McKinsey model	Movement model
Definition of issues	By top management, often through external consultants	Broadbased, involving the stake-holders
Designing of change	Centralized and according to a blue print	Interactive, participative and according to the merging consensus
Improvization and innovation	Modest	Widespread and deep
Content of change and innovation	Mostly related to competitive strategy and focus, and supporting system, structures and processes	Systematic changes needed to rectify an emotionally disturbing, widely shared gap in the effectiveness or status of the organization
Kind of leadership	Transactional (centering around incentives, rewards and punishments) and change initiated through the top level	Transformational (envisioning, mobilizing and empowering) and widespread, level-wise initiatives for change

TABLE 17.1 *(continued)*

Parameter	McKinsey model	Movement model
Value emphasized	Focus on commercial and efficiency related issues	Stress on quality of life, development, social contribution and core social values
Empowerment of staff	Formally circumscribed (formal delegation of operating authority constrained by policy framework, formal controls and MIS)	Widespread autonomy restrained by internalized norms and peer group control, in addition to free expression and participation in shaping systematic changes
Learning	Partial, mostly at the top level, confined largely to strategies, systems and structures	Collective, organization wide and deep, and emphasis on human relations
Motivation	Calculative and extrinsic, based primarily on financial incentives	Intrinsic, powered by identification with a cause or a superordinate goal
Results	Modest, but relatively certain	Potentially very large, but relatively uncertain
Costs	Potential large costs in terms of rationali-zation, divestiture, downsizing and demotivation	Potential large costs in terms of the movement going haywire

Managerial Implication

The above models provide two alternatives of managing major change initiatives in organizations. Each one of them has its own advantages and limitations. For example, McKinsey model is highly transactional and has professional oriented approach that can provide immediate results but may last only for a short-term. In contrast, Movement model is highly relationship-oriented that may give result in long run but can provide sustained benefits. Therefore, organizations must adopt an approach that most suits to its requirements, and alternatively they could draw their own using the inputs of both the models.

COOPERS AND LYBRAND MODEL FOR MANAGING CHANGE RESISTANCE

All types of employees working in all types of organizations and in all types of situations make attempts to resist all types of change programmes. This resistance is not necessarily a negative phenomenon but in most of the cases it is a very natural reaction. This resistance can manifest in many ways that range from merely expressing protest to outright sabotage of the company's products and assets. For an organization, failure to recognize this resistance will have more far reaching consequences. Therefore, organizations must anticipate and plan to deal employee resistance constructively. Coopers and Lybrand, one of the world-class management consultancy firms developed a model to manage employee resistance. The model comprises a number of recommendations as indicated below:

1. Communicate often with employees fully and honestly describe the changes that will take place as well as the reasons for them.

2. Assess employee readiness for change.

3. Remove unnecessary barriers to change, such as rules and regulations that make no sense in view of the planned changes.

4. Engage in test projects to determine the effectiveness of change and then report the results of those projects to all employees (even if the results are not the ones anticipated).

5. Demonstrate leadership's commitment to change by engaging in behaviours desired of employees, and make it clear that management is totally committed to the change and expects the employees to be as well.

6. Develop ways to help make the proposed changes more acceptable (even desirable) to employees.

7. Maintain absolute honesty and integrity at all times.

8. Determine in advance exactly how employees will have to change and what they will have to do to ensure success for the planned change.

9. Involve employees in the planned changes as much as possible that is, encourage them to adopt a positive attitude by giving them a vested interest in success.

10. Develop HR policies that support the planned change.

11. Provide ongoing training and education to ensure that employees have the skills necessary to make the changes.

12. Reward desired behaviour and establish disincentives for undesired behaviour.

Managerial Implication

The above change resistance management model was developed drawing insights from a number of real life change programmes. The implementation of above described actions reported to have led the organizations to handle resistance very effectively. These resistance management plans are also believed to have been used to prepare the employees for change successfully. Therefore, the practical value of these prescriptions in managing resistance is immense. These help all managers, particularly HR managers who can draft the above described points as check list while handling the change management programmes in their organizations.

TEN-STEP MODEL FOR TRANSITION MANAGEMENT

The most important activity in any change programme is preparing the organization for transition. Unfortunately, this is generally neglected due to various reasons. The prominent reason among these is that organization feel impatient to spend considerable efforts in planning before acting. This is because, most of the managers feel no progress during preparation phase and they will be unduly eager to get onto the implementation of change programme. This misplaced eagerness leads them to act without thought, resulting in failures. Therefore, the critical activity that can assure the success of change programme lies in preparing organization for transition. The corporate change guru, William Bridges in his book titled *Surviving Corporate Transition* published in 1988 presented an insightful model consisting ten steps that keep organization ready for smooth transition. These are:

1. Describe in the most fundamental terms possible the change that is going to affect the unit in question and the resulting changes that are likely to occur within the unit as a result.

2. Look ahead and identify those individuals and groups that are going to be plunged into transition by these changes.

3. Assess the transition—readiness of the organization—as measured by its training and communication systems, its structural flexibility, its cultural dynamism, and the morale of its personnel.

4. Analyze the political implications of the changes you are preparing to make.

5. Set a challenging but realistic pace for the transitions that the changes are going to require, even if the time table for the changes themselves (as announced by the organization's leaders) is unrealistic.

6. Create a representative group of employees to serve as a transition monitoring team which is charged with the job of keeping track of what is happening to people during the transition period.

7. Identify the new skills and knowledge that will be required for the new beginning, and find or develop training and educational programmes that will provide them.

8. Review the communication resources within your unit and between the unit and the rest of the organization, and make such changes in the communication channels as are necessary to keep people feeling informed and listened to.

9. Create incentives, both long term and ad hoc to reward people for doing what the new situations requires them to do and be.

10. Plan from the very beginning to celebrate the different phases of transition and to represent it in symbolic ways.

Managerial Implication

The ten-step transition model offered many managerial prescriptions that help managers in preparing their organizations for any corporate transition. It is a comprehensive checklist presented in a simplified manner tailored to suit the practical scenario. As the model drives, failure in preparing the organization reflects the failure of any corporate change management programme. The observance of ten steps assures the managers in leading their organizations through success in the event of transition.

GROUP MODEL FOR ACHIEVING CHANGE IN PEOPLE

Most of the 21st century management problems are related to people issues directly or indirectly. These people related problems are concerned with achieving change in their work behaviours. A number of methods have been proposed, tested, reviewed and implemented to push the change initiatives with least resistance and high success. However, resistance continues to exist and success remains a limited experience in organizations. There is one method that can make people welcome and achieve change in a person's behaviour. That method is seeking groups as medium as well as target of change. However, there are two challenges in using groups: First is gaining commitment of groups to perform as medium of change and second is acceptance level of these groups among employees. Dorwin Cartwright in his seminal paper titled "Achieving Change in People: Some Applications of Group Dynamics Theory" published in *Human Relations* in 1951 stipulated eight critical principles adherence of which can ensure groups as medium and target for achieving change in people:

1. If the group is to be used effectively as a medium of change, those people who are to be changed and those who are to exert influence for change must have a strong sense of belonging to the same group.
2. The more attractive the group is to its members the greater the influence that the group can exert on its members.
3. In attempts to change attitudes, values, or behaviours, the more relevant they are to the basis of attraction to the group, the greater will be the influence that the group can exert upon them.
4. The greater the prestige of a group member in the eyes of the other members, the greater the influence he/she can exert.
5. Efforts to change individuals or subparts of a group, which, if successful, would have the result of making them deviate from the norms of the group, will encounter strong resistance.
6. Strong pressure for changes in the group can be established by creating a shared perception by members of the need for change, thus making the source of pressure for change lie within the group.
7. Information relating to the need for changes, plans for changes and consequences of change must be shared by all relevant people in the group.
8. Changes in one part of a group produce strain in other related parts, which can be reduced only by eliminating the change or by bringing about readjustments in the related parts.

Managerial Implication

These eight principles help managers as guidelines in implementing the change through groups. The model as such is based on strong fundamentals of group dynamics. Therefore, it possesses enormous practical value. The model also offers two useful insights to HR managers for putting them into practice. Firstly, it promotes using groups as medium and target of change in organizations, which is a profound idea in pushing change in people. Secondly, the eight principles work as a checklist in adoption of group mechanism to attain change goals.

WHO MOVED MY CHEESE

Often we do not want to change even when things change. We suffer due to this resistance. How to overcome this inner resistance? How to deal with change? Why to invite change? How change benefits us? Answer to these common questions in uncommon style are provided in the book titled, *Who Moved My Cheese* authored by Dr. Spencer Johnson, Fellow of Harvard Business School, which was published in 1998. Dr. Johnson narrates the serious story of change management in an incredibly lighter way that leaves us thoughtful. It comprises of three sections: (i) A Gathering, (ii) The story of who moved my cheese and (iii) A discussion. The story goes like this:

The book begins with A Gathering, wherein former classmates have lunch and chat in a realistic manner about how much their lives have changed since high school. They agree that things have certainly turned out differently than they thought, and notice that they often 'don't want to change when things change'. Then one of them, Mr. Michael narrates the story of "Who Moved My Cheese" to the others.

The story revolves around two mice, Sniff and Scurry, and two little people Hem and Haw. They live in a maze and spend their time running around, looking for, finding and eating cheese. Cheese is a metaphor for what we want to have in life: a job, a relationship, money, a big house, freedom, health, recognition etc. There are different approaches taken by those hoping to acquire Cheese. Sniff is good at sniffing out cheese, and Scurry excels at Scurrying after the cheese once he knows where it is. The two mice don't really think about things, they just react to them. As for Hem and Haw, they are a bit complicated. They use their brains a little more than the mice do, thinking things through, instead of scurrying blindly off into the maze. One day, the mice and the little two find a huge mound of cheese in the maze. Hem and Hew decide that this mound of cheese is so large they never have to think about finding more. They feel comfortable and settle down when suddenly they are caught unaware. Their cheese is gone—Sniff and Scurry are ready to handle this situation, and get back to looking for more cheese immediately. Ham and Hew, however, mope around, complaining that someone moved their cheese. They feel they are entitled to the cheese they worked hard for. While Sniff and Scurry had quickly moved on, Hem and Hew continued to hem and haw. Both the little people visited the maze time and again with the hope of finding cheese but in vain. The situation has not changed. At one point of time Haw realizes that instead of being depressed, he must do something to get new cheese. He wonders where are Sniff and Scurry? Do they know something which we don't? After repeated struggle, he finds new cheese and also reunites with his pals Sniff and Scurry. Haw vows to change his ways by being ready for things to change the next time. He sure learned something from those two mice! Sure, they may be vermin, but they know a thing or two about change. Meanwhile, Hem continues to yell "who moved my cheese" and hopes someone will keep it back for him.

Once, Michael finishes telling the story, his friends sit there for a few moments of thoughtful silence and start discussing the great relevance of the story. Some of them begin to see just how much they really are like Hem and Haw or Sniff and Scurry.

Managerial Implication

The implication is well written on the wall. We should not be too attached with the way we perform or create permanent structures that make us difficult to change when things change. It is applicable to organizations and individuals equally. The uniqueness of the story is that it is applicable to all kinds of scenarios of change: something very small personal habit, to big organizational change. Let us be ready for keep moving with the change!

THE NEUTRAL ZONE

Change is fundamental to all kinds of institutions, organizations and societies. Everybody agrees to this. Volumes have been written on it, and discussions have never seem to end. Despite all this, change and its management remained as elusive as it were at least in practice. Even highly acclaimed models have not succeeded in managing the change in its entirety. A few models regarded as highly effective in a few organizations didn't show the same or similar results when they are adopted or replicated in other organizations. There are instances, when change undergoes a massive change while its implementation is in progress. Many change specialists probed these issues in depth in the hope of finding answers, particularly why some change programmes succeed and others end up as failures.

A plausible answer came from the thought leaders of the decade: William Bridges of William Bridges Consultancy and Susan Mitchell of Mitchell Consulting Group in their paper titled "Leading Transition: A New Model for Change" published in the book *Leader to Leader* in 2000. In brief, they point out that change programme in organizations fail because of lack of leader's (top management) clear understanding about the change. A change is an external phenomenon consisting new structure, practices, systems and policies that organization and its leaders are trying to bring about while *transition is internal*, i.e. a psychological reorientation that people have to go through before the change can work. A classic mistake occurs in misunderstanding this process. Leaders believe that change will bring transition. In other words, transition is assumed as automatic and taken for granted as a consequence of change. The result of this assumption will be that systems, policies etc. might have changed on paper but practice remained the same as it was. Therefore, the first lesson in change management ought to be mastering the transition process. Managing transition is a challenging task, as it requires the people to undergo three phases as explained below:

- Phase-I: *Saying Goodbye.* It involves motivating people to unlearn and leave the ways and disengage the methods being followed for accomplishment of their functions. Sometimes, they may have to be asked to give those functions themselves. It is like asking people to vacate their bases in search of new ones.

- Phase-II: *Shifting to Neutral.* This is the most difficult phase in transition. It is a stage that lies between leaving old and finding new. It generates confusion, chaos and uncertainty in the minds of people. The success of transition and change depends on the effective management of this phase called as Neutral Zone. This is also an uncomfortable phase that drives people either to find new ways or withdraw to old. Therefore, the time to be spent here must be minimized to the lowest possible.

- Phase-III: *Moving Forward.* As the transition reaches the third stage, there will be people (i) who are through with new ways, (ii) who are stranded due to frightened neutral zone syndrome and (iii) who refuse to give their old ways. This phase demands people at neutral zone must be helped to move to third phase while people at first phase must be pulled. At the end of third phase, all people must behave in new ways and work on new functions.

Managerial Implication

The concept of neutral zone has many practical implications. Firstly, we must understand that knowledge of transition management is a must for all managers. This assumes importance because of our limited understanding about how transition precedes change management. Secondly, it offers a systematic picture of three phases through which the transition could be managed successfully. Thirdly, it cleverly points out the gap between desired and actual change that happen due to mismanagment of transition. Fourthly, HR managers could be highly benefited from the insights provided here which they could use in different contexts of people management.

STRATEGIC INFLECTION POINT

Andrew S. Grove, chief executive of $ 10 billion Intel, the computer chip company, in his global best selling book titled *Only The Paranoid Survive* published in 1996 presented a change model which he called 'strategic inflection point'. Strategic inflection point is a time in the life of a business when its fundamentals are about to change. That change can mean an opportunity to rise to new heights. But it may just as likely signal the beginning of an end. A strategic point can be deadly when unattended to. Companies that begin a decline as a result of changes rarely recover their previous greatness. What is an inflection point? Mathematically, we encounter an inflection point when change of the slope of a curve (referred to as its second derivative) changes. For instance, going from negative to positive. In physical terms, this is where a curve changes from convex to concave, or vice versa. So is with strategic business matters too. An inflection point occurs where the old strategic dissolves and gives way to the new, allowing the business to ascend to new heights. However, if you don't navigate your way through the inflection point, you go through a peak, and after the peak the business declines.

Many things can trigger a strategic inflection point: intense competition, a change in regulations or changes in technology. When a strategic inflection point occurs, the current ways of running your business no longer work. Yet, managed well, a strategic inflection point can be turned to your advantage and your business can emerge stronger than ever. Grove highlights the criticality of inflection point by saying; the things I tend to be paranoid about vary. I worry about products getting screwed up, and I worry about products getting introduced prematurely. I worry about factories not performing well, and I worry about having too many factories. I worry about hiring the right people, and I worry about morale slacking off. And of course, I worry about competitors. I worry about other people figuring how to do what we do better or cheaper and displacing us with our customers. But these worries pale in comparison to how I feel about what I call strategic inflection point.

Managerial Implication

HR managers must understand the strategic inflection point model for two reasons. Firstly, they need to know that (i) every organization has to pass through stages when it has to alter its fundamentals, (ii) organizations and individuals should never be allowed to be complacent, and (iii) things which worked today doesn't work tomorrow in the ever changing world. Secondly, they need to enable line managers and key leaders to turn the event of strategic inflection point into an opportunity rather than a threat by developing right culture, right aptitude and right attitude.

MODEL FOR SUCCESSFUL CHANGE AGENT ROLE

The quality of change programme implementation depends on the quality of change agents and how effective they are in facilitating the change. It is useful to organizations to train a few resource persons as change agents who will be helpful in managing changes in the organization. Organizations usually equip such managers with training on change agent skills like inter-personal processes, communication, teamwork etc. Though the imparting of these skills is important it is essential to equip them with the kind of role they shall play in facilitating change. The ideal model for change agent role came from the classic work of Herbert Shepard in the form of his paper titled "Rules of Thumb for Change Agents" published in *Organization Development Practitioner* in 1975. There are eight principle rules, if followed that could transform anyone as successful change agent:

- Rule-I: *Stay alive.* It means staying alive with your purpose. A change agent must keep himself/herself totally involved in the process as a facilitator. It also involves using one's skills, emotions, position and labels rather than being used by them.

- Rule-II: *Start where the system is.* The rule implies that one should diagnose the system in a systematic manner. The change agent must understand the operating culture, history and dominant ethos of organization before commencing the actual work. He or she also must build rapport with people involved in the change process,

- Rule-III: *Never work uphill. This rule comprises six sub-rules.* (i) don't build hills as you go, (ii) work in the most promising arena to start with, (iii) build resources in terms of teams and team operating procedures, (iv) Don't overorganize as it consumes a lot of valuable time, (v) win-lose strategies to be avoided because they deepen conflict, and (vi) play god a little.

- Rule-IV: *Innovation requires a good idea, initiative and a few friends.* Little that can be achieved alone and independently. Most of the ideas and initiatives come from collaborations and group performance. Again, quality of ideas and initiatives depend upon the quality of group members. Therefore, choose quality people to perform the role of resource persons.

- Rule-V: *Load experiments for success.* The new things and processes shall be tested first and experimented on a group that is most likely to cooperate and succeed the test.

- Rule-VI: *Light many fires.* The success of change initiative comes from involvement of many subsystems in organization. Therefore, efforts shall be made to involve as many people as possible. Especially, people who will be affected by change must be given adequate opportunity to participate and own the change process.

- Rule-VII: *Keep an optimistic bias.* The change agent is usually flooded with the destructive aspects of the situations he enters. There will be resentments, indifferences, politicking and bitter struggles among groups and individuals participating in change programme. Change agent must be optimistic of facilitating the group to emerge as united force and shall not be frustrated.

- Rule-VIII: *Capture the moment.* Change agent must utilize the situations appropriately for appropriate purposes. If the timing is not proper, even the best of interventions with best of intentions can fail to yield any results.

Managerial Implication

The practical implications of this model include (i) emphasizing on a vital element that a change agent is one who religiously follow these practical eight rules while facilitating a change programme and not one who merely possesses a few tips on change process and (ii) these rules help change agents to charter their plan of change in a systemic manner. This model also offer remarkable learning for HR managers and OD practitioners in terms of assisting them as a standard checklist of activities they need to perform behavioural management. Finally, knowledge of this model enable managers to meaningfully participate in change management activities.

Chapter 18

Audits, Assessments, Measurements and Evaluations

Certainly, this can be considered as the litmus test for HR practitioners. More and more organizations and top managements solicit reliable, tangible and measurable data for all activities of HR function. Unless, it is presented in a systematic manner, a clear need, purpose, meaning and benefit to the company is explained, companies may not consider or commit any resource allocation to HR function. Further, HR practitioners are rightly being asked to prove worth, utility and contribution of HR function to the people and organization in terms of human capital and bottom line. This means that HR practitioners must be well conversant with survey technology and should be capable of interpreting the data and inferring the lessons from it. The methods of mere personal observations and reflections, anecdotal and descriptive presentations have taken a back seat.

Thirty ideas focusing on audit, assessment, measurement and evaluation of various HR functions such as culture, communication, stress, career, competency, personality, organizational climate, leadership, training, teams, intellectual capital, human capital etc. are dealt with in this chapter. These thirty classics could equip HR practitioners with essential ingredients of HRM assessment and measurement.

FICTION AND FACT ABOUT HR AUDITS

Most of the people in organization including HR managers believe that auditing HR activities is just impossible because of its subjectiveness and abstractedness while others turn it down saying HR audit creates HR problems and reports generated out of such audits will not be useful. Assessment experts namely Adrian Furnham and Barrie Gunter destroyed these myths with logical explanation in their book titled *Corporate Assessment* published in 1993. The myths of HR audit are:

Fiction	*Fact*
You can't measure things as abstract as corporate culture or climate.	HR audits can, when properly designed, effectively tap into and generate workable operational definitions and measures of an organization's culture and climate.

Fiction	*Fact*
You can't tell what information to collect.	Many useful clues can be obtained through pilot works (initial interviews with key individuals, open ended discussions with small group of employees and so on). Therefore, to a large extent you can decide what information an audit must yield.
You can't calculate the benefits of an audit (return on investment).	Though, it is not easy to demonstrate exactly the direct or immediate financial benefits of a HR audit, but there are often ways of calculating the cost of not doing such an audit. For example, failed mergers and acquisitions can often reflect an inability of distinct corporate cultures to work effectively together. An early audit might have identified the problems to come and indicated the ways of avoiding them.
Auditing can only be used in respect of production and financial matters.	It is a traditional belief that where numbers/balance sheets are available, there only audit is feasible. There are techniques now available to audit performance, morale, training etc.
There are too many factors that affect an audit to pinpoint anything useful.	A good HR audit can take into account any factors that relate to organization and provide focused information. Multivariate statistical techniques can measure the individual or combined effects of any number of variables/responses.
Senior people in the organization would not even look at the feedback report from the audit.	Executive summary/myth breaking findings/systematic report means senior management will read the report entirely, because of the importance of information.
Audits can exacerbate employee discontent.	HR audits can reduce rather than worsen organizational problems. If employees are not provided with a constructive mechanism by which to express their discontent and dissatisfaction, it may manifest itself in more serious and destructive ways.
Data from HR are regarded with scepticism.	Scepticism can be easily dispelled if the audits are done in a detailed and professional manner.

Managerial Implication

HR managers should not only have absolute belief in practicality of HR audit but also must impress upon all in the organization about its viability and usefulness. However, the trust and reliability of such audits and their reports can be established only through their utility to employees and organization. Therefore, an audit should have a clear objective at first place. To fulfil the objective, HR managers must be well familiar with audit systems and the way it can be utilized.

MODEL FOR HRD AUDIT

There are number of techniques and models organizations employ to evaluate the efficacy/ utility/effectiveness of HR function. The model developed by Advisory Board of HR Professionals of American Management Association is not only comprehensive but also contemporary. HR head/chief of organization himself/herself can conduct this audit with inputs from self and other related departments. The audit enables HR chief to collect factual information about HR department, evaluate and analyze the information and evolve action plans. The audit model consist of four parts as briefly presented here:

1. *Information gathering.* Sixteen HR sub-functions such as (i) HR department mission, (ii) HR department organization, (iii) Quality of HR team, (iv) Labour relations, (v) Recruitment and selection, (vi) Education, training and development, (vii) Employee relations, (viii) Benefits, (ix) Compensation, (x) HR planning, (xi) Organization development, (xii) Diversity and equal employment opportunity, (xiii) Safety and environment, (xiv) Security, (xv) Equipment and facilities and (xvi) Documentation and information systems are covered under the audit. There are number of items for each sub-function to which HR chief (user) must assign a number ranging from 0 to 1000 in order of priority. Some of the items that are not applicable to some departments can be crossed (x) with no value. The aggregate score to all the items should not exceed 1000.

2. *Evaluation.* The numerical ratings of the user are to be compared with key weightages (Advisory Board weightages) provided in the instrument. Here, detailed explanation (justification) is given, about why a particular numerical value is assigned to each item in the key. However, user can disagree with that explanation of an item. Such disagreed statement values are to be noted down separately.

3. *Analysis.* Here, users are to total the numerical value thus assigned to each sub-function. Then the user is asked to examine other factors that will assist him/her in understanding how well the activity denoted by each item is being performed. Finally, the user will have one more opportunity to repeat the assigning numerical value to each item in the light of both the user's earlier values and key values. At the end of this process, user will gain understanding of his/her department's strengths and weaknesses.

4. *Action planning.* Based on the assessed strengths and weaknesses, user will be guided to prepare action plans for improvements. It is advised that user on identification of areas for strengthening must select a maximum three areas for action at a time.

John H. McConnell, president of the consulting firm McConnell-Simmons authored a remarkable book presenting this audit model. The title of the book is *Auditing Your HR Department,* published in 2000.

Managerial Implication

The model helps HR managers not only to assess the strengths and weaknesses of their respective departments but also enables them to gain a large perspective of a business oriented HR function. The simplicity of the model and its user-friendly approach is an added advantage. HRD audit is the first step in the direction of professionalizing HR function in organizations.

MODEL FOR CULTURE AUDIT

The importance of understanding and managing organizational culture has grown manifold in the recent past. However, culture means different things to different people. The methods employed to study culture also differed across the organizations. This difference in methodologies has led them to draw different inferences and conclusions of culture. For example, quantitative studies often study the overt cultural dimensions such as how people talk, perform and behave whereas qualitative methods like case study formats focused on covert behaviour such as underlying assumptions shared beliefs and customs. However, it is well acknowledged that studies focused on covert dimensions of culture were largely accurate in their assessment of culture.

Alan Wilkins in his insightful paper titled "The Culture Audit: A Tool for Understanding Organisations" published in *Organizational Dynamics* in 1983 proposed a twin factor criteria to understand and assess the culture: (i) shared assumptions and (ii) taken for granted/shared meanings that people assign to their social surroundings. This criteria is useful because (i) we can identify what kind of assumptions (culture) are productive/relevant to organizations and (ii) we can understand how to influence these assumptions. But it is difficult to audit the assumptions because of two reasons such as (i) people don't speak of assumptions directly and (ii) some assumptions contradict overtly stated norms, so people are reluctant to admit them.

Therefore, we must adopt an informal audit method to assess the culture, i.e. the shared assumptions and meanings. This can be done through:

1. *Observation.* A combination of consistent and random observation of people's behaviour at work helps to know how they act and react in a given situation. This data should be corroborated with past data if available or and crosscheck with people who worked earlier in the organization. All these individual observations can be accounted for a dominant group characteristic including the underlying assumption. However, observers must be careful to take broad enough samples to determine how representative their findings are because people have natural tendency to cover up some assumptions.

2. *Stories.* There will always be some stories in circulation in the organization that employees share. All these must be collected, documented and analyzed to understand the patterns. This leads us to know the assumptions behind such stories.

3. *Language.* The way people speak in different occasions, slang, words, expressions etc. indicate something a group shares. Sometimes there will be unique expressions in an organization to express a particular thing. This uncovers the shared assumptions.

4. *Customs.* The manner in which decisions are taken and methods used to solve the problems by the employees must be documented. The study of such documents reveals the similarities and shared *modus operandi*.

5. *Patterns.* How a particular event or incident is viewed or valued by employees may differ from organization to organization. For example, a reward or punishment that is well-received in one organization may not invoke same response from other organization. These patterns help us to understand the assumptions of behaviour.

Managerial Implication

Audit of culture and its management is crucial for organizations to infuse motivated and productive work behaviour. Organizations no longer can take it for granted that people just respond to their overt overtures or regulations or written contracts or norms. More important for them is to know what people share at shop floor and assumptions behind them because these are more powerful than management imposed customs in motivating or demotivating employees. HR managers must take lead in understanding, assessing and managing culture for shaping world-class work organizations.

AUDIT TECHNIQUES FOR ORGANIZATIONAL COMMUNICATION

Communication process and its effectiveness are vital to functioning of any organization. We employ various methods and channels for communication flow in the organization like upward, downward, horizontal etc. The systematic study of these methods, channels, tools of communication in the form of audit provide us with very useful data. This data so obtained from communication audit can be used to improve the communication through (i) using right channels/tools suiting to the situation/occasion, (ii) minimizing the cost on communications (iii) removing the barriers and (iv) creating a communication policy and strategy. The techniques in communication audit are:

1. *Structured and unstructured interviews.* Data can be obtained on effectiveness of various communication channels and their comments/suggestions to improve the communication.

2. *Questionnaire.* Both open ended and forced choice questionnaire can be developed with a clear objective to collect the data either from all the employees or identified group.

3. *Analysis of telephone bills.* The cost incurred on telephone bills, frequency, purpose and subject of issue can provide important data.

4. *Network analysis.* Use of this technique can yield information on patterns of organizational communication, senders, receivers, blockages etc.

5. *Communication logs.* In this technique, employees will be requested to maintain a diary of communication for a specified reasonable period. This provides us with data that can be useful to understand communication needs and habits of each employee.

6. *In-tray and out-tray analysis.* How an employee or group of employees clear their letters, memos, correspondences, circulars etc. and the type they receive in a normal course will be analyzed.

7. *Critical incident technique.* In this method, employees will be asked to narrate the important events/experience where communication helped or thwarted any activity.

8. *Use of media.* Degree of use of different methods and purposes like telephone, e-mails, postal mails, written communication, oral communication, formal and informal interaction can be accounted for. This data clarifies us the importance of each method in the organization in its priority.

Managerial Implication

Communication has occupied the centre stage in today's organizations. Studies prove that communication pitfalls are responsible for a number of problems in organizations. There is also a view that communication creates more problems than it solves because of bad management of communication. Therefore, HR managers must take up the challenge and make a start. First step in this direction is taking stock of the situation through a systematic audit of communication. Based on this, proper communication channels can be put into use and a communication policy can be developed.

MODEL FOR STRESS ASSESSMENT

Modern jobs are fraught with danger of stress. The motivational strategies like job enrichment, incentives, rewards, awards, promotions may obtain superior performance from employee in short-term but these are also potential sources for job stress, if not managed timely and appropriately. Sometimes they may have fatal consequences that makes these motivational strategies not only irrelevant but also counter productive. Therefore, HR managers must conduct and coordinate the studies intended to understand the sources, factors and implications of stress in organization. Broadly, there will be two kinds of stress:

1. Environment induced stress like economic recession, uncertainty in business environment, competition, changing technology, and changing products.
2. Organization induced stress like complexity of management, which demands high level of consistent performance, increasing pressure/targets, unstructured job profiles, enhanced responsibilities, employment insecurity, sharp reward and punishment measures.

Ross Maynard presented a stress assessment tool called Occupational Stress Indicator (OSI) in a paper titled "Stress in the Workplace" published in *Management Accounting* in 1996. This is a diagnostic tool that helps to obtain an objective and accurate measurement of sources of stress in organizations. It is based on a structured questionnaire that seeks employees' opinion regarding events that they find particularly stressful and the methods they adopt to cope with them. Answers are elicited on their perceptions about their job, health status, and behavioural pattern under different situations. Analysis of the responses helps to generate a report on the sources and effects of stress that may be group/department/organization specific.

Organizations can use the analysis report for variety of purposes like (i) to understand the avoidable and unavoidable stress on the jobs, (ii) to draw plans to weed out the avoidable stress, (iii) to develop programmes to develop coping skills for functional stress and (iv) to minimize the organization induced stresses.

Managerial Implication

Studies prove that stress is becoming a major area of concern to managements particularly to HR managers. Unfortunately, avoiding or removing stress altogether from workplace is an impossible task. However, HR managers must make efforts to identify sources of stress, particularly organization induced in order to minimize them. If left unassessed or unattended, it may become a formidable block in realizing the potential of employees apart from resulting in dysfunctional effects to the organization. The above described indictor of occupational stress may be useful as a model to devise your own organization or department specific stress assessment tools.

MODEL FOR CAREER ASSESSMENT

Career assessment is a double-edged sword. Proper assessment helps employees to realize their potential and enables organizations to match right people to right positions. In contrast, pitfalls in career assessment could cause catastrophic consequences to both of them. People find joy and meaning in work when they choose careers that are compatible with their intrinsic interests.

Outstanding people are those whose personal interests are matched with their work demands. This realization has struck many organizations that people should be placed in trades they like to be in. The challenging task here is many of us do not have complete knowledge of our own occupational interests since any occupation will have multiple faces that include functional and emotional side of it. Therefore, employees need to be subjected to a series of career assessments tests in order to obtain the most realistic data. Broadly, career-planning assessments are four types as illustrated below which when used in combination can form as model:

1. *Career interest assessment.* This helps to understand an employee's interests, aptitudes, and preferences of work life. The data collected using this technique will be plotted, compared with standard data of different occupations, which provide the result of best-suited occupation. This also contribute for deeper understanding of one's self in terms of occupational preferences. Paper-based test, simulations, questionnaires and interview methods can be used as a part of this assessment.

2. *Skills assessment.* It involves assessing the type, degree and intensity of skills an individuals possesses. It also provides the data about transferability of skills and preferences of the individual in using these skills. For this purpose generally skills are classified into three: hands-on skills, minds-on skills and people-related skills. Most occupations use these skills in different combinations and permutations with varied emphasis. The individual skill data will be compared with standard occupational skill data bank to determine the matching occupation.

3. *Personality assessment.* This provides data regarding personality traits, personal work style including work settings in which a person can be happiest, work settings to avoid, key strengths, endurance to work stress, decision making capability, communication and conflict management capabilities and inter personal relationship profile. This also provides data on leadership, learning and preference for team vs individual work. There are many tools such as FIRO-B, PF-16, Birkman tests, and leadership tests used in data collection.

4. *Values inventory.* This assessment reveals value profile, particularly work related value preferences of an individual. This also helps to clarify one's value state. Here also paper-based tests and interview method will be used to collect the data.

Managerial Implication

Many organizations experience difficulties in building work motivation in people. This, they need to realize because of mismatch between individual career preferences and organizational career placements. Many employees spend years of their work life in frustration because of this mismatch. Therefore, organizations need to implement comprehensive methods to assess the career interest of employees. In this process, the above model helps as a basis. Secondly, organizations tend to carryout career assessment using one or two methods like skill assessment or leadership inventory. These individual assessments cannot provide reliable data for career related decisions. Therefore, as described above, organizations must choose comprehensive model for career assessment.

MODEL FOR ASSESSMENT CENTER IMPLEMENTATION

Assessment centers are complex exercises that demand professional planning and execution. Further, an organization that intends to implement assessment center must be clear in its objectives. Implementing just out of curiosity or as experimentation or since it is the latest thing to do may result in serious problems. Therefore, organizations must adopt it after serious thought and with clear understanding of its utility, challenges and pitfalls. We need to undergo the following steps for systematic implementation of assessment center:

- Step-I: *Identify the need.* We should define the purpose, objective and scope of the exercise based upon identified need of the organization.
- Step-II: *Determine the criteria.* This is the planning part of the exercise. This may comprise of methods to be followed, instruments to be employed to suit the data collection purpose and description of analysis tools etc.
- Step-III: *Train the people.* An orientation programme followed by training on assessment center methodology and philosophy should be conducted exposing the identified people who will be involved in conduct of the initiative.
- Step-IV: *Design the assessment center programme.* With the help of expert and involving team members decide the content and schedule of assessment center.
- Step-V: *Conduct the pilot test.* The designed assessment center content should be administered on a group of people as a pilot study.
- Step-VI: Analyze the pilot study results using the requisite quantitative and qualitative tools and check for reliability of the data.
- Step-VII: Incorporate the suggestions/shortcoming observed during pilot study experience and finalize the assessment center content and schedule.
- Step-VIII: *Communication.* All employees identified for being covered under assessment center testing must be informed well in advance. Such communication must invariably take care of all the aspects such as purpose, method and schedule of the event
- Step-IX: *Implementation.* Now implement the assessment center as per schedule and in an objective manner.
- Step-X: *Analysis and report writing.* Analyse the data with predefined techniques and write the report in a clear manner. Distribute the draft report among a few key resource persons seeking comments. Based on this, write the final report in a classified manner.

Managerial Implication

This 10-step model is fundamental to implementation of assessment center. Lack of clarity or bad planning or no planning could land the exercise futile. We must note that assessment center is a comprehensive and integrated method in the assessment technology. Trying to do it in a casual manner defeats its objective. HR managers must study and equip themselves formally not only in assessment center techniques but also in its methodology, particularly in the method of analysis, interpretation and report writing.

ASSESSMENT CENTER TECHNIQUES

In assessment center, a combination of techniques/tests will be used in a continuous exercise that may last for 2/3 days to assess a person's managerial potential. These techniques include the following:

1. *Job related exercises.* These exercises targeted at understanding participant's job related behaviour against the job demands such as decision making style, communication abilities, job related aptitude etc.

2. *Group discussion exercises.* This is targeted at assessing participant's interpersonal effectiveness, problem solving and leadership capabilities. Group discussion exercises can take several forms but there are two main types: one is cooperative group discussion where participants are required to analyze a set of information and to come up with recommendations within an allotted time frame. These exercises are also called as non-assigned roles because participants are all given the same information and no one is assigned any particular role. The second is competitive group discussion in which participants are required to persuade and negotiate in order to achieve the best deal they can. Here, participants usually receive common information as well as information that is exclusive to them. They need to sell a viewpoint to other team members. This is also called as assigned role exercise since participants will be assigned particular roles.

3. *Oral presentations.* Participants will be asked to make presentation on a given topic. This helps to assess the participant's communication and presentation skills.

4. *Role-play.* Participants will be assigned particular roles which they must assume and perform. This elicits the multidisciplinary capabilities of the participant.

5. *In-basket exercises.* The participants will be asked to clear papers/make correspondence on a set of issues and take decisions. These papers and issues may include urgent, long term, policy, operational, HR, finance related etc. The participants way of dealing, deciding the priorities will be studied.

6. *Interview exercises.* The participants will be assessed using one to one and one to group interview methods in which participants are supposed to answer the questions posed to them

7. *Analysis/case exercises.* Participants will be provided with contradictory and disorganized information, to classify and interpret them to assess the reasoning and analytical capabilities.

8. *Decision-making games/exercises.* Hypothetical situations will be presented to participants, which they need to solve through decision-making.

9. *Conflict management assessment.* Either paper pencil based tests or hypothetical alternatives will be presented to participants who on careful study should choose the best course of action.

Managerial Implication

The specialty of assessment center is in its use of multiple methods and multiple assessors to profile a person's strengths and weaknesses apart from managerial potential. This method is extensively used for recruitment, promotion and developmental purposes. Readymade methods to assess aptitude and attitude tests based on above techniques are also available like FIRO-B, MBTI. PF-16 tests, Campbell skill inventory survey, String skill inventory test, 360 degree appraisal method, Interpersonal communication inventory, and Thomas-Killman conflict mode instrument to name a few. However, organization must use these readily available instruments in combination with organization specific tests that must be developed suiting to its requirements. The above description of assessment center techniques will be useful for this purpose.

DEVELOPMENT CENTER

Development center is somewhat broader in its application and usage than assessment center though it employs assessment center methodology for data collection. For example, assessment center method is used mainly for recruitment or career planning whereas development center method is targeted at general and specific development of employees. The principle features of Development Center are captured in detail in the book titled *Assessment and Development Centers* authored by Iain Ballantyne and Nigel Povah published in 1995. They say leaner and flatter organizations of today are continuously striving for making their people more effective. Similarly, concepts such as empowerment, learning organization and never ending push for quality means that people are being encouraged to take a broader and more positive view of the need to develop. These trends relate neatly to the development center, a powerful diagnostic tool which helps people identify where to start their development. The following clarifies the role and process of development center:

1. *It is not a pass/fail event.* The purpose of the method is to pave a way for development plan and it has no implications to the decisions like recruitment, promotions etc. as in assessment center.

2. *Duration and cost.* This is an ongoing process and usually take more time and costly than assessment center because it seeks more data and seeks cross checking.

3. *Ownership of the data.* Employee is viewed as owner of the data collected through development center unlike in assessment center where the ownership of the data lies with management.

4. *Feedback occurs during the event.* The feedback of the data analysis will be made available to the participants on the spot. This enables them not only to understand it in the same context but also enables to draw plans for development.

5. *Development occurs during the event.* The event itself generates great awareness apart from providing clues for the development.

6. *Focus on learning and development.* The main objective is to stimulate learning and development. Therefore, participants will be encouraged to reflect on the findings and analysis. They also will be encouraged to draw lessons for learning and build self-plans for development.

Managerial Implication

Development center is an improved version of assessment center in a way. This helps to instill development motivation among employees. Unlike assessment center where employees may have apprehensions since that has relevance to career related matters, development center can invoke honest and natural responses and feedback since it is voluntary and purely development focused. HR managers who are development-focused have a valuable option in the form of development center. However, it demands wholehearted commitment and professional preparation.

FIVE-PHASE MODEL FOR COMPETENCY ASSESSMENT AND DEVELOPMENT

There is no need to emphasize the vitality of close link between management development and business strategy, because it has become a fundamental knowledge. The question remains is, how to achieve this close link between the two in organizations. Many experts suggested many ways, but the highly practical and workable seems to be the route of competency development. The secret of successful competency development lies in its scientific assessment. Harbridge Consulting Group, a London-based management consultancy, developed a model for competency assessment whose efficacy is proved through its application in a few organizations. This model consists of five phases as discussed below:

- Phase-I: *Strategic review.* The first stage of assessment is reviewing the company's vision, mission and its objectives on the long-, medium- and short-terms. If these are not available, efforts shall be made to draft them. Based on this review, strategic areas of the business competence will be defined.

- Phase-II: *Strategic areas of competence.* This phase involves clarifying and confirming the critical success factors for the business strategy, so that areas of strategic competence can be identified. A strategic area of competence is defined as an area in which the organization must be competent, if it is to succeed in its mission.

- Phase-III: *Identification of competency requirements.* The competencies are identified at three levels: (i) the requirement of the business as reflected in the strategic areas of competence, (ii) the job itself, in terms of both business, professional/technical requirements, personal and managerial competencies, and (iii) the organization in terms of the culture and therefore the behaviours required, and the level at which the individual operates.

- Phase-IV: *Application.* Strategies to bridge the gaps between assessed competency levels, i.e. current competency levels of business, organization and jobs and defined strategic area of competence (difference between phase-II results and phase-III) will be drawn.

- Phase-V: *Job and business performance.* The strategies drawn at phase-IV should be crystallized in such a way that these are integrated around jobs and business of the organization.

Managerial Implication

It is a pragmatic model that helps organizations in designing their own method of conducting competency assessment and development. As stated earlier, competency development can be a prime vehicle in attaining the sharp linkage between management development and business strategy. Every organization needs to have its own competency assessment and development model suiting the internal and external business environment. HR managers must take a lead in driving their organizations for this crucial activity.

SEVEN PROBLEMS AND THEIR SOLUTIONS IN PERSONALITY ASSESSMENT

Personality assessment is pivotal to all types of HR assessments in organizations. The most widely employed method in these personality assessments is questionnaire method. Despite its popular usage and utility, managers express apprehensions about the method. Their suspicions include: (i) genuineness/validity of information collected using questionnaires, (ii) ability and willingness of employees to participate in such assessment, (iii) usefulness of the information gathered, (iv) cost factor etc. There is no doubt that some of these are real problems. However, solutions are available to overcome them. Neville Bain and Bill Mabey in their book titled *The People Advantage* published in 1994 identified seven problems organizations encounter with personality assessments and proposed practical solutions. These are given here as:

TABLE 18.1

Problems in Personality Assessment	Solutions
1. They can be faked	While this is true to some degree for many assessment methods, it is a relatively small problem in the use of good personality questionnaires.
2. They will undermine the interview	The questionnaire should supplement the interview. Both are vulnerable alone. In combination they can produce rich insights to personality. Try using a questionnaire in advance to set specific probing areas for the interview.
3. They may include obtrusive, irrelevant questions	This may indeed have occurred where non-occupational questionnaires have been used. Look at questionnaires whose content has been developed or at least reviewed for occupational relevance.
4. They are expensive to use	On a comparative basis, vis-à-vis other options, this is not true. There may be an initial investment in training an internal user and some instruments which are licensed.
5. They may not work as good as interview	This is an issue of the relative validity of different approaches. Call for publishers to show you their validation data. Separately, enquiries can be made of independent specialists from professional bodies.
6. Candidates may be put off by personality assessment	Any form of testing can be threatening to candidates. The solution lies in good administration and the provision of feedback. There are explanatory leaflets to be sent in advance; administration should be thorough and sympathetic; feedback should be accurate and relevant.
7. Management loses ownership of the decision-making process	The overall objective is to gather information against a clear person specified for the job. The personality questionnaire is just one input. It should be kept in perspective with other issues of ability, technical competence and experience, relevant training, personal circumstances and the like. Decision-making on a balanced input basis remains management's prerogative.

Managerial Implication

Questionnaire method is an essential technique in personality assessment exercise. The above solutions help managers to overcome the problems they face in using questionnaires. The explanation also drives a relevant issue that in assessments, we must use a combination of methods that may include questionnaire administration. Excessive dependence on a single method create problem in terms of capturing the wholistic and most reliable picture of an individual's personality. Further, combination of methods serve as crosschecks and raiders.

PSYCHOMETRIC INSTRUMENTS FOR HRD

Psychometric instruments have become prime tools to HR managers in their efforts to enhance the business prospects as well as individual effectiveness. According to the psychometric scientists, Tuvia Melamed and David Jackson, Psychometric tests such as ability tests, personality questionnaires, and occupational interest inventories and job analysis techniques can be used to serve multiple purposes. They illustrated the extent to which psychometric instruments can contribute to HR effectiveness and business strategies in their paper titled "Psychometric Instruments: Potential Benefits and Practical Use" published in *Industrial and Commercial Training* in 1995. The practical use of the psychometric instruments in HRM include:

1. *Recruitment and selection.* Aptitude tests and personality profiling questionnaires can be used as an aid to identify possible strengths and weaknesses against particular job requirements. The information can be used in a selection interview to investigate in what way an individual is likely to behave and perform in new or different work settings and assist in making better quality decisions on placements.

2. *Job profiling.* Job profiles can be produced in the form of job and person specifications by using commercially produced packages specifically designed for the purpose. Comparing the psychometric data for prospective candidates with the job profile information produces job match reports.

3. *Personal development.* Aptitude tests, career inventories and personality profiling questionnaires can be used in various combinations to help individuals understand themselves more fully and how also their behaviour impinges on others.

4. *Team building.* Personality profiling questionnaires, particularly those designed to tackle team issues, can be used to assist in team building, on as well as off-the-job, by identifying complementary personality types and associated behaviours as part of a process for improving team effectiveness.

5. *Career counselling.* Career inventories are particularly useful in the process of career counselling, often providing a degree of acceptable objectivity to candidates. As a further enhancement to the process, aptitude tests and personality profiling questionnaires can provide additional information to give a more thorough, comprehensive and objectively derived estimate of a candidate's capabilities and suitability for adopting new career.

Managerial Implication

Sometimes, it sounds to be ironical that companies take keen interest in informing their employees about how the company is performing, what are the new products or services being planned, how it wants its employees to participate in company vision and mission building etc. but they lack in demonstrating the same kind of keenness in informing the employees about their attitude and aptitude profile. Appraising the employees about their profile should be the beginning of any HRD effort. The above text provides a glimpse of the various uses of psychometric tests. HR managers must identify the areas where psychometric tests can be and should be used. The data obtained using these instruments will be reliable. Therefore, developmental planning of employees can be planned based on this data. A psychometric driven HRD will help, both the employees and organizations.

INSTRUMENTS IN MEASURING ORGANIZATIONAL CLIMATE

There are a number of instruments experts, academicians and practitioners use to measure organizational climate. These include the following (Table 18.2) selective ones:

TABLE 18.2

Title of the instrument	Measurement dimensions/Sub-scales	Developed by
Organizational Climate Questionnaire	1. Structure 2. Responsibility 3. Reward 4. Risk 5. Warmth 6. Support 7. Standards 8. Conflict 9. Identity	Litwin, G. and Stinger, R. (1968), *Motivation* and *Organizational Climate*, Boston: Harvard University Press.
Organization Practice Questionnaire	1. Conflict and consistency 2. Decision timeliness 3. Emphasis on analytic method 4. Emphasis on personal development 5. Formalization 6. Goal consensus and clarity 7. Communication adequacy 8. Information suppression and distortion 9. Job pressure 10. Adequacy of planning 11. Smoothness of horizontal communication 12. Selection on ability and performance tolerance of error 13. Top management receptiveness 14. Upward information requirements 15. Violation in chain of command 16. Workflow coordination 17. Adaptability 18. Adequacy of authority	House, R. and Rizzo, J. (1972), "Toward the measure of organizational practices: Scale development and validation", *Journal of Applied Psychology*, 56, pp. 388–96.

TABLE 18.2   (*continued*)

Title of the instrument	Measurement dimensions/Sub-scales	Developed by
Survey of Organizations	1. Technological readiness 2. HR primacy 3. Communication flow 4. Motivational conditions 5. Decision-making practices	Taylor, J. and Bowers, D. (1972) Survey of Organizations: A Machine Scored Standardized Questionnaire Instrument, Michigan University.
Psychological Climate Questionnaire	1. Job and role characteristics 2. Leadership style 3. Organizational subsystems	Jones, A. and James, L. (1979), "Psychological climate: Dimensions and relationships of individual and aggregated work environment perception", *Organisational Behaviour and Human Performance*, 23, pp. 201–50.
Organizational Climate Description Questionnaire	1. Disagreement 2. Hindrance 3. Espirit 4. Intimacy 5. Aloofness 6. Production emphasis 7. Trust 8. Consideration	Halpin, A. and Croft, D. (1963), *The Organisational Climate of Schools*, Chicago: University of Chicago Press.
Organizational Climate Questionnaire	1. Competent 2. Responsible 3. Practical 4. Risk-oriented 5. Impulsive	Lawler, E., Hall, D., and Oldham, G. (1974), "Organizational climate: relationship to organizational structure, process and performance", *Organizational Behaviour and Human Performance*, 11, pp. 139–55.
Organizational Climate Measures	1. Autonomy 2. Conflict vs Cooperation 3. Social relations 4. Structure 5. Level of rewards 6. Performance-reward dependency 7. Motivation to achieve 8. Status polarization 9. Flexibility and innovation 10. Decision centralization 11. Supportiveness	Pritchard, R. and Karasick, B. (1973), "The effects of organizational climate on managerial job performance and job satisfaction", *Organizational Behaviour and Human Performance*, 9, pp. 126–46.
Perceived Organizational Climate	1. Individual autonomy 2. Position structure 3. Reward orientation 4. Consideration	Dieterly, D. and Schneider, B. (1974), "The effect of organizational environment on perceived power and climate", *Organisational Behaviour and Human Performance*, 11, pp. 316–37.

Managerial Implication

The above-described instruments are time tested, used on large samples and their reliability and validity is established. These are beneficial to HR managers in two ways: (i) Adopting one of the above instruments that suit to your organizational need and setting or (ii) develop your own instrument with the help of these instruments. Measuring organizational climate is important for organization to take appropriate actions on various fronts. HR managers must take lead in this.

TOOLS IN ORGANIZATION ASSESSMENT

Organizational improvement and renewal on continuous basis has become an essential condition for companies to survive in the ever-changing scenario. Assessment of organizational climate, health, learning capabilities, etc. provides managers with rich data to determine the strategies for organizational improvement. A few important instruments that help in organizational assessment are described in Table 18.3.

TABLE 18.3

Assessment tool	Purpose	Dimensions/Scales	No. of statements (Reference)
MAO-C (Motivational Analysis of Organizational Climate) by Udai Pareek	To study organizational climate with special regard to motivation. The instruments consist of 12 dimensions of organizational climate and 6 motives such as: achievement, expert influence, extension, control, dependency and affiliation	1. Orientation 2. Interpersonal relationship 3. Supervision 4. Problem management 5. Management of mistakes 6. Conflict management 7. Communication 8. Decision-making 9. Trust 10. Management of rewards 11. Risk taking 12. Innovation and change	72 statements (Pareek, Udai (1997), *Training Instruments for HR Development*, New Delhi: Tata McGraw-Hill).
Organizational climate index by George Stern and Carl Steinhoff	Measures organizational climate	1. Abasement–Assurance 2. Achievement 3. Adaptability–Defensiveness 4. Affiliation 5. Aggression–Blame 6. Avoidance 7. Change–Aameness 8. Conjunctivity–Disjunctivity 9. Counteraction 10. Deference–Restiveness 11. Dominance–Tolerance 12. Ego achievement 13. Emotionality–Placidity 14. Energy–Passivity 15. Exhibitionism–Inferiority avoidance 16. Fantacised achievement	300 statements (Stern, G.G. (1970), *People in Context*, John Wiley).

TABLE 18.3 (*continued*)

Assessment tool	Purpose	Dimensions/Scales	No. of statements (Reference)
		17. Harm avoidance–Risk taking	
		18. Humanities–Social science	
		19. Impulsivenss–Deliberation	
		20. Narcissism	
		21. Nurturance	
		22. Objectivity–Projectivity	
		23. Order–Disorder	
		24. Play–Work	
		25. Practicalness–Impracticalness	
		26. Reflectivenss	
		27. Science	
		28. Sensuality–Puritanism	
		29. Sexuality–Prudishness	
		30. Supplication–Autonomy	
		31. Understanding	
Organization Health Survey by P.T. Kehoe and W.J. Reddin	Measures organizational health	1. Productivity 2. Leadership 3. Organization structure 4. Communication 5. Conflict management 6. HR management 7. Participation 8. Creativity	80 statements (This instrument can be obtained from Organizational Tests Lt., Fredericton, N.B. Canada)
The Campbell Organizational Survey by David Campbell	To collect information from the employees within an organization about their feelings of satisfaction or frustration with various aspects of work, such as feedback, top leadership, diversity, and organizational planning.	1. The work itself 2. Working conditions 3. Stress-free 4. Co-workers 5. Diversity 6. Supervision 7. Top leadership 8. Pay 9. Benefits 10. Job security 11. Promotions 12. Feedback 13. Planning 14. Ethics 15. Quality 16. Innovation 17. General contentment 18. Overall index	The instrument can be obtained from reidlondonhouse@ncs.com

Managerial Implication

The above instruments help HR managers not only to diagnose the organizational functioning but also enables to develop right solutions and strategies to improve the organization. HR managers focused on developmental side of organizational management must implement survey technology using assessment techniques on a regular basis.

TOOLS IN PERSONALITY ASSESSMENT

Personality assessment is one of the most popular and relatively well-tested means in understanding people. This has a critical role in assessment center also. There are many instruments that organizations use for this purpose. Four of the most popular tools are briefly described in the following, as Table 18.4:

TABLE 18.4

Assessment tool	Purpose	Dimensions/Scales	No. of statements (Reference)
MBTI (Myers-Briggs Type Indicator) by Katharine Briggs And Isabel Briggs Myers	To discover your preferred type or natural preferences in dealing with both your inner and outer worlds when you are at work. It provides your overall psychological type across all of your life's activities.	It indicates four major types: 1. Introverts–Extroverts 2. Feeling types–Thinking types 3. Intuitives–Sensing types 4. Perceptives–Judging types It also indicates sixteen combinations of personalities	124 statements. (The instrument is registered trademark of Consulting Psychologists, Palo Alto, California)
16 PF (Personality Factor—Fifth Edition) Test by Raymond Cattell, Karen Cattell and E.P. Heather	Measures levels of warmth, reasoning ability, emotional stability, dominance, liveliness, rule consciousness, boldness, sensitivity etc.	1. Reserved vs warm 2. Concrete vs abstract 3. Reactive vs emotionally stable 4. Deferential vs dominant 5. Serious vs lively 6. Expedient vs rule-conscious 7. Shy vs socially bold 8. Utilitarian vs sensitive 9. Trusting vs vigilant 10. Grounded vs abstracted 11. Forthright vs private 12. Self-assured vs apprehensive 13. Traditional vs open to change 14. Group oriented vs self-reliant 15. Tolerated-disorder vs perfectionist 16. Relaxed vs. tense	Contains five forms of questions with different range of responses. (The instrument is a registered trademark of NCS assessments, USA; can be obtained from assessments @ ncs.com)
MMPI (Minnesota Multiphasic Personality Inventory by S.R. Hathaway and J.C. McKinley	Measures personality traits	1. Hypochondriasis 2. Depression 3. Hysteria 4. Psychopathic deviate 5. Masculinity–Femininity 6. Paranoia 7. Psychasthenia 8. Schizophrenia 9. Hypomania	566 statements (Dahlstrom, W.G. and G.S. Welsh (1960), *An MMPI Handbook: A Guide to Use in Clinical Practice and Research.* Minneapolis: University of Minnesota Press).

TABLE 18.4   *(continued)*

Assessment tool	Purpose	Dimensions/Scales	No. of statements (Reference)
Thurstone Temperament Schedule by L.L. Thurstone and T.G. Thurstone	Measures preferred personality style	1. Active 2. Vigorous 3. Impulsive 4. Dominant 5. Stable 6. Sociable 7. Reflective	140 statements (It is registered trademark of Science Research associates, Inc, Chicago-60611)

Managerial Implication

These instruments are highly reliable and their validity has also been established. The data obtained after administering these instruments can be used for variety of purposes that include: (i) career planning of employees, (ii) development of training and development plan and (iii) placing of right personality style for right positions. HR managers must conduct personality tests and retests and should use the data appropriately.

TOOLS IN INTERPERSONAL RELATIONSHIPS ASSESSMENT

Interpersonal relationships effectiveness is prerequisite not only for creating organizational harmony but also for effective performance of organizations. Therefore, managers must constantly need to assess the interpersonal relationship status in the company. The tools provided here as Table 18.5, will be helpful in such as assessment.

TABLE 18.5

Assessment tool	Purpose	Dimensions/Scales	No. of statements (Reference)
FIRO-B (Fundamental interpersonal relationships-Behaviour) by Will Schutz	Measures an employee's (i) behaviour towards others and (ii) behaviour wanted from others in terms of inclusion, control and affection	1. Inclusion (expressed) 2. Inclusion (wanted) 3. Control (expressed) 4. Control (wanted) 5. Affection (expressed) 6. Affection (wanted)	44 statements (Schutz, W.C. (1966), *A Three Dimensional Theory of Interpersonal Behaviour*, California: Science and Behaviour Books).
FIRO-F (Fundamental Interpersonal relationships-Feelings) by Will Schultz	Measures an employee's feelings in the areas of significance, competence and lovability	1. Significance (perception of others) 2. Significance (wanted to be perceived by others) 3. Competence (perception of others) 4. Competence (wanted to be perceived by others) 5. Lovability (perception of others) 6. Lovability (wanted to be perceived by others)	44 statements (Schultz, W.C. (1966), *A Three Dimensional Theory of Interpersonal Behaviour*, California: Science and Behaviour Books)

TABLE 18.5 (continued)

Assessment tool	Purpose	Dimensions/Scales	No. of statements (Reference)
Interpersonal Communication Inventory by Millard J. Bienvenu	Identifies patterns, characteristics and styles of communication	1. Self-concept 2. Listening 3. Expressing 4. Angry feelings 5. Self-discipline	24 statements (Pfeiffer, J.W. and J.E. Jones (1972), *The 1972 Annual Handbook for Group Facilitators*, California: University Associates
Survey of Interpersonal Values by Leonard V. Gordon	Measure certain critical values involving the individual's relationships to other people or their relationships to him/her, which are important in the individual's personal, social, marital and occupational adjustments.	1. Support 2. Conformity 3. Recognition 4. Independence 5. Benevolence 6. Leadership	90 statements (Pfeiffer, J.W and J.E. Jones (1972), *The 1972 Annual Handbook for Group Facilitators*, California: University Associates
Interpersonal rating by Robert Freed Bales	Measures self-report, inter-personal perceptions and interaction process	1. Material success and power 2. Devaluation of self 3. Conservative group beliefs 4. Rejection of conservative group beliefs 5. Equalitarianism 6. Individualistic isolationism	26 statements (Bales, R.F. (1970). *Personality and Interpersonal Analysis*, New York: Holt, Rinehart, and Winston
Psychological Audit for Interpersonal Relations by Richard Stephenson	Measures a person's pattern for interpersonal relations	1. Social status 2. Intellectual rigidity 3. Family cohesiveness 4. Social extraversion 5. Political conservatism 6. Self-rejection 7. Aggressive hostility 8. Physical affection 9. Monetary concern 10. Change and variety 11. Dominant leadership 12. Nurturing helpfulness 13. Order and routine 14. Aesthetic pleasures 15. Submissive passivity 16. Psychological support 17. Emotional control 18. Dependent suggestibility 19. Outdoor interests 20. Self-acceptance	500 statements (Jones, J.E. and J.W. Pfeiffer (1975), *The 1975 Annual Handbook for Group Facilitators*, California: University Associates

Managerial Implication

These instruments were developed based on rigorous research and statistical validity. HR managers must familiarize themselves with administration of these instruments. They also can develop their own tools for assessment of interpersonal relationships in their organizations. For this, the dimensions and interpretation methods used in these tools can help as a route map.

TOOLS IN LEADERSHIP AND MANAGEMENT DEVELOPMENT ASSESSMENT

Assessment of leadership programmes, leadership status surveys, leadership styles etc. is an essential activity in management development efforts. A few selective instruments are illustrated below, in Table 18.6, that help to assess managers' leadership capabilities and to provide feedback to them. Managers depending upon the context and need can use one or more instruments as a part of management development initiative.

TABLE 18.6

Assessment tool	Purpose	Dimensions/Scales	No. of statements (Reference)
The Denison Leadership Development Survey by Daniel Denison and William Neale	To provide leaders and managers with feedback on a set of 12 leadership skills and practices that can impact bottom line organizational performance.	1. Involvement 2. Adaptability 3. Consistency 4. Mission	96 statements (The instrument can be obtained from survey director of Denison consulting at jrichards@ denisonculture.com)
MDQ (Management Development Questionnaire) by Alan Cameron	To identify a manager's strengths and weaknesses and pinpoints areas for development.	1. Managing change 2. Planning and organizing 3. Interpersonal skills 4. Results orientation 5. Leadership	160 statements (The instrument can be obtained from HRD Press, 22 Amherst Road, Amherst, MA)
LLQ (The Leatherman Leadership Questionnaire) by International Training Consultants, Inc	Measures the participant's knowledge of good leadership behaviour	1. Assigning work 2. Career counselling 3. Coaching employees 4. Oral communication 5. Managing change 6. Employee complaints 7. Employee conflicts 8. Employee counselling 9. Decision making 10. Delegating 11. Discipline 12. Handling emotions 13. Goal setting 14. Handling grievances 15. Conducting meetings 16. Giving positive feedback 17. Negotiating 18. Performance appraisals 19. Performance standards 20. Persuasion 21. Making presentations 22. Problem solving 23. Selection interviews 24. Team building 25. Termination interviews 26. Time management 27. One-on-one training	339 statements (The instrument can be obtained from International Training Consultants Inc, P.O. Box 35613, Richmond, Virginia-23235)

TABLE 18.6 (*continued*)

Assessment tool	Purpose	Dimensions/Scales	No. of statements (Reference)
Thomas-Kilmann Conflict mode instrument by Kenneth Thomas and Ralph Kilmann	To measure an individual's relative use of five conflicts handling modes in situations where his/her wishes differ from those of another person.	1. Competing 2. Collaborating 3. Compromising 4. Avoiding 5. Accomodating	30 statements (Kilmann, R.H. and K.W. Thomas (1974), *Developing a Forced-Choice Measure of Conflict-Handling Behaviour: The Mode Instrument*)
Leadership assessment Survey by CCI Assessment Group	It is a 360-degree feedback instrument that focuses upon an individual's leadership skills and abilities. It is extensively used for managerial and leadership development.	1. Initiative/Risk taking 2. Quality of results 3. Delegating 4. Planning/Goal setting 5. Technical competency 6. Mentoring 7. Personal integrity 8. Empowerment 9. Motivating 10. Problem solving/ Decisions 11. Diversity 12. Vision 13. Communicating 14. Coaching 15. Creativity/innovation 16. Team work	96 statements (*CCI Assessment Group*)

Managerial Implication

The systematic assessment of current availability of leadership potential is important to plan developmental activities. In this effort, survey technology plays a vital role. Managers committed to build leadership for organizational performance must use reliable instruments and conduct survey as regular as possible to benchmark the individuals' performance. The above tools are widely used and very contemporary. Therefore, understanding the use and interpretation of the above tools helps HR managers in their leadership development assignments immensely.

TOOLS IN TEAM ASSESSMENT

Assessment of teams' performance and their effectiveness has become important with the increasing use of teams in organizations. This assessment helps organizations not only to understand the status of team functioning but also gives scope for their improvement. The systematic assessment contributes for strengthening the teams to achieve organizational performance. Three highly reliable tools that help to measure the teams' effectiveness, performance and their learning are illustrated in Table 18.7.

TABLE 18.7

Assessment tool	Purpose	Dimensions/Scales	No. of statements (Reference)
Cross Functional Team Effectiveness Inventory by Gaylord Reagan	Used as action research tool to focus team members on aspects of cross functional teams, such as: (i) key factors for team success, (ii) team processes and (iii) team outcomes	1. Team context 2. Team process 3. Team outcomes	38 statements, The 1998 Annual, Volume 1, Training: Jossey-Bass
Team Hope Survey: Enhancing Performance in Teams by Susan B. Wilkes, Terry L. Hight, John D. DelCarmen and Melissa Figueiredo	It measure the team's sense of optimism and hope	1. Where (purpose and goals) 2. Way (methods and plans) 3. We (cohesion and caring) 4. Will (motivation and confidence)	20 statements The 2000 Annual; Volume 2, Consulting: Jossey-Bass
A survey for Team Learning by Barbara Pate Glacel	To measure the team behaviour to achieve high performance	1. Invest time 2. Manage differences 3. Gain full participation 4. Achieve results	28 statements The 2001 Annual; Volume 2, Consulting: Jossey-Bass
Teamwork questionnaire by High Performance System, Inc	To provide teams a method of identifying the team members' perceptions of how well the team is performing on three dimensions: Human, operational and cultural.	Shared leadership 1. Cooperation 2. Communication 3. Commitment 4. Mistakes 5. Happiness 6. Goalsetting 7. Problem solving 8. Adaptability 9. Decision-making 10. Talents 11. Trust 12. Opinions 13. Cohesion 14. Values 15. Rules 16. Competition	18 statements (the instrument can be obtained from **hpsys2aol.com**)

Managerial Implication

The above tools enable managers dealing with HR and teams to assess their contribution and also health of teams. The familiarization with administration of these tools and interpretation of scores obtained help them to implement team working in a systematic manner. The above tools are user friendly and simple to use at regular intervals.

SELECTIVE TOOLS IN HRM

A few assessment instruments are given below in Table 18.8 which will be useful to HR managers in their mission to build organizational learning capabilities, systems thinking practices, career management, HRD climate and so on.

TABLE 18.8

Assessment tool	Purpose	Dimensions/Scales	No. of statements (Reference)
Innovation Capability Audit by Dave Francis	To assess an organization's capacity for innovation.	1. Innovation leadership 2. Strategic advantage 3. Prudent radicalism 4. Exceptional individuals 5. Full competencies portfolio 6. Capable implementation 7. Selective empowerment 8. Innovation demanded 9. High enrolment 10. Continuous learning 11. Respect for mastery 12. Fruitful linkages 13. Apt organizational form 14. Supported champions 15. High-Performing New Product/Process Development 16. Guiding mental maps 17. Sound decision processes 18. Resourced initiatives	54 statements The 1998 Annual, Volume 2, Consulting: Jossey-Boss
Systems Thinking: Best Practices Instrument by Stephen Haines	To assess an organization's practices against the best practices of organizations that use systems thinking.	1. Systems thinking basics 2. Six levels of organizational systems 3. ABCs of a yearly strategic management cycle 4. Organization as an open system 5. Rollercoaster of change 6. The learning 7. Organization Strategic Management System overall	50 statements, The 2002 Annual, Volume 2, Consulting: John Wiley & Sons
The Perception of Empowerment Instrument by W. Kirk Roller	To measure the empowerment dimensions of autonomy, responsibility and participation.	1. Autonomy 2. Participation 3. Responsibility	15 statements (Spreitzer, G.M. (1993). Psychological Improvement in the Workplace: Construct, Definition and Validation, Los Angeles: University of Southern California

TABLE 18.8   (*continued*)

Assessment tool	Purpose	Dimensions/Scales	No. of statements (Reference)
Organizational Learning Diagnostics by Udai Pareek	Helps to identify the stage of organization learning i.e. Innovation phase/implementation phase/stabilization phase.	1. Experimentation and flexibility 2. Mutuality and teamwork 3. Contingency and Incremental planning 4. Temporary systems 5. Competency building	23 statements (Pareek, Udai (1997), *Training Instruments for HR Development*, New Delhi: Tata McGraw-Hill)
Organizational Learning Capability by S. Ramnarayan	To study learning capability of the organization and also for diagnostic purpose.	1. Clear focus on Objectives 2. Attention to Integration and among departments/functions 3. Attention to vertical integration 4. Sensitivity to people potential and needs 5. Concern for long term planning and success 6. Support for experimentation? creativity 7. Environmental scanning 8. Concern for development of capabilities	46 statements (D.S. Sarupriya, T.V. Rao and P. Sethumadhavan (1996), *Measuring Organisational Climate*, Ahmedabad: AHRD
The Career-Dimension survey: asking the right Career-Development questions by Caela Farren and Beverly Kaye	To discover what key areas need to be improved in career Development System	1. Future perspective 2. Organizational systems and practices 3. Work design 4. Managerial support 5. Individual career Management concern	20 statements: The 1996 annual, Vol. 1, *Training:* Pfeffer & Company.
HRD Climate survey by T.V. Rao and E. Abraham	To study HRD climate and Organizational Diagnosis	1. Positive problem solving 2. Recognition and reward 3. Growth and development 4. Innovation and change 5. Experimentation 6. Interpersonal openness and risk taking 7. Top management commitment to HRD 8. Commitment to competence development 9. Personnel policies 10. Positive attitude and objectivity 11. Developmental climate 12. Interpersonal helpfulness and team spirit	38 statements (D.S. Sarupriya, T.V. Rao and P. Sethumadhavan (1996). *Measuring Organisational Climate*, Ahmedabad: AHRD

Managerial Implication

HR managers of current genre must apply tools and instruments to capture the existing realities, climate and capabilities in the organization for diagnostic purposes. The application of these tools yields comprehensive data, which can be deployed to improve organizational functioning.

ENNEAGRAM

Enneagram is an age-old model originated from spiritual teachings of the Sufi Muslims that helps to identify the personality type of a person. It is similar to Myers-Brig Type Indicator but a sharper method in terms of identifying the underlying motivations and fixations of a personality type. There are nine types of personalities in Enneagram model as described below:

- Type-1: *Reformers.* These types are rigid, perfectionists and always want to be right. They are moralistic, self-critical and want to reach highest standards in whatever they engaged in. Their inflexibility creates problems for others and sometimes to themselves.

- Type-2: *Helpers.* This type gives more importance to love, affection and relationships. They will be emotional, make themselves indispensable and sometimes very possessive that is potential enough to create problems to others. They may indulge in violent behaviour in the situations of rejection of their love

- Type-3: *Motivators.* These types are career driven and attaches great value to success and winning. Though they like scoring points over others, they still accommodate others emotions. They work hard but still think that they lag behind and or not making enough efforts.

- Type-4: *Romantics.* This type is characterized by deep sensitivity, emotions, love, affection, care and spiritual. They can exhibit a wide range of emotions and deeply touchy. They are inconsistent and pulled apart between many people and many interests.

- Type-5: *Thinkers.* As the title suggests, they are very incisive, analytical and deep thinkers. They lead isolated and independent life. They are as well as very cynical, critical and satisfying them is very difficult. Capable of thinking in new ways and provide perspectives not thought of so far.

- Type-6: *Loyalists.* They are trustworthy and values trustworthiness. It is safe type and do not like to harm anyone. They are fun loving and get along with people and are always found in the midst of company of many people. But they can be suspicious of others very easily because of their obsession with trustworthiness.

- Type-7: *Enthusiasts.* They experiment with everything. Open to learning and practice many things. This leads most of them as generalists. Tend to be bored with anything easily that makes them less perseverant.

- Type-8: *Confronters.* Dominant, assertive, very loud and confronting authority all the time are the characteristics of this type. Fights, confrontations and challenging something, energize most of them. They exhibit protecting attitude towards persons whom they like.

- Type-9: *Mediators*. This type is easy going, nothing serious, and open to all sides of an issue and sees merit in all of them. Sometimes, they go with the flow and do not have anything of their own.

The latest book that can provide comprehensive knowledge on the subject is *The Wisdom of the Enneagram* authored by Don Richard Riso and Russ Hudson published in 1999.

Managerial Implication

This instrument has gained popularity in the recent years on account of its reliability. Many tools based on this model are in circulation that include (i) Riso-Hudson Enneagram Type Indicator which has 144 questions and (ii) The New Enneagram Test consisting of 36 questions. Administration of these instruments helps to identify the dominant personality type of a person. This knowledge is very useful to self as well as to others like managers in proper understanding of an individual's personality.

MANAGEMENT SKILLS AND STYLE PROFILE

This instrument developed by HR Decisions Ltd., based in Vancouver, Canada is useful to assess (i) general management skills and style and (ii) cognitive abilities of front line managers. This instrument is also used to assess the managerial skills of supervisors being upgraded them to managerial cadre. The methods such as (i) brain storming exercises (ii) in-basket exercises and (iii) paper-based tests are conducted to assess the managers on 10 dimensions as described below, in Table 18.9.

TABLE 18.9

S. No.	Dimension	Measures
(a) Management Orientation Dimensions		
1.	Administrative/planning orientation	Planning, scheduling, arranging, coordination of tasks, and effective time management
2.	Interpersonal orientation	Including others in decision making, and operating via direct interpersonal contact, rather than impersonality
3.	Task control orientation	Organizing, training, directing, and monitoring subordinates and keeping in touch with all job and ask operations
4.	Action orientation	Taking action on things now, rather than later, and by making independent decisions, rather than utilizing opinions of others
5.	Reflective orientation	Getting information, understanding the background of problems, and operating with caution, deliberation and discussion
6.	Service/performance orientation	Providing customer service, and helping the organization to perform at a higher level to provide goods and/or services.
(b) Management Performance Dimensions		
7.	Resourcefulness	The number of imaginative, creative solutions generated in response to some typical managerial problems

TABLE 18.9 (*continued*)

S. No.	Dimension	Measures
8.	Productivity	The quantity of work produced: the number of actions accomplished or attempted in the completed exercise
9.	Organizational insight	The level of understanding of the issues and problems represented in the exercise
10.	Quality of Judgement	The appropriateness and effectiveness of the actions taken in the exercise

The instrument also provides picture of an individual's strengths and weaknesses on the above-illustrated dimensions.

Managerial Implication

Numerical values could be assigned to each of these dimensions. Management profile of an employee can be determined by comparing the scores so obtained on above dimensions with benchmarks. Organizations can create benchmarks themselves by administering the instrument on a group of managers. The highest ever scored can be drawn as standard for this purpose because benchmark adopted in other organization may not be totally relevant to your organization.

MODEL FOR HR MEASUREMENT

The saying that *Something, which is not measurable, is not manageable* has picked up momentum in all business organizations. This has spread to all functions including HR. Several factors that include (i) increasing HR cost, (ii) to identify and cut down avoidable expenditure on HR, (iii) to enhance accountability in HR function, (iv) to eliminate value free services, (v) to compare the costs with global benchmarks in that industry etc. have given a fillip to measurement exercises in organizations. There is albeit, no standard measurement system that can be straight jacketed to the needs of a company, a few key inputs are provided here that may help the companies to design a tailor made HR measurement system.

- Step-I: *Determine the objective of measurement.* The measurement purpose may be (i) financial assessment to illustrate cost and benefit value, or (ii) a non-financial value assessment that to understand organizational health/commitment of employees, or (iii) a micro assessment that provide the benefit/loss of conducting each function like training, pay cost of HR staff vis-à-vis services rendered by them or (iv) a combination that encompasses financial and non-financial purposes.

- Step-II: *Classify HR activities* in the company in terms of (i) tangible that are easily measurable like technical training and (ii) intangible that are difficult to measure in terms of numbers like behavioural training. Note that it is the distinction between easy and difficult and not the impossibility because everything in HR is measurable but only the methods differ depends upon tangibility and intangibility factors.

- Step-III: *Develop measures for tangible HR activities.* There are many methods that are in vogue in organizations. One method is based upon deductive logic. It means, you have organized a management development programme for 20 managers for 3 days in-house. An expenditure of one lakh rupees is incurred. It would have been two-lakh rupees expenditure if this programme conducted by an external agency. Therefore, the saving is to the tune of a lakh rupees. Take the other example. A standard consultancy agency charges Rupees two lakhs to evaluate 20 persons on managerial skills. The saving or loss will be the difference between your expenditure and this fee. The other is based on deductive logic. For example, had you not taken care of registering the company under Contract Labour (R&A) Act, a penalty of ten thousand rupees and criminal proceedings could have been instituted.

- Step-IV: *Develop measures for intangible activities.* There may not be clear benchmarks in terms of external fee as mentioned in step-III. For example, a new appraisal system that is implemented in the organization for which an expenditure of Rupees ten lakhs was incurred. Measures to assess to what extent it achieved its own objectives should be adopted. This can be an indication of its utility. Similar method may be followed in case of long term HR programmes like culture building and so on.

Managerial Implication

Measurement of HR activities is a potential opportunity for HR managers to prove the worth of HR in a language that is understood by all. This also enables them to play a strategic role. However, one must be careful from a syndrome that measurement often leads them to implement only those HR activities whose worth can be established easily. There may be some activities, which provide core strength to organizations in long term. Therefore, emphasis on short-term assessment must be viewed critically. Finally and undisputedly, measurement helps organizations and HR managers to deploy resources fruitfully.

MODEL FOR PERFORMANCE MEASUREMENT

Performance management is the backbone of HRM whereas performance measurement standards and methods are cardinal to performance management system. Every organization follows some kind of measurement, which it believes is the right type to assess the performance of employees. It is also an undeniable fact that some of the measurement standards in vogue in organizations are disputable, ambiguous, irrelevant, deficient and counter productive. Some are end in themselves and still others are complex and cumbersome to handle. Therefore, organizations should develop an appropriate, rational and a pragmatic performance measurement system that serves to attain equitable HRD in organizations. There are a few basic rules that an organization must adhere to while developing performance measurement standards. A model has been developed and published in 1995 by Kenneth Rose in the journal *Quality Progress* titled "A Performance Measurement Model" consisting these fundamentals. A step-by-step approach is followed in the model as described below:

- Step-I: A group of people concerned with different functional areas and performance measurement meets. It starts with exploring answers to the questions concerned with the identification of performance dimensions: general and specific to each function.
- Step-II: The next step is to identify specific goals with respect to each performance dimension. For example, the goal of training dimension is to arm the employees with all the organizationally/technically/functionally required skills.

- Step-III: Here we identify the indicators related to each goal. These indicators reflect what is important for successful performance. The definition and scope of each indicator is standardized to ensure a common understanding.

- Step-IV: Determine the comparative importance indicators. For example, two successful performances of two activities may not be equal in terms of their utility to the organization.

- Step-V: Identifying the right methodology to measure the indicators is the next step. The measurement methods may include quantitative or qualitative or both depending upon the nature of indicators of a performance dimension.

- Step-VI: Conduct a pilot study and analyze the results for incorporating changes. This should be followed by communication to all employees about new performance measurement system to be implemented from a prospective date.

Managerial Implication

The success of performance management is largely contingent upon the relevance of performance indicators and objectivity of measurement system. More importantly, success of performance measurement is vital to organizations because it is interlinked with other systems like compensation, career planning, separations etc. Therefore, HR managers must commit adequate resources to develop and execute a scientific performance measurement. There may be many methods organizations follow to measure the performance of their employees. It is difficult to adopt a system of one organization in another even though they may be in the same industry given their differences in other human systems, culture, and history. Hence, HR managers must focus on having their own and in this process the above model helps as a road map.

SEVEN-STEP MODEL FOR TEAM MEASUREMENT

Measuring team performance is one of the most challenging functions in HRM. It is challenging since it demands consideration of (i) what is to be measured, (ii) what measurement techniques should be used, (iii) the level of measurement, i.e. whether measurement is to be carried out at individual level and aggregate it for team, or should be measured at team level and (iv) the varieties in teams that require different methods of measurement etc. Based on his vast experience in team performance measurement, Jack Zigon of Zigon consultants developed a seven-step process for measuring the results of work teams in 1998. The salient features of this model are:

- Step-I: *Review the existing organizational measures.* Mostly, organizations follow unidimensional measures like financial or commercial or operational. However, a more integrated approach may be appropriate. Team measures should clearly linked to all the aspects of team performance and such measures should be clearly known to team members.

- Step-II: *Define team measurement points.* There are four alternatives in defining team performance points: (i) team customer diagram, (ii) team accomplishments pyramid, (iii) work process mapping and (iv) accomplishments which support organizational measures. Selecting the best alternative to measure team performance is the main activity in this step.

- Step-III: *Identify individual team member accomplishments, which support the team.* Role result matrix technique can be used to measure an individual performance from the team perspective. Role result matrix is a table, which identifies the results each team member must produce to support the team's accomplishments or work process steps.

- Step-IV: *Weigh the accomplishments.* In this step the relative importance of each accomplishment is discussed and agreed upon. Weights can be used to help teams to discuss priorities and agree on what is really important.

- Step-V: *Create measure for each accomplishment.* Measures are the yardsticks used to judge how well the team produced each accomplishment. General measures tell what is important, about each accomplishment. There are four general measures: quantity, quality, cost and timeliness. Specific measures describe in numeric or descriptive terms which parts of the accomplishment the team wants to track. There are two specific measures: (i) numeric measures that use numbers to evaluate the accomplishment and (ii) descriptive measures that use words to evaluate the accomplishment.

- Step-VI: *Develop performance standards.* After creation of measures as described in step-V, developing the performance standard becomes easy. For numeric measures, ask yourself, how much is the team expected to produce? Or what level of performance the team must achieve to help the organization attain its goals? For descriptive measures ask, for example, what customers are saying about product quality/service?

- Step-VII: *Develop a feedback system.* Use these steps to develop feedback: (i) decide what data to collect, (ii) decide which source the feedback should come from, (iii) decide whether all data or sample data should be collected, (iv) determine when to collect data, (v) determine who should collect data, (vi) review the existing reports and (vii) decide the format for evaluation of feedback data.

Managerial Implication

All organizations use some kind of teams. For some organizations teams are essential and critical to organizational performance and these may be incidental to others. Regardless of the extent of utility and criticality of team, it is important for organizations to develop a method of measuring team performance. In this attempt, the above model helps immensely. Measurement, apart from helping organizations to understand the contribution of teams, also helps teams to adopt clearly defined goals for team as well as team members.

FOUR C MODEL FOR EVALUATION OF HRM POLICIES AND PRACTICES

The effectiveness of HRM policies and practices could be enhanced only through enhancing their efficacy in organizations. This efficacy could be achieved only through the means of continuous appraisal and evaluation of HRM. However, many experts have suggested many methods for this evaluation. Among them, the most comprehensive and logical is 4C model of evaluation. The HRM specialists namely Michael Beer, Bert Spector, Paul Lawrence, Quinn Mills and Richard Walton are the authors of this model who presented it in their book titled *Managing Human Assets* published in 1984. They argued that HRM effectiveness must be evaluated in terms of their consequences. These consequences can be of four types as discussed below:

1. *Commitment.* To what extent the HRM policies and practices enhance the commitment of people to their work and their organization? Commitment means that employees will be motivated to hear, understand, and respond to management's communications about changes with implications for wages, work practices, and competency requirements. The mutual trust will be there to enable management's message to be more believable to employees and to enable management to be responsive to employee's legitimate concerns as stakeholders.

2. *Competence.* To what extent do HRM policies and practices attract, keep and develop people with skills and knowledge needed by the organization and society, now and in the future? Competence means that employees in the firm will have the versatility in skills and the perspective to take on new roles and jobs as needed. Through a positive attitude toward learning and personal development fostered by policies that encourage and reward learning, employees will be more capable of responding to change.

3. *Cost effectiveness.* Cost effectiveness means that the organization's HR costs—wages and benefits and indirect costs such as strikes, turnover, and grievances, have been kept equal or less than those of competitors.

4. *Congruence.* What levels of congruence is generated HRM policies and practices generate employees? Higher congruence than competitors means that the firm has shaped work systems, reward systems, and flow policies so that there is a higher coincidence of interest among management, stakeholders and workers.

Managerial Implication

Most of the people question the utility of HRM because they hardly come across any efforts to demonstrate the benefits of HRM to the employees and organization. HR managers also struggle to convince the top management and other stakeholders the effectiveness as well as the utility of HRM practices. In this backdrop, the above model is of great help. The model is also much acclaimed for its integrative approach. Further, it provides the macro basis of evaluation, i.e. the evaluation of HRM in terms of its consequences to four areas termed here as 4C's in this model.

FOUR-LEVEL MODEL OF TRAINING EVALUATION

Companies spend substantial amount of money, energy and time on training and development of their employees. Training is one function that receive overwhelming attention in all types of organizations. Therefore, it is also essential for companies to accrue the proportionate benefits. This warrants continuous evaluation and improvement of training design and implementation. Organizations employ a variety of methods in evaluation of training programmes. However, seeking feedback on a predesigned format soon after completion of the training programme has been the most commonly used evaluation technique. However this alone will not fulfil the criteria of a systematic training evaluation procedure. Many trainers, training specialists, consultants, academicians and practitioners had come up with many models for evaluation of training but all of them has some or other limitations. A four-level training evaluation proposed and developed by Donald Kirkpatrick remained a classic and the most comprehensive model that has enormous practical value. These four levels are briefly described here:

- Level-I: *Reaction.* This involves assessing the reactions of participants at the end of the training course in terms of their satisfaction with course coverage, faculty standards, infrastructure facilities, courseware, teaching methodology and the like Usually, a predesigned format will be used for this purpose. In some cases, course director may seek oral feedback directly from the participants. According to an estimate of *Training Magazine*, almost hundred per cent of the trainers and training institutes perform this level-I evaluation.

- Level-II: *Learning.* This involves assessing the amount of information the participants learned. Mainly, paper-based reference tests will be used as a part of this method. In this, the acquired knowledge of the participants will be tested seeking answers to questions based on the course syllabus. This may involve a descriptive version or multiple choice or simple one or two line answers. This level-II evaluation help to understand the effectiveness of training delivery in terms of participants learning.

- Level-III: *Transfer.* This involves assessing the benefit of training to the work in the real world. Level-III evaluation can be conducted anytime after six weeks to six months of training delivery. A variety of methods such as seeking feedback from functional heads, survey, competency assessment, observation and interviews with trainees and their co-workers will be implemented. This help to understand the utility of training at functional level.

- Level-IV: *Business results.* This is an organizational level involvement the contribution of training to the bottom line of the company. This may be in terms of business turnover, profits, sales, market capitalization etc. This is the most difficult part of the valuation. This usually carried out once in a year using survey techniques and business and training data.

Managerial Implication

This is the most popular and commonly used evaluation model in organizations. This model offers option to the evaluators whether to use a single level of evaluation or all four levels. In order to gain comprehensive insight, it is advisable that organizations must do the evaluation using all levels. This is particularly so when investment on training is substantial. This also increases the accountability of training function and training administrators significantly apart from providing valuable data for improving the training management. HR managers and trainers must adopt it in organizations, as this is the most comprehensive training evaluation model available to practitioners.

RETURN ON INVESTMENT OF HUMAN CAPITAL   ②⑨⑦

Despite prophesying human capital as a strategic value, there are hardly any constructive efforts to measure the contribution of human capital to the bottom line of the company. Fortunately, the mounting costs of human costs are driving the organizations to assess the value of such costs and their worth. However, assessing the value or return on the investment of HR is not as easy as auditing other inert resources like finance, materials or machinery. It is rather complex given the relative abstractness of HR contribution. There is a greater need to evolve objective measures that are capable of assessing the return on investment of HR in organizations. Jac Fitz-Enz, father of human performance benchmarking, addressed this need in his SHRM award winner book titled *The ROI of Human Capital* published in 2000. Based on 20 years of qualitative and quantitative research, it provides an effective methodology for measuring the effect of employee performance on the bottom line, he proposed gauging of human costs and productivity at three levels:

1. *Enterprise*—through analysis of five corporate indicators: (i) cost, (ii) time, (iii) volume, (iv) errors and (v) human reactions

2. *Functional*—assessing work functions and process improvement in terms of: (i) service, (ii) quality and (iii) productivity

3. *People*—assessing value added by five basic HRD activities: (i) planning, (ii) acquiring, (iii) maintaining, (iv) developing and (v) retaining people.

This model also explains how to integrate these three levels in a single, end-to-end system of human capital valuation with the aid of formulas and scorecards for measuring and monitoring at every step. Further, four steps are prescribed in assessing the impact of human capital. These are:

- Step-I: *Perform a thorough situation analysis.* It consists of four actions: (i) determine what the business problem is: service, quality or productivity (SQP), (ii) measure the current performance level, (iii) show how the current performance is affecting competitive advantage/disadvantage, and (iv) establish what are the critical processes in the situation.

- Step-II: *Determine a plan of action.* It involves three actions: (i) find the source of the problem. The problem will be found within or among the people, equipment, material, the process or the product, (ii) decide what the best solution is and (iii) agree on a solution, plan the action and do it.

- Step-III: *Measure impact.* It involves (i) once action has been taken, allow an appropriate amount of time, and measure the effect, positive or negative, (ii) what kind of change occurred? how much? Examine the basic indicators: cost, time, quality, error and human reaction and (iii) determine what caused the change; is it because of action taken or extraneous?

- Step-IV: *Measure value.* Through two actions: (i) within the organization, show how, where, and when service, quality and production changed in the business unit and (ii) whether the problem was identified correctly, and the action taken was effective, there should be positive effects in terms of increased sales, customer satisfaction, higher margins etc.

Managerial Implication

ROI of human capital analysis helps organizations in two ways: Firstly, it provides results of current human capital value of an organization through objective analysis using relevant indicators. Secondly, it contributes for drawing plans to enhance the value of human capital in a meaningful manner. Therefore, HR manager must master these techniques and philosophy of measurement and methodology. This is one more opportunity to demonstrate not only the value of HR in our organizations but also the value of HR function and its managers.

TWELVE INHIBITING FACTORS IN IMPLEMENTATION OF HR COSTING AND ACCOUNTING

Despite the seriousness of organizations to assess the utility and cost of HRs, many of them haven't succeeded in its implementation. Organizations encounter numerous difficulties that include technical, ethical, social and emotional constraints in pursuing HR costing and accounting. These difficulties encourage organizations to withdraw and discourage some who are intending to implement. However, top management and HR managers know that they cannot avoid this because of its utility and essentiality in optimizing the HR costs. Therefore, understanding the kind of difficulties that arise while implementing HRCA will help in preventing and proactively managing them. Professor Ulf Johnson of Stockholm University identified twelve factors that inhibit successful implementation of HRCA based on the study of seven Swedish world-class organizations. He presented the study details, data and analysis in the paper titled "Why the Concept of HR Costing and Accounting Does Not Work: A Lesson from Seven Swedish Cases" published in *Personnel Review* in 1999. These twelve inhibiting factors are:

1. Lack of knowledge among organizations about HRCA indicators, standard costs, causal relationships
2. Lack of knowledge among organizations about HRCA models
3. Inefficient information systems in organizations that restrict to produce the relevant HRCA information
4. Lack of top management attention, appreciation, commitment and demand for costing and accounting of HR
5. Reward systems in organizations not directed towards HRCA targets
6. No HRCA targets
7. Hesitation of organizations in implementing HRCA on ethical grounds
8. Action in accordance with HRCA information conflicts with established rules
9. HRCA information not integrated with other financial information
10. Managers feel being controlled due to HRCA target orientation
11. Lack of openness for new ideas discourage to push the initiative of HRCA
12. Managers feel they have no time to think and act on HRCA

Managerial Implication

HR manager's primary responsibility in the changing scenario is to enable the organization to assess the utility of HR. In order to achieve this they need to implement HR costing and accounting. To achieve this, they are required to act on five issues. Firstly, organize the knowledge about HRCA models, operational indicators, methodology and its benefits as well as spread the knowledge among all the managers. Secondly, obtain top management commitment to the effort. The top management acceptance to such initiatives mostly depends upon HR manager's own sincerity and knowledge about the subject. Thirdly, make an attempt to reorient the HR system towards the objectives of HRCA. Fourthly, involve as many employees as possible in the initiative, particularly in the implementation stage. Finally, utilize the data generated from HRCA for development and optimization of HR and abstain from drastic actions such as downsizing and reward reorganization in the initial stages.

ELEVEN TECHNIQUES IN MEASURING INTELLECTUAL CAPITAL

Intellectual capital has become the cardinal resource of organizations. Innovation of products and services, quality, cost effectiveness, technological edge or any other measure will be dependent upon one factor, i.e. intellectual capital of an organization. Though it has been playing a central role right from the origin of agriculture revolution, realization struck the organizations during information revolution that this is one resource having all the virtues and uniqueness. Therefore, the measurement of intellectual capital become important in order to (i) understand the current status of intellectual capital and (ii) to draw plans to enrich and enhance the intellectual assets.

Intellectual capital is classified into three groups: (i) Human capital that exist in the minds of people: knowledge, competencies, know-how, (ii) Structural capital that refers to information systems, data bases and (iii) Customer capital that include customer relationships, brands and trademarks. Insofar, there are 11 techniques that are used in evaluating the intellectual assets. These are:

1. *Balanced scorecard.* Three indicators such as customers, internal business process and learning are used here to assess the human capital value.

2. *Benchmarking.* This is comparing your own scores on set of pre-identified areas of intellectual capital against the benchmarks created by world leader.

3. *Relative value.* This evaluates the progress. For example, how many employees have the ability to use the existing database to reply the customer queries.

4. *Competency models.* This is a process in which successful employees and behaviours are calculated in terms of monetary value in correspondence to the wealth generated by them and extrapolation of it to the quantity generated by all employees with relevant discount proportion.

5. *Calculated intangible value.* This is created by comparing the return on assets against the average return on investment of the total industry.

6. *Business worth.* This is calculating the worth of information/knowledge on three counts: what is the loss if the existing knowledge becomes nil in the organization, what will be the gain if existing knowledge doubles and what will be the value of this knowledge in immediate future, like after 6 months/one year.

7. *Business process auditing.* This measures how information enhances value in given business process, such as accounting, production, marketing and so on.

8. *Subsystem performance.* It is the method used to measure the progress/contribution of a single function at a time

9. *Micro lending.* The value of an institution/society that can attract lending without collateral security forms as a measure to evaluate intellectual capital.

10. *Brand equity valuation.* The popularity of brand, its pricing, distribution channels, etc. forms as indicators of intellectual assets.

11. *Knowledge bank.* It is also called as salaries model in which pay roll bill will be considered as intellectual capital.

Managerial Implication

The future of present organizations certainly rests on its intellectual capital. The evaluation of intellectual capital in the organization helps in many ways. Firstly, it generates awareness in terms of value of intellectuality and its relative value. Secondly, it enhances the accountability for various acts and decisions. Thirdly, the exercise provides x-ray for organization's intellectuality enabling organization to take right measures to improve the worth. HR managers must acquire the proficiency of various measurement techniques, identify the appropriate technique and implement with the help of line managers and corporate planning experts of your organization.

HUMAN CAPITAL ACCOUNTING TECHNIQUES

HR professionals during the current decade came under pressure to prove worth of HR in terms of balance sheet. The human capital exists at four levels in any organization: (i) basic knowledge of employees, (ii) skills or abilities of employees to solve day-to-day problems, (iii) abilities of employees to solve complex problems and (iv) creative and futuristic abilities. Human capital accounting involves evaluating the sum of all these assets of abilities of your employees. There are many techniques organizations use in accounting the human capital that includes monitory and non-monitory techniques. Such as:

1. *Replacement cost model.* It is a cost that would have been incurred today to replace the HR presently employed. This involves three basic steps in cost analysis: (i) Recruitment cost, (ii) Training cost and (iii) Separation cost.

2. *Opportunity cost model.* It is a competitive bidding method whereby all managers will be encouraged to bid for an employee. The bid rate of such employee is considered as equivalent to the sum of investment.

3. *Salaries model.* It is also known as Lav and Schwartz Model of Discounted Value. The accounting involves three steps: (i) Classification of employees into homogenous group profiles, (ii) Estimation of earnings of each such group and (iii) Calculation of the present value of earnings of each group vis-à-vis cumulative salaries of each group, using an appropriate discounting rate.

4. *Adjusted Present Value Model.* Two steps are involved in this model. The first step is to compute the present value of future wage payment for five years. The second step is to find out the efficiency ratio. This ratio is applied to adjust the present value of the future wage payments. The resultant figure is the value of human assets.

5. *Stochastic Model.* Here the movement of an employee from one position to another position would be considered over a time period and used statistical probability used to forecast the person's association with a particular position in each of the time period to establish the value of an individual.

6. *Non-Monitory Techniques.* Skill inventory, Attitude Measurements, Potential and Competence availability etc. form the non-monitory techniques. These are assessed using survey methods and check lists.

Managerial Implication

A formal evaluation of human capital has many benefits such as (i) it makes good economic sense, (ii) increases accountability in HR investment, (iii) accounting establishes worth of HR and (iv) accounting leads to focus on value added activities. However, choosing a right method, applying and producing a human capital account is a tough job even to some of the best financially familiarized HR executives. But it is easy to understand and implement with some efforts if some one is serious enough. Human capital accounting is a great opportunity to organizations in general and HR professionals in particular to show the worth of their HR in an undisputable manner.

References

Abelson, Robert, *Theories of Cognitive Consistency*: *A Source Book*. Chicago: Rand McNally (1968).

Adams, Scott, *The Dilbert Principle*. New York: Harper Business (1996).

Adams, Stacy J., "Inequity in Social Exchanges" in L. Berkowitz (Ed.), *Advances in Experimental Social Psychology*, New York: Academic Press (1965), pp. 267–300.

Ali, Abbas J., Manton Gibbs and Robert C. Camp, Human Resource Strategy: The Ten Commandments Perspective. *International Journal of Sociology and Social Policy*, **20**(5, 6), (2000), pp. 114–132.

American Society for Training and Development, "Models for Excellence" (1983), p. 29.

Applebaum, Steven H. and Loring Mackenzie, "Compensation in the Year 2000: Pay for the Performance", *Health Manpower Management*, **22**(3), (1996), pp. 31–39.

Argyris, Chris, *Personality and Organisation*. New York: Harper Collins (1957).

_____, "Organisational Learning and Management Information Systems", *Accounting, Organisations and Society*, **2**(2), (1977), pp. 113–123.

_____, "A Leadership Dilemma: Skilled Incompetence", *Business and Economic Review*, **1**, (1987), pp. 4–11.

Armstrong, Michael, *A Handbook of Management Techniques*. London: Kogan Page (2001).

Bain, Neville and Bill Mabey, *The People Advantage*. London: Macmillan Business Books (1994).

Baird, Lloyd and Ilan Mesholaum, "Getting Pay-off from Investment in Human Resource Management", *Business Horizons* (1992), Jan.–Feb., pp. 1968–75.

Ball, Ben, "Career Management Competences: The Individual Perspective", *Career Development International*, **2**(2), (1997), pp. 74–79.

Bandler, Richard and John Grinder, *The Structure of Magic*. NJ: NLP Seminar Group International (1975).

Bandura, Albert, "Self-Efficacy: Toward a Unifying Theory of Behavioural Change", *Psychological Review*, **84**, (1977), pp. 191–215.

_____, *Social Learning Theory*, Englewood Cliff, NJ: Prentice-Hall (1977).

Barner, Robert W., *Executive Resource Management: Building and Retaining An Exceptional Leadership Team*. Mumbai: Jaico Publishers (2001).

Barnes, Ralph, *Motion and Time Study: Design and Measurement of Work*, New York: John Wiley & Sons (1968).

Barney, Jay B. and Patrick M. Wright, "On Becoming a Strategic Partner: The Role of Human Resources in Gaining Competitive Advantage", *Center for Advanced Human Resource Studies*, Cornell University, Working Paper, (1997), pp. 97–09.

Baruch, Yehuda, "Organisational Career Planning and Management Techniques and Activities in Use in High-Tech Organisations", *Career Development International*, **1**(1), (1996), pp. 40–49.

Bate, S., *Strategies for Cultural Change*, London: Butterworth-Heinemann (1995).

Becker, Brian and Mark Huselid, "HR as a Source of Shareholder Value: Research and Recommendations", *Human Resource Management Journal*, **36**, (1997), pp. 39–47.

_____, "Strategic Human Resource Management", *Human Resource Management Journal*, **38**, (1999), pp. 287–301.

Becker, Brian, Mark Huselid and Dave Ulrich, *The HR Scorecard: Linking People, Strategy and Performance*, MIT: Harvard Business School Press (2001).

Beckhard, Richard, "The Confrontation Meeting", *Harvard Business Review*, March–April, (1967), pp. 155–159.

_____, *A Model for the Executive Management of Transformational Change* (1989).

Beer, Michael, Bert Spector, Paul R. Lawrence, D. Quinn Mills and Richard E. Walton, *Managing Human Assets: The Ground Breaking Harvard Business School Programme*, New York: The Free Press (1984).

_____, *Managing Human Assets*. New York: The Free Press (1984).

Belasco, James A., *Teaching the Elephant to Dance*. New York: A Plume Book (1990).

Benne, Kenneth D., Leland Bradford and Ronald Lippitt, "The Laboratory Method", in, Leland Bradford, Jack Gibb and Kenneth Benne, *T-Group Theory and Laboratory Method*, New York: John Wiley & Sons (1964).

Bennis, Warren, "The Secrets of Great Groups", *Leader to Leader*, Chapter 31, No. 3, Winter (1997).

Bennis, Warren and Burt Nanus, *Leaders: The Strategies for Taking Change*, New York: Harper & Row (1985).

Best Practices, LLC, *HR Systems of World-Class Companies*. Chapel Hill, NC (2000).

Blake, Robert R. and S. Jane Mouton, *The Managerial Grid*. Houston: Gulf Publishing (1964).

Blancero, Donna, John Boroski and Lee Dyer, "Transforming Human Resource Organisations: A Field Study of Future Competency Requirements", *Center for Advanced Human Resource Studies*, Cornell University, Working Paper (1995), 95-28.

Blanchard, Kenneth and Spencer Johnson, *The One-Minute Manager*, New York: William Morrow (1983).

Block, Peter, *Flawless Consulting: A Guide to Getting Your Experience Used*, San Diego, CA: University Associates (1981).

Brand, Adam, "Knowledge Management and Innovation at 3M", *Journal of Knowledge Management*, **2**(1), (1998), pp. 17–22.

Brauchle, Paul E. and David W. Wright, "Training Work Teams", *Training and Development*, March (1993), pp. 65–68.

Bridges, William, *Surviving Corporate Transition*, New York: Currency Double Day (1988).

Bridges, William and Susan Mitchell, "Leading Transition: A New Model for Change", *Leader to Leader*, No. **16**, Spring (2000).

Brooke, Tunstall W., "Culture Transition at AT&T", *Sloan Management Review*, Fall, **25**(1), (1983).

Brooks, Jr. and P. Frederick, *The Mythical Man-Month*, Reading, Mass.: Addison-Wesley (1975).

Buckingham, Marcus and Curt Coffman, *First, Break All the Rules: What the World's Greatest Managers Do Differently*, Simon & Schuster (1999).

Burdett, John O., "Forty Things Every Manager Should Know About Coaching", *Journal of Management Development*, **17**(2), (1998), pp. 142–152

Burns, Mike and Adrienne Rosen, "HR Aspects of a Takeover", *Career Development International,* **2**(5), (1997), pp. 219–224.

Burns, Tom and G.M. Stalker, *The Management of Innovation*. London: Tavistock (1961).

Buzan, Tony, *Mind Map Book*, New York: Penguin Books (1993).

Cairns, Heather, Global Trends in Executive Development, *Journal of Workplace Learning*, **10**(1), (1998), pp. 39–45.

Cakar, Figen and Umit S. Bititci, "Human Resource Management as a Strategic Input to Manufacturing", *International Working Conference on Strategic Manufacturing*, August 26–29, Denmark (2001).

Cameron, Kim S., "Strategies for Successful Organisational Downsizing", *Human Resource Management,* **33**(2), (1994), pp. 189–211.

Campbell, Don, *Mozart Effect*. Washington: Avon Books (1997).

Cartwright, Dorwin, "Achieving Change in People: Some Applications of Group Dynamics Theory", *Human Relations*, **4**(4), (1951), pp. 381–392.

Cattell, Raymond Bernard, "Theory of Fluid and Crystallised Intelligence: A Critical Experiment", *Journal of Education Psychology*, **54**, (1963), pp. 1–22.

Champoux, Joseph E., *Organisational Behaviour: Essential Tenets for a New Millennium*, Cincinnati: South-Western College Publishers (2000).

Charan, Ram, Steve Drotter and Jim Noel, *The Leadership Pipeline: How to Build the Leadership Powered Company*. New York: John Wiley & Sons (2000).

Ciampa, Dan and Michael Watkins, *Right, From the Start*, Boston: Harvard Business School Press (1999).

Cipolla, Carlo M., *The Basic Laws of Human Stupidity*, Bologna: The Millers (1976).

Conger, J. and R. Kanungo, "Toward a Behavioural Theory of Charismatic Leadership in Organisational Settings", *Academy of Management Review,* October (1987), pp. 637–647.

Crossan, Mary M., Henry W. Lane and Roderick E. White (1999), "An Organisational Learning Framework: From Intuition to Institution", *Academy of Management Review*, **24**(3), pp. 522–537

Dalton, M.A. and G.P. Hollenback, "Best Practices in 360 Degree Feedback Process", *Center for Creative Leadership*, Greensboro, N.C. (1997).

Davenport, Thomas, *Knowledge Management Case Studies*, Graduate School of Business, University of Texas (1997).

_____, "Some Principles of Knowledge Management", *Strategy and Business*, First Quarter (1996).

Denhardt, Robert, Janet Vinzant Denhardt and Maria Aristigueta, *Managing Human Behaviour in Public and Non-Profit Organisations*, Thousand Oaks: Sage Publications (2002).

Despres, Charles and Jean-Marie Hiltrop, "Human Resource Management in the Knowledge Age: Current Practice and Perspectives on the Future", *Employee Relations*, **17**(1), (1995), pp. 9–23.

Devanna, Mary Anne, Charles T. Fombrun and Noel M. Tichy (1984), *Strategic Human Resource Management*, New York: John Wiley & Sons.

Dixon, Nancy M., *Common Knowledge*, Boston: Harvard Business School Press (2000).

Dobbins, Richard and Barrie O. Pittman, "Self-Development: The Nine Basic Skills for Business Success", *The Journal of Management Development*, **8**(6), (1997), pp. 521–667.

Dyer, L. and G.W. Holder, *HRM: Evolving Roles and Responsibilities*, Washington D.C.: American Society for Personnel Administration (1988).

Eric, Berne, *Games People Play* (1964).

Farkas, Charles De, Philippe Backer and Allen Sheppard, *Maximum Leadership*, London: Orion Books (1995).

Fein, Michael, "Job Enrichment: A Re-Evaluation", *Sloan Management Review*, **12**, (1974), pp. 69–88.

Felkins, Patrica K., B.J. Chakris and Kenneth Chakris, *Change Management: A Model for Effective Organisational Performance*, New York: Quality Resources (1993).

Festinger, Leon, *A Theory of Cognitive Dissonance*, California: Stanford University Press (1957).

Fielder, Fred E., *A Theory of Leadership Effectiveness*, New York: McGraw-Hill (1971).

Fisher, Dalmer, *Commentaries in Organisations*. St. Paul, MN: West Publishing Company (1993).

_____, *Communication in Organisations*. Mumbai: Jaico Publishing (1998).

Fitz-Enz, Jac, "On the Edge of Oblivion", *HR Magazine*, **41**(5), (1996), pp. 85–88.

_____, *The ROI of Human Capital: Measuring the Economic Value of Employee Performance*, New York: AMACOM (2000).

Flynn, James R., "IQ Gains Over Time", in R.J. Sternberg (Ed.), *Encyclopaedia of Human Intelligence*, New York: Macmillan (1994), pp. 617–623.

Folger, Robert and Russell Cropanzano, *Organisational Justice and Human Resource Management*, London: Sage Publication (1998).

Fombrun, C., N.M. Tichy and M.A. Devanna, *Strategic Human Resource Management*, New York: John Wiley & Sons (1984).

Forret, Monica, Daniel Turban and Thomas Dougherty, "Issues Facing Organisations When Implementing Formal Mentoring Programmes", *Leadership and Organisation Development Journal*, **17**(3), (1996), pp. 28–31.

French, Wendell and Cecil Bell Jr., *Organisation Development: Behavioural Science Interventions for Organisation Improvement*, Englewood Cliff, NJ: Prentice-Hall (1983).

French, Wendell L., Cecil H. Bell Jr. and Robert Awake, *Organisational Development and Transformation*, Boston: McGraw-Hill (2000).

French, Wendell, L. and Robert W. Hollmann, "Management By Objectives: The Team Approach", *California Management Review*, **17**(3), (1975), pp. 13–22.

Fulmer, Robert M., Philip Gibbs and J. Bernard Keys, "The Second Generation Learning Organisations: New Schools for Sustaining Competitive Advantage", *Organisational Dynamics*, Autumn (1998), pp. 7–19.

Furnham, Adrian and Gunter, Barrie, *Corporate Assessment: Auditing a Company's Personality*, New York: Routledge (1993).

Galbrith, J.R. and D.A. Nathanson, *Strategy Implementation: The Role of Structure and Process*, St. Paul, MN: West Publishing (1978).

Garavan, Thomas N., Pat Costine and Noreen Heraty, "The Emergence of Strategic Human Resource Development", *Journal of European Industrial Training*, **19**(10), (1995), pp. 4–10.

Garavan, Thomas, Patrick Gunnigle and Michael Morley, "Contemporary Research: A Triarchy of Theoretical Perspectives and their Prescriptions for HRD", *Journal of European Industrial Training*, **24**(1), (2000), pp. 65–93.

Gardner, Howard, *Frames of Mind*. New York: Basic Books (1983).

Gates, Bill, *Business @ the Speed of Thought*, New York: Penguin Books (1999).

Gatewood, Robert and Hubert Field, *Human Resource Selection*. Auburn University: Dryden Press (1994).

Geert, Hofstede, *Culture's Consequences: International Differences in Work Related Values*, Baverly Hills, California: Sage Publications (1980).

George, Stephen, *Uncommon Sense: Creating Business Excellence in your Organisation*, New York: John Wiley & Sons (1997).

Goleman, Daniel, *Working with Emotional Intelligence*. New York: Bantom Books (1998).

Gongla, P. and C.R. Rizzuto, Evolving Communities of Practice: IBM Services Experience. *Knowledge Management*, **40**(4), (2001), pp. 1–19.

Gordon, William, *Synectics*, New York: Harper & Row (1961).

Greiner, Larry E. and Vorginia E. Schein, *Power and Organisational Development*, Addison-Wesley (1988).

Greiner, Lary, *Organisational Change and Development*, Homewood: Richard Irwin Press (1970).

Grove, Andrew S., *Only the Paranoid Survive: How to Exploit the Crisis Points That Challenge Every Company,* New York: Bantom Books (1996).

Guilford, J.P., *The Nature of Human Intelligence*, New York: Basic Books (1967).

Guns, Bob, "The Chief Knowledge Officer's Role: Challenges and Competencies", *Journal of Knowledge Management*, 1(4), June, (1998), pp. 315–319.

Hammel, Gary, "Strategy as Revolution", in John Seely Brown (Ed.), *Seeing Differently*, Boston: Harvard Business School Press (1997).

Hammer, Michael and James Champy, *Reengineering Corporation*, New York: Harper Business (1992).

Hamzah, A. and M. Zairi, "People Management: Where is the Evidence of Best Practice", *Training for Quality*, 4(4), (1996), pp. 37–44.

Harari, Oren, "Back to the Future of Work", *Management Review*, 82, (1993), p. 35.

Harrison, Lawrence E. and Samuel P. Huntington, *Culture Matters: How Values Shape Human Progress,* New York: Basic Books (2000).

Heider, Fritz, *The Psychology of Interpersonal Relations*, New York: John Wiley & Sons (1958).

Hersey, Paul and Kenneth H. Blanchard, *Management of Organisational Behaviour*, Englewood Cliffs, N.J.: Prentice-Hall (1982).

Herzberg, Frederick, B. Mausner and B. Snyderman, *The Motivation to Work*, New York: John Wiley & Sons (1959).

Hoeksema, Ludwig and Geert de Jong, "International Co-ordination and Management Development: An Application at Pricewaterhouse Coopers", *Journal of Management Development*, 20(2), (2001), pp. 145–158.

Honold, Linda, "A Review of the Literature on Employee Empowerment", *Empowerment in Organisations*, 5(4), (1997), pp. 202–212.

Hughey, Aaron W. and Kenneth J. Mussnug, "Designing Effective Employee Training Programmes", *Training for Quality*, 5(2), (1997), pp. 52–57.

Hull, Clark Leonard, *Principles of Behaviour*, Chicago: The University of Chicago Press (1943).

Hultman, Kenneth E., "It's a Team Effort", *Training and Development*, Feb. (1998), pp. 12–14.

Iain Ballantyne and Nigel Povah, *Assessment and Development Centers*, Hampshire: Gower (1995).

Iles, Paul, "Sustainable High Potential Career Development: A Resource Based View", *Career Development International*, 2(7), (1997), pp. 347–353.

Ingo, Hoffmann, "Knowledge Management Tools", in, *Knowledge Management Best Practices in Europe*, Kai Mertins, Peter Heisig and Jens Vorbeck (Eds.), (2001), pp. 74–94, London: Springer Publishers.

Janis, Irving, *Victims of Group Think*, Boston: Houghton Mifflin (1972).

Johnson, Spencer, *Who Moved My Cheese*, Putnum Publications (1998).

Johnson, Ulf, "Why the Concept of Human Resource Costing and Accounting Does not Work: A Lesson from Seven Swedish Cases", *Personnel Review*, 28(1/2), (1999), pp. 91–107.

Kakabadse, Nada and Andrew Kakabadse, "Outsourcing: A Paradigm Shift", *The Journal of Management Development*, **19**(8), (2000), pp. 670–728.

Kalra, Satish Kumar, "Human Potential Management: Time to Move Beyond the Concept of Human Resource Management?" *Journal of European Industrial Training*, **21**(5), (1997), pp. 176–180.

Kane, Bob, John Crawford and David Grant, "Barriers to Effective HRM", *International Journal of Manpower*, **20**(8), (1999), pp. 494–515.

Kanter, Rosabeth Moss, "Power Failure in Management Circuits", *HBR*, Jul.–Aug. (1977), p. 65

_____, *The Change Masters*, Simon & Schuster (1983).

_____, "The Enduring Skills of Change Leaders", *Leader to Leader*, No. 13, Summer (1999).

Kanter, Rosabeth Moss, Barry A. Sten and Todd D. Jick, *The Challenge of Organisational Change: How Companies Experience it and Leaders Guide it,* New York: The Free Press (1992).

Kaplan, Robert S. and David Norton, *The Strategy Focused Organisation: How Balanced Scorecard Companies Thrive in the New Business Environment*. Boston: Harvard Business School Press (2001).

Katzenbach, Jon R., *Real Change Leaders*, London: Nicholas Brealey Publishing (1996).

Katzenbach, Jon R. and Douglas K. Smith, "The Discipline of Virtual Teams", *Leader to Leader*, **22**, fall, 2001.

Kelley, Robert, *How to be a Star at Work*, New York: Times Books (1999).

Kets de Vries, M. and Miller, D., "The Neurotic Organisation", *Psychology Today*. November, (1984), pp. 27–34.

Khandwalla, Pradip N., "McKinsey Versus Movement Management: The Two Modes of Major Change", in, Anup K. Singh, Rajen Gupta and Abad Ahmed (Eds.), *Designing and Developing Organisations for Tomorrow*, New Delhi: Sage Response (2001).

Kirkpatrick, Donald, *Evaluating Training Programmes*, San Francisco, CA: Berrett-Koehler Publishers (1994).

Kolb, David A., *Experiential Learning: Experiences As the Source of Learning and Development*, Englewood Cliffs, NJ.: Prentice-Hall (1984).

Kotter, John, *Leading Change*, Boston: Harvard Business School Press (1996).

Lawler III and E. Edward, "The New Plant Revolution", *Organisational Dynamics*, Winter, (1978), pp. 10–22.

Lawler, Edward E. and Susan, A. Mohrman, "Quality Circles after the Fad", *Harvard Business Review,* Jan.–Feb. (1985).

Lee, James, *The Gold and Garbage in Management Theories and Prescriptions*, Ohio: University Press (1980).

Likert, Rensis, *The Human Organisation*, New York: McGraw-Hill (1967).

Locke, E.A. and G.P. Latham, *Goal Setting: A Motivational Technique That Works*, Englewood Cliffs, N.J.: Prentice-Hall (1984).

London, Manuel and Stephen Stumpf, *Managing Careers*, Massachusetts: Addison-Wesley (1982).

Longenecker, Clinton O. and Laurence S. Fink, "Improving Management Performance in Rapidly Changing Organisations", *Journal of Management Development*, **20**(1), (2001), pp. 7–18.

Luft, Joseph and Hari Ingham, *Of Human Interaction*. California: National Press Books (1969).

Luoma, Mikko, "Developing People for Business Success: Capability Driven HRD in Practice", *Management Decision*, **38**(3), (2000), pp. 145–153.

Luthans, Fred and Robert Kreitner, *Organisational Behaviour Modification and Beyond*, Scoott, Foresman (1985).

Mahieu, Carla, "Management Development in Royal Dutch/Shell", *Journal of Management Development*, **20**(2), (2001), pp. 121–130.

Mansfield, Richard, "Building Competency Models: Approaches for HR Professionals", *Human Resource Management*, **35**, (1996), pp. 7–18.

Marilyn, Wood Daudein, "Learning from Experience Through Reflection", *Organisational Dynamics*, Winter, (1996), pp. 36–48.

Marwick, A.D., "Knowledge Management Technology", *IBM Systems Journal*, **40**(4), (2001), pp. 814–830.

Maslow, Abraham, H., "A Theory of Human Motivation", *Psychological Review*, (1943), pp. 370–396

May, Andrew, "Developing Management Competencies for Fast Changing Organisations", *Career Development International*, **4**(6), (1999), pp. 336–339.

Maynard, Ross, "Stress in the Work Place", *Management Accounting*, July–Aug. (1996), pp. 63–64.

McCampbell, Atefeh Sadri, Linda Moorhead Clare and Scott Howard Gitters, "Knowledge Management: The New Challenge for the 21st Century", *Journal of Knowledge Management,* **3**(3), (1999), pp. 172–179.

McClelland, David, *The Achieving Society*, Princeton, NJ: Van Nostrand (1961).

McGregor, Douglas, *The Human Side of Enterprise*, New York: McGraw-Hill (1960).

Meisel, Edward (Ed.), *The Essential Writings of Alexander*, New York: Thames & Hudson (1989).

Melamed, Tuvia and David Jackson, "Psychometric Instruments: Potential Benefits and Practical Use", *Industrial and Commercial Training*, **27**(4), (1995), pp. 11–16.

Merton, Robert E., "The Mathew Effect in Science", *Science*, **158**, (1968), pp. 56–63.

Milas, G.H., "How to Develop a Meaningful Employee Recognition Programme", *Quality Progress*, May, (1995), pp. 139–142.

Morton, Clive, *Becoming World Class*, London: Macmillan (1994).

Neft, Thomas J. and James M. Citrin, *Lessons from the Top*, New York: Currency Doubleday (2001).

Nelson, B., "Motivating Employees with Informal Awards", *Management Accounting*, **77**(5), (1995), p. 30.

Nicholls, John, "Getting Empowerment into Perspective: A Three Stage Training Framework", *Empowerment in Organisations*, **3**(3), (1995), pp. 5–10.

Niehoff, Brian P., "A Motive Based View of Organisational Behaviour: Applying an Old Lens to A New Class of Organisational Behaviours".

Nininger, James, R., *Managing Human Resources: A Strategic Perspective*, Ottawa: The Conference Board of Canada (1982).

Orsburn, Jack D., Linda Moran Musselwhite and John H. Zenger (Eds.), *Self-Directed Work Teams: The New American Challenge*: Illinois: Business one Irwin (1990).

Osborn, Alex F., *Applied Imagination*, New York: Charles Scriber's Sons (1963).

Ouchi, William G., *Theory Z: How American Business Can Meet the Japanese Challenge*, New York: Avon Books (1982).

Oudtshoorn, Van Mike and Laurie Thomas, "A Management Synopsis of Empowerment", *Training for Quality*, **3**, (1995), pp. 25–32.

Parkinson, Cyril Northcote, *The Parkinson's Law*, Boston: Houghton Mifflin (1958).

Peter, Lawrence J., *The Peter Principle*, New York: Morrow (1969).

Peters, Tom, *Thriving on Chaos*, New York: Harper & Row (1987).

Peters, Tom and Robert Waterman, *In Search of Excellence: Lessons from America's Best Run Companies*, New Delhi: Harper Collins (1982).

Peters, Tom, Robert Waterman and J.R. Philips, *Structure is Not Organisation*, Business Horizons (1980).

Pfeffer, J., *Competitive Advantage Through People: Unleashing the Power of the Workforce*, Boston: Harvard Business School Press (1994).

Pickett, Les, "People Make the Difference", *Industrial and Commercial Training*, **32**(6), (2000), pp. 225–229.

Pilditch, James, *Winning Ways: How Companies Create the Products We all Want to Buy*, New Delhi: Viva Books (1992).

Popoff, Frank, "Reflections on Succession", *Prism*, Third Quarter (1996), pp. 109–116.

Pratt, Danielle, *The Healthy Scorecard: Delivering Breakthrough Results that Employees and Investors Will Love*, Trafford Publishing (2001).

Price, Alan, *Human Resource Management in a Business Context*, International Thomas Business Press (1997).

Pucik, Vladimir, "Strategic Alliances, Organisational Learning, and Competitive Advantage: The HRM Agenda", *Human Resource Management*, **27**(1), (1988), pp. 77–93.

Reitsma, S.G., "Management Development in Unilever", *Journal of Management Development*, **20**(2), (2001), pp. 131–144.

Revans, Reg, *Action Learning: New Techniques for Management*, London: Blond & Briggs (1980).

Richard Riso, Don and Russ Hudson, *The Wisdom of the Enneagram*, New York: Bantom Books (1999).

Robbins, Harvey and Michael Finley, *Why Teams Don't Work: What Went Wrong and How to Make it Right,* London: Orion Business Books (1997).

Robinson, Alan G. and Sam Stern, *Corporate Creativity: How Innovation and Improvement Actually Happens,* Berrett-Koehler Publishers (1997).

Rokeach, M., *The Nature of Human Values,* New York: Free Press (1973).

Rose, Kenneth, "A Performance Measurement Model", *Quality Progress,* Feb. (1995), pp. 63–66.

Rosen, Robert and Patricia Digh, *Global Literacies: Lessons on Business Leadership and National Cultures,* Simon & Schuster (2000).

Roth, Robert, *Maharshi Mahesh Yogi's Transcendental Meditation,* Maharshi University Management Press (2000).

Rothwell, William J., Robert K. Prescott and Maria W. Taylor, *The Strategic Human Resource Leader,* Davis Black Publishing (1998).

Rotter, Julian B., *Social Learning and Clinical Psychology,* New York: Prentice-Hall (1954).

Salas, Eduardo, C. Shawn Burke, A. Jannis and Cannon-Bowers, "What We Know About Designing and Delivering Team Training: Tips and Guidelines", in Kurt Kreiger (Ed.). *Creating, Implementing and Managing Effective Training and Development,* San Francisco: Jossey-Bass (2002).

Samson, Danny and David Challis, *Patterns of Excellence,* London: Prentice-Hall (1999).

Schein, Edger, *Organisational Culture and Leadership,* Boston: Jossey-Bass (1985).

_____, "How Career Anchors hold Executives to their Career Paths", *Personnel Journal,* **52,** (1975), pp. 11–24.

Schneider, Benjamin, "HRM—A Service Perspective: Towards a Customer-Focused HRM", *International Journal of Service and Industry Management,* 5(1), (1994), pp. 64–76.

Senge, Peter M., *The Fifth Discipline. The Art and Practice of The Learning Organisation,* London: Random House (1990).

Shafer, Richard A., Lee Dyer, Janine Kilty, Jaffrey Amos and G.A. Ericksen, "Crafting A Human Resource Strategy to Faster Organisational Agility: A Case Study", *Center for Advanced Human Resource Studies,* Cornell University, Working Paper, (2000), pp. 2000–08.

Shepard, Herbert A., "Rules of Thumb for Change Agents", *Organisational Development Practitioner,* Nov. (1975), pp. 1–5.

Shimko, Barbara Whitaker and Marshall S. Swift, "Choose an HR Star for Competitive Edge", *Management Decision,* 38(9), (2000), pp. 616–625.

Simon, Herbert, *Models of Bounded Rationality.* Cambridge, MA: MIT Press (1983).

Sinha, Jai B.P., "The Nurturant Task Leader", *ASCI Journal of Management,* 8(2), (1979), pp. 109–119.

Skyrme, David, "Fact or Fad? Ten Shifts in Knowledge Management", *Knowledge Management Review,* July–August, (1998), pp. 6–8.

Spearman, Charles Edward, "General Intelligence: Objectively Determined and Measured", *American Journal of Psychology,* **15,** (1904), pp. 201–293.

Stace, D. and D. Dunphy, "Beyond Traditional Paternalistic and Developmental Approaches to Organisational Change and Human Resource Strategies", *The International Journal of HRM*, **2**(3), (1991), pp. 477–495.

Sternberg, Robert J., *Beyond IQ: A Triarchic Theory of Human Intelligence*, New York: Cambridge Press (1985).

Storey, John, *Developments in the Management of Human Resources*, Oxford: Blackwell (1992).

Thorndike, Edward Lee, *The Fundamentals of Learning*, New York: Columbia University Press (1932).

Thurstone, L.L., *Primary Mental Abilities*, New York: Appleton Century Croffs (1938).

Tichy, Noel M. and Eli Cohen, "The Teaching Organization", *Training and Development*, **52**, July (1998), pp. 27–33.

Tolman, Edward C., *Purposive Behaviour in Animals and Man*, New York: Appleton Century Croffs (1932).

Tovey, Laura, "Competency Assessment—A Strategic Approach", *Executive Development*, **7**(1), (1994), pp. 16–19.

Tuckman, B.W., "Developmental Sequences in Small Groups", *Psychological Bulletin*, June, (1965), pp. 384–399.

Ulrich, Dave, *Human Resource Champions: The Next Agenda for Adding Value and Delivering Results,* Harvard Business School Press (1997).

US Department of Labour, *Government as a High Performance Employer*, SCANS Report for America (1998).

Vroom, V.H., *Work and Motivation*, New York: John Wiley & Sons (1964).

Waterman, R. Jr., Tom Peters and J.R. Philips, "Structure is not Organisation", *Business Horizons*, **23**(3), (1980), pp. 14–26.

Weber, Max, *Bureaucracy Theory*, Oxford University Press (1946).

Weisbord, Martin K., "Toward Third Wave Managing and Consulting", *Organisational Dynamics*, Winter, (1987), pp. 64–79.

Weisbord, Marvin and Sandra Janoft, *Future Search: An Action Guide to Finding Common Ground in Organisations and Communities,* Berrett-Koehler (2000).

Weiss, David S., *High Impact HR: Transforming Human Resources for Competitive Advantage,* John Wiley & Sons (1999).

Weiss, Tracey B. and Franklin Hartle, *Reengineering Performance Management: Breakthrough in Achieving Strategy Through People*, Florida: St. Lucie Press (1997).

Wertheimer, Max, *A Source Book of Gestalt Psychology*, New York: Harcourt Brace & Co (1938).

Whitaker, Barbara and Marshall Swift, "Choose an HR Star for Competitive Edge", *Management Decision*, **38**, (2000), pp. 616–625.

Wilkins, Alan L., "The Culture Audit: A Tool for Understanding Organisations", *Organisational Dynamics*, Autumn, (1983), pp. 24–38.

Wilson, Graham, *Self-Managed Team Working*, London: Pitman Publishing (1995).

Wimer, Scott and Kenneth Nowack, "13 Common Mistakes Using 360 Degree Feedback", *Training and Development*, May (1998), pp. 9–80.

Winfield, Ian, "Toyota UK Ltd: Model HRM Practices?" *Employee Relations*, **16**(1), (1994), pp. 41–53.

Wright, Patrick M. and Lee Dyer, "People in the E-Business: New Challenges, New Solutions", *Center for Advanced Human Resource Studies*, Cornell University, Working Paper, (2000), pp. 2000–11.

Wright, Philip C., Gary D. Geroy and Maura MacPhee, "A Human Resources Model for Excellence in Global Organisation Performance", *Management Decision*, **38**(1), (2000), pp. 36–42.

Zigon, Jack, A Seven-Step Process for Measuring the Results of Work Teams (1998), www.zigonperf.com

Author Index

Subject Index